THE CROWN AND THE PEN

THE CROWN AND THE PEN

The Memoirs of a Lawyer Turned Rebel

Bereket Habte Selassie

The Red Sea Press, Inc.
Publishers & Distributors of Third World Books
P. O. Box 1892 P. O. Box 48
Trenton, NJ 08607 Asmara, ERITREA

The Red Sea Press, Inc.
Publishers & Distributors of Third World Books

P. O. Box 1892　　　　　　P. O. Box 48
Trenton, NJ 08607　　　　　Asmara, ERITREA

Copyright © 2007 Bereket Habte Selassie
First Printing 2007

All rights reserved. No part of this publication may be reproduced, stored in a retrieval system or transmitted in any form or by any means electronic, mechanical, photocopying, recording or otherwise without the prior written permission of the publisher.

Book and cover design: Saverance Publishing Services

Library of Congress Cataloging-in-Publication Data

Bereket H. Selassie
  The crown and the pen : the memoirs of a lawyer turned rebel / Bereket Habte Selassie.
    p. cm.
  ISBN 1-56902-275-5 (hardcover) -- ISBN 1-56902-276-3 (pbk.)
  1. Bereket H. Selassie. 2. Lawyers--Ethiopia--Biography. 3. Judges--Ethiopia--Biography. I. Title.
  KRP110.B47A3 2007
  340.092--dc22
  [B]
                              2007015161

DEDICATION

To Asgede, Finot and Sebene

All my love…

And my blessings to Noah and Asa

May you continue to be the source of joy to all who love you!

Table of Contents

Appreciation	ix
Prologue	xi

PART I: CHILDHOOD YEARS AND BEYOND

Chapter 1:	Village Life: Boyhood in the Village	3
Chapter 2:	Early Schooling: Faith and Fascism	17
Chapter 3:	Into Haile Selassie's Kingdom	41
Chapter 4:	Continuing Education: From Harar to the "Wingate."	55
Photos		69

PART II: OUT OF AFRICA......AND BACK

Chapter 5:	In England as the Sun Sets on the Empire	83
Chapter 6:	Law School and the Start of my Problems: My First Taste of Shoan Intrigue	101
Chapter 7:	An Emperor Meets the Future	121
Chapter 8:	A Shaken Emperor Makes Concessions:	141

PART III: INSIDE AN EMPIRE

Chapter 9:	Between Law and Clandestine Politics	165
Chapter 10:	As the Sun King Becomes Africa's Father	181
Chapter 11:	From Government to Academia...and Politics	195
Chapter 12:	Banished but Undefeated	215
Photos		243

PART IV: WORLD BANK, REVOLUTION, AND "DIPLOMACY"

Chapter 13:	As Fate Would Have It	257
Chapter 14:	Journey to the Unknown	281
Chapter 15:	Among the Guerillas—a Lawyer Turned Outlaw?	299
Chapter 16:	Transition to New Life and Work	327
Index		353

Appreciation

For a number of years now, many friends and colleagues have urged me to write my life history. I resisted writing my memoirs mainly due to time constraints; but the reason I gave to my friends was a facetious one—I was too young to write it; only retired people write their memoirs. It was not until late 1997 that I was persuaded to start thinking about writing. When I hesitated, my colleagues at the University of North Carolina at Chapel Hill, Professors Julius Nyang'oro and Michael West, forced me to do it by organizing a mini-conference in Chapel Hill to which they invited some old friends to a one-day meeting at which they grilled me with questions about my life from the cradle to the grave work of constitution making! That grave work will be part of the planned second volume of my memoirs—Insha'Allah!

Those who attended the meeting were (in alphabetical order):

Hussein Mohamed Adam, Kassahun Checole, Mohamed Hassen, Ruth Iyob, Jim Paul, Rich Rosen, Said Samatar, and Gloria Steinem. Plus Julius and Michael, of course. Having interrogated me about people, events and issues surrounding my life and work (all tape-recorded), they had planned to come out with a book, which was to be the basis for a more detailed memoir that I would write eventually. As part of their methodology, Julius and Michael wrote to selected friends and colleagues to send them letters objectively assessing my life and work. The majority responded positively, and copies of their letters were passed on to me.

The planned book was postponed indefinitely mainly due to Michael's move to another university, and Julius's busy schedule as chair of the African and African-American Studies Department. However, their book project spurred me on to write my memoirs. For that I owe Julius and Michael a debt of gratitude.

I also want to express my deep appreciation to the following people for making pictures available to me:

Mezgebu Gebre Amlak for the pictures of General Aman Andom,

Dr. Aklilu Habte for the picture of the group with Presidentr Kwame Nkrumah,

Woizero Selamawit Woldeamanuel for a picture of her brother, Dejasmach Workneh.

Dawit Habteyesus for the picture of the "twelve evangelists."

Prologue

KING AND KING'S COUNSEL

Of all the dramatic events of my life, none stand out more vividly in my mind than those of September 10, 1967. That day marked for me a break with the past and the beginning of a new, revolutionary phase. It was as if the accumulated frustrations of the previous years—all the contradictions between my core beliefs on the one hand, and my life as a government lawyer on the other—were now brought to the surface. It was a moment of truth, and, like all moments of truth, it induced in me a liberating sense of clarity, albeit one fraught with anxiety about my fate.

I was awakened early by a knock on my bedroom window. It was a cool morning with a clear sky. The rest of the family was asleep when the house servant knocked at my window. I opened the window and asked him what was the matter, quietly, so as not to wake my wife and children. He said, equally quietly, that there was a policeman waiting outside who insisted on seeing me. I leaned out to look for myself and, true enough, there was a uniformed policeman standing by the gate.

I went out in my pajamas and dressing gown and greeted the policeman, who stood no ceremonies; he just told me curtly that I must go with him. I asked him why and where, "To the Ministry of Security," he answered.

"But why? And why at this hour?"

"I don't know sir; all I know is that I have my orders to take you there." He added, more politely, "You'd better hurry up and get dressed."

I got dressed as fast as I could, taking care not to awaken my wife, our five-year-old son and our eight-month-old daughter who were also sleeping; so I walked out of the bedroom and went to the gate as if nothing out of the ordinary had happened. In fact I told the night guard to tell my wife that I had gone out to take care of an urgent matter and would phone her later. Whatever the reason for this unusual summons to the Ministry of Security, I decided that the family must not be alarmed.

After talking to the night guard, I turned toward the garage, taking my car keys out of my pocket. I was about to open the car door when the policeman said there was no need for me to take my car; I was going in the police van. I knew then that I was in trouble. I followed him to the police vehicle, parked outside the compound. Inside the van were two plain-clothes men who did not bother to return my greeting. One of them, a sinister-looking man in his thirties, had an Uzi submachine gun, which he nursed on his lap, as a warning for me not to do anything rash. This is serious stuff, I thought, and my mind raced back and forth, reviewing the past to find possible reasons for this arrest. That was what it was, and I prepared for the worst.

We headed toward the Ministry of Security, which I knew very well from my previous life. As it was early, there was not much traffic. Before we turned from the main thoroughfare, Churchill Road, to the road leading to the Ministry, the traffic stopped us and Tamene Workineh, whom I knew from my school days at the Wingate, saw me. He was standing on a corner, waiting for the lights to change. He was about to cross the road but on seeing me he stopped, turning his gaze toward the van which was moving slowly. I was seized with an inexplicable desire to shout his name. It was one of those moments when in trouble, you search for a way out of your predicament, a moment when a ray of hope shines like sunlight through rolling clouds. A flash of thought passed through my mind: in case something bad happens to me, at least someone who knows me had seen me in a police van. Surely, my schoolmate must have noticed the license plate of the van. Just in case....

And then I lost sight of him.

We reached the Ministry of Security after some twenty minutes. The van stopped at the back entrance. The gray stone building built by the Italians during their occupation of the country had never looked colder; the sight of it sent a chill down my spine. I was led out of the car and escorted by the Uzi-carrying security man to the office of the Minister on the second floor. We walked up the wide marble stairs, our steps echoing across the corridors, and reached the office of the Minister. A police constable stood guard at the door, and my escort gave his name and told him the Minister was expecting us. The constable went inside and came back after a few seconds and gave a go-ahead sign.

The security man knocked at the door and, after he heard a voice say "come in," he opened the door and pushed me forward. The push was hard and I cannot say how much that small act irritated me. It was worse than if he had hit me. Here I was, a former Minister of the Emperor, and here was a junior officer of the police inflicting on me a small but humiliating indignity. He would not have dared even to look me straight in the eye when I was His Excellency, the King's Counsel. Being a thoroughbred Ethiopian, he would have been obsequious and respectful. But when you are down, respect goes out of the window and aggression takes its place. You become fair game for all those who resented your rise in the first place. I could not stomach that act of indignity. I immediately returned

Prologue

it in kind; I gave him a backward jab with my right elbow, so hard that it must have hurt. I didn't even turn to see how he felt.

He announced my presence to the Minister and withdrew. Damn him!

I was now in the tender care of His Excellency Mr. Kifle Irgetu, Minister of Security, a man known for his ruthlessness and furious loyalty to the Emperor and the imperial system. Kifle was a swarthy, unsmiling, hard-hitting man in the law enforcement business. Special imperial enforcer would be more accurate. He was of medium height and stocky build, with black eyes that never wavered or blinked when they were fixed on you; the way that a cat looks at its prey before it pounces, playing with it before its final disposal.

I knew Kifle rather well; there was no love lost between us when I was Attorney General. He was from an older generation; in the 1950s, when I was a law student in London, he was a senior security official of the Ethiopian government. Years later, we worked at more or less the same level; but he was, of course, more powerful because of his closeness to and trust of the Emperor. Kifle had trained in Belgium as a police officer before the 1935 Italian invasion of Ethiopia. He had worked in various capacities as a security officer as well as a provincial governor. He was finally promoted to the powerful position of Minister of Interior, with all security matters under his jurisdiction.

The Ministry of Interior was like a government within a government. No one (except the Emperor, of course) could hold it to account for anything for which there should be accountability in the eyes of the law. The law had been my business, but the arms of the law at my disposal as Attorney General could do very little to penetrate the walls of the secret government. I had run-ins with officials of the Security Department on a number of occasions, and many in the department held grudges against me. This was in addition to my outspoken advocacy of the rule of law and the observance of human rights, which was anathema to the security people.

And now it seemed that fate landed me in their dark domain; my life could be in their hands. There I was standing in the august (or rather, awful) presence of His Excellency, who was busy signing papers and did not even seem aware that I was there. But I knew that it was a power play, a not–so-subtle exercise of psychological pressure. He did not rise to greet me, nor ask me to sit down, as he would have done in days gone by. That was a customary courtesy not denied even to adversaries in normal circumstances. But this was not a normal circumstance; I was at his mercy, and I stood there awaiting his pleasure. As I watched him reading and signing the papers from a pile of dockets, I made a mental calculation that at that rate, I would be standing there for hours. Then in the middle of his interminable signing chore, he spoke to me without taking his eyes off the file. Without any word of explanation he said that I had been summoned to appear before the Emperor. Delivered in an even and neutral voice, the announcement sounded ominous. I did not know whether to feel relieved or apprehensive.

Two weeks before, I had returned from two years of advanced legal studies in London University, my alma mater, preceded by a one-year of fellowship at the UCLA Law School. I was scheduled to teach law at the newly opened Law School of Haile Selassie I University. Immediately on my return, I had met the Dean of the Law School, Professor Johnston, and some members of his all-American faculty. I had already been assigned office space and elected, in absentia, member of the Faculty Council. I was expected to start teaching the following week; instead I found myself summoned to the Emperor. Only the Emperor and perhaps his Minister of Security knew what fate awaited me. An audience with the Emperor was not new to me, but whereas previously, I was summoned with the decorum befitting a high-ranking member of the government and ushered in with appropriate courtesy, this time I was forcibly taken to his imperial presence and treated as a virtual prisoner.

The memory of September 10, 1967 in the Imperial Palace is so vivid that when I think of it, I get the feeling that it is happening now. The Minister takes me there and deposits me in the ante-chamber, then disappears into the Emperor's inner chamber. I wait alone sitting on a couch, observing the ebb and flow of the movers and shakers of the Ethiopian empire. The atmosphere of tension and fear is such that I begin to feel apprehensive with premonitions of mortality. Is this going to be my final hour, before the curtain of life descends on me? It is an oppressive thought brought on by an oppressive environment. There was a time when I went in and out of this center of power and intrigue without any sense of danger, even though I never felt comfortable in it.

As I saw them come and go looking inebriated with power, I knew that to these privileged of the empire, who lived under the favor and reflected glory of the "Sun King," the imperial palace was the one place where they felt validated, because it distinguished them from the ordinary mortals. Far from being oppressive, it was to them, an elevated and elevating ground distinguishing them from the masses. Even when they were sometimes subjected to humiliating treatment at the hands of palace orderlies, it was worth it. That was the pain they had to suffer for the gain of imperial favor and to redeem themselves from being ordinary. Those who have gained daily access to the palace must, therefore, consider themselves as specially redeemed. Not I; I never felt redeemed in that sense even at the height of my power.

Now here I am alone in the palace ante-chamber, and no one speaks to me as I wait.

After four hours, someone finally calls my name, and I get up and move toward the inner sanctum where the empire's business is determined. I am gently reminded by a kindly palace chamberlain (there were some kindly souls even there!) not to walk too fast. My heart is pounding, but strangely enough, the anxiety that assailed me while I was waiting is now gone, replaced by a sense of calm. I am told to wait at the entrance; the Emperor's soft voice is audible though I cannot hear the words. Then the Emperor's *aide de camp* appears from within and motions for me to move forward, directing me toward the Emperor's chamber. I walk past the red curtains and find myself face to face with His Imperial Majesty. He is sitting behind his huge mahogany desk, while Prime Minister Aklilu Habtewold and Kifle Irgetu stand to his right. To his left, standing and taking notes, is his deputy private secretary, Yohannes Kidanemariam.

Prime Minister Aklilu, a Sorbonne-educated lawyer, is in his late fifties, of medium height with light brown complexion. He has broad shoulders, and his prominent forehead, beady eyes and aquiline nose dominate his face. His gray hair gives him an air of distinction, enhanced by his well-tailored light gray suit. Aklilu's claim to fame, one that he treasures above everything else, is that he managed to have Eritrea delivered to His Imperial Majesty on a silver platter. There are differing views on who did what in the matter of the disposal of Eritrea, but Aklilu always reminded whoever listened to him that his contribution was second to none. Indeed, it was to be his final plea to the Commission of Inquiry investigating the role of the government during the Wollo famine of 1972-1974. Alas! It did not help him.

The Emperor looks up and we stare at each other, eyeball to eyeball. It is one of those moments when, all of a sudden, out of nowhere a sort of madness gets hold of you and all fear is gone. It is difficult to explain or justify such glorious feeling in the face of peril. All I know is that suddenly, "His Imperial Majesty" disappears and I see only a human figure in the form of a frail, if commanding, old man who will die a human death one day, just like me and all other humans. Another side of me, the side of caution, reminds me that the Emperor holds my life in his hands, but the holy madness that displaced that caution prevails for a moment. This must be the moment that saints and martyrs embrace as their destiny, come what may. I am no saint but I share that glory, if only for a short while. In my own case the source of that momentary and dubious glory is the knowledge that in our past relationship as Emperor and subject, I stood on the side of justice and fairness even when he did not.

I will have occasion later to describe the Emperor's personality. For now, it is enough to say that he and I had a complex and strained relationship from the beginning. He had mixed feelings about me. I suspected he rather liked me for my assertive and open-minded Eritrean character. He had dealt with Eritreans of the previous generation and was familiar with our independent ways. But as the all-powerful King of Kings, he had expected me to bend to his will, which I rarely did when honor and principle were at stake. The "battle of wills" started soon after my graduation from Law School when I was presented to His Majesty. He asked me where I wanted to work, as was his wont in those years, and I told him my aim was to practice law as an independent attorney. He was quick in his answer which startled me. In a dismissive tone, His Imperial Majesty told me that was impossible; I must work for the government. When I disputed his order that I was to work for the government, he flew into a temper tantrum, as had been rarely witnessed, and let loose a torrent of harsh words to put me in my place. It was the "counsel of the wise" to the would-be King's Counsel. Some of those who witnessed the event told me later that I was lucky to escape with mere counsel. His Imperial Majesty had the power of life and death over his subjects of whom I was one, I was reminded, in case I didn't know, or had forgotten. I did not have the right to choose what kind of work I can do; he did, and he ordered me to work in the Ministry of Justice, and that was that. The powerful do what they may, the powerless what they must. A sobering thought, one with which I was launched into my career in government service.

His Imperial Majesty, Haile Selassie I, Elect of God, Conquering Lion of the Tribe of Judah, King of Kings, Defender of the Faith....could order his subjects to do anything he wished. According to tradition, codified in the Revised Constitution of 1955, the Emperor's person is sacred, his power indisputable, his dignity inviolable. In short, his word is law.

The remarkable fact about Emperor Haile Selassie, at least during the time I worked in his government, is that he used his absolute power sparingly, preferring "wise counsel" or reprimand before taking drastic steps. Had it not been so, I would have already been punished several times over. The problem for me was that I took His Majesty at his word when he talked about law and justice in his empire.

Now, on September 10, 1967, as the Emperor and I face each other, eyeball to eyeball, man to man, it is clear to me that I had gone too far.

My offenses (there were three) and punishment (I survived as is clear) I will relate in the pages that follow. I mention this imperial encounter because it was a turning point in a career that took me from village boy to student, government official, Eritrean freedom fighter, and diplomat.

But let us begin with the boy; or more properly, his village...

PART I
CHILDHOOD YEARS AND BEYOND

Chapter 1

BOYHOOD IN THE VILLAGE

The village of my birth is in the Hamasien region of eastern Eritrea, an area one British traveler described as "the land of the thousand villages." Imagine a land and a people living as in biblical times. As I recall it in memories of my childhood years, it is a wonderland.

I see in my mind's eye the Adi Nifas of childhood, and the surrounding area: a land of rolling hills and green meadows, dotted with villages invariably lying on hilltops. The modest, rectangular-shaped stone houses are arranged in rows, each row of houses facing one direction. The roofs are covered with dried mud placed over wooden planks, curved from the middle towards left and right so as to allow rain water to drain. This place is in Africa, but to experienced travelers it gives the impression of the Middle East.

The inhabitants of this land, whom Herodotus described as the people with burnt faces, wear clothes made of cotton and consisting of tight-fitting trousers, long shirts and a *netselas* (toga), or *gabi*, wrapped around the shoulders.

Adi Nifas

Lying five miles to the north of Asmara, the Eritrean capital, my birthplace was founded by the legendary Asgede. Beneath the commonplace name, Adi Nifas, which literally means windy village, lies concealed the pride of its inhabitants. Starting from their common ancestor, the illustrious Asgede, the people of Adi Nifas and their kith and kin elsewhere in the highland, believe that it had pleased the Almighty to bestow upon them a special favor. There was even a time when elements of *Deqi-Asgede* (descendants of the illustrious one), elevated themselves into an aristocracy lording it over others. Even today, in this age of enlightenment (!), many feel pride from the simple fact of being counted as one of *Deqi-Asgede*.

Adi Nifas lies on a hill at the edge of a steep escarpment overlooking the eastern lowlands that reach the western coast of the Red Sea. To the east, a vast area of high mountains and deep valleys finally gives way to the sandy plains of

Semhar, bordering the Red Sea. Some two centuries before the Christian era, this geographical proximity to the Arabian Peninsula would lead to waves of migrations of Arabs who crossed the Red Sea and eventually settled in the highlands. Their advent changed the ethnographic and cultural landscape. Today's Arabs call us "Habesh," meaning mixed race.

In my childhood, I used to hear some elders say that on a bright day you could see the shining waters of the Red Sea, and every time I heard that I would strain to see the sea, but always fail. My failure, I later found out, was not only because of the distance, but due to the interposing mountains. So, either the elders were exaggerating (which they are not supposed to do) or they saw the sea from another vantage point, probably the mountain called *Ri'si Adi*. The elders also spoke of two kinds of winds blowing on the village: the wind from the sea (*Nifas baHri*) and the wind from the desert *(Nifas BereKa)*; the one blowing from the east and bearing moisture and potential rain, the other blowing from the west and bringing dry air and dust.

The word "sea" used to conjure up, for me, distant lands beyond the mountains that stood between my village and the world out there. The Arabian Peninsula lay on the other side of the Red Sea. Aboy Bashai Tella, one of the venerable elders of our village, a village historian and a close friend of my father, spoke tantalizingly of the historic Red Sea port of Massawa and the time he spent there in his youth, learning Arabic. In the ordinary village parlance of my mother tongue, Tigrigna, the word *baHri* (sea) was, in fact, used to describe the whole lowland area adjoining the Red Sea. In earlier centuries, what is today known as Eritrea used to be known as *Midri BaHri* (the Land of the Sea).

The English traveler's reference to the thousand villages, though hyperbolic, gives a sense of the density of the population of the area, which was made up of settled farmers with a few cattle herders, living off a relatively fertile land. Earlier visitors like the eighteenth-century British traveler, James Bruce, were struck by the peculiar cultural milieu and religious practices. For the area forms part of the larger region in northeastern Africa where Christianity gained a foothold in the fourth century, followed by Islam four centuries later. Indeed, for centuries, Christianity and Islam competed, sometimes not peacefully, for the allegiance of the population of the area. The outcome was that the people of the highlands of Eritrea (and of neighboring Ethiopia) remained predominantly Christian, while the people in the eastern and western lowlands became Muslim.

Orthodox Christianity and Sunni Islam have been the dominant religions. Catholic and Protestant missionaries, mostly European, began to arrive in the early decades of the nineteenth century. These two faiths remain minority denominations today, albeit vibrant and grudgingly recognized by the general public, the adherents of the Orthodox faith. A succession of regimes tolerated Catholics and Protestants, but Italian colonial authorities favored the Catholics and harassed Protestants.

Today, as yesterday, the inhabitants of the Land of the Thousand Villages and beyond, including the land further south beyond the river Mereb, see them-

selves as a special breed. This has been as much a source of strength as a curse. As children, we grew up with our heads filled with grand ideas of a privileged place on earth. That such a claim may offend reason and clash with reality—like the misery of people's lives—is irrelevant. My people, these proud people, sustain their pride through a set of myths and legends, not all of them of their own invention. After all, didn't Homer write about our ancestors as the "blameless Ethiopians?" Didn't he report that the gods visited those blameless beings once a year for a grand feast, choosing them instead of the Egyptians? Who are we to doubt Homer!

My people never tire of reminding Egyptians that the life-giving Nile, the source of their sustenance, springs from the belly of our land. It is even possible, some might fancifully add and rub it in, that it was this that prompted the Greeks to prefer us and not them, in their annual visit for the divine feast.

> For Zeus went to the blameless Aithiopians at the Ocean yesterday to feast, and the rest of the gods went with him. On the twelfth day he will be coming back to Olympos."(The Iliad, Book One, lines 423-425).

Fanciful? Perhaps, but the use of legends to bolster national ideology is not peculiar to us. But perhaps we have erred on the side of fancy for far too long.

I, for one, find this inordinate pride about being the source of the Nile a bit tacky. Need I remind my fellow "Habeshas" that, except for the time of the Pharaohs, there has not been famine of biblical proportions in Egypt? Whereas our people, on both sides of the Mereb, have been visited with the scourge of war and famine for as long as I can remember.

It Takes a Village—Growing up in a Community of Values

I passed my childhood until the age of twelve in my village of birth. Childhood is like a magic circle when it is a happy one, as mine was. The now famous dictum, "It takes a village to raise a child," is one that I can attest to, based on my own experience. Every older villager felt an obligation to minister to the wellbeing of any village child.

Which one of the myriads of memories to record? For reasons hard to fathom, some jump out of the past—out of the dark recesses of the mind—and rush onto you. There is the story of the rabid dog, for instance, an incident in which I was snatched by a neighbor and taken to her home. The woman, who had a boy of four (my age) did not wait to get permission from my parents. She snatched me and took me into the safety of her house because a rabid dog was on the loose. She took it upon herself to be *in loco parentis* for that moment of danger. Her son and I huddled together for some time. We heard people outside, one of these voices being that of my father who was looking for me. The woman opened the door and told my father I was safe in her house. Within minutes a deafening shot rang in the neighborhood, followed by cheers of approval. We were frightened out of our wits, but we ventured out to see what was going on. I saw the village chief, Aboy Kentiba Ghidey, with his rifle and my father talking to him. He had just shot the dog dead, and immediately after, it was pulled away for burial by a couple of village elders.

It was the first time that I heard gunfire and saw a rifle. Aboy Kentiba Ghidey was a veteran soldier of the Italian colonial army and knew how to wield a gun. He was what was known as warrant chief in British colonial service, that is to say, not a hereditary chief, but one granted by a colonial power. His duties consisted of adjudicating disputes pertaining to customary law, as well as acting as conduit or point of contact for the colonial authority, transmitting orders to the village community. He was well-liked by the villagers.

Apart from the usual games and the pleasant indulgence of the elders, a typical village boyhood involved first, herding lambs and goat-kids from the age of six or seven, followed by herding of sheep and goats, from the ages of seven or eight to ten. Then one was promoted to bigger livestock, like cattle. About the time I turned seven, my first job was to tend to lambs and kids in the proximity of our village within sight and hearing distance of parents or other village elders.

In their early teens, village boys were initiated into the world of agriculture, helping on the farm during the sowing and harvest seasons. The boys were taught how to yoke the oxen, how to assemble the plough and its accessories, and how to fasten the assembled plough to the middle of the yoke, which was already fastened onto the necks of the two oxen. Above all, boys were taught how to hold the handle of the plough (*irfi*) and drive the yoked oxen. The aim was to keep the ploughshare in the hard soil and avoid its slipping out and goring the feet of the oxen. Like all things, it took patience and practice. All the boys (not girls) learned this. Traditionally, though this is changing now, girls' chores lay in the domestic area, helping their mothers' cooking and preparing food.

At harvest time, all able-bodied members of the family, including girls, were expected to participate in cutting the crop with sickles and placing it in conical stacks to dry in the field. Again, everyone took part in weeding long before the crop was ready for harvest. Both weeding and harvesting were tiresome, back-breaking work. Whenever the head of the household was absent due to illness, death or other reasons during a harvest season, village social custom decreed that the harvest was gathered through a cooperative effort known as *wefera*, in which members of the extended family pitched in to help. For other purposes such as tilling the land, a widow might lease land in *firqi* or *meselless*. The former involved partnership of equal division of the produce, while in the latter a third was given to the owner of the farm.

I was still learning all this as a boy when I escaped to a different world, as I will explain. But there was an incident in which my elder brother, Tekeste, who had been tilling the land, asked me to take over the handle of the plough (the *irfi*), because he needed to pass water. Tekeste had always been indulgent with me and defended me against village bullies. That particular day I think

he wanted me to feel like a man and boast to my peers that I could handle my *irfi*. I say this because I know he could have simply stopped the tilling, leaving the ploughshare lying loose on top of the ground, and the oxen wouldn't have moved. Anyway, at first it looked easy and I held on to the *irfi*, but soon the ploughshare slipped out of the ground. I was not skilled enough (or may be not strong enough) to handle the *irfi*; in no time the ploughshare gored the foot of one of the oxen. I cried for help, whereupon Tekeste interrupted Nature's call and rushed back to take over. Fortunately, the ox was not badly hurt, but from then on, I was given up as hopeless. My father reprimanded Tekeste and told me that I was not cut out for farming; my destiny lay elsewhere, he said. May he rest in peace!

A Family of Three Girls and Six Boys

We were a large family, like most families at that time. Traditionally, a large family was devoutly wished by everyone, as a kind of a biological insurance against death, at a time when modern medicine was not available to protect children from the hazards of many diseases. And boys were preferred over girls because, once married, a girl left her family to become part of the family of the husband, invariably living in a village far from her village of origin. She was thus a "loss" to her family in economic terms—in terms of her participation in the family's labor—although in social and emotional terms she was still a member of the family.

My mother gave birth to ten children, one of whom (the first) died in infancy. Nothing was said about that infant in our family; it is possible that he was stillborn, and it was taboo to talk about stillbirth in village societies. Then two girls were born, Hanna and Bissrat, followed by three boys—Tekeste, Simret and Bereket (myself). Next to me, came Mebrat, a girl, followed by three boys: Tewelde-Birhan (Tewlede), Daniel and Elias.

As I write, there are four of us living: Bissrat, Tekeste, myself, and Elias. The first to die was Daniel, who expired at twelve years of age, a few weeks after my father's death in early 1950. I was in London studying, and I was later told that Daniel died, literally, of grief.

There is a sad story concerning Daniel's death, which I must relate. When he was eight years old, he and Tewelde, who was eleven, found a rusted but unexploded hand-grenade left by retreating Italian soldiers, early in World War II. The two boys started playing with the grenade, thinking it to be some kind of toy. It exploded injuring them both. Tewelde received minor injuries in the leg and hands. Daniel, who received the main impact of the explosion, was badly injured; he lost one eye, and the other eye was partially blinded. He also lost his left hand and three fingers of his right hand. His face was severely disfigured. I was studying in Harar, Ethiopia, when this happened. It was a devastating piece of news.

Daniel was a special child and I am overcome with grief when I think of him and the unfulfilled promise that he represented. He was an extremely bright boy with an incredible memory. I remember reading to him from the Bible, and asking him to relate it to me later and he would recount it all faultlessly. I would also teach him English words and sentences, and he would repeat them perfectly when I tested him many days later. In educational terms, he was far above his peers and even surpassed those in higher grades. His brilliance was noticed by my father who always looked out for and encouraged talent

It was a matter of great sadness for me and the rest of our family that such a promising life as Daniel's was cut short. After his injury, my father had a plan to put Daniel in the care of a famous Bible scholar, Haleqa Tewelde-Berhan, who happened to be blind, to receive classical education of Orthodox Christian scholars. My father had begun to pay special attention to Daniel ever since his injury, so when he died, Daniel was obviously stricken with grief beyond repair. I was told that he sat by my father's deathbed every day, enfolded in sadness and fearing the worst but hoping for his recovery. Alas! His worst fears overcame his hopes and, as *rigor mortis* set in, his agonized pleas moved everyone to tears. "Oh God, do not forsake me, do not forsake me. Have mercy on me, oh God!" he cried out.

Daniel died a week or so after father's death.

He is buried in the village cemetery, near father. The first thing I did after my return from my studies abroad in 1956 was to visit the cemetery. It was, at once, an act of homage and a ritual in conformity with village tradition, a ritual that constitutes society's defiance to Death's dominion.

As I stood by the graves of my father and my brother, one of my father's favorite passages of the Bible rang in my ears, and one that I later chose for the gravestone of my brother Tewolde, following his untimely death on Christmas Day 1995. The passage is from the 2nd Epistle of the Apostle Paul to Timothy (2nd Timothy for short), chapter 4, verses 7-8:

> I have fought a good fight, I have finished the course. I have kept the faith. Henceforth there is laid for me a crown of righteousness, which the Lord, the righteous judge, shall give me at that day; and not only me, but unto all them also that love his appearing.

Hanna, our oldest sister, was the next to die in 1962, aged only 42, and after her, my brother Simret died in 1988. A little over seven years later, Tewelde died on Christmas Day 1995. The last sibling to leave this mortal coil was Mebrat who departed in 2001. Of all of my deceased siblings, Mebrat suffered much, not only because of the loss of her husband and two sons in the war of liberation, but because of a debilitating cancer that caused her much pain before she was mercifully delivered from it.

I would be remiss if I completed this family narrative without including Aboy Hailu. A quiet and gentle man of sturdy build—short but compact— Aboy Hailu was very much part of our family, even though he was no blood relation. He was an Ethiopian from the district of Wadla-Delanta in central

Ethiopia, as I would learn later from my older brother Tekeste. Aboy Hailu had been part of the family ever since I can remember; I was told that he appeared on the scene when I was a toddler. My father decided to allow him to stay in our household, and he stayed on presumably because he felt comfortable in a home in which the head of the household, and later some of us could speak to him in the language he understood—Amharic. Throughout his life as a member of the Habte Selassie family, Aboy Hailu diligently took part in all the duties of the household, including farming, weeding, harvesting, and looking after the animals.

I remember, throughout my childhood, many people came to serve briefly as seasonal workers especially during the harvesting season. They would come, serve, take their wages and leave never to return. Aboy Hailu came and never left. As he became a permanent fixture of the homestead, villagers stopped referring to him as *Amharaicum* (Your Amhara servant) and called him Aboy Hailu, instead, using the same term of respect used for elders of the village. When he died the entire village community turned up at his funeral, and he was mourned as a member of the community.

Aboy Hailu went to his grave without revealing to anyone the reason why he left his birthplace. No one except perhaps my father knew where he hailed from, and why. Did he leave a family behind? If so, why did he leave them and stay away from them forever? Did he perhaps commit a serious crime and flee the scene of the crime never to return? These were questions that many people wondered about but never asked loudly. My mother often said that she noticed a change in the expression of his face, with misty eyes whenever my brother Tewolde, as a small boy came near and snuggled on his lap. She speculated that he must have left a small boy of Tewolde's age behind. Toward the end of his life, he would reveal to my brother Tekeste that he hailed from the district of Wadla-Delanta in central Ethiopia. Why Aboy Hailu revealed that piece of information in his last years is a mystery; perhaps he felt that whatever it was that had sent him out of his birthplace happened so long ago, no one would hold him to account for it. Or perhaps it was nostalgic memories that haunted him in old age. He suffered from some dementia in the last years of his life and was cared for by the members of the family who were close by, notably my mother.

The Ties That Bind

Now in the traditional communities where I spent my childhood years, attending a funeral of a family member is an obligation of the greatest moment affecting all members of the extended family. In the village community, funerals and weddings are perhaps the most important social indices of group cohesion. They form part of the ritual of expressing solidarity, of finding and asserting one's place in the scheme of things. According to rules of tradition, all the members of the extended family embracing the larger kinship group, as well as neighbors and friends, are required to be present at these occasions, especially at funerals. Even if you are not present at the funeral you are required to visit the bereaved, pay homage and commiserate, expressing regrets and explaining your absence. This custom has survived even in cities, but not to the same extent as in the villages.

Funeral occasions also provide the opportunity and venue for reconciliation of enemies and rebuilding bridges, thus restoring social solidarity. If the deceased is the main breadwinner of the bereaved family, the elders of the immediate family must also discuss plans of helping the widow and her children get by until they can get back on their feet. Whenever there is neglect of such traditional duties, the village gossip will begin to be heard. The village girls, those adorable creatures and paragons of virtue and barometer of moral outrage, will begin their songs of disparagement, putting all concerned to shame. The sheer shame of it will invariably cause correction or redress of the wrong or omission.

Nor are such songs limited to omission with respect to funerals and the like. They can also voice society's moral sanction in cases of people who commit adultery or similar misdeeds. I can still remember the withering attack leveled at my favorite uncle, Bashai Asfaha, for allegedly committing adultery with the widow of one Gebretsadiq. My good uncle protested, denying the allegations, but to no avail; once the rumor reaches the sensitive ears of village girls, there is no point in protesting. Out comes the song and it is repeated throughout the season until another song aimed at another villager takes its place.

The only sibling at whose funeral I was present was Tewelde. This was so because I happened to be living in Asmara at the time, engaged in some of the most exciting events of my life, as head of the Constitutional Commission of Eritrea. All the other siblings died while I was away: Hanna when I was in Ethiopia; Simret and Mebrat when I was in the United States; and Daniel, while I was studying in England, as I have already related. I could have been at Mebrat's funeral but, by 2001, I had run afoul of the current regime and could not return to my birthplace.

My Parents of Blessed Memory

My mother, Letehaimanot Negassi, was a generous and gentle soul, loved and respected by all the people of our lineage and beyond. I last saw her, frail and old, in February 1975, in circumstances I will describe in another chapter. She died in Asmara in 1978, while I was involved in our armed struggle for independence from Ethiopian occupation. There was no way I could attend her funeral, for I was on the top of the list of "criminals" wanted by the Ethiopian government, dead or alive.

Qeshi Habte Selassie Gulbot, was a legendary figure, known throughout the area of the "thousand villages." His fame had become a source of pride not only to members of his immediate family but to his entire lineage group. I am referring to the person who determined the course of my life, from childhood on—my father of blessed memory. The word *Qeshi,* attached to his name, means priest, for in addition to being a revered community elder and consummate advocate in traditional law, my father was also a Protestant pastor.

My father's fame rested on character and charisma. He was known for his fearless uprightness, honesty, generosity and eloquence of speech. All who knew him attest to these qualities. The followers of his faith speak of his masterly delivery of sermons. Those who frequented the law courts speak with admiration of his arguments in court pleadings. In both undertakings he was known to hold his listeners spellbound. A striking figure, at six feet four inches, he was revered because he always performed the tasks of an elder in good conscience and with due humility. He represented indigent villagers in court, without monetary consideration. He stood for the underdog, including defenseless women. He also tendered wise counsel to individuals and groups who came to our house seeking it. The memory of the endless flow of people to our house, their complaints or questions, and my father's responses after listening to them, is etched in my mind. For some reason, my father let me sit at his feet listening to what went on. Could he have discerned in me a future lawyer who would follow in his footsteps? He never said so, but occasionally hinted that I was destined to go far.

I always thought it remarkable that the people of our village had such high regard for my father despite his conversion to the Lutheran Protestant faith from Orthodox Christianity, the faith of his forefathers. The overwhelming majority of Christians in our country subscribe to the Orthodox faith, and my father had been an ordained Orthodox priest. His conversion had convulsed the village; yet his standing in the community was not adversely affected by it, although a few stalwarts distanced themselves from him. Several attempts were made by prominent Orthodox pastors and other village elders to persuade him to return to the "Mother Church." They failed and their failure provoked the village girls to express the communal disappointment by singing in a rhyming couplet, addressed to his mother, Itye Sebene:

Adey Itye Sbene
Habtes'mber fanene
Intelemmenuwos
Melisu'mber genene.

(O Mother Itye Sbene/Habte has revolted
And the more they pleaded with him,
the more he became adamant).

I have not been able to establish the exact date of his conversion, but I think he must have been in his mid-to-late-twenties, which would put it around 1917 or 1918. My reason for this supposition is based on one simple fact of family history: Hannah, the oldest child in the family was baptized and brought up as a Protestant, as were the rest of us.

There is an interesting anecdote related to my father's conversion. My mother was a devout Orthodox Christian and had married my father according to the Orthodox marriage rites. Apparently the pressure was too much for her after my father converted, so she ran away to Beleza, her village of origin. She must have been about sixteen at the time. Beleza is three miles from Adi Nifas.

The reception my mother got in Beleza was not surprising in view of our traditions with respect to a married woman's place. Grandma Birheen told her daughter in no uncertain terms that her place was with her husband, come what may, adding the oft-quoted remark, "Even if he becomes a Muslim." My mother related this to me with a broad grin, as she repeated the last remark. I must say, I have always blessed my grandmother for sending my mother back to her husband, because otherwise I would not have come to this world. Grandma Birheen was a woman of enormous beauty and grace, features that my mother inherited.

Italians in Our Village

As I look back to the innocent years of my childhood, many events claim a place in my memory—of games we played, of the changing seasons and traditional activities that correspond with the seasons, of visitors from near and far, of Selassie Hamle, the annual celebration of the village patron (Selassie being the Holy Trinity), and so on. Being very close to Asmara, our village was frequented by curious Italian visitors who regaled us kids with gifts. I remember with impish pleasure some of the not-so-innocent things that I did. On one particular occasion, a group of Italian tourists wanted to take pictures of us. Most of us had heard that if an Italian took a picture of your face, you could fall prey to the Devil and become haunted by him, so we would turn our faces or cover them with our hands. In order to induce our cooperation the Italians showed us a fistful of coins and started throwing them to the ground. Two children raced to pick up the coins one by one. Obviously, the Italians found this amusing and roared with laughter.

More coins were thrown on the ground. This time, I beat the rest; I made a split-second calculation and instead of picking up the coins one by one, I scooped up the soil where most of them had fallen, put it onto the front part of my cotton *qemis,* then sat down and coolly picked out the coins. Amused at the sight of native boys fighting over coins, the Italians laughed uproariously; one of them pointed to me and cried, "bravo, bravo!" and gave me more coins, presumably as a reward.

When it was all over, I ran to my mother and proudly presented her with my catch. The story of my "exploits" became the number-one news item in the village that day and for many days thereafter.

My first awareness of the presence of aliens in our midst, people who looked different from us, was when Signor Ventimale, the Italian owner in a fertile part of our village land, came to the village with his two young daughters. I must have been about five years old, and the girls were about the same age. The occasion created a stir: we village children were excited and intrigued to see the girls, who seemed to us like dolls with their clear blue eyes and straight brown hair tied with ribbons. None of us wore shoes or had seen that kind of dress. The girls seemed to be equally intrigued by us, for they touched our hair and giggled and we giggled back. When I exclaimed, "They laugh like us!" their father turned to me and said in Tigrigna, "Of course they laugh like you; they are just like you."

Iwway kemana yizareb'yu" (Oh, he speaks like us) I exclaimed.

"Yes, just like you; and just like you, I was born in Eritrea," he said in flawless Tigrigna without a trace of foreign accent, patting me on the head.

The girls must have enjoyed their experience among us, because they were engaged in a long talk with their father who seemed to hesitate first and finally gave in, saying, "*va bene.*" He then turned toward us and asked us if we would like a ride on his truck.

Would we!

Ventimale drove his truck, filled with excited village children, all the way out to his plantation and back.

As we grew older, we came to know the gentle Ventimale more closely. He sent his wife and daughters to Asmara for the girls' schooling and he lived on the farm. We never saw the girls again, but we saw him from time to time as we watched our flocks in the nearby grazing area. His farm was fenced off by giant aloe plants, thorny acacia and other trees and shrubs, bordered by a small stream. On the outer side of the stream was a large tract of green grass, which was used by the village community for grazing cattle. The spring lying between the farm and the commons was also used for watering the cattle. A portion of the commons was enclosed for the use of the Italian's cows, and when our flocks strayed into Ventimale's preserve, they were impounded by his servants. When Ventimale was present he would only reprimand us and let us off with a warning. But if this happened during his absence, the head warden of his farm would demand payment in the form of grain for his personal benefit.

Seasons of Work and Play

Our life of shepherding was not all work and no play. We played games and took part in the celebrations and feasts that came with the changing seasons. Activities in village life, whether they are related to work or play, are defined by seasonal cycles. In springtime, which starts in March, villagers get busy ploughing and otherwise preparing the ground for sowing and planting. In general, the ground is ploughed three times before sowing. The first stage of ploughing takes place in March. It is designed to prepare the ground so that it will be soaked when the small rains occur. The second stage deepens the process so that more rain will be absorbed. The third stage takes place when the seed is sowed. The seed may be wheat, barley, taff, maize or other grains, as well as beans, peas, chickpeas and flax.

During this period there is little time for play. Children help in small ways while learning the farming process by watching adults. The rainy season starts in mid-June and ends in late August. During this period, the green fields turn less and less green until finally they turn yellow or grayish yellow as the grains mature, nearing harvest. Autumn, which starts in September and ends in December, is the harvest season. Harvest is followed by the dry season, which starts in January and ends in March or April. And the cycle goes on, year after year, unless there is drought, as seems to be the case increasingly in recent years.

Festivities correspond with the changing seasons. *Meskel* (the finding of the cross by Queen Helena) and *TeHambeley* come between September and October. *Timket* (Epiphany) comes in January, right after *Lidet* (Christmas). Most festivities and weddings take place after the harvest season, when the grain stores are full and people can afford to spend. Perhaps the most colorful festivities in the year take place during Timket, when villagers come out to meet, sing and dance on village squares around the church, or near a river or lake. In Eritrea and Ethiopia, *Timket* is celebrated with more fanfare than *Lidet*.

Meskel is more enjoyable for children because that is the time when they are the actors in the drama. I have fond memories of the *Meskel* celebration, when village children gather wood for torches to light up the evening, and go marching to the farthest corners of the fields, chanting "*Hoyye Hoyye—Ho.*" We village boys neither knew nor cared much about the legend of the discovery of the True Cross by an ancient queen called Helena; we only cared about getting the best-burning wood to last through the night of celebration, during which one of the older boys leads the chanting in rhyming words, telling the stories of local heroes and villains, some of them with gaudy details.

> *Aba'brham Agua—*
> *Ho!*
> *kigoyyi tegoga*
> *Ho!*
> *Ab'brahm TiTu*
> *Ho!*
> *kigoyyi TeriTu.....etc.*

Perhaps the most enjoyable time is the wedding season from January to March/April. It is a time of good food and dancing and singing, a time also when older boys flirt with village beauties. There is much mischief as well. When an out-of-town bride is brought to the village of the bridegroom, the village girls on the groom's side give the poor young bride a rough reception, taunting her and singing songs of abuse and disparagement until the best man comes to her rescue and chases them away. The best man is by custom bound to protect the bride as much as he can, even from the bridegroom's spousal abuse.

In extreme cases, the village girls can sneak past the best man and place burning pepper underneath the bride's nose, thus causing her to sneeze violently, at which point the best man might use his whip and avenge the bride's hurt dignity. Whenever I hear of hazing by students in American universities, or its British equivalent, "ragging," I am reminded of the petty cruelties committed by village girls in fulfillment of a silly custom.

Memories, memories...Memories of days gone by, that will never return. Are the boys of the present generation in the village doing the same things? I am sure the traditions continue in somewhat changed form. Modern schooling and its demands have no doubt impacted aspects of village life and the old ways of play. For one, soccer has replaced traditional games of *Qarsa, Timbi* and *TewesseT*.

Some customs die hard, such as the free portion reserved for children from the fruits of the earth in harvest time. It was called the shepherd's portion. By custom, children were allowed to help themselves to ripe grains and legumes before these were claimed by their owners. Children were allowed to roast or bake and eat them to full satisfaction, but not to take them away to the market or even to their home. But children being children, they sometimes abuse the custom, as the following story shows.

One day, during the harvest season, my friend Solomon Gebrehiwet and I got greedy. After helping ourselves to a reasonable portion, we decided to take more. The more we took, the more we became greedy, and we ended up gathering baskets full of unharvested peas and beans. We carried it in three or four trips and stored it in a cave so that we could eat it later. While we were busy carrying our treasure trove, the land warden, a wily man named Gebretsadik, surprised us and caught us red handed. We were terrified and pleaded with him not to tell our parents. He would not budge, and that same day in the evening, Solomon and I got a fair beating on the backside by our respective fathers. Our action might have become the source of village songs by the girls, but in order to avoid that shame, our parents must have done some favor to Gebretsadik, for we didn't hear of it from anybody afterward. And we of course kept it to ourselves, vowing never to do it again.

Chapter 2

EARLY SCHOOLING—
FAITH AND FASCISM

❖❖❖❖❖❖❖❖❖❖❖❖❖❖❖

My mother's village of origin, Beleza, had been one of the outposts of Swedish missionary activities for a long time. It had a school and a clinic, that served the local community, and had become one of the magnets of Protestant education until it was taken over by a Catholic Mission on the order of the Italian colonial authorities. This happened after the Italian invasion of Ethiopia in 1936. Catholic missionaries began frequenting our village. One incident stands out in my memory.

It was a warm afternoon in early May. The sun was shining from a blue sky. A group of us, aged five or six, were playing on one of the village playgrounds when five nuns appeared on the scene, unannounced. Three were Italians, dressed in snow-white habits with headscarves to match, and two were Eritrean who acted as interpreters; the latter wore khaki habits and headscarves. One of the Italian nuns was carrying a satchel. We ran after them, wanting to touch the golden cords dangling at their sides.

Suddenly, the nun carrying the satchel opened it and took out a fistful of chains with medallions of the Holy Mother, and distributed them to all of us. We were all excited, as we had never seen anything so beautiful. I ran home to show my medallion to my mother. My father was away on some legal case.

"Isn't she lovely, mother," I said excitedly, pointing to the medallion. I had already hung it round my neck.

"Yes, she is wonderful," mother replied absent-mindedly. She was cooking the evening meal, which must be ready before father returns. Then she looked at the medallion more closely and said, "I don't know if your father will allow you to wear it."

"Why not, mother?" I asked with the anxiety of a five-year-old child fearful he might lose what he considers a most beautiful object. When I pressed her, she said that the Protestants do not believe in the Holy Virgin Mary. "That is all I can say; the rest your father will explain to you."

"Are we Protestants against the Holy Mary?"

"No, we are not, not really. It is very complicated. Ask your father."

I was disappointed and was determined to keep my medallion. "Didn't grandma Birheen say that I am the Holy Mary's special child?"

"Yes, you are. Don't ask me any more," mother said with finality, handing me some roasted wheat. "Here, have some *qolo*."

After father returned, I showed him the medallion and asked him to let me wear it. He could see I was excited and didn't want to hurt my feelings. But he gently instructed me on the question of intercession by the Holy Mother and the Saints: telling me that there was no need for intercession, according to Protestant theology. He told me that this was one of the differences between the Protestants on the one hand and the Catholics and Orthodox, or Copts, on the other. He said that Jesus had died for us so that there would be no need for any mediator between us and God. Jesus, he said, was the Way, the Truth and Salvation, quoting chapter and verse from the New Testament.

I had to accept father's word but my heart was with the medallion. Later, I reminded mother that father did not actually order me not to wear the medallion. She smiled and said, it is okay to wear it but don't show it. That made me the happiest child. And I reminded my mother, again, of grandma Birheen's words about me being a special child of the Blessed Mary. My mother became Protestant by marriage, but I suspect that at heart she remained an Orthodox. As I grew older, she also allowed me to steal away in the dead of night to join Meskel and other celebrations, of which father did not approve.

A Woman of Beauty and Grace

Just the mention of her name brings back a rush of memories of my long-departed grandmother. One particular event remains prominent in my memory and keeps coming back—the incident of the lost sheep and my flight to my grandparents' home.

It was already dark when I arrived at their house in Beleza. After feeding me, grandma tucked me into bed and kissed me good night. I did not sleep the whole night, having lost my sheep, and got up early in the morning the next day. This too I remember as if it is happening now...

It is dawn in Beleza, an idyllic pastoral scene.

The first crimson rays of sunlight over the hills announce the arrival of a new day in April. I had just stepped out to pee against the wall of the house, facing east. Having emptied my bladder and admired nature's wondrous sight, I go back to bed and lie awake thinking about my fate. I try to tune out the memory of yesterday's events by listening to nature's morning music—the sweet chorus of birds chirping, mixed with the cry of lambs and goats; a donkey's mournful bray from afar, which sounds like a broken French Horn; and the crowing of a late-rising rooster.

The rooster prompts my grandfather to observe, "What a hopeless creature! Where was he when the others were doing it at the right time?"

"He must have been created for late-rising men," grandma says.

"Or late-rising women," retorts grandpa, which draws a hearty laugh from her. This laughter fills the house and gives me a mysterious sense of cheer and comfort. I smile and stifle a laugh. I should not invade their private moment of good humor, for though I have known them to tease each other in private, grandma keeps the lid on and maintains customary decorum in front of others. According to the golden rule that keeps the family together, a woman must not only respect her husband, but she must be seen to respect him.

A male voice from a nearby house calls someone, presumably his son, reminding him of his early morning tasks. Lying in bed, I imagine the poor boy yawning and stretching, and probably complaining as he rises to do his chores. For that is what I do some mornings when my father or older brothers call me to wake up. The thought brings back the memory of what happened yesterday. The peaceful and leisurely village life does not feel so peaceful this particular morning.

Earlier, grandma Birheen had thrust a teaspoonful of white honey into my mouth when she saw that I was awake. She did that every time I spent the night with them. The idyllic pastoral morning and the sweet honey does not erase the pang of guilt I felt for coming to Beleza yesterday in the late afternoon. I had run away from my village but I did not inform my grandparents why I ran away. Of course, grandma is perceptive and must have known something was wrong; I certainly did not come for a family visit at that hour of the day. At age seven, you just don't pack up all of a sudden and walk five kilometers to visit your grandparents. Not without parental consent or knowledge.

But this morning my grandparents do not seem in a hurry to find out why their beloved grandson had come alone at night. Grandma Birheen takes her time and gives me time and space to come clean, which she knew I would sooner or later. She must know that a discreet silence, accompanied with tender care and attention would yield better results than rough interrogation. Besides, it was not in her nature to force people to talk.

As for grandpa Negassi, he normally leaves such things to his perceptive and gentle wife of forty years. He is busy seeing that the family's domestic helper and farm hands do their morning duties, like milking the animals before releasing their young to suckle what is left over. A good shepherd knows how much to take and how much to leave for the young animals.

I hear Grandpa's baritone voice booming from the front porch of the house, talking to the shepherd boy who tends to the sheep and goats during the day. "Woldai, be sure to leave some for the lambs; don't milk too much."

"Don't worry, Aboy Negassi; I know when to stop."

"And give some hay to the bulls."

"I already have."

"Good boy. Your lunch should be ready any time now. You must start early to get to the common pasture before the other boys."

"I will Aboy Negassi."

I can now smell the aroma of grandma's cooking, mixed with her favorite incense, which she lit as she roasted the coffee beans—the staple first intake of all adults in the village, their eye-opener. The mixed aroma, which comes in waves, stimulates my appetite. Breakfast can't be too long in coming now. As if pulled by the prospect, I scramble out of bed and put on my clothes and join grandma. The fire in the *iton* has warmed the room.

Is this the right moment to tell her? I hesitate and then decide to be out with it. How much longer can I keep it in? "Grandma," I say, wishing to tell my sad story.

"*Yey Wedey* (Yes, my son).

I chicken out momentarily and ask her, instead, what she is cooking.

"I am cooking the usual food for the morning and for the rest of the day." She steals a look at me. "You will pass the day with us, won't you?"

I can't hold it any longer. "Grandma," I begin, "I didn't tell anyone that I was coming here. I ran away."

"Why, honey? Is anything the matter?"

"Yes. I lost the sheep."

"Where?"

"Near SheKa Abi; by the big lake. I was playing with my friends when I last saw them grazing on the pasture nearby."

A pall of silence envelopes the house. Then Grandpa comes in from the front porch and Grandma tells him my story. He does not say much; he just asks a rhetorical question: "Where could they have gone?"

"Do you think the hyenas might have eaten them?" I ask, hoping for a reassuring, negative answer.

"Nah. They must have strayed to a neighboring village and been taken hostage. Or perhaps the warden of a private estate has impounded them and is holding them for ransom. Yah, I am sure that's what it is. Don't you worry, your little head, my boy."

There are none sweeter than grandparents, especially in times of distress. It is hard to describe the calming effect of their wise words.

"But we must take you home. Your mother must be worried sick," grandma says. She knows that I would not go alone because of my fear of punishment. If my sheep have been devoured by hungry hyenas, I will be severely punished. "And I will take you myself," she adds.

All grandmothers are special, but mine is doubly special.

My anxiety is somewhat relieved. But there is no telling how father will take it this time. A year ago, I lost two sheep to a fox, because I was engrossed in a game with the village boys and forgot all about the sheep. It was at the end of my first year, after my promotion to sheepherder. That time, while I was playing, a fox had stalked the flock of sheep and killed one. Another fox wounded another

sheep and left it because some passers-by drove it away. The wounded sheep ran towards the area where we were playing, with blood running from its neck. Some one spotted it and we all ran to see. When I discovered that it was one of mine, I was shocked and angry and immediately ran to recover the scattered flock of about fifty sheep. I have hated foxes ever since.

That day in the evening, I reported the events to my mother with great trepidation. My mother scolded me but was able to intercede with my father, saving me from punishment. Her argument was that I was too young, only in my first year of herding experience. She also played on his favorite theme, that I had shown more promise as a student, and that my future lay in studies not in the life of a farmer.

But I do not look forward to confronting father this time. This time, no intercession from mother can save me from punishment.

The Sheep Are Found

Back in Adi Nifas with grandma Birheen, I expect her to take me to our house to face my parents. Instead she takes a circuitous route and brings me to my uncle Asfaha's house. Uncle Asfaha, or Aboy Bashai Asfaha as we called him, is comfortably seated on a wooden chair, under the awning of his front porch. He is wearing the traditional white *gabi* (toga) with one end wrapped around his left shoulder, which frees his right arm. He waves his flywhisk with his right hand, chasing the flies, while he absent-mindedly strokes his goatee with his left hand. It is a warm afternoon and the sun is shining brightly. A group of village boys are sitting at his feet, waiting to hear his wonderful stories. The boys' expectations are suddenly dashed as my grandma approaches him and whispers in his ear. He tells the boys to come back tomorrow, as he has to attend to an urgent matter.

"What brings you here, Birheen," my uncle asks, and grandma relates the story of my lost sheep "Bereket is worried the hyenas might have eaten them," she says.

"What hyenas? The sheep are all well; Tesfai, my son, is looking after them today. He volunteered to look after the sheep until Bereket's return," he said, stroking my head gently as if to express his joy in seeing me back safe.

"Where were they found?" grandma asks. I myself am speechless.

"They were impounded by Ventimale's warden and held for ransom because they had strayed into his garden and eaten his cabbage."

"Blessed Mother of God!" exclaims grandma, who is a devout Christian. She never failed to remind me and my mother that I was a special child of Mary (*Wedi Mariam*) because I was born on *Mariam Gunbot(* St. Mary's Day in May), the day of annual celebration. According to her, this makes me a special ward of the Blessed Mother. "No harm shall befall him," she had repeatedly told my mother, especially whenever I fell ill during infancy.

And it is true! As I hear my uncle, I become dizzy with happiness. My grandma then tells me to follow her to meet my anxious parents. It is as if a heavy burden has been lifted from my head. Once more I was saved from parental chastisement. Now I can enjoy the rest of the day while cousin Tesfai looks after my sheep. Long live the extended family!

After the incident of the lost sheep, my father decided to enroll me in the school that my two brothers were attending. My farming days were done.

Scuola Vittorio

Education in my childhood was of two kinds. The first kind was Orthodox Church education; the second was modern education in either Christian mission schools or government schools organized by the Italian colonial administration. In a traditional society like the one where I grew up, people generally resisted the introduction of modern education, so very few people sent their children to modern schools. The resistance to the mission schools was based on confessional or denominational reasons. Orthodox Christians feared that their children might be converted to the Catholic or Protestant denomination. In the cities, things were better; with urbanization, people began to see the advantages of modern education and did not hesitate in sending their children to school.

My father was one of the few enlightened village elders who believed in the value of modern education. This was largely due to his association with Swedish Protestant missionaries, as well as to his observation of the practical effects of modern education. He thus sent the three oldest boys, Tekeste, Semret, and myself to the Scuola Vittoriao Emauele III in Asmara. My older brothers started two years ahead of me, because I was too young to start with them.

Before I started school in Asmara, I was instructed in the Tigrigna language, reading and writing. Our house was used as a school for many village children during the dry season when there was no farming activity. But the majority of the village boys were first schooled in the traditional Orthodox Church manner. When they reached the age of five or six, their parents would send them to the head of the village church, the *Quese Gebez,* who either taught them himself or assigned another teacher. The traditional technique consisted of loud repetition of assigned texts. The teacher would lead the pupils who repeat what he reads many times over until they know it by heart. This technique made them weak in writing and comprehension.

Being the son of a Protestant pastor, I was not sent to the Church school, but I could hear my friends repeating the lessons day in day out. I used to get envious and ask my friends, Solomon Gebrehiwet and Tekeste Dirar to teach them to me. At times I even sneaked into the churchyard where the *Yeneta* (professor.) was teaching his pupils and pretended to be one of them. To this day, I can repeat some of the lessons in Geez. When my father found out, he told me that if I was interested in Geez, he could teach it to me which is the origin of my rudimentary knowledge of our classical language.

 Early Schooling—Faith and Fascism

When I was enrolled at the *Scuola Vittorio Emanuele III*, or Scuola Vittorio, as it was commonly known, I was just past seven, three years younger than Semret and six years younger than Tekeste. Until that time, as I noted before, we were all home-schooled, Tekeste and Simret as well as other older boys serving as teaching assistants. The principle was, "Each one teach one," with my father supervising the teaching assistants. Our house served as a school until a village school was opened much later, on the initiative of my father and two other village elders who were his close friends, Tedla Gebremedhin and Teclemicael Aghias.

When I think of going to the Italian school, the first thing that comes to my mind is how hard it was. At that tender age I hated the early rise and walk, barefoot in the mornings. My brothers and I had to get up early and walk five miles from the village to Asmara. We would start just before sunrise and walk carrying our lunch in our satchels, traveling early in the morning and returning home before sunset. It was cold and the stones on the rough road hurt my toes, as I occasionally stumbled. But our father placed a high premium on learning and impressed upon me that I should overcome all obstacles that stood in the way of my educational progress. On lucky days, a kind bicyclist would stop to give me a ride.

I have a vivid memory of my first day at the Scuola Vittorio. The four of us, my father my two brothers and I traveled from Adi Nifas and made our way to the school ground which was filled with hundreds of children waiting to be called. My father left me with my brothers and went to attend to other business. The bell rang and Tekeste and Simret went to their classes, leaving me outside with the crowd of newly enrolled boys. We stood there, hundreds of six-and seven-year-olds, in rows and rows, waiting for our names to be called. Tekeste had instructed me that when my name is called I was to shout *"presente."*

I waited for what seemed an eternity, feeling faint under the scorching sun. Eventually, my name was called. I didn't respond the first time, because I was not sure, but when it was repeated, somehow the word *"presente"* came out of me in a hoarse voice. It sounded like somebody else's voice and I didn't know what to do next. Then an usher motioned me forward, past a nun who was reading the names, to a door through which boys whose names had been called before mine were slowly entering.

I attended the first grade in Scuola Vittorio, where Italian Catholic nuns taught us the Latin alphabet, elementary geography, and history of Italy. The name of my teacher escapes me, but I remember she was a tall, smiling nun with protruding teeth. Some unkind soul gave her the nickname *mefles* (beaver) which stuck. The first day in *prima classe* (grade one) we sat on long wooden planks joined to benches. Suddenly the door opened and our teacher, dressed in a white flowing robe with matching headpiece, entered smiling, followed by a greyhaired Eritrean gentleman called Yeneta Yohannes. Some one told us to rise and we did. The nun said "Good morning, children !" in Italian. A few of the students responded, also in Italian. These were, we were later told, students from last year who had not made it to the next grade; that was why they knew how to respond. They were called the *sclusi* (Italian for excluded).

The class started with a pep talk from Yeneta Yohannes. The nun/teacher then made a long speech, which Yenet Yoannes translated to Tigrigna. She ended her speech by promising us that before long we would be able to understand and speak Italian. And we would be good servants of the colony. She turned to Yeneta Yohannes with the same charming smile and told him that his role as interpreter would be ended soon; they both laughed and he left us in her tender care.

I had seen Yeneta Yohannes at the school ground, earlier that day; upon seeing him, my father had rushed toward him and he in turn started rushing toward my father, and they gave each other the customary greetings by touching each other's shoulders repeatedly. I remember my father taking off his hat and Yeneta Yohannes admonishing him and insisting that he put on his hat. Concerning this custom of courtesy and mutual respect, I also remember a similar incident, years later, when I was studying at the Geza Kenisha School. My father and I were going toward the Asmara cereal market, past the Great Mosque. He was mounted on his favorite grey-colored mule and I was walking by his side. Suddenly the Asmara muezzin started his call to prayers, and my father immediately dismounted and took his hat off. I asked why, and he said, "It is out of respect for the faith of others. The man is crying *Allahu akber* (God is Great), calling the Muslim faithful to prayers. The Muslims call Him Allah, we call Him *Igziabher* (God), but "He is the same God and we must respect their hour of prayer."

I have always remembered that lesson and tried to live by it.

I also learned later that, although they had their political differences, my father and the muezzin, Aboy Imam Musa, were good friends. Tahir Imam Musa, the muezzin's older son, and I became good friends in the late 1960's when I was exiled in Harar and he was an employee of a company in Dire Dawa. In 1975, Tahir became one of the many kidnap and murder victims of the military government of Mengistu Haile Mariam.

Fascism and Schooling

To go back to my early schooling, the most dreaded moments in the whole experience were the visits of Fascist cadres, who would storm into the class unannounced to harangue us about Mussolini and his greatness, about the glorious Fascist Party and about "bella Italia." As we understood Italian more, they would tell us how we must grow up to be loyal subjects of the King of Italy, "*Sua Maiesta, Vittorio Emanule Terzo, Re d'Italia, imperatore d'Etiopia.*" (His Majesty, Victor Emanuel III, King of Italy, Emperor of Ethiopia).

At the end of each harangue, the Fascist cadre would shout:

"*Salute il re!*" (Salute the king).

And we were taught to respond, "*Viva il re!*"

Then he would shout, "*Salute il Duce!*" (i.e. Mussolini). And we would shout back, "*a noi!*" (For us).

This ritual salutation to the leader of the Fascist party and the puppet king was also sometimes repeated at the end of each class, with the nun leading the chorus this time. This was presumably a case of rendering unto Caesar what is Caesar's; one hopes that their religious conviction did not make the good nuns susceptible to fascist propaganda.

The school lay in the indigenous zone of the city, which was divided into the Italian zone and the indigenous zone. Under the system of racial segregation, no Eritrean was allowed to live or work in the Italian zone. According to Italian colonial policy, Eritrea's indigenous populations, the *indigeni (natives)*, were only allowed education up to the fifth grade. It was a policy designed to produce native clerical and sub-clerical workers to serve the colonial purpose. The highest position an *indigeno* (native) could aspire to was to be a clerk in a company or a government office. One such clerk, and a proud one at that, was my former brother-in-law, Yoseph Gebremicael (my oldest sister, Hannah's husband). I well remember Yoseph as an object of admiration as a *scrivante* (clerk) in some small commercial enterprise.

Yoseph's arrival home from work on a new bicycle was an occasion of great curiosity among the neighborhood people. Clearly he had "arrived," he had made it! But it would not last long; he was recruited as a soldier (an askari) in the colonial army, probably willingly because soldiers were paid more, plus it was an adventure for a young man of twenty-four. He was lucky to survive the war, but brought back VD and gave it to my poor sister. The marriage ended in divorce.

The few people who were able to obtain education beyond the fifth grade were students in Catholic and Protestant missionary schools. In the case of Catholics, the few students proceeding to higher secondary (and some university) education were those chosen for the priesthood. Some defected from the priesthood and did well in their academic education, but instead of returning to Eritrea they went to Ethiopia where they would serve the ungrateful Emperor Haile Selassie with great distinction. An example of these was Lorenzo Taezaz, an Eritrean who was sent abroad to study theology. For reasons best known to himself, Lorenzo left the priesthood school and eventually obtained a doctorate in law from Montpelier University in southern France. He finished his education in the late 1920s and returned to Ethiopia, where Ras Teferi Mekonen (later King Teferi) had been crowned as Emperor assuming the throne name of Haile Selassie. Lorenzo was the principal advisor of the Emperor when Italy invaded Ethiopia in 1935. When the Emperor addressed the League of Nations in Geneva in 1936, Lorenzo helped draft the speech that propelled the Emperor to world fame.

Lorenzo's service to Ethiopia did not end there. After the Emperor settled in England as an exiled king, he sent Lorenzo back to find out how the Ethiopian patriotic resistance was doing. At great risk to life and limb, Lorenzo went to the guerilla-held areas in northern and central Ethiopia and reported back to the Emperor. It was during those visits that he contracted the disease that would finally kill him at the age of 47. He died while serving as Ethiopian Ambassador to the Soviet Union, a hardship post for the man who had been the first foreign minister after the Emperor's return to his throne. Lorenzo's fate was regarded by Eritreans as metaphor for the Emperor's treatment of Eritreans who served him. It contributed to the disaffection of the next generation, leading to the rising nationalist sentiment among the young that would eventually crystallize in the formation of an armed struggle for independence.

In the case of Protestants, there were a few who were taught by missionaries, mostly Swedish and one Italian, in small teacher training centers. The most famous Italian Protestant pastor (a Valdese) was Pastor Tron. Among his students was Woldeab Woldemariam, one of the founding fathers of Eritrea's movement for independence. Other Eritrean Protestants went to Ethiopia, such as Efrem Tewolde-Medhin and Dawit Ogbazghi. The first served as teacher and school administrator before the Italian invasion and as Ethiopian ambassador after the Italians left in 1941. The second served in various administrative posts, ending as Minister of State at the Ministry of Foreign Affairs until December 1960. He was among those ministers and other dignitaries who were killed by the leaders of the 1960 failed coup d'etat.

The activities of Protestant Missionaries were closely monitored and some curtailed, especially after Mussolini became dictator of Italy in 1923. The Swedish Mission Scool in Geza Kenisha, Asmara, was ordered closed, and mission schools and clinics were also ordered shut down. Some of the Swedish missionaries left for Ethiopia and elsewhere.

Between Town and Country

Even while living in the city, the strong roots of the village followed me. Every weekend, my brothers and I returned to the village, living and working like village boys. During the school break we helped in the farming activities, including weeding (which I hated) and harvesting. Hanging out with my village friends, I either proudly displayed my knowledge acquired at Scuola Vitorio, or conversely sought information on their progress in the Church school.

I was happiest to be in my village during harvest time because that was the fun time. Harvest time is the most favored season in village life because it heralds the coming of weddings and other festivities. It is also the time when the elders gather in the *Baito* to discuss village affairs or to gossip, or to sit in their front porches for afternoon chats.

The mere mention of the word songs brings back memories of my uncle Asfaha's story; and it is a compelling one. Of the village elders my revered uncle Bashai Asfaha was the most popular among us children. Uncle Asfaha was a born story teller who would hold us spell bound for hours by his tale of village heroes and other delectable stories. In our case, the story of village heroes begins with Asgede, the common ancestor of Adi Nifas. Every child must know his or her lineage by memorizing the names of ancestors to the seventh line. This was principally to avoid marriage within the circle, because all members within the circle of seven generations are considered blood brothers and sisters.

One fine morning after the harvest season was over, uncle Asfaha was regaling us with stories of heroes and villains.

"Remember," he was saying jabbing a finger to emphasize a point, "remember that you belong to a proud lineage. And you have relatives all over the land. Do you know where you have such relatives, many Deqi-Asgede?"

"No, tell us," cried the assembled village children.

"Wherever he went conquering land, Asgede did not sleep at night alone. He took the best looking girl and made her his wife."

This was greeted by loud cheers and merriment.

"Yes, wherever he went, he had children from the daughters of local chiefs from the highlands of northern Hamasien through Habab all the way to Sahel."

"Do these relatives come to visit us, uncle?" a boy wanted to know.

"Yes, occasionally. They live very far from here, but they do come from time to time. After some reflection, he added, "We are a proud people and our tribe is large and powerful. That is why no one dares mess with Deqi-Asgede."

My Uncle and Village Gossip

The sun was slowly descending on the western horizon. And, although it was at least an hour before sunset, parents were calling for their young shepherd children to make sure that they are coming back before it grew dark. Suddenly, the sound of *kebero* was heard nearby accompanied by songs. It came nearer and nearer until it drowned all our talk and Uncle Asfaha was forced to stop his story telling. The girls burst upon the scene and begin a *guayla*. The *kebero*'s tom tom begins and they go round and round singing a song that we were not able to hear from the distance but became clear now. The boys who were huddled at the feet of my uncle now join the girls in the *guayla,* one by one. I also join before I hear the words, because if there is anything in the world that can wean children out of the charmed circle of a story teller, it is the *guayla*

I look back to the porch where we were sitting; my uncle has apparently thought the better part of valor is discreet disappearance. He must have discerned his name and the message of the village girls long before I heard it. For the song was a song of censure leveled at him.

As we dance round and round in the guayla, going anti-clockwise, I can hear the song clearly.

Geza la'elai geSkum aitiKidu
Asfaha hilala deisebeitu lemidu
Wei gada wei gado/Bishimel teteKendido!

The Crown and the Pen

Dam-didam! Dam-didam! Dam-didam!

They repeat the song of censure aimed at my dear uncle, again and again ad nauseam.

[Roughly translated, the song said:
Do not venture to the upper part of the village
For Asfaha, the philanderer has been fornicating.
Oh what a scandal, what a scandal!
Would that I could cane him on the backside!].

As the dance reaches the climax, the lead singer sounds a refrain that is repeated by the others. Even the boys who had been under my uncle's charmed circle join in the refrain, but I break rank and get out of the circle. Standing alone, I hear them repeat the refrain:

"Thirty lashes on the backside!" says the lead singer.
"Thirty lashes on the backside!" repeat the rest.
"Thirty lashes on the backside!"
"Thirty lashes on the backside!"

It goes on and on. I decide to go home; I did not want to witness my uncle's ritual flogging.

As I look back to those days and review the event and the song of the village girls who were mostly in their early teens, once more I am tempted to compose a theory, discerning reason in the rhyme.

The wrong supposedly committed by my uncle (sleeping with a woman other than his wife) is not a crime under the law of the land and is not, therefore, subject to legal penalty. But it had been preordained by society that such an act should not go unsanctioned, in one way or another. "Thirty lashes on the backside" ritually intoned by village girls becomes a form of punishment, no better, and certainly no worse, than a scandalous article in the National Enquirer. The difference is that the former is made for social solidarity, the latter for profit, even though they both include some entertainment value.

My uncle, the object of the song of censure, is a kind and generous man with an impish sense of humor. He has always been popular especially with women. He was "a lady's man" who could win a young woman's heart even in his late fifties. We called him "Aboy Bashai", bashai being a honorary military title. It is a corruption of the Old Turkish title Pasha.

It turns out that the song of the girls is based on a rumor that has been circulating about his affairs with a woman. No sooner had it reached the sensitive ears of the village maidens than they composed a song of censure. Such a song is a variation on a theme: if you stray from the preordained moral path you must face public censure. These kinds of songs serve the ends that the press is supposed to serve in modern times, expressing public disapproval on errant behavior through adverse publicity.

As I reflect on it today, I imagine the elders in the distant past for some reason choosing to be above the fray, delegating such delicate but necessary duty to the young. They consider the young, in their pristine innocence, to act as guardians of good behavior and thus maintain social solidarity. But of course it is the adults who instigate the young by causing information to spread through the "grape vines." And it is all done for a cause and without malice.

You see, in the end, it is a matter of survival; it boils down to maintaining the integrity of the community. To that end, various members are assigned various tasks. The sociologists have a fancy term for this but I will not use it; I prefer the method of the storyteller, who has his place as guardian of values just as the guard on duty has his specific task. As an Italian scholar and ethnographer of the peoples of the Horn of Africa region has written, the customary rules of the society (Eritrean society in this instance) act as unarmed guards in the scheme of things. This is true whether we are talking about criminal offences, family matters or community affairs.

People in Eritrea, as in most African countries, live mostly by these values, as more than sixty percent of them live in the rural areas. By and large, they define their values and interests in terms of the community first and the individual second, seeing their freedom less in individual competition and more on cooperation. To put it pedantically, people's participation in community life rests on the social nature of being and the organic being of society.

I repeat, in the end it is a matter of survival—this community thing; this banding together and forging ties that bind. It is invested with moral and religious values so that it can endure across decades and centuries, across generations. We embellish it, adorning it with myths and legends of heroic ancestors, and we claim a common ancestor. My uncle Asfaha, (Aboy Bashai), was unique in weaving tales of heroic ancestors, as he was trying to do that morning before he was overtaken by the consequences of his not-so-heroic deed. But that weakness of his—all too human and pardonable—was also a necessary part of the tribal tale: the young must be aware that even the elders—even the highest leaders—have human weaknesses. They must be sanctioned mildly, but they are not to be impeached for "High Crime and Misdemeanor!" Only ritual flogging by blameless nubile village maidens.

Crime and Punishment

Societies are defined as much by their geographical boundaries as by the limits they set on themselves—by the moral and legal norms governing the behavior of their members. The fancy name for this is normative order. Such normative order is perceived by its adherents to be more or less permanent, recognized as the distilled essence of historical experience: of the wisdom of the ages, so to speak. It is not surprising, therefore, that historically, those members of society who overstepped the bounds of the normative order have at times been dealt with in a manner that would seem to us today extremely harsh. Criminal justice, as a system of sanctions, is the nerve center of a society's normative order. It dramatically expresses some of society's deeper values and sentiments, and is thus a measure of the character of that society.

In Africa, traditionally evolved law constituted as the living law of the people and was viewed as permanent. But the coming of the Europeans with their own system of law tended to be disruptive. Yet African customary law persisted surviving the colonial experience. Thus a dual system of law emerged with colonial law existing side by side with African law. In this respect Eritrea was no exception.

No crime is left unpunished, but the punishment does not always fit the crime. Again, considerations of social solidarity intervene as mitigating factors in meting out punishment. The following story will serve to illustrate this point.

When I was about ten, a murder was committed in my village. It was one of those moments of turmoil in our village life. Confusion and alarm spread among the people of Adi Nifas and of neighboring villages that heard about the sad episode.

Abraham Geresus, my own kinsman of the BeHailai lineage, had killed one Tesfamariam of the AdifiChen lineage. Homicide is a rare phenomenon in village life. This was why this story drew the interest of people throughout the area. Tempers had flared up to boiling point. "Blood for blood," had cried some hotheads among the party of the deceased. A few were gearing up to settle scores through vendetta killing, even though vendetta killings had not been known to occur in living memory, being prohibited by legislation. Nonetheless wild stories spread about the circumstances and motives of the homicide, adding fuel to the fire. Some elders of Adi BeHailai considered taking to a safe hiding place to avoid vendetta killing. Mothers rushed to shelter their boys because vendettas are aimed at the male part of the culprit's side. While mothers fretted the elders of both sides were holding meetings continually to prevent the situation from going out of control. One solution suggested by the culprit's side was to offer blood money together with a marriage arrangement. In such arrangements, customarily, a girl would be wedded to a son from the victim's side.

Meanwhile, a criminal case was brought against Abraham in the criminal division of the High Court presided over by an Italian judge. Now according to Italian criminal law, murder is punishable by death, unless there is an extenuating circumstance. In this case, the deceased had started the fight, having provoked the culprit. The fight erupted after an ox belonging to the victim fell into a lake apparently frightened by the bicycle horn that Abraham had blown. The victim then started the fight, attacking Abraham and verbally assaulting him. Abraham had got off his bicycle and was pleading with the victim saying that it was not his fault. When the victim continued his assault, Abraham, who was slightly built, picked up a stone and hit the victim on his head. The victim died instantly. Thus there was extenuating circumstance at least to reduce the ultimate punishment from death to imprisonment.

The elders of the village had found a way to resolve the case and the attorney of the accused requested that the case be handled in accordance with customary law of the village. The request was granted, the case settled according to customary law and peace and harmony restored to the village. Abraham lived to produce more children, one of whom, Dr. Afewerki, is a prominent medical doctor.

The Coming of the British

As I was growing up as a subject of Italian colonial rule, I heard sentiments of opposition to Italian rule. These sentiments were mixed with stories and rumors, mostly coming in the form of bits and pieces of whispered conversations between my father and some of his friends in the Protestant community. When the Second World War broke out and Italy joined Germany as a member of the Axis Powers, there was hope that the days of the Italians in Eritrea were numbered, despite the propaganda of the Italian colonial government to the contrary. The Protestant community, having been singled out for victimization by the fascist administration, was particularly enthusiastic about this. Protestant exiles living in the Sudan and other expatriates fanned the fires of Eritrean freedom in conjunction with Ethiopia's liberation from fascist occupation.

Then the war came closer home to Eritrea. I remember the day when British air force planes bombed the Asmara railway station. I was with my father and my two older brothers in one of the farm fields when we heard the sound of a huge explosion coming from the direction of Asmara. My father ordered my older brothers to unfasten the oxen and take them to pasture. We then headed to our village, where there was a mixture of excitement and confusion. Many of the village elders came streaming to our house to seek my father's view on what was happening. Of all the things that my father said in response to these inquiries was the phrase, "It is the beginning of the end of our enslavement. May it be the will of the Lord, that the Italians are defeated." He asked all present to kneel down with him and he prayed. He would repeat these prayers daily until the defeat of the Italian armed forces in the Spring of 1941, when the victorious British-led Allied troops came marching in.

After British and Allied Forces defeated and replaced the Italians, and not long after the incident in which I gored the foot of one of the oxen, my father sent me to attend school at the newly reopened Swedish Missionary School, known as Geza Kenisha. The director of the school was none other than Woldeab Woldemariam, who would be one of the leading lights of the Eritrean freedom fight and, together with Sheikh Ibrahim Sultan Ali and others, is regarded by Eritreans as the founding father of the new Eritrea. With Woldeab and Mesfin Gebrehiwet (his deputy) at the helm, the Geza Kenisha School had the reputation as the best school at the time. Prominent people, irrespective of the denomination to which they adhered, sent their children to that school.

I was placed in the Second Grade, even though I was old enough to be at Fifth Grade. But in those days, classes had a mixed age group; there were three or four boys who were older than me in that class.

My reading and writing and knowledge of the Bible was of a standard to place me on the Fifth Grade, but I lacked knowledge in Math and English and other subjects like Geography and History. My Second Grade teacher was Seare Kahsai who was fair but a strict disciplinarian. On the first day of his arrival in the class, he inspected the students, slowly from the front to the back of the class room and telling students to sit up and not to talk. He was an unsmiling, serious teacher who did not joke in class or get engaged in the usual banter with his colleagues.

But he was a typical caring teacher, who impressed upon his students to be diligent, not to waste time playing too long. I will relate what happened on one occasion and the effect it had on me and on my studies.

Teachers as Parents—Village Values at Work

One evening after school hours, my friend Zerit and I were playing late into the evening on the school ground. I had stayed overnight at a friend's house and because his residence overlooked the school ground, Seare saw me playing with my friend who was also a class mate. It was a time after six when children were supposed to be inside their houses. The following morning, he asked me to repeat the assigned lesson; I did not know the answer because I did not study, and when my friend whispered repeating the answer, Seare was gently critical of both of us. He was more severe on my friend who was older than me. "You should have advised him to learn his lesson instead of playing beyond normal playing hours," he told Zerit who had by then bowed his head in shame. He then turned to me and asked a rhetorical question: "Tell me this, Bereket, did Aboy Keshi (referring to my father by his pastoral title), choose you of all your siblings to come here to play?" My bowed head fell deeper than that of my friend. Although uttered in the form of a question, it was a cutting remark; I felt its sting and never again played beyond the normal hours. Indeed I became a star student. At the end of the school year, I was top of my class.

Seare taught us Tigrigna, Bible studies, and arithmetic. My other teachers and the subjects they taught us in Grade two were: Abraha Gebreselassie (English); Aba Woldeab (Amharic); Tsegai Iassu (geography); Teccletsion Debas (history). And the school director, Woldeab Woldemariam, would occasionally come in and quiz us in English and geography. The geography teacher, Tsegai told me later that he was quizzing us in geography because he wanted to find out if he (Tsegai) was doing his job properly, because he was appointed at the special recommendation of Woldeab. Tsegai eventually became a faithful disciple of Woldeab when the latter became a leading politician in favor of Eritrean independence.

Aba Woldeab, who should not be confused with Woldeab Woldemariam, was an interesting man with a background in Orthodox Christian Church education, and he studied and lived in Ethiopia for many years. Like my father, he converted to the Protestant denomination later in life. He spoke perfect Amharic and insisted on a correct enunciation of Amharic words when we read passages. Occasionally, he would venture into Geez, the ancient language. Because my father had started me off in both Amharic and Geez, I was way ahead of my classmates and thus became Aba Woldeab's favorite student.

We students liked his stories; our favorite time with him was when he told us stories mostly based on the Bible. He had a dramatic style of story telling that made the stories come alive. He would have made a great novelist or dramatist. Unfortunately, Aba Woldeab had a drinking problem and when he knew he was going to be late or absent he would ask me to supervise the class during his teaching hours. I cooperated for a while, but Aba Woldeab's absence and my role was found out. One day, I was summoned to the office of the director, who was Mesfin Gebrehiwet at the time. [Woldeab Woldemaraim had accepted a job as Information Officer with the British Caretaker Administration]. Mesfin asked me a few question to make sure the story of Aba Woldeab's absence was true. I told him the truth and he dismissed me without a further word. Aba Woldeab must have been reprimanded because he did not ask me to repeat my previous role. But there were occasions when he came smelling of drink and his teaching would be incoherent as he rambled on, jumping from topic to topic. On such occasions the older boys would ask him embarrassing questions such as whether he had any relation with women while he was a student at the famous Monastery called Waldiba. He had often told us stories of life in the Monastery where he studied under famous teachers of whom he spoke with fond remembrance, and the wicked boys used that to pose these questions. His answer was always the same: "No women were allowed in the Monastery; we cooked our meals ourselves taking turns. Every one was required to work, contributing to the monastic life, each according to his ability. It is a very strictly organized society," he said once and, staring at the older boy who posed the embarrassing question, added "some of you might learn a thing or two in discipline if you were placed in Waldiba." And there would be a roar of laughter.

I heard later that he was dismissed from his teaching position and that he earned a living as a dress-maker with near starvation income. But he spent his little income on drinking. I also heard that some of his former students, including the older boy who used to make fun of him, contributed to help him get by. When he died they made similar contributions towards the funeral expenses.

It is remarkable that whenever I meet my old classmates of those days, we always talk about Aba Woldeab more than anybody else. It is strange how one remembers such characters more than others. Memories of people and events are selective; the mind cannot remember everything at the same time: it recalls selectively from the memory bank those that had been embedded in it due to extraordinary pain or pleasure. Among the pleasurable events that I remember from those days are the Christmas Carols that Woldeab Woldemariam taught us during the Advent Season, including "Gloria...In Excelsis Deo..." We stood around him in groups as he played the Church organ and led the hymns, occasionally hurling an adjective of rebuke on some who sang out of tune. I remember, for example, he used the word "*Gobiye!*" (Turtle) stopping his music and glaring at one boy called Girmai MeleliK, because he kept singing out of tune. The unfortunate boy earned the name Gobiye since then, until the day he died.

I was promoted to Grade Three. The class master was Paulos Bkhit, a mild-mannered man who could be rough when provoked. I was ordinarily a well-behaved student, having been brought up to respect elders and be kind to everybody, without distinction. But occasionally, I would lapse into unnecessary childish things. One day, we had a visitor in our class. He was an elderly, dignified gentleman whose village of origin, Tsaazega, was the same as our teacher's. The gentleman's name was Aboy Yohhannes who was the father of a girl in the class, named Ttsion. As he and our teacher were conversing, Aboy Yohannes uttered a Tigrigna expression of surprise, "*Weike Deqei!*" Some irresistible impulse pushed me to do something I regretted for ever; I repeated the remark loudly to the amusement of the class. If the teacher or his guest were displeased at that moment, they did not show it. But after the guest had left, the teacher asked in a calm but serious manner, "who said that?"

Silence.

He repeated the question. More silence.

Peer solidarity required that there would be no pointing of fingers. I was quivering and although I wanted to say it was me, I didn't dare and no one would expose me. I thought he would let it pass; after all, it was an innocent remark. But no, he wouldn't let go. He said, "no one is going to leave this classroom until I know who made that remark; every one is going to remain here all night until I know."

It was getting close to four o'clock, time for class dismissal and dinnertime. I thought that the cat would be out of the bag soon anyway, so I may as well make a clean breast of it and face the consequences.

I raised my hand and said, "it was me."

"You!?" Paulos could not believe his ears; I was a model student, well-behaved, polite and always good in my class assignment. Besides, being from the countryside like me and knowing my father, he was obviously deeply disappointed.

"Come out here," he said and I left my place and went forward.

"Wham!" And I saw stars.

Before I knew where it came from he had landed a slapping blow on the left side of my face then on the right. Left –right, again and again. What hurt most was the thick silver ring he wore on his left ring finger. When he had enough, he said,

"Get out."

I went out crying, not so much with the pain though I was smarting with an awful pain on my head. I cried more for the shame and for disappointing one of my favorite teachers. Although he had said he would report me to my father, he never did. The next time he saw me he advised me seriously not to fall in the company of bad city boys and get spoiled. It was a good advice and one that I remembered.

That was the last time I made a childish remark like that.

One day, years later when we met in Ethiopia, I reminded him of the incident. He remembered and said smiling almost embarrassed, "whenever I hear your name mentioned I think of that unfortunate incident." He added with a smile, "especially now that you are an important person."

I answered "Ayya Paulos, maybe it is because of the care and concern you teachers showed, including the deserved punishment, that I have become what I am."

And I meant that, and it pleased him immensely.

I was promoted to Grade Four, Tecletsion's class. But it was to last only a few months until I left for Ethiopia in February 1945. Next to Aba Woldeab, Tecletsion Debas was another character in the school. He was a popular teacher and a gifted artist. He also had a beautiful calligraphy; the school certificates, including the ones announcing the prizes were written in his hand, as mine was at the end of my Third Grade exam. He taught us history, and he spoke of historic figures like Churchill and Stalin as though they were his school mates.

Colorful Characters

I have fond memories of my years at the Geza Kenisha School. In my class, there were class clowns and the usual victims of boyish malice. There were also those who would become famous or notorious, years later. Among those who were class clowns was Kidane Haile who later became a notable soccer player. An older class clown was Kibrom Zeilo who later became a district judge. A victim of boyish malice (especially of Kidane Haile) was Gebreab Garoy who became an elementary school teacher. Kidane's antics were varied and could be vicious, and they were not limited to Gebreab. One day Kidane procured from God knows where, a foul-smelling dried leaf and placed it under Aba Woldeab's desk. As we all watched the teacher who was grading papers, there was an anticipation of great fun exacted at the expense of our teacher. We saw him sniffing and frowning with distaste. We all laughed and he suspected foul play. He sniffed again, this time drawing more of the air and then began looking around. He found the source of the smell, picked it up, threw it in disgust and got up from his chair. He surveyed the room as we all smirked and sniggered.

"Who did this?' he asked, looking around the room.

"Bereket" he said, turning to me, "who was it? You can tell me. You *must* tell me."

I told him that I didn't know who did it. It was a bald lie, of course, but the choice was between lying, and telling the truth and suffering the consequence of being ostracized by my classmates.

In any case, Aba Woldeab's suspicion fell on the right target. He knew from previous experience that the only boy capable of such a trick was Kidane Haile. So, he got closer to where Kidane was sitting, stared at him for a moment and said, "I know it is you, you *Qeleblabba*."

It was his favorite Amharic adjective of disfavor, meaning wayward. Some of us used it against each other in mock imitation of him. One day, I had just used it against one of my friends when he suddenly appeared. And hearing what I said, smiled amiably, but warned, "Make sure, you don't become one." He could be kind and forgiving, but not to some of the students like Kidane. On this particular occasion—which became known as the "stinking incident"—he was not in a forgiving mood. He repeated his favorite Amharic expression of disapproval, pulled Kidane by the ear and set about slapping him, as Kidane wriggled and whimpered, protesting his innocence!

Many of my classmates have since departed to meet their maker; some have done well while others not so well. One case of interest from among my classmates who had the natural ability to do well but ended up engaged in devious ways is that of Haile Kahsai. Haile came from a well-to-do family, his father being a prosperous businessman. Like many children of the well to do, Haile Kahsai was a spoilt child who apparently did not feel the pressure to succeed in life on his own merit. He had a nonchalant attitude to studying and spent most of his spare time playing and generally having fun like going to the cinema all the time. He frequently entertained the rest of us telling stories of films he saw, mostly films about cowboys and Indians.

Looking back now and upon reflection, I think some of his attitudes to life and his adventure (or rather misadventures) later in his life might have been influenced by the pictures he saw. Hollywood's dream machine has had an impact on the lives of many young Third World people, beyond belief.

His father sent Haile to attend high school in Addis Ababa. But instead of studying Haile ended up becoming a con-man. He developed a scheme of confidence trick. His first known trick was to convince mothers in Asmara who had children studying in Addis Ababa that their children were suffering from hunger and privation and needed money to be sent to them. Many a mother trusted Haile and gave him money which of course did not reach the target. He was eventually caught by the police and imprisoned in a police station. But he escaped and made his way to the Sudan and from there to Egypt and then Europe. The manner of his escape and how he continued to con people is a story by itself. In addition to what I can only describe as a hypnotic power of convincing people to do what he wanted them to do, Haile was also a good actor. I will give an example to illustrate his daring and ability.

In the Fall of 1952, I was in my second year law studies at the University of London. I was sitting in the library of the London School of Economics (LSE) when I was approached by a smiling man who stood over me and said "hello Bereket." I looked up and couldn't believe my eyes. There he was, smiling mischievously and before I could recover from my shock, he had the gall to tease me.

"I hope I am not interrupting you in your study," he said.

I got up, we shook hands and he suggested that we go outside for a chat. He stood no ceremonies. "Is there some quiet place where we can have lunch? I am hungry," he said. We got out of the library and made our way to the university cafeteria. When we got there, he protested; he said he wouldn't have it. What! On a blessed day like this, old friends' meeting! No, we must go to a good restaurant. My protest was brushed aside and we went to a nearby restaurant.

After we ate, true to form, he offered to pay, taking out a wad of British Pound notes and watching me to see that I am suitably impressed.

All the time I was curious to know what he was doing in London, and as if he read my mind, he told me that he was on a world tour. He had won a lottery and is using the money to see the world before he settles down to study economics.

"What are the entrance requirements for LSE ?," he asked.

The gall! The sheer impertinence of the man!

I knew that he did not complete sixth grade, and he must have known that I knew, but didn't care. A con man, like a rapist, only thinks of having his will on the particular victim of the moment. Like the proverbial biased judge, his mind is made up; he wouldn't be confused by the facts. Haile's mind was only focused on what he set out to do at that particular moment. The facts are too tedious and inconvenient and therefore are to be ignored at will. At will, that is the key point.

Then he tried to pull a fast one on me, again with the same disrespect for facts and for the "victim's" intelligence. After he paid for the lunch and tipped the waitress handsomely, he produced from his pocket the Communist Manifesto. Before I could ask him why he bought it, he launched into a lecture about Marxism and Leninism and how we must help the suffering masses to liberate themselves from class oppression and exploitation.

The man had intelligence and knew how to influence people appealing to what he thinks makes them amenable to his scheme. Only, that time, he mistook his target. He was obviously misinformed that the LSE was a den of communists and therefore he wanted to impress me that he was "one of us." I disabused him of that misapprehension at which point he quickly changed tune. He said he was only educating himself and we talked about his plans.

The next day, he went to the Ethiopian Embassy and convinced the Ambassador that he was the son of Tedla Bairu, the then newly elected Chief Executive of Eritrea, and that he lost his wallet. He needed only one hundred pounds which he had asked his father to transfer to him soon. The good ambassador believed him and loaned him the money. He disappeared from England and was seen in Paris next where he tried to con Zewde Gebreselassie, using the same tactic that he had used in London. Only Zewde, who had graduated from Oxford and was in Paris on government business, was too shrewd for him.

After an adventurous life in Europe and the Middle East, Haile Kahsai was finally caught by the Egyptian police. Meanwhile he had met a Dutch girl who fell in love with him and whom he finally married. They settled down in Addis Ababa and later in Nairobi, both of them working for KLM, the Dutch Airlines.

Once when I met him in Addis Ababa, I tried to remind him of our meeting in London. He totally denied such a meeting!

He may be right in concluding that some memories are better left forgotten.

During the time of my school days at Geza Kenisha, I changed residence three times. In the first few months while I was attending Grade Two, I was staying with my sister Hannah before she separated from her husband, Yoseph. He had been recruited in the newly established police force and he was given a two-room house called Agdo or tukul in the area called Deposito. His younger brother Araia and I lived with them, sharing the same bed. We then moved to Geza Banda Habesha, where they rented a better two-room house in a compound owned by Aboy Geresus, a well known Protestant preacher and church elder. I walked to school with his two sons, Tekie and Seyoum and their cousin Habteab Yohannes.

I did not stay there long because Hannah and Yoseph separated. Although the house was better, life for my sister had become daily hell and I suffered with her. Yoseph would come in late at night drunk and he would beat Hannah. Here I will make a confession that I have told only a few people.

One weekend, when everybody had gone out, Hannah and Yoseph started arguing. She always won an argument, because not only was she extremely bright, she also had right and reason on her side. When he was beaten in argument he resorted to violence. This time he not only slapped her but he threw her to the ground. I was outside in the compound reading my assigned Bible passage when I heard the argument and her call for help. After he threw her to the ground, he proceeded to whip her while his foot was on her neck. I threw down the book and rushed inside. When I saw what he was doing, I got out to the compound and looked for something to hit him with. There was a stove in which she had lighted a piece of wood for cooking purposes. I took hold of the burning wood, rushed back to the room and, yelling, "let go of my sister, you bastard," pushed the burning wood onto to his bare back. He emitted an agonized cry and let go of my sister. Then I ran for it and never returned. They were separated immediately thereafter.

I often joked to friends to whom I told this story that my revolutionary consciousness was raised forever by that incident! That incident was certainly one of the factors that helped determine my attitude towards women's rights.

After that, I moved to my aunt Ellen's place in the center of the commercial district. My aunt had an eating place where *mess* and *siwwa* (local drinks equivalent, respectively, to wine and beer) was also served and all kinds of clients frequented the place. And, although my aunt was good to me, my father was never happy about the arrangement. He put me there only because there was no alternative at the time, and he didn't want me to interrupt my studies. I stayed there some five months, but fortunately my sister Bissrat and her teacher husband, Fissehaie Bahta, had moved back from the countryside to Asmara. So, until my departure for Harar, I lived with them in the Idaga Hamus area at a place called Geza Nistrom.

The place was named Geza Nistrom after the Swedish missionary who first built a mission school and place of worship there for the adherents of his denomination. His branch of the Lutheran evangelical denomination was a split from the larger one in Geza Kenisha. People who knew of the origin of the split say that it was not based on doctrinal differences, but rather on personality clash, in this case between Nistrom and another Swedish missionary, Kolmodin. To this day, they remain separate churches.*

The period of my stay at Geza Nistrom was one of the happiest in my life. It was the time when I formed lasting friendships with Isaac Abraha, Tesfazghi Gebrehawariat and Habtegiorgis Indrias. These three, among others lived in Geza Nistrom and we went to and from the Geza Kenisha School together, most of the time. I was especially attached to the gentle Tesfazghi with whom I walked slowly to school and back, because one of his legs was wooden, resulting from an accident at the Scuola Vittorio the year before I joined that school. One of my brothers had been with him when the accident occurred and told me that it was the good Yeneta Yohannes who carried him, bleeding profusely, to the nearby hospital and thus saved his life. But his leg had to be amputated. Tesfazghi joined us in Harar some six months after Isaac and I got there, and he and I passed the secondary school entrance examination and entered the Wingate School together, as I will relate later.

---

* In 2006, the two merged to form the Evangelical Lutheran Church

Chapter 3

INTO HAILE SELASSIE'S DOMAIN

❖❖❖❖❖❖❖❖❖❖❖❖❖❖

Eritreans and the Story of a Legendary King

I first heard about Ethiopia and the world-famous Emperor Haile Selassie when I was a boy of four or five. At that time, my father and some of his close friends who frequented our house referred to him as King Teferi. Teferi was his given name. They spoke in whispers about "the exiled king." They called him by that name even though he had assumed the throne name, Haile Selassie, at his coronation in 1930. It was with the name Teferi that he had become well known as a popular and progressive ruler. His fame had spread across the Ethiopian border, to the then Italian colony of Eritrea and beyond, as the cult of Rastaferianism (Rastas) demonstrates.

Before the advent of Italian colonial rule in Eritrea, the relation of Eritreans and Ethiopians was alternated between periods of peaceful coexistence and Ethiopian domination. Various feudal lords of Ethiopia competed for the allegiance of the inhabitants of what was at one time called *Midri BaHri* (the land bordering the sea). The local lords competed with one another for the upper hand and, in the competition, sided with one or another of the feudal lords within Ethiopia. In this process of political struggle for dominion versus autonomy, aggrieved Eritreans often traveled to Ethiopia to present their cases to the overlord of the day—from Emperor Teodros in the mid 19th century, to Emperor Yohannes of Tigray after Teodros. In the early period of Italian occupation of Eritrea, (early in the 20th century), thousands of Ethiopians were recruited into the Italian colonial army to fight against the Libyan leader, Omar Mukhtar. After the end of the Libyan campaign, hundreds of them settled in Eritrea and married Eritrean women.

As for the attitude of Eritreans toward the central Amharas of Shoa, much was determined by what Emperor Menelik did to Eritrean soldiers after he defeated the Italians at the battle of Adwa in 1896. Menelik released Italian prisoners of war, but ordered that the Eritreans be punished severely; on his order many a man's right hand and left leg were amputated. As can be imagined, this did not endear Menelik to Eritreans. Forty years later, when Mussolini planned his invasion of Ethiopia in 1935, Italian propaganda played on the horrible deeds at Adoa in order to secure Eritrean allegiance to Italy's cause. Added to this was the history of slavery in Ethiopia. When Ethiopia applied for membership of the League of Nations in the early 1920's, some members of the League objected on the grounds that Ethiopia practiced slavery. Slavery had actually been abolished by that time, and Ras Teferi (the future Emperor Haile Selassie) answered objections by reminding the League that he had abolished slavery. Ethiopia was admitted to the League (for all the good that this would do). Italian propaganda especially during Mussolini's rule (1923-1945), would not stop painting Ethiopia in a bad light.

Meanwhile, Teferi (Haile Selassie) did his own counter-propaganda, with the help of supporters from Europe and missionaries as well as the Ethiopian Orthodox Church. Historically, the Orthodox Church formed a critical link between the peoples of Eritrea and Ethiopia. With the coming of Catholic and Protestant missions, a further people–to–people link was forged along confessional lines. Indeed, several mission-educated Eritreans crossed the border to escape Italian colonial rule and to serve in the Emperor's government. Others went straight to Ethiopia from their studies in Europe and the Middle East. To mention the best known, there were: Ephrem Teweldemedhin, Lorenzo Taezaz, Dawit Ogbazghi and Sereqebirhan Gebrezghi. It is interesting to note that two of them (Lorenzo and Sereqebirhan) were Catholic, and two were Protestant.

I remember the story of Nigus Teferi (Tafari) because I used to sit at the feet of the elders listening to their conversations. The memory remains vivid in my mind especially because there was this song of lamentation that they used to sing in muffled voices about an exiled king. The Tigrigna song went like this:

> Iti Nigus abbei keidu--------Abei keidu?
> Tesedidu ab zei'Adu---------Ab zei'Adu

The song asked. "Where did the king go----where did he go? And the answer follows: "He was exiled to a distant land-----to a distant land." I forget the rest of the words, but I remember that they went on singing as if the song offered an answer to some question they needed answered.

In later years, when I became familiar with Ethiopian history, I would learn that at the time when my father and his friends were lamenting his exile, Emperor Haile Selassie was living in exile in Bath, England. Clearly, they were behind the times; they had no news of his whereabouts because any talk about him was a criminal offence. But his legend was a palpable force in the minds of many Eritreans, particularly among the literati.

Italian propaganda against Haile Selassie and his country became even more virulent after Italy invaded and occupied Ethiopia in 1936. I became aware of such propaganda while studying at the Scuola Vittorio Emanuele III School. Some of the nuns who taught us at the school occasionally made reference to *il negus* (the king, meaning Haile Selassie), in disparaging terms. On one occasion, our teacher instructed one of the school guards called Aboy Seleba—a one-armed and one-legged men to tell us about the backward nation called Ethiopia and its savage practices. Aboy Seleba had been a soldier and had fought at the battle of Adoa (1896), where he lost his arm and leg. No, he was not wounded in the war, his limbs were amputated at Menelik's orders. He was one among many unfortunate Eritreans whose right arms and left legs were amputated on the order of Emperor Menelik. Had I not heard it from Aboy Seleba himself, a venerable and dignified old man, I would have found it hard to believe.

As it can be imagined, then, the attitude of Eritreans toward Ethiopia was a mixed one.

To return to Haile Selassie, I remember that in the Italian text used in the school (the *sillabario*), there was a passage which I never forgot. It spoke about the glory of Italian victory in the 1936 war on "Abyssinia" (Ethiopia), the defeat of the Ethiopian army and of Haile Selassie's ignominious retreat. A passage in the text, a favorite of some of the teachers, went like this: *"Nella via di Ashenghe, il negus fu sbaragliato e costretto a una fuga precipitosa."* (On the way to lake Ashenghe, the king was routed and forced to a hurried flight).

It was all designed to demean Ethiopia and the Ethiopians and to glorify Mussolini's Italy. But some Eritreans, including my father, compared and contrasted the ways of an alien (European) ruler with those of a neighboring fellow African. With the latter, they felt kinship and shared certain cultural values. Apparently it was a hard choice and, as my father wrote later during the debate on Eritrea's future, the choice was made in favor of association with an African neighbor as against a European occupier.

It was thus only a matter of time before my father would decide to send me to Ethiopia for further education and to find my destiny there, as Eritreans of the previous generation had done.

My fateful journey to Ethiopia began in early 1945. One fine day in February, I had just returned from school to my sister Bissrat's house where I was staying, when I found my father waiting for me. This was unusual; it was after five in the afternoon; and if he spent the day in Asmara on business, he normally would leave for the village long before that time. So I became curious as to what detained him. I found out soon enough that he was there to stay the night at my sister's house, which he rarely did.

Bissrat served us both tea and wheat bread. My father looked at me smiling and asked me about school. What lessons did I learn that day, was I going to be first in my class again, and other questions that fathers ask their children. He was very relaxed, so I knew there was something pleasant he was going to tell me. But I did not dream of what came next. My father told me that my friend Isaac Abraha and I would travel to Ethiopia in a few days time.

No words could describe my happiness when my father smilingly told me this piece of good tidings. It was all arranged, he said ; we would travel to Addis Ababa under the care of Haile BeraKi, a member of our extended family, who was going there to bring back his long-lost brother, Iman. From Addis Ababa, we would travel to Harar where we would be lodgers at the Mission School under the care of the Swedish missionary, Anton Jonsson.

The next day, instead of going to school, Isaac and I were taken by our fathers to the market to do some shopping, mainly for clothes and leather sandals. We were both 13 years old and, at that time, fully covered shoes were not worn by most boys of our age. They bought us leather sandals. I remember that when it came to paying, my father did not seem to have the proper amount; so he casually asked his friend, Qeshi Abraha (Isaac's father), to pay for both of us. Qeshi Abraha did so without question or hesitation. I did not hear the words "lend" or "borrow," just "would you pay for both, my friend." Such was the nature of their friendship, one based on trust and mutual care. I am sure the money that Qeshi Abraha put up was returned in kind another time. They belonged to a tight-knit fraternity; apart from being members of the Lutheran Protestant Church, they very close friends.

When my father died in 1950, during my second year in England, it was Qeshi Abraha who broke the news to me indirectly. He wrote a letter to his son, Dawit, who was studying economics at Manchester University, and Dawit phoned Worku Habtewold, my former classmate at the Wingate, asking him to tell me the sad news. Dawit also forwarded his father's letter to Worku. I will never forget how Worku invited me to lunch and gently broke the news, then handed me Qeshi Abraha's letter of condolences and expression of personal loss that he felt on the death of his best friend.

The Journey to Addis Ababa

Preparation for an adventurous journey is an exciting thing; perhaps more enjoyable than the journey itself, or at least equally enjoyable.

In February 1945, World War II was winding to an end, but my friend Isaac and I neither knew nor cared about the momentous events going on in world history, nor of other events that were not connected to our narrow world of youth. While waiting for our date of departure with eagerness and youthful impatience, Isaac and I were filled with news of Ethiopia, the mythical "promised land" of our imagination. Haile Selassie, by then a world-famous leader, had been restored to his throne by British and Allied Forces, only three and a half years earlier. The legends that I grew up hearing about the exiled king produced in my mind a picture of a perfect kingdom. But the reality that I later experienced was to dispel very quickly any notion of a perfect kingdom. Indeed, a large part of this memoir is a record of the saga of struggle within and against that "promised land."

The departure, when it finally came, started with tearful farewells and good wishes from friends and relatives. Isaac's mother wept her eyes out; my mother braved it until I was out of her sight, but I was later told that she began weeping soon after I left. We thought we were traveling by bus. But that was not possible; instead we were loaded onto the back of a lorry owned by Habtetsion, a kinsman from Adi Nifas. That was our first shock, but it did not dampen our enthusiasm and great expectations. The driver of the lorry, Kidane, was a hearty type and also another kinsman from Adi Nifas. He saw to it that we were given the best place on the back of the lorry, cushioned with sacks and other material. Whenever he stopped for refueling or resting, he would come to us, buy us tea and joke about the journey.

Kidane spoke volubly about sundry matters, but one remark that has stuck in my mind was his repeated admonition to us not to fail our parents and squander our luck. He told us about our luck compared with our fathers; he reminded me that when my father in his youth went to Ethiopia for further education, he and his companions traveled on foot, begging for food all the way. "So, remember", he would conclude, "you are very lucky to have an uncle like me." And he would roar with laughter, showing a missing front tooth. We liked him.

Years later, after my return from studies in England, I found both Kidane and Habtetsion and thanked them for what they did for us. They were surprised that I did not forget the favor. I saw Habtetsion last when he came to visit me in my office of the Constitutional Commission of Eritrea. He showed me a picture of his martyred son, Arefaine, taken while he was undertaking military training in China in the late 1960's. He said it was given to him personally by his son's comrade-in-arms, Isaias Afwerki (Current President of Eritrea).

Kidane's task was, we later found out, to take us as far as Dessie, a little over 600 kilometers from Asmara. That leg of the journey took five days; today it would take a day and half, at most. There were delays all along the way. In some towns, we would wait the better part of the day; it was all a mystery to us. What we didn't know then was that Kidane and our guardian Haile had to keep negotiating with different authorities, including the British immigration officials and their local employees. Our travel was facilitated or handled by Kidane, who was the savvier of the two. To this day, I don't know how we were able to cross the Eritrea- Ethiopia border without passport or other documents. I assume that there was a tacit understanding between the British and Haile Selassie's government on travel across the border, though I have found no documents to that effect.

The journey was smooth until we reached the town of Adi Grat in northern Ethiopia, a short distance from the Eritrea-Ethiopia border. Ah, the border! The border and its function of dividing peoples is a concept that I found strange even at that age, and that I would grapple with all my adult life. It is a subject that haunts post-colonial Africa and one to which I will return. At Adi Grat I came face to face with a reality that would become more complex as I went deep into Haile Selassie's mixed kingdom, a country that an Italian scholar had termed a museum of peoples (*un museo di popolo*).

We spent the first night at Adi Grat at the home of a local grandee who was Eritrean by origin but was an important employee of the Ethiopian regional administration of Tigray. It bears emphasis and repetition that Haile Selassie used trained Eritrean manpower to his advantage for many years. This particular local grandee may have been an education officer of some importance, because we were taken to a school and ushered into a class where third graders were learning arithmetic, in Amharic. Even at that age, I was perplexed by the incongruity of the fact that Tigrigna-speaking children were being taught in a strange language. As events demonstrated years later, the language question was one of the great issues of contention between the Ethiopian authorities and subject peoples. Eritrea and later Tigray led the way in this battle, as we shall see.

Of course, the key to the riddle that was a mystery to me then is that Amharic was the Emperor's language. It is an old logic of empires: the subject people must be made to learn the occupier's language. They must know the ways of their masters, or there will be no advance, no promotion etc.

Years later, I was traveling on this same road, running for my life, fleeing from the military government of Mengistu Haile Mariam. My Tigrayan friend, Desta Woldekidan, drove me all the way from Addis Ababa to Mekele, the Tigray capital, as I will relate later. When we reached a point near the border between the provinces of Tigray and Wollo, he stopped the car upon seeing some shepherd boys waving at us. We got out of the car and approached the boys. Desta asked one of the boys, "Are you Tigraway or Amharai? "

The boy hesitated for a moment, looked at his friends, and then answered quietly, "Tigraway, of course." (In Tigrigna, he said *Tigraway imbey*.").

As we resumed our travel, I ask Desta, "What do you think the answer would have been, had you asked the question in Amharic?"

"He would have given the same answer."

"How can you be certain?"

"Because I know that, although Haile Selassie arbitrarily lopped off this part of Tigray and put it in Wollo, the people in this area are still adamantly Tigrayan in sentiment."

I have no reason to doubt or second-guess Desta.

Some twenty years later, I asked a similar question to shepherd boys on the Eritrean-Tigray border. I stopped at a point in the Zalambesa area that juts out into and is encircled by Tigray territory. The people in the entire region are related by blood and intermarriage, cutting across the artificial borders fixed during Italian colonial rule and dividing them into Eritreans and Tigrayans (Ethiopians). It is an example, among many throughout Africa, of the power of the nationalist ideology produced by boundaries. The fact that the boundaries were arbitrarily fixed makes no difference; once fixed, the boundary creates a new set of identities, dividing people that were one before.

The boy answered my question emphatically, saying "Eritrean of course. (*Eritrawi imber*) The answers of the two shepherd boys were similar, both given in Tigrigna, but the latter considered himself to be Eritrean. It is conceivable, of course, that had I put the same question to another shepherd on the Tigray side of the boundary, the answer would have been "*Tigraway imber*." ("Tigraway of course")

In another area, where Eritrea meets the Sudan, the Benamir people live on either side of the border; they are the same people. But there, too, the border has created a new national consciousness. Once in a Khartoum hotel, I was served by a waiter who heard me speak in Tigrigna. He was a Benamir by ethnicity, but an Eritrean Benamir and proud of being Eritrean. I am Eritrean of the Tigrigna ethnic group and so not related to him ethnically. Pointing to one of his colleagues in the hotel who was Sudanese Benamir (and speaking to me in Arabic), he launched into a tirade against the inefficiency of "these Sudanese." "We Eritreans should run this place," he said with a smile. The man was berating his own kith and kin and identifying with me on the basis of a new identity created by colonial rule. This is one of the paradoxes of the post-colonial African reality.

Back to our journey. When we started from Adi Grat on our way to Dessie, the back of our lorry was full and we found ourselves squeezed between adults who did not care much about our discomfort. So when we stopped in Weqro, we complained to Kidane, who told us to be patient; it would only be for a short distance. He also whispered to me that this was what he had to do as a favor to some local authorities (*balabats*) who otherwise would make life difficult for him in future travels. And so we settled to a rather uncomfortable journey, cramped between relatives of the local *balabats* and suffering their scowling faces and insolent remarks about "these pushy Eritreans." They spoke in the same language, our mother tongue Tigrigna, though in a different accent; yet they saw us as foreigners. This I found difficult to understand then, particularly because a family from the Adi Grat region had lived in our house for a number of years during my early childhood. The head of the family was a gentle old man we knew as Aboy Tirfe, and his son, Ye'bio, was very close to my brother Simret. We did not see them as foreigners; others might have, but I didn't.

As the lorry made its tortuous way to Mekele, the Tigray capital, I withdrew into a sullen mood, listening to the chattering men and ignoring their scowls. Mekele at the time was a small town. We didn't stay there long, but the short stop impressed me with a view of a struggling people, many poorly-clad children much younger than me milling around the city center and addressing each other as *atum,* which is the respectful form of address reserved for older people where I came from. We left Mekele late in the afternoon and proceeded toward Dessie.

On this eventful journey through northern Ethiopia, nothing impressed us more than the incredible sight of the Ambalaghe mountain range. As we started climbing the winding road built by the Italians, the lorry huffed and puffed and heaved up the steep slope of Ambalaghe. It was a great relief to reach the summit pass after the harrowing climb. Then the descent towards the Alamata plains began. That awe-inspiring sight remains etched in my memory. Soon after we crossed the Alamata plains we saw differently-clad people speaking a different kind of Tigrigna which I had difficulty understanding. Kidane told me they were called the Raya. I would learn later that these fascinating people are a cross between the Oromo and the Tigrigna people, and their language was influenced by that fact. And further south, there was a variation on the same theme—mixing between the Oromo and the Amhara.

We reached Dessie in the afternoon of the fifth day of our departure from Asmara. We were taken to the home of Ayya Leggese, where we passed the night. We said goodbye to Kidane in Dessie because he had to go back to Asmara. His last words to me were: "Don't waste your time fooling around. Your father and all of us expect much from you. Be good and God be with you." I had misty eyes when he left us.

Early the following morning, the gentle Ayya Leggese took us to an Eritrean restaurant and treated us to the most delicious *fuul* I have ever tasted. He then put us on a bus going to Addis Ababa, for a much more comfortable journey than the one we had been through. With us, of course, was Haile BeraKi, who carried and ate his own provisions brought from Adi Nifas; he neither offered nor took anybody else's food. Even when our gracious host, Ayya Leggese, invited him to eat *fuul* with us he declined, but accepted tea.

Our journey to Addis Ababa took one day. Except for one incident at the start of our journey, the trip was relatively uneventful. An incident occurred just before the bus departed from Dessie. The driver, a hefty Italian, was about to start the engine when a slightly-built but furious-looking man entered the bus. He was dressed in traditional Ethiopian dress, carrying a scimitar in a scabbard. The driver told the man there was no room and asked him to get off the bus. The man, who probably had been a guerilla fighting the Italians, flatly refused to get off. To make his point very clear, he put his right hand on the handle of the scimitar and shook it with a flourish, and with flashing eyes said, "*Imbi alwerd'm!* (I will not get off!).

The poor driver was scared and did not know what to do. He looked left and right for support, while stepping back all the time presumably to avoid being hacked to death.

Fortunately, one of the passengers who spoke Italian offered his own seat to the armed man and asked the driver if he could sit with him near the driver's seat. The driver gratefully accepted the offer and we were on our way. No one spoke to the armed man who had meanwhile withdrawn into a sullen mood. Isaac and I were sitting right behind him. He kept muttering *"Banda hullu!"* (damned collaborators!), and I understood his anger to be aimed at those Ethiopians (and Eritreans), who had collaborated with the Italians during the five-year Italian occupation of the country. They were called *bandas*. The scimitar man's irrational mutterings were presumably aimed at the passenger who spoke Italian. (This kind of irrational charge was flung at me later at my school in Harar, although I was too young to "collaborate").

A few hours later, he got off at a place called Kombolsha, to everyone's relief.

"*Meno male,*" cried the Italian as soon as the door closed behind the departing armed man. It is the equivalent of "good riddance," and many among the passengers laughed in agreement.

The rest of the journey to Addis Ababa was uneventful, except for the tunnel of Tarma Ber, between Debre Sina and Debre Birhan, which was built by the Italians during their five-year rule of Ethiopia. It was the first time I had passed through a tunnel.

When we arrived at the bus stop in Addis Ababa, there was no one to meet us. That was when my kinsman Haile became very useful. He had been given a letter from our fathers addressed to Aya Geresus Habtu, who lived in an area called Gulele. So he called porters to carry our bags and lead us to the place. After walking for an hour or so, passing a thickly forested area, we arrived at a clearing surrounded by eucalyptus trees, where we saw some children playing. I asked one of the boys if this was Aya Geresus's house, and was told it was. My Amharic even then was quite good because my father had taught me and I had improved it at the Swedish missionary school in Asmara.

We were received by the lady of the house whose name was Tsehai. She asked us to come in; Isaac and I did, but Haile wanted to go looking for his brother. Tsehai wouldn't have it that way; she insisted that he stay for dinner, stay over the night, and look for his brother the following day. Eventually, Aya Geresus came and added his voice to Haile's staying. Haile gave Aya Geresus an account of our trip. We stayed with this very hospitable family for a few days. I came to know the children, especially those who were around my age. Noah, the oldest boy was a year or so older than me. His younger sister, called Ariam, was very beautiful. We lingered in her bright company enjoying her laughter. It was not the first time that I felt stirrings of adolescent (or pre-adolescent) feelings, but this one was special. Thinking that she was beyond reach, I settled to the idea of considering her a sister and treating her like one.

Years later, Ariam would marry a high-ranking police officer, General Mebrahtu Fisseha. Next to Ariam was Mekbib, who later joined us at the Harar Mission School. Then came Biniam, a boy, and another girl, Ti'gist, who was a toddler at the time.

We had such a pleasant and memorable time with the Geresus family that we hardly felt the time pass.

Three days later Haile came back to announce that he had found his brother, Iman, who was living with an Ethiopian woman in what in some countries, is known as "common-law" marriage. He did this even though he had a wife waiting for him back home. Nor was his case untypical. No wonder he did not go back at the end of the war, in which he had been a soldier with the Italians—a *banda*! Many Eritreans who had come with the invading Italian army, had taken Ethiopian "common-law" wives. Some did not go back home but the majority did.

Haile took us with him to attend a wedding. A relative of Iman's Ethiopian wife was getting married, and insisted that we attend. We were treated to a sumptuous meal consisting of many different types of food. Haile worked hard at persuading Iman to go back with him, no doubt to the chagrin of the Ethiopian woman. She, by the way called him Gabre, not Iman. Iman had been one of my early childhood role models—a strong sportsman who was kind to young people. I was close to him and so, in a moment of levity probably aided by the drinks which they insisted that Isaac and I take, I teased him by calling him "Gabre" in the woman's accent. Although he was embarrassed, he just smiled at me indulgently. In other situations, I might have been scolded or even whacked.

Looking back now, I suspect that the change from Iman to Gabre signified a process of change—his long absence from his home and wife and his association with this woman might have led to an identity change, a process that was rudely interrupted by the arrival of an elder brother. Evidently Haile persuaded Iman that his home and duties lay elsewhere, for they left for Eritrea soon thereafter. Such was the authority of elders over their younger brothers, according to custom and tradition.

That was the last time I saw the two brothers.

The Journey to Harar

Aya Geresus took Isaac and me to the Railway Station, called Leghar, which is the corrupted form of the French, La Gare (the railway). It is the Addis Ababa station of the Addis-Djibouti railway.

It was to be our most eventful journey, one that would test our stamina and intelligence in a foreign land with people speaking languages we did not understand. To begin with, we were exposed to the stifling crowded railway station; I had never seen such dense crowds. Although I had walked past the Asmara railway station and seen it at its busiest, there was no comparison. The pushing and shoving, the deafening din of the motley crowd, shouting in different languages, and the pungent smell coming from the butter-soaked heads of the women mixed with odor of sweat under the hot February sun, proved overwhelming. This was my introduction to Haile Selassie's kingdom—my epiphany. No one seemed to care about the possible hazards of two boys being trampled under the feet of the jostling crowd in the platform of the station that day.

As he said good bye to us, Aya Geresus reminded us we were to get off at the Dire Dawa station and told us that there would be people from the mission to meet us on our arrival. After he managed to get us, with great difficulty, into the crowded train, bound for Djibouti via Dire Dawa, we were on our own in a strange land among strange people. We were not accompanied by any elders as we were on the Asmara-Addis Ababa journey; nor was there anyone among the passengers to whose care he could entrust us. Right from the time the train gave its strange hooting and started moving, strange faces stared at us with curiosity and watched our prized possessions, which consisted of two middle-sized suitcases. The one belonging to Isaac was brand new and was much more attractive than mine, which was old. Wary of the people eying our suitcases, we whispered to each other to hold onto them tightly, placing them close to our legs.

During the first part of the journey between Nazret (then known as Adama) and Awash, we were entertained by a peculiarly-dressed man who sang and danced an Oromo dance. He had an enormous lion's mane as his headgear and was very impressive. He sang and danced in our cabin and then moved on to other compartments and did his act all over again. No one was giving him money for the performance, nor did he seem to expect or demand any. We had never seen anything like it and we wondered what the man wanted. Years later, after I joined government service, I learned that the security service of the imperial government used different tactics to collect information. The man with the lion's mane could well have been a special agent dressed up to fool the passengers, looking for people on a government list of suspects.

As the train sped across the rolling hills, grassland, and savannah of eastern Shoa and Hararghe provinces, we began to feel tired. We took turns sleeping and watching our luggage; I was in charge at first. Then Isaac woke up and told me it was my turn to sleep which I gratefully accepted. All this time, there was a petty trader who was smiling at us and offering us bananas. We declined but thanked him in Amharic. It was getting dark and I was getting sleepy but had forced myself to stay awake until Isaac woke up to take his turn in watching our bags, after which I went to sleep.

I had a nightmare, dreaming of robbers boarding the trains. One of the robbers was about to attack me with a knife when I woke up, perspiring. When I looked around, I found Isaac sound asleep. I shook him by the shoulder, woke him up and made fun of him for falling asleep on his watch. He rubbed his eyes and looked around him and underneath his seat; then said, "Where is my suit case?" I said, "I don't know, I just woke up…Wait a minute, that man, the smiling merchant!"

"Oh my God," Isaac cried. He ran off looking for him from compartment to compartment. He came back shaking his head and said, "He is gone. He must have run off with it. It is my fault, I shouldn't have fallen asleep."

"Don't blame yourself," I said, "He must have been waiting for both of us to fall asleep before he took his chance."

"Yes, but how could he have gone out without being seen by the others? And where did he go? How could he just disappear while the train was moving?" Isaac asked in desperation. He then fell silent, resigning himself to a prospect without spare clothes. We kept looking around, thinking of everyone as a culprit; we looked at everyone in our compartment. No one seemed to care. Some were asleep and others were standing looking out of the window and breathing the cool night air, as the train went on its merry way towards Dire Dawa, our destination.

The petty trader, who had been all smiles and watching us like a vulture circling above carrion, had made off with his booty. Poor Isaac looked dejected and I tried to comfort him. "Look, Isaac," I said, "don't worry; you can wear my spare kaki shirt until we have new clothes made when we reach Harar." He shook his head. "He must have jumped out when the train slowed for a bend," he said. He then added, "The bastard!"

"Yah" I agreed, "The son of a bitch!" We kept silent for the reminder of the journey.

It was early in the morning when we arrived at Dire Dawa. The sun was out shining brightly and it was warm already. The place was full of hustle and bustle though not quite as crowded as the Addis Ababa station. The platform was full of Somali men, women, and children clad in colorful dress and shouting. The women especially, with their stately build and slow walk, shouted louder and more freely than women in Addis Ababa. They were quite a sight to behold and made one feel welcome.

An elderly gentleman approached us hesitatingly and asked if we were indeed the two boys he had been waiting for; we said we were, whereupon he said "Thank God" and asked to help carry our bags. I carried my bag and Isaac was just carrying himself looking more dejected than when he found his bag missing. When the man who came to meet us asked for his bag, Isaac was too embarrassed to say that his was stolen. I had to say it for him and repeated the dreary story to the man's amazement. I forget his name but I remember him as a very kind and gentle soul who told Isaac not to worry, reassuring him that the mission would find him some clothes from the school supplies.

He took us to the home of pastor Tsegaye, who was in charge of the Dire Dawa branch of the Lutheran Evangelical Mission. Pastor Tsegaye was an elderly man in his mid-fifties, short and stocky in build, with a shock of gray hair. He had an engaging personality with a cheerful disposition. He quizzed us on the long journey and marveled at the fact that we had come all the way from Asmara by ourselves. When we told him that we were unaccompanied only during the Addis Ababa-Dire Dawa segment, he still expressed admiration; he also reassured Isaac that a way would be found to help him. He then ordered a domestic helper to prepare food for us. Suitably replenished and refreshed and reassured, we spent the day exploring the market in the company of a student of the Mission school who was a couple of years older than us. Dire Dawa is a hot place, though at the time we arrived the weather was mild. It is a city that sprang up during the construction of the Addis Ababa railway, called the Franco-Ethiopian Railway. Then we had dinner and went to bed early.

The following day we were put on a bus to Harar, some fifty miles from Dire Dawa. The climb from the lowlands of Dire Dawa to the highlands of Harar along the winding road up Dengego Mountain is quite stiff, though not comparable to Ambalaghe. From the top of Dengego all the way the historic city of Harar, past the Alemaya (Haremaya) lake, is a beautiful landscape of farms and grassland. The road is lined with eucalyptus trees almost all the way.

At the Harar bus station, we were met by Barnabas Teklemariam and Iasu Gebrehawariat. The station was located in the *"botega"* area, a commercial center built by the Italians. From the bus station we were taken to the mission boarding school, where we were immediately settled in one of the dormitories. It would be my home for the following eighteen months. We were told that we would be studying, not at the mission school but at the Haile Selassie Elementary School of Harar, also run by M. Anton Jonsson.

The following morning we were taken to M. Anton, who took each one of us by the ear and asked in good but heavily accented Amharic *Indihu lijye, sint new idmeh* (So, how old are you, my son?) He always used the word, *indihu* even when it did not make sense. (We made fun of it, asking each other stupid questions using *indihu lijye*. He was a gentle man of God who practiced what he preached, as much as it was possible. A Swedish missionary who had defied the Italian Fascist occupation of Ethiopia in 1936, he became a legend in the years following liberation of Ethiopia. He was fondly remembered by those he helped during the dark days of Fascist occupation, when he took hundreds of Ethiopians across the frontier to Kenya, and for five years tirelessly labored to bring them necessary supplies. As such he was well known to the Emperor.

But what I have always remembered, along with others who knew him in those days, are his Sunday sermons in Amharic at the small mission church. He always wept as he preached. Some unkind types called him "Weeping Willow." He was always dressed in a white suit with a white toupee to match. He traveled the short distance from the mission to the school and back in a single-horse carriage. Although as a Protestant missionary he preached the gospel from an angle different from that of the established Church of Ethiopia, he was regarded with favor and respect by the church authorities. This was not only because of his service to the nation, but also due to his character. He never went out of his way to challenge the established church. He also paid due homage to the learned men of the church like Aleka Lemma, as borne out by the memoirs of Mengistu Lemma, the Aleka's poet son, and my friend.

M. Anton told Isaac and me that we would start school the next day; I would attend fourth grade and Isaac third grade, based on our standing in the Asmara school. We reported this to Barnabas, whom we saw as our mentor. He was some fifteen years older than us, an elder brother and father-substitute combined. We went to him for emotional support or for guidance on many matters. He had started school rather late in life, so I used to help him in both math and English. But his knowledge of the Bible was very good, because his father was one of the well-known Bible scholars of Eritrea. In fact I had heard my father say that he was the best and he was known among his peers by the nickname of *Assertu*, a title given to scholars who mastered all the major subjects in biblical studies.

Iasu (Joshua), who was among the first to be sent to Ethiopia around 1943, was about four years older than us and also became our elder brother and guide during our first days in Harar. There were a few other boys and a couple of older men of Eritrean origin, and we became a tightly-knit community. There was also the wonderful Addei Tiblets, wife of of Ato Tedla, an early "pilgrim" to Ethiopia and a Protestant missionary. Her husband had died long before our arrival, and Addei Tiblets had raised her children by herself with the help of the mission. When we arrived in Harar, two of her children, Berhe and Heriyti, were studying there. An older brother, Haileab, had gone to the Haile Selassie

I Secondary School in Addis Ababa and thence to Beirut. The oldest brother, Mehreteab, was an officer in the Ethiopian army.

We were always welcome at the home of Addei Tiblets, where we frequently went when we missed home and native food. In later years I would be close to two of her children in rather special circumstances, which is why I list their names here and which I will take up later.

Our adventurous journey to Harar thus came to a conclusion. We were in the eastern end of the Ethiopian empire, in the midst of people speaking different languages and practicing different religions. There was the powerful minority ruling group, the Amhara. There were the Oromo, who are the majority and were referred to as Qottu by the others. And there were the Adere, or Harari as some writers prefer to call them, who lived within the historic walled city, the *jogla*. One could find a sampling of other ethnic groups, like the Gurage and Wolamo (Wolaita), as well as a few Arabs and a handful of Turks. The Turks were remnants of the days when Egypt held sway in the area for a few years as agent of the Ottoman Turkish Empire in the nineteenth century. A visit to the market in the walled city of Harar, of which I would be mayor one day, revealed the reality of the empire, the economic and social reality. For now I'll leave it there.

Chapter 4

HIGHER EDUCATION:
FROM HARAR TO "THE WINGATE"

The Lutheran Evangelical School in Harar was a boarding school housing about a hundred elementary school students at the time of our arrival.

Whenever I think of that school, I can't help reflecting on the role European missionaries played in African education and even political development. African leaders like Nkrumah and Nyerere were products of such missions.

When Isaac and I arrived in Harar, the school was run by the famous Swedish missionary and humanitarian Monsieur (Musse) Anton Jonsson, generally known as Musse Anton. Musse Anton was also director of the government-run school, the Haile Selassie I Elementary School (HSIS) of Harar. It first started as a boarding school, catering to the Ethiopian exiles Musse Anton had taken to Kenya and helped between 1936 and 1941. The school eventually expanded, admitting students from the general population in Harar, so that the majority of the students at the time of our arrival were day students.

Out of those who lived as boarders at the mission school, seven of us attended the HSIS; we ate our breakfast and evening meal at the Mission and walked to the school. On weekends we stayed in the mission compound and could go out for visits or to the market in the walled city only by permission of the mission authorities. Iasu had been the first to enjoy the special privilege of attending the government school while residing in the mission compound. He was joined by the Gebreamlak brothers, Menbere and Hailu, and later Isaac and myself. After a few months Dawit Abraha (Isaac's older brother) and Tesfazghi (Iasu's younger brother) were added, and after Dawit and Tesfazghi, came the irascible and quarrelsome Bereket Goitom (BG) who got into trouble soon after his arrival. BG was a good soccer player but was notorious for kicks and jostling of other players.

On one particular occasion, while we were playing in the mission compound, he jostled a proud man from Gonder, named Tasew. Tasew, who was one of the biggest boys in the mission, took offence and ran after BG challenging him to a boxing bout. Tasew knew nothing about boxing, as I could see from the way he held his hands hanging loose. BG immediately got hold of his shirt and using that as a prop leaped up and gave Tasew a nasty *testata* (head butt) on his chin, which sent Tasew reeling with a bleeding mouth. Some bigger boys intervened and took Tasew to the mission clinic, while BG was summoned to the office of the director, who at the time was the stern pastor Stark, who had succeeded Musse Anton. Stark told BG that he would be expelled and we expected him to go the next day. But Stark relented the following day and let him off with a severe warning, due to the solicitations of Barnabas, who made an undertaking to be responsible for BG's good behavior.

The subject of our special status was talked about in whispers among the mission students. and some of their teachers. The reason that we were privileged to go to the HSIS, unlike the other boarders, was that the mission school did not at the time provide education beyond third grade. Yet there were bright students at the mission school who could have entered HSIS. Indeed, some of these complained about being discriminated against, but were told in no uncertain terms that they were lucky to be boarders at the mission school.

Student life in Harar at the time was marked by patriotic songs and endless marching and gymnastics. The patriotic songs were mostly composed by local literati, including one by the poet Mengistu Lemma. Some of the songs denigrated those who collaborated with the enemy during the Italian occupation, and praised the *arbegnas* (patriotic forces). This was to be expected such a short time after Ethiopia's liberation from Italian occupation (only three or four years earlier), and when nationalist passions were fresh and raw.

Life in the mission compound was not bad; the food was average by Ethiopian standards of the time, consisting of porridge in the morning and typical staples like *injera* and cheap *wat* in the evening. Meat was served once a week and lentils twice a week, while fruits and vegetables were rarely provided, even though Harar is famous for the abundance of its fruits. When we were hungry in between meals, we would sneak into the kitchen and ask *Inkoyye*, the chief cook, to give us *injera*. She was a generous and kind person and always complied.

Naturally, I missed home and family, but the little community of Eritreans and especially my friends, Isaac and Tesfazghi, was a source of comfort. I wrote home a few times and my father answered me each time. In one of his letters, he told me the sad news about the accident in which my two younger brothers were involved, as I have already written. Barnabas and Iasu helped as elder brothers, acting as a kind an extension of village elders. Adei Tiblets also became a substitute mother, telling us that she always prayed for us and knew that "the Lord would be with his people." She was a deeply religious woman and an inspiration to many. Barnabas and Iasu also helped as elder brothers. In fact, it was as if the village values of care and concern were transported to this distant land. Above all, what sustained us was our concentration on our studies and I, for one, was soon to be rewarded in a special way as a result of that concentration.

Among students at the time, there was talk of the newly opened secondary schools in Addis Ababa. The first to be opened was the Haile Selassie I

Secondary School, called Kotebe after the area where the school was located, northeast of Addis Abba. Then in 1946 the General Wingate Secondary School was opened. Earlier, students from another Harar school, had passed the exam and joined the Kotebe School. One of these was the poet/dramatist, Mengistu Lemma, whom I would later meet and befriend in England. The other was Haileab Tedla, Adei Tiblets' son.

Early in 1946, when I was attending fifth grade, a secondary school entrance examination was given to sixth graders in Harar. To the surprise of all of us, Dawit Abraha passed and Iasu did not. Six months later, another examination was given and fifth graders in the two schools of Harar were allowed to take it along with sixth graders. There came another surprise, one that shook Harar like an earthquake. Five of us passed: I topped the list as number one, Tesfazghi came number two, Menbere came third and two boys from the other school (the Ras Mekonen School) came fourth and fifth. And we were all accepted at the new Wingate School, or the Wingate, as we came to call it. The first shock, when Dawit passed and Iasu did not, had to do with the fact that Iasu had been first in his class the previous year, whereas Dawit was not even mentioned. The second shock was that I passed the secondary entrance exam from the fifth grade and all those who took it from the sixth grade had failed.

This story created a legend about me that would be replicated at the Wingate and that would haunt me later, after I matriculated and went to England, as I will explain.

The Wingate School: An Elite School with a Competitive Spirit

We "the secondary boys," as our teachers proudly referred to us, were put on a bus taking us to Dire Dawa and then on a train bound for our final destination, Addis Ababa. The train journey was uneventful, unlike the one Isaac and I had taken a year and half before.

It was dark the evening we arrived in Addis Ababa. We disembarked and were taken by bus to a meeting place outside the Technical School in the center of Addis Ababa. I remember a distinguished looking man with dark complexion and a tenor voice calling our names after we got off the bus and assembled at the entrance of the Technical School also known then as Gondrand. He was a Ministry of Education Officer in charge of logistics. His name was Mekonen Zewde. I would meet him again two years later, when he was tasked to take care of our necessities for the journey to England.

When I think of Mekonen Zewde, I cannot resist telling of a funny incident involving him. One morning, a few days before our departure for England, we went to see him at the Ministry of Education. It turned out that, after all our necessities had been purchased and we were ready to go, someone had forgotten about buying us handkerchiefs. My classmate Worku Habtewold, who had an anarchic streak, told Mekonen Zewde about it. In response, Mekonen said nonchalantly that there was no money left from the allocated budget.

"All right, then, we'll do what we have done all our lives," Worku said, "We will do this on the streets of London and in our schools." And, waiting to make sure Mekonen was watching, he turned his head sideways and blew his nose loudly with the use of his forefinger and thumb, thus discharging snivel and flinging what remained on his fingers to the ground. He then wiped his fingers on his coat sleeves, as Mekonen Zewde exploded into hysterical laughter.

"Don' think I won't do it," Worku said.

By that time Mekonen had recovered and pleaded, "Oh no, please. No, we'll find the money somehow." He started laughing again, looking at Worku and shaking his head in amazement. We got our handkerchiefs the afternoon of the same day.

Worku was three or four months ahead of me. I met him the morning after our arrival at the Wingate. The five of us from Harar, the "secondary boys" and pride of HSIS, had been transported by bus from the meeting point to the Wingate. The five were: Tesfazghi, Menbere, Zewde Seyoum, Worku Mekasha and myself. We were received by the headmaster of the school, Mr. Harry Lawrence, who called our names and inspected our faces one by one, making fun of some of us but otherwise welcoming us warmly. We had arrived after dinner time, so we were treated to hot meals and tea before we were taken to our assigned dormitories.

The following day, we were placed in what today would be grade nine but was then called grade one (Secondary). At the time of our arrival, the Wingate had been open for just over a year. The headmaster was an ambitious man who wanted his school to do as well as, if not better than, the Kotebe School. One of his policies was to administer fortnightly tests to all the classes and, after a few such tests, promote the best two or three students from the lowest to the next grade, right up to the top grade. At the time the top grade was the third grade (grade eleven in today's system). I was promoted to second grade after about a month and before the end of the year to the top grade.

In the Spring of 1947, the headmaster decided to create a fourth grade, calling it the "Matriculation Class." He consulted with the teachers and selected four of us to be in that class. The four were: Kahsai Tesfai, Tesfalul Tesfai, Worku Habtewold, and myself. There followed an intense education process under which the teachers tutored us, preparing us for the London Matriculation Examination, or Matric for short. This was the equivalent of a school leaving certificate examination, and the students who passed Matric would enter any one of the universities of Great Britain.

We became the object of envy among many of our schoolmates, and also of pride. The competitive spirit that was engendered by our selection to beat the odds and "show them" was palpably expressed in the sentiments of the majority of the Wingate students. We had to show the Kotebe that we could pass Matric in record time. It is the same competitive spirit that animates the fans of football teams. However, a few also looked on us as the sacrificial lambs, or the guinea pigs, in the scheme of the British to show their superiority to all others.

The feeling of superiority among the British was evident in the attitudes and remarks of some of our teachers. And most of us bought into it, convinced that the British had the best university education in the world and that it would be a privilege to pass the London Matric and enter one of them. It was like pursuing the Holy Grail. The Ethiopian Ministry of Education, with the Emperor at the head, also entertained a similar bias. Some of the ministers and other dignitaries sent their sons to the Wingate, not always succeeding of course, because the entrance requirement was beyond the capacity of many of their boys. A few of the aristocratic families had sent their sons to England for university education. Four of the best known of these were: Amaha Aberra, Endalkachew Mekonen, Michale Imru and Zewde Gebre-Selassie. Endalkachew would become the ill-fated first Prime Minister after the Emperor was shaken by the coup-makers of 1974, as we shall see. The others occupied various high positions in Haile Selassie's government.

The best proof of a pro-British bias on the part of the Emperor's government was the fact that all those who passed Matric were sent to England, while those who failed were sent to the United States and Canada, although in some cases the students were given a choice. Some of the Kotebe boys who passed Matric, like the legendary physicist, the late Yohannes Menkir, chose to go to the United States. Being curious on this point, I asked Yohannes Menkir, years later, why he chose the United States. He told me he had learned from some of his teachers at the Kotebe, that there were top-notch universities in the United States and Canada, and also that life in England after the war was miserable and he was not willing to be a victim of such misery.

After a little over a year of intense study that was like hard labor, with the teachers as taskmasters, our labors as a class of matriculants were rewarded with spectacular success. Out of the four, three of us passed in all the required subjects, and one (Worku) was "referred" in English. (Being referred meant that the student was required to take again only that one subject in which he had failed; had he failed in more than one, he would have been required to take all the subjects again.) By contrast, out of twenty of the Kotebe students who took the exam, five passed, if my memory serves me well. This became the number one topic of conversation among the students and government officials for many weeks, and we were lionized wherever we went.

Thus in two years I would complete secondary education and begin university studies.

The memory of the summer of 1948 is one of the most pleasant in my entire life. I had also won first prize in the final exam and was awarded a watch and a book by Emperor Haile Selassie, who acted as the Minister of Education at the time. But at the time that I received the prize, in June of that year, we had not yet heard the results of the London Matric exam. So I left for vacation to Asmara by bus, together with several Eritrean students also going back for vacation. It was a vacation filled with great expectations mixed with anxiety.

It was while I was passing the summer break that the news of the results of the Matric examination came. One of my English teachers, Mr. Victor Menage, sent a telegram to the Geza Nistrom residence of my sister Bissrat to break the good news.

I wasn't there when it arrived. I had borrowed my brother-in-law Fissahie's bicycle and gone to pass the weekend in Adi Nifas. On my way back, I ran into Mrs. Tegbaru (mother of Dr. Nerayo, a kinsman and distinguished Eritrean freedom fighter) who was on her way to Adi Nifas. I stopped to greet her; in fact as soon as she'd seen me from the distance, she waved for me to stop. For she happened to be carrying one of the sweetest pieces of news that ever warmed my heart. Aya Fissehaie had told her to deliver it to me.

Tegbaru simply said, "there is a message for you; it came yesterday from Addis Ababa" and gave me the telegram. I remember the exact words. It said:

"KASSAYE AND BEREKET PASSED MATRIC[STOP] TESFALUL NOT KNOWN YET [STOP] HEARTIEST CONGRATULATIONS" After I read the telegram, I embraced Tegbaru and gave her a tight hug until she cried, "What has happened? It must be very good news."

"Yes you blessed woman," I said, "the best news in the world," and rushed on to Asmara.

I had always loved the gentle Tegbaru, and that incident added more to my warm regard for her. At that time, Dr. Nerayo, her first-born and my favorite kinsman, was only six years old, and I must have told him this story, scores of times, in later years!

Pride filled my heart, pride that was fanned by the sycophantic gloating of my fellow Wingate students. Perhaps the gloating was worse in the case of the teachers who saw things in special kind of competitive light. The rivalry between the Wingate and Kotebe schools had taken on an international aspect. The Wingate was British-operated, whereas the Kotebe School was run by Canadians and Swedes, later joined by Americans. This rivalry was subtly encouraged by the Emperor and his government. It is well-known that the Emperor played on the different interests of the foreign powers. Besides, His Imperial Majesty loved tugs-of-war, both in the literal and figurative sense, and we students became sometimes victims, and at other times beneficiaries, of these contests.

So off we went to Enagland. Once in England, I was enrolled in a pre-med preparatory school, first in London and later in the spring of 1949, at the Croydon Polytechnic. The plan was to enter a medical school in the University of London, after two years of pre-med studies at the Polytechnic. Now one of the consequences of my speedy passage through the secondary education and passing of the Matric exam was that I was hard-pressed to compete with my British classmates. My Wingate teachers had given me a sound educational background in all the relevant subjects that I had to pass to enter into a university. But although there was depth in that education, it lacked coverage especially in science subjects. The science subjects were critical because I had decided to study medicine.

The Wingate Legacy

The legacy of the Wingate School was epitomized by one anniversary event. On May 18th 1971, the Silver Jubilee Anniversary of the Wingate School's establishment was celebrated in the presence of Emperor Haile Selassie, Prime Minister Aklilu Habtewold and Cabinet Ministers. Earlier, representatives of the more than 3,000 graduates of the school had met and formed a steering committee to plan the celebration. The meeting elected me to chair the steering committee and execute the plan. Also elected was Solomon Deresa as secretary. I had known Solomon briefly when he attended my class in Ethiopian constitution and government in the late 1950s and we got on very well. We shared many views about social and political issues. Since then he became better known as a poet and critic after he and anther Wingate alumnus, Gedamu Abraha, started an English Weekly newspaper.

Solomon was quick to point out the widening gap between the "haves and have-nots" and that the educated generation should do something about narrowing the gap. This led to a long discussion in the Steering Committee as to what we alumni of the Wingate can do to lead the way in meeting the challenge. One practical suggestion was to establish a scholarship trust fund to pay for the education of the best students from poor families, beginning with ten scholarships a year. And someone was assigned the task of finding out the cost of such a scholarship, so that alumni could be asked to make contributions annually as well as donors from among the business community in Addis Ababa. The ever-resourceful Solomon suggested that we call the scholarship fund "Development Unlimited."

Thus, the occasion provided the alumni an opportunity to look back in gratitude for the good fortune and to search for ways of helping in modest ways children from deprived families to be given the same opportunities as we were given. As a social gathering of old schoolmates, it opened new doors making it possible for the reunions of old friends who recalled "the best years" of their lives with nostalgia. At the same time, it posed intellectual and moral challenges to a privileged group of professional people with an earnest desire to give back to society in some way. At first there was confusion and lack of clear consensus on what the alumni could do to meet the challenge. The idea of meeting the challenge raised two questions: first, what did the Wingate stands for? Second, what did the Wingate contribute to the intellectual growth of its students?

Did the Wingate stand for something special?

Clearly, the Wingate School was an elitist school with stringent entrance qualifications and, as such, did not cater to the vast majority of students. This raises the question whether the reward of merit eventually helps in creating better opportunities for more and more people so that in the end others will join the circle of the privileged? Solomon's suggestion of the scholarship fund "Development Unlimited" tentatively provides the answer to this question.

The occasion of the Jubilee anniversary provided a golden opportunity for us to reflect on our achievements as well as what we needed to do to make a contribution to the society at large. The presence of the Emperor and his speech gave the idea further impetus and emboldened some of the timorous souls to think that what was considered unthinkable can be done. Such was the power of official (the Emperor's) stamp on events and issues at the time even to highly educated professionals, many of them products of the Wingate School. Ethiopian Herald covered the event with pictures of the Emperor and his Prime Minister visiting a science lab put up for the occasion by Wingate alumni. There were many exhibitions demonstrating the extent of the school's contribution to education of professionals. Using the opportunity, the Emperor related the history of the founding of the school. In one of those rare moments when the Emperor expressed profuse thanks to his British benefactors, he explained why the school was named after British General Orde Wingate. In explaining it, the Emperor also claimed a role in the anti-fascist military campaign of 1941 that some might question. In his address, the Emperor said the following:

"At a time when We, during World War II, waged the campaign to oust the Fascist invaders from Our country at the head of Our army, the late General Orde Wingate was Our close military advisor. General Wingate ...played a great role during the campaign against the Fascists and it was in recognition of his gallantry that we were pleased to name this school after him. Our consent to establish and name the school after the late Major General Orde Wingate, besides commemorating the late British General, was also in full realization of the need of training Ethiopian students in various educational fields so that they may actively participate in the national growth and development programme We laid out for our country. "

As leaflets were dropped from Ethiopian air force planes piloted by former Wingate students organized for the task by the Steering Committee, the Emperor's speech droned on, haranguing us, "the former and present students" of the school to serve the country "with perseverance and moral uprightness in their respective duties." Whereas his Cabinet and the other guests flinched as the leaflets dropped, he did not even look up to see the floating papers. People admired his sang froid, but the truth is that he had been forewarned about it. Indeed, we could not have done it without the agreement of the Palace Minister whom we consulted and who secured the Emperor's consent.

We had to show the Minister the draft of the leaflets, which contained quotes from one of the Emperor's speeches. The one we chose was, "Change begets change; the man who says I will go thus far and no more is indeed foolish." Among the members of the steering committee, there were those who argued against using this quote, which they thought was too provocative. But the majority who were for change argued that this is a direct quote from his own speech and in any case, he liked being associated with progress, so he won't object to it. The argument carried the day and, as predicted, he did not object to it.

The Emperor commended the school's Alumni Association for establishing the Trust Fund. But he lost no time to add an admonition; no one was surprised when he reminded us that our gestures "should not be limited to this school." "As you are presently serving in various capacities," he told us, "you should also be deeply concerned in the efforts *We* are making towards educating Our people and improving their ways of living." (It was royal "We.")

In other words, no matter how worthy any one else's undertaking, it cannot be allowed or presumed to upstage the work of His Majesty. Who did we think we were, after all, mere products of his great handiwork, to talk about trust funds and educational opportunities for his needy subjects when he is doing it and has done it all his life! Weren't we the products of His educational policy and generosity? Isn't the fact of our very presence at the celebration—doctors, engineers, lawyers and other professionals—evidence of His Majesty's foresight and munificence?

In any case, we listened with rapt attention and enjoyed our jubilee immensely both during the afternoon ceremonies on the school ground and in a an evening gala where champagne and whiskey flowed and we danced to the wee hours of the morning. The majority of Wingate graduates that had obtained graduate degrees, were in the engineering and medical fields. Among those who studied the social sciences and humanities and who had attained high government office, there was one who had not only climbed the ladder of officialdom but had married into the imperial family. His name was Kasa Woldemariam. We were contemporaries at the Wingate, but not close friends. Our paths would cross later in less auspicious circumstances, when he was appointed President of the University by imperial appointment and was instrumental in denying me the right to teach law at the University, as I will relate in another chapter.

Before the Emperor gave his speech, there was a welcome speech by the director of the school, followed by the British Ambassador and by myself representing the school's Alumni. Ambassador Campbell praised the work done by former and current directors of the school for what they did to bring the school to a high standard. And the director of the school praised his teachers.

The Wingate Teachers

I will give a brief sketch of some of my teachers at the school.

There was first Mr. Lawrence, the headmaster, who taught us English literature and composition. He was a colorful figure and somewhat controversial. He was good as a teacher but was erratic in his methods of teaching. He only taught us for a couple of months until others took over from him, but he would act as substitute teacher whenever the others were absent. His administrative duties as headmaster must have proved too much for him to continue teaching on a continual basis. Lawrence was dramatic in his teaching with the touch of an actor, which made him interesting. On reflection, I think he spent too much time play-acting and amusing us. But some of his antics are memorable. As headmaster he made sure that we went to bed early and had enough rest. He would make sure that the school rules were obeyed by making occasional spot checks. He also relied on the British system of head boys and prefects, who acted as his agents to enforce the rules. But he relied more on his own cat's walk method of inspection. During one such inspection he discovered some of us reading after hours, using the corridor lamp which flooded our dormitory through the window. The following morning he ordered a meeting of the whole student body. After we were in the assembly hall, he came marching in followed by the prefect and some head boys. No sooner had he got on the platform than he began to fulminate. As always he would strut on the stage before exploding.

"I won't allow it, I won't, I won't!" he said and stood there angrily surveying the silent and puzzled assembly of curious students. On such occasions his eyes flashed with anger, but it was anybody's guess whether it was genuine anger or acting. The suspense was palpable and in the ensuing silence one could virtually hear a pin drop.

Then he asked, "Who were the boys that I saw reading after hours last night?"

He waited a few seconds and then commanded:

"Come on, come on; out with it!"

I got up and raised my hand, followed by the two other culprits. He told us to come to stand on the platform facing the assembled students who were obviously enjoying our humiliation. He then gave us a sermon on obedience and observance of school rules. He would let us off this time, he said with a warning, but any more breach of the rules and we would be "dealt with severely." He knew that standing on the platform facing the students with our heads bowed in shame was one form of punishment. Our sense of shame was not really for breaking what we thought was a silly rule, but for what our peers saw as taking advantage over them by studying while they were sleeping. The teasing that followed confirmed this beyond doubt. Mediocre students always find ways of getting back on bright students, teasing them sometimes into submission and mediocre performance. As it happened, I was never affected that way.

Even as he scolded us, Mr. Lawrence was playful and gently made fun of us thus taking the punitive sting out of the episode. His theatrical performance was not limited to the assembly of students as was the case when he scolded us for reading after hours. As he went round the dormitories, with cat's paw performance, he would surprise students engaged in compromising situations. A rare example of such compromising situation was his discovery one Saturday evening of two older students drinking Tej (local wine) brought in from a nearby Tej house. He was not amused! Another occasion that I remember him sneaking in was when he walked into our dormitory while we were studying for Matric. One of the four matriculants, Worku Habtewold, was wrapped in a blanket resting after a whole day of study. Lawrence poked Worku with his cane but Worku did not respond.

"Is he dead," Lawrence asked, whereupon Worku, who was equally theatrical, flipped his blanket to the side and exclaimed:

"Ah! Did you say: is he dead?! May you die, sir!"

That took Lawrence by surprise; he just walked out and went back to his house.

Lawrence's theatricality was demonstrated during the school production of Bernard Shaw's Saint Joan, in which he played a part. My classmate Worku and I were given some minor roles acting as two angry monks, which only involved our exclaiming "Protestantism!" when the word was uttered by one of the characters. But we were proud to be part of a famous play in which all the other roles were played by Englishmen, mostly our teachers. The part of Joan of Ark was played by Mrs. Gurnell, our Math teacher. Lawrence played the part of a major character in the play; I remember him strutting upon the stage and playing his part with gusto thus giving lots of fun to the Wingate student body that comprised the majority of the audience.

The play was enacted in the presence of His Imperial Majesty, Emperor Haile Selassie. At the end of the play, the Emperor shook the hands of all those who took part in the play, including Worku's and mine. Worku and I were later invited to a British Council buffet dinner organized by a Mr. Littler, the Council's representative; we were two proud students who did not know which of the array of European food displayed on a huge table to eat. I had not seen so much food with so much variety displayed at one time, until that day. Finally we had to ask one of our teachers to tell us about the food; the gentle Mrs. Gurnell became our gastronomic guide.

The British Council produced English plays several times during my time at the Wingate which our English teachers recommended us to see. That and my reading of English novels and plays led me to be interested in English literature. In fact by the beginning of my third year in England I had read most of Shaw's plays.

Of the two others who taught us English, Mr. Victor Menage and Mr. Stephen Wright, Menage was a young teacher who was preparing for his MA while teaching us, while Wright was an established English scholar who had worked as a librarian at the Bodlean library in Oxford University. They both knew Amharic, both written and spoken, and both taught us translation from English to Amharic and from Amharic to English. Wright also taught additional lessons in English grammar and composition. Of the two, the older Wright who must have been in his fifties at the time, had deeper knowledge of Amharic language. In fact he even knew Geez, the "Latin of Ethiopia," and was a stickler for accuracy not only in grammar but in using the right letter in Amharic, as our correspondence shows. Stephen Wright was also a character in his own right, who amused us with his stories and English humor. He did not like us to think too much about examination. He once proposed that if any one of us mentioned the word examination, he would throw a chalk or even an eraser at us. If, on the other hand, he mentioned the word any one of us can do likewise. And in one of his lessons he mentioned the word test, whereupon, Worku threw an eraser at him, which he ducked and then asked Worku in puzzlement why he did that. Worku said that test and examination have the same meaning. Wright then expounded to the embarrassed Worku the different use of the word test and that in the sense in which he had used it, did not have the meaning of examination.

It was a rare privilege and real pleasure to be in Stephen Wright's class. He was an iconoclast and did not spare his paymasters and compatriots in his criticism. Because he was paid by British Council, he once jokingly described his work as peddling British culture. We corresponded while I was studying in England mostly at the time when I was editor of the Student Journal, The Lion Cub. He was obviously an English patriot, but loved Ethiopia and had an English sense of fairness and decency, as his criticism of my editorial shows.

He retired in Ethiopia and the last time I saw him, I was mortified to find that he could not remember me, one of his star students. He was suffering from advanced case of Alzheimer's disease.

Menage eventually did a Ph.D in Turkish language and history at the School of Oriental and African Studies (SOAS) of the University of London where I met him in 1966 while I was doing my Ph.D. He had an appointment as a lecturer in Turkish. I was pleasantly surprised that he still remembered Amharic and spoke it well.

Other teachers were: Mr. Gurnell (science) and his wife (maths). I never heard anyone call Gurnell by his first name, so I don't know it. He was a very good teacher and, by all accounts, a good scientist. He taught us both chemistry and physics. His wife taught us mathematics. The Gurnells were a childless couple and devoted to each other. As I have already stated, he was in charge of sports in addition to his science teaching. I remember one day, while he was out in the football field supervising some athletic activities, it started raining. We had been watching the track athletes running and some jumping when the rain suddenly came pouring. We ran back to the school compound but were soaked, and there was Mrs. Gurnell anxiously waiting for her husband, standing near the gate holding an umbrella with her right hand and his jacket with the left. I'll never forget the look of worry on her face, almost like that of a worried mother waiting for her child. At times, she even expressed this maternal care towards her students, especially the young and vulnerable among them.

Then there was Major Wainwright who taught us geography, and Mr. Lawrence alternated with Mr. Menage teaching us history. History taught by these gentlemen was, of course, European history. But we were also taught Ethiopian history using Tecletsadik Mekuria's Ye-Itiopia Tarik (Ethiopian History). A variation with modern history was current affairs taught by both Lawence and Menage.

We also had an Amharic class taught by the new graduate of the Teachers' Training School. His name was Milion Neknik and he eventually got scholarship to a university in Wales to do a degree in education. Milion was appointed Minister of Education after the fall of Emperor Haile Selassie's government in 1974, which was to be a short-lived appointment.

At the time when I was at the Wingate School, there was a group of about fifteen Teachers' Training School students at the Wingate under a special arrangement with the school and the Ministry of Education. Their classroom was separate but they were taught by the Wingate teachers most of the subjects taught at the secondary school level. Most of these students became teachers while a few were employed in various administrative positions of the government administration and in diplomacy. This special arrangement was not repeated, for in the meantime teacher training schools were established in several places to cater for the needs of the country. They were older than the average Wingate student and thus provided a maturity and the protection of elder brothers in some situations when such was needed. This was especially true in sports such as soccer, in which they took part with the rest of the Wingate students, which enabled the Wingate team to excel, from time to time. As I played with the Wingate's first eleven, I especially remember three: Lakew Yigletu, Haile Keleta and Abate Mengiste. Indeed, the part these took in the school team's success endeared the whole group to the Wingate students, leading to a lasting friendship among some of them, long after they left the school.

Competition to enter the Wingate was open to boys from the different parts of the country. This fact made the school (and other schools) a unity building educational institution. There were occasional fights between students caused by some difference in ethnic background, but it was always resolved amicably by the students themselves. Politics complicated by ethnicity was at times the cause of misunderstanding and strife. Although this was not the case during my time at the Wingate, I was informed that, in later years, on at least a couple of occasions, Eritrean students were involved in conflict with the rest of the students. This conflict was connected with the growth of national consciousness among Eritreans as manifested in University and upper secondary school students.

As we shall see, the Eritrean question became a matter of great controversy and division among students in Addis Ababa University and elsewhere. On the whole, students with progressive leanings supported the principle of self determination of Eritrea, *up to and including secession*. However, this was unpalatable to the majority of Ethiopian students reflecting the attitude of the government. It divided the student movement that eventually spawned the revolution of 1974, and it became the litmus test on how a progressive movement was defined. The growth of political awareness among Ethiopian students with progressive leanings was expected to resolve some of the outstanding contradictions, including the one concerning Eritrea. It is a matter of great interest that in 1969, Tilahun Gizaw, the president of the Addis Ababa University that year, was killed by unknown persons, presumed to be members of the special Security Service of the government, immediately after he successfully resolved a conflict between Eritrean and other students of the Wingate. As I will write in more details later, I was myself in a similar mediation between conflicting Eritrean and Ethiopian students at the Teacher Training Institute of Harar.

When I was a student at the Wingate, such questions were unknown. There were petty jealousies based on personal competition for higher grades and such mundane student concerns. Some individuals occasionally tried to give personal conflicts ethnic color, but nothing of serious consequence happened. Certainly, there were no group fights between Ethiopians and Eritreans as happened in 1969.

In my matriculation class, out of the four three of us were Eritreans. And Worku Habtewold, the only Ethiopian, fell to the ethnic temptation; at some moments of weakness due to frustrations in falling behind in his grades, he would create tension in the class. As the four of us were studying he would sing some Amharic war songs using words such as "banda" (enemy collaborator), referring to the three of us. On one occasion, Tesfalul (one of the three), replied in kind and a horrific row ensued. Kahsai and I became conciliators. After that event the three of us agreed to say nothing even if Worku became aggressive or provocative. Outside our classroom, some among the petty mediocrities tried to use Worku's frustrations to push the ethnic agenda and harass us. To his credit, Worku never became their tool and after each of the few clashes we had, we mended fences and continued a cordial relation to the very end when all four of us left for England.

Twelve Eritrean Evangelcal Christian pastors. My father is in the middle among those seated. (Circa 1930).

Myself with my father taken in 1948, just before I left to study in England.

London, 1954. Ethiopian Students in England.

The author and Ethiopian delegates with Dr.Kwame Nkrumah, Panafricanist and first President of Ghana. The group picture was taken during the All African Peoples Conference, held in Accra, December 1958, convened by Nkrumah.

Accra, Decemeber 1958, at the All African Peoples Conference. I am on the outer right and Tedla Tebeje is on the outer left of the picture. The man in the center is the leader of the Togo delegation.

1958 Ethiopian Delegation mixing with other delgates. Accra.

Accra, December 1958. Ethiopian Delegation to the All African Peoples Conference, with other delegations.

My mother with infant Asgede, my first born Taken in 1962.

February 1962. Mr. Nathan Marein, Attorney General of Ethiopia, with High Ciourt Judges, on the eve of his retirement and my succession to the office.

At my desk circa 1963.

Addis Ababa, 1963. With Minister of Labor, Getahun Tessema (with his back to the camera) and Dr. Seyoum Gebreigziabher.

With Woldeab and EPLF fighters in Rome.

Los Angeles. March 1965, at the UCLA Law School with Professor Don Hagman.

Dejasmatch Takele Woldehawariat, Legendary Ethiopian Arbegna and revolutioanry. Chief Justice (1959-1963). Picture taken during his banishnment, circa 1965

Hakim Gara, Harar, 1968. With Governor General Workneh, and General Haile Baikedagne, Commandant of Harar Military Academy.

Emperor Haile Selassie planting a tree at Hakim Gara, July 1968.

Hakim Gara, Harar. During Tree planting exercise.

Tree plating on Hakim Gara, Harar. Deputy Governor General, Meharenna Minda is planting a cedar tree.

Jijiga, 1968, Negotiating the restitution of the spoils of war with Somali delegation. General Mehreteab Tedla showing Somali delegate a juicy morsel. Isn't peace better than war? he says.

Harar, 1968. Governor General, Workneh Woldeamanuel, explaining a city building project to Emperor Haile Selassie, at the time when I was an exiled mayor of Harar. In the forefront, in balck suit, is the venerable Ras Imru, my benefactor.

Dire Daw, 1968. With Ethio-Japanese Textile Company manager, Nishidati, at the end of an arbitraton, which I umpired.

PART II
OUT OF AFRICA... AND BACK

Chapter 5

IN ENGLAND AS THE SUN SETS ON THE EMPIRE

On a fine October morning in 1948, a group of excited students met at the small Addis Ababa airport. Four of us were matriculants from the Wingate Secondary School and twelve were from the Haile Selassie I Secondary School (Kotebe). Wingate boys were: Kahsai Tesfai, Tesfalul Tesfai, Worku Habtewold, and myself. Each group was brought to the airport by their respective schools in vehicles supplied by the Ministry of Education. Mothers and sisters wept on the shoulders of their loved departing sons or brothers, even as we laughed and joked with each other.

The airport then was very small before the modern Bole Airport was built in the 1960s. We were all shepherded into the tiny passenger lounge, by the ground hostess, a good-looking woman in her early- or mid-twenties. Her name was Almaz; and we all stared at her, particularly as she wore red lipstick, which made her more attractive. One of the Kotebe boys tried to flirt with her and when she did not respond to his attempts, he made a nasty remark about her lipstick. She ignored him and soldiered on, taking care of business, checking everyone's ticket and travel documents and telling the members of the public to stay beyond the dividing line consisting of ropes hitched on wooden stands at both ends. A couple of mothers who arrived late begged Almaz to let them through in order to kiss their sons goodbye, and she smilingly obliged, telling them to make it quick. All eyes were fixed on Almaz, who kept waving her left hand to show a wedding ring as a sign to would-be flirts that she was married.

At last we were called to board the plane and said our goodbyes to the weeping relatives. As we filed toward the airplane, a DC6 belonging to the newly established Ethiopian Airlines, Mr. Lawrence, our headmaster, was heard shouting, "Goodbye, Captain." Worku, who was nicknamed "captain" by Wingate students, smilingly acknowledged the good wishes and waved goodbye. Lawrence had often bantered with Worku, affectionately teasing him about the blanket that he always wore when it got cold, and Worku telling Lawrence to be grateful that he was in Ethiopia instead of England where it was freezing. So the rest of us did not mind Worku being singled out for a special goodbye by our headmaster. We saw it as their final banter.

The DC6 took off and made an arc, flying over the city and then over the Intoto mountain range. It was on its way to Cairo, via Asmara, my home town. It was my first time in an airplane; I saw for the first time how the city and the land around it looked like from the air. I sat near a Kotebe student by the name of Meaza Workineh, who turned out to be so funny that we laughed all the way. I remember the first remark he made to me was to ask if I was prepared for *blukbash*. When I asked innocently who he was, Meaza laughed and said, "It is not a he, it is an it." He then pulled out an envelope from the pocket of the back of the seat in front of him and said, "When *blukbash* comes, this is where you deposit it." The word happened to be a Turkish military title, comparable to non-commissioned officer (NCO), adopted by the Italians and given to their "native" soldiers. During the Italian occupation of Ethiopia (1936-1941), many of these NCOs acted as the colonizers' point-of-contact with the population and were feared and despised by the people. Meaza himself, it turned out, did not experience the Italian occupation because he was one of the several thousand Ethiopians who went over to Kenya as refugees.

As it happened, only a couple of the passenger-students suffered from airsickness and used the blukbash envelope. I was not one of them.

We arrived at Asmara after a flight lasting an hour and a half. When we landed we were greeted by a group of people including my father and several of his friends. Earlier, I had written to my father from school telling him about life at the Wingate and about my classmates. I was surprised to learn that my father remembered Worku by name and wanted to meet him. For some reason he referred to him as Workineh (literally, "you are gold")! I, therefore, asked Worku to come out of the waiting room and meet my father, which pleased him enormously. It was the last time I saw my father and, as I have already written, it was Worku who told me the news of my father's demise, in 1950. He broke the news with deep emotion, expressing his happiness that he at least met him, albeit briefly. Although we had our differences in later years, I always had a soft spot for Worku and was deeply saddened at his death. He was one of the numerous victims of the Derg.

We flew from Asmara to Cairo, arriving after some six hours' flight. We were put up at the Heliopolis hotel in central Cairo. It was during the first Arab-Israeli war and there was a curfew. I remember people scrambling from their chairs in the garden outside the hotel when the siren sounded and rushing back to the lobby, and some young lovers hugging, presumably afraid of an Israeli attack. That is etched in my mind, together with the sound of wooden shoes click-clacking on the streets of Cairo. In later years, after the Nasserite revolution, as I passed through Cairo, I noticed the disappearance of wooden shoes and their replacement by more decent footwear, among other improvements.

We stayed in Cairo a few days and were taken to the Ethiopian embassy, where we were treated with Coca Cola. It was the first time that I ever tasted

Coca Cola, and it seemed to me more delicious than any I tasted in later years. The ambassador, Fitawrari Taffese, was a kindly man in his fifties who gave us the usual pep talk about how Ethiopia waited for her educated children to rescue her from ignorance and backwardness. He was a member of the Shoan Amhara nobility known as the Adisghe most of whom were big landlords who exploited the peasants, who handed over three-quarters of their produce to them.

Later that day, my fellow traveler Meaza commented that the ambassador and his kind were the cause of the country's backwardness. It was the first time I heard an Ethiopian student express such a "radical" view. We parted company in Paris. Meaza and most of the Kotebe group left for the United States of America, while we, the students of the Wingate and one student from Kotebe, Beyene Woldegabriel, flew to England after a restful night in a Paris hotel.

We were met at the airport by a portly Englishman with a ruddy face and humorous disposition, presumably sent by the British Council, or perhaps by Philips and Randall, our education agents who also acted as bursars of our monthly stipend. We were taken to the Osborne Hotel in the Bayswater area of central London, where we stayed until we were placed in different lodgings. Apart from the population density, the thing that impressed me most about London was the fog and the early sunset. Among the residents/guests of the Osborne were a few Americans and Europeans as well as English people. During the evenings for the first few days, we were visited by Ethiopian students who had been sent to England a year ahead of us. These included the poet Mengistu Lemma and the Eritrean, Habte-Ab Bairu, both students at the London School of Economics, and Belai Abai, who was studying science at the University of London.

The visits and encouragement of these senior students helped brighten an otherwise gloomy arrival. It is worth remembering that England, and especially London, had emerged from World War II only three years earlier. Practically everything was rationed; the only thing that was not rationed was water. As winter approached, it got colder and colder. The hotel rooms were heated with gas, which was activated by inserting coins in a meter. Our Ethiopian friends, who had experienced one of the coldest winters the previous year, advised us on how to make optimum use of our meager monthly stipend of twenty-five pounds. There were times, toward the end of the month, when I had to make a choice between heating the room the whole night and going without lunch the following day. The woolen clothing that the Ministry of Education officials had bought us in Addis Ababa helped, but there were times when I wore two pullovers under my coat.

A few words about my other companions who were sent to different places: Kahsai was sent to Edinburgh, Tesfalul was sent to Loughborough to study engineering and Worku was sent to a preparatory school in the west of England to study English, which he had failed in his Matric. He passed in the summer of 1949 and was enrolled at the London School of Economics. Kahsai entered the University of Edinburgh's prestigious medical school and would become one of Ethiopia's earliest medical doctors until his untimely death in 1976. Tesfalul developed mental problems and was repatriated around 1950 after several attempts at cure and rehabilitation failed.

I spent the winter studying physics, chemistry and biology at a special preparatory school in London not far from the Osborne Hotel. It was part of the preparation toward entering medical school. It was a tough assignment. My science education had left much to be desired and I hated chemistry, especially lab work. In the spring of 1949, Phillips and Randall decided to enroll me at Croydon Polytechnic, south of London, to study pre-med. Accordingly, they found me a nice landlady, a Mrs Startin, with whom I stayed the spring, as one of five boarders, including an East-Africa-born Indian who was at the Polytechnic, studying medicine. His name was Amir Kanji, and we became good friends, but whereas he stuck with medicine, I was to leave it in favor of law.

While studying science in the pre-med course, I became interested in literature and politics, which took much of my study time. I switched to law partly influenced by people I met at the International Language House (ILH) in East Croydon, to which I moved from Mrs. Startin's toward the end of 1949. There were many Africans, Caribbeans and Asians at the ILH, all interested in national and international politics and debating and arguing all the time. Through the experience of these debates as well as my wider readings, I developed a more acute awareness of political and social issues.

My social life also changed from that of a shy schoolboy who was limited to going to the cinema. I started frequenting dancing halls with friends, including Amir Kanji. I was seventeen-going-on-eighteen and awkward at first. After I took some dancing lessons, I gained more confidence and began flirting with English girls my age. But until I went to Paris in the summer of 1950, my experience did not go beyond venturing onto the ballroom floor, flirting and occasional kissing. The hundred-odd Ethiopian students in England used to meet twice a year in those days, once around Christmas and once during the summer. One Ethiopian student I met at these gatherings was Zewde Haile Mariam, with whom I became a close friend. Zewde was interested in studying law, and I began to think about it more seriously.

Perhaps the most important reason for the final switch from medicine to law—the moment of truth, so to speak—was when my biology teacher, Dr. Boyd, showed us a cadaver. "One day soon, you will all be expected to perform an operation, first on the cadaver then on a live body," he said with a smile. Then he turned his gaze on me.

"What say you, Selassie?"

"I don't think I am cut out for this, sir," I said.

"Why is that?"

"I am squeamish and can't stomach the sight of blood," I said.

"We all go through this, my boy, you will get used to it," he said, or words to that effect.

"No, Dr. Boyd," I remember saying to the kindly Scotsman, "If I change as a result of doing more incisions and seeing more blood, then something in me that I value will change. And I don't want that something to change."

Having made that remark, I asked for his pardon and left the Polytechnic for good. The next day, I went to London looking for my friend Zewde. I told him about my decision, to his delight, and together we decided to start legal studies.

That was in 1950. By that time our educational agents, Philips and Randal, had been fired and replaced by one Mrs. Holland. When I told Mrs. Holland, who was herself a lawyer, that I had made a switch to law, she was extremely displeased and said that I might not receive my stipend or might even be repatriated back to Ethiopia. A time of tension and uncertainty followed, during which I delved into more books on philosophy, politics and literature. That was when I read most of George Bernard Shaw's plays, as well as much socialist literature. As for my monthly stipend, Mrs. Holland did not make good on her threat, for I continued to receive it.

Summer Work and Extracurricular Activities

During the summer months, I got occasionally employed doing menial work to supplement the monthly stipend that was sometimes not adequate to cover my extracurricular activities, which included travel to Europe and studying French and Italian. This began after my first visit to Paris in the summer of 1950 when my friend Zewde Hailemariam and I had an enthralling time, experiencing our first taste of "sinful delights" in that City of Light.

Some of the extracurricular activities in London included weekend visits to the British Council off Oxford Street, in a medley of cultural events in which foreign students were entertained by visiting actors and lecturers, as well as engaged in dancing. The dancing part was the more popular segment of what the British Council offered. It was in these dancing sessions that I made friends with girls from the European continent. Obviously, it was mainly the financial demand implied in these extracurricular activities on the meager resources of a student that drove me and a couple of my friends to seek work for extra income. On a couple of occasions during the summer months, I was employed picking apples and strawberries at a place called Wysbich in Cambridgeshire. Students from Sweden, Germany, France and Ireland frequented these summer works; and although the work was tedious, it was relieved by delightful events in the evenings. Though not comparable to the Paris night clubs, with their music and dance, or to the cultural medley and dancing floor of the British Council, evenings in these summer work camps were no less delightful.

They were certainly far better than working in the kitchens of the Lyons Restaurant in the Marble Arch area, where in my first summer work I had a nasty experience at the hands of a woman kitchen manager. The story of my kitchen joust with the Cockney manager is memorable for my outlandish response to her unjust order and her reaction to my response; for it became the talk of the kitchen staff for a long time judging by the reports to me given by a couple of West Indian workers, who witnessed the occasion, and who continued to work there.

It happened in my first week of work as a kitchen hand, involving washing dishes. It was steaming hot in the kitchen and I had been washing hundreds of dishes and wiping them and placing them on trays and placing them on a rack. One day, toward the end of the work-day before I was due to leave for an evening rest, I was tired and needed to rest a while; so I stopped washing dishes and was standing outside the kitchen when the said manager came charging and furiously gave me a piece of her Cockney mind for stopping work. As punishment for my crime, she ordered me to scrub the floor of the entire kitchen area, a more tedious and unpleasant work than washing dishes.

It must have been her tone and language as well, of course, as my tired bones, but I decided to challenge her there and then. So I stood upright and looking her straight in the eyes said I would not scrub the floor. She could not believe her ears. It was clear to me that no worker in that menial job had ever challenged her authority before.

"You what!" she exclaimed

"You heard me; I will not scrub the floor."

"Yes, you will. Scrub the floor, I say, right now," she said pointing to a mop and cloth and a pail of water at the corner of the area. Her determination to humiliate me only whetted my appetite for a showdown.

"And I said **no, I will not**. Didn't you hear me? Are you deaf?"

"You call me deaf!" She screamed and repeated it turning to the kitchen staff, who had stopped work and come to witness the drama.

"I will show you what I am made of. You will be dismissed and you will get nothing at the end of the fortnight. No wages!!" At this point I took the apron off my waist and threw it at her, slowly walked up the stairs leading to the first floor, and equally slowly turned my face and said, "You can stuff the wages up your bloody arse." (I swear I had never used such vulgar language before that occasion and, as what follows demonstrates, I must have been possessed by some spirit!)

Before she recovered from that (for me) uncharacteristic excessive response, I found myself stretching out my right arm. Boring my eyes into hers, I said: "May the spirit of my ancestors, sitting on the Obelisk of Axum and on the rock-hewn churches of Lalibela, haunt you all your wakeful moments and pursue you to your grave!" The poor woman turned red all over from her neck up her entire visage and was left standing there speechless. The other members of the kitchen staff were equally intrigued and speechless. They must have thought that it was some mysterious magical curse pronounced on the hapless woman who, I was told later, never raised her voice at any one of them after that extraordinary event. From then on, I started telling some gullible souls that my curse could wreak untold damage on anyone who crossed me. I added that my tongue was tinged with black spots, which testified to the potency of my curse. It was all said in jest, of course, but some took it to heart!

I left Lyons Restaurant, never to return even to claim my wages. How different and pleasant was apple picking in Cambridgeshire!

The summer of 1950 was marked with sadness for me. Following the death of my father in January of that year, the death of Bernard Shaw in the summer of 1950 added more sadness. Shaw had become my intellectual godfather and a kind of father substitute following my own father's death. I was not depressed but was very sad. To borrow a line from a friend who lost her husband: "Depression means nothing matters. Sadness means everything does." And so it was with me; I put all my energy into reading Shaw's works and understanding their message. I had begun searching for a mission in life and for a field of study that would enable me to fulfill that mission.

The hiatus between giving up medical studies and beginning with law was one of tremendous intellectual growth and discovery. In addition to reading and widening my intellectual interests, I also became involved in Left politics, as well as in Ethiopian student politics. Shaw's writings, among others, had helped me define my mission. I was elected secretary of Ethiopian students in Great Britain as well as editor of their journal, *The Lion Cub*. It was a time of the beginning of political awakening in Africa, when demands for independence from colonial rule were being made by African leaders. It was the time of the Mau Mau war in Kenya. It was also the time of the start of the Korean War, when Ethiopia's Emperor Haile Selassie sent a contingent of his Imperial Bodyguard to Korea to fight on the side of the West against North Korea and its Chinese allies.

As the Sun Sets on the Empire

In one of his memorable statements, Winston Churchill said that he was not appointed Her Majesty's Prime Minister to "preside over the dissolution of the British Empire." He added that "the sun shall not set" on the Empire. Clearly, that was not his finest hour in terms of prophecy. In London, the empire's metropolis, colonial people from British Africa, India and other British possessions mingled in universities and student conferences, in clubs and common rooms, in positive interaction. Many frequented Speakers' Corner at Hyde Park to hear orators openly denouncing British exploitation of colonial peoples and demanding that the empire be ended and the subject peoples freed. All socialist and communist forums and publications advocated the termination of the colonial empire.

London brought different peoples from the colonial empire to share the same experiences of prejudice and discrimination. Many expressions of prejudice were subtle, but others were not. Some boarding houses cast decency aside and put out notices that read:

> Cats, Dogs, and Blacks not allowed to reside in these premises.

There were variations on this theme, with Persians, or Indians substituting for Blacks. Commenting on this vulgar trend, an Indian speaker at Hyde Park quipped that the fate of the British Empire would be determined by British landladies.

My generation of Africans saw the gradual loosening of the bonds of empire, together with the awakening of people and the organization of liberation movements throughout Africa and Asia. Students played a catalytic role in this process, adopting the cause of any liberation movement as their own cause, organizing protest and fund-raising meetings and inviting prominent personalities to speak and debate. The role of African students was made effective by student associations, organized regionally both in England and on the continent, especially in France. There, the support of Left parties for the cause of African liberation was much more explicit and aggressive. Thus the Senegalese leader and poet, Leopold Sedar Senghor, was a member of the Socialist Party of France and was indeed, an elected member of the French National Assembly in post-war France. So was Felix Houphuet Bigny of the Ivory Coast. Similarly, Ahmed Sekou Toure of Guinea, a labor union leader, was a member of the French Communist Party, albeit an independent and thus uncontrollable member. Both Senghor and Sekou Toure would lead their respective counties to independence, becoming their first presidents. In a later chapter, we shall note their participation in the creation of the Organization of African Unity (OAU).

My first interaction with African students in France was with my friend Zewde Haile Mariam. We found that the French-speaking African students felt more at home in France than those of us studying in Britain did. I remember being asked by French-speaking African students whether I was French or English (*vous-etes francais ou anglais?*). My frequent answer, "neither" (*ni l'un, ni l'autre*), was greeted with puzzled looks. African students felt more at home in France because of the relative absence of color prejudice. Black men dated and married French women without anybody raising an eyebrow, whereas in England there was no such easy acceptance, although the decency and live-and-let-live attitude of the British did not allow or lead to any nasty confrontations.

Official French policy in their African colonies was one of assimilation, even though one reads of ugly incidents in which the scum of Europe aspired to become, and did behave as, the aristocracy of Africa.

In contrast to the British policy of indirect rule made popular by Lord Lugard, French policy was direct rule. Under the British policy, African traditional chiefs were used as points-of-contact with the African populations, playing critical roles in the maintenance of security as well as in the collection of revenues. Indirect rule reflected British pragmatism in maintaining respectful distance from the "natives." The policy fit in well with the legendary British "reserve," which I experienced during my ten years in England. And French direct rule fit well with the French character of more robust social interaction at practically all levels, among individuals and groups. This too was my experience in France. In addition to the French penchant for direct speech and sociable

nature, could it also stem from the French revolution's declaration of *liberte, egalite, fraternite*? I leave it there, in the form of a question, because I have no way of proving one way or the other.

As Secretary of Ethiopian Students Association in Great Britain, I was able to invite two African political figures to be our guests of honor and address the students on their respective countries' plights. One was Seretse Khama of what was then known as Bechuanaland (today's Botswana), who came with his English wife, Ruth. As a traditional Chief, Seretse Khama was expected by the British colonial authorities to behave in certain ways. One of those ways was not to marry an English woman! When he and Ruth fell in love and announced their prospective wedding, he was warned against it, but the wedding took place nonetheless. In consequence of this "crime," he was banished from his land and "exiled" to Britain. He later returned in triumph to lead his people to independence and be elected their first president.

Another African leader was Mbuyu (Peter) Koinange, who had somehow managed to persuade the colonial authorities in Kenya to give him permission to travel to Britain, where he told of the Mau Mau war and the harsh reprisals exacted by the authorities. The leader of Kenya's emerging political movement, Jomo Kenyatta had been detained under allegations of fomenting the rebellion. At that time there were no Kenyan students in England, and it fell on us as their neighbors, as well as other African students and British friends, to take up the cause. Most notably, the Left section of the British Labor party, led by Aneurin (Nye) Bevan, took up the cause of African liberation and raised the issue repeatedly in Parliament.

I remember meeting Mr. Bevan after a speech he gave in Paddington and talking to him about the Kenya situation. I was emboldened to approach him because of his fiery speech, in which he challenged the British government to free the colonial peoples "on whose backs we have prospered for so long." As other admirers accosted and button-holed him, he asked his wife, Jenny Lee, to take down my name, address and telephone number. What impressed me most about that meeting was Mr. Bevan's simplicity and grace as well as his willingness to take time to listen to a young and unknown African student whom he had never met before. This particular experience was part of my growing political awareness: I was learning that principled commitment to the cause of democracy and justice makes no distinction based on race or ethnicity. This is one of the articles of faith of socialism which became my cause for years to come.

I adopted the Labor Party as my own, especially the Left faction led by Nye Bevan. I read their publication, *Tribune* and other socialist publications such as the *New Statesman and Nation*. I also attended some meetings of the Communist party of Great Britain (CPGB) and read its organ, the *Daily Worker*. But I found the CPGB dogmatic and disempowering; I would later find out that this was because Moscow was calling the shots in what communist parties worldwide did or said. So, I stuck to democratic socialism as my guiding ideology.

In later years, I was gravely disappointed when a Labor Prime Minister, Harold Wilson, who had been a Bevanite in his early career, did not have the courage of his convictions on the Rhodesian question. Harold Wilson sided with "kith and kin," supporting the white minority and ignoring socialist principles of universal brotherhood. In 1965, Wilson betrayed the African people's democratic right of self determination by allowing Ian Smith to get away with his defiance of world opinion and announce UDI (Unilateral Declaration of Independence) of Southern Rhodesia (today's Zimbabwe). It took fifteen years of bloody guerrilla war before majority rule could be established. Rhodesia and Kenya were similar in that a significant white settler community owned the best land, having driven the Africans off. Whereas in Kenya an amicable settlement was made accommodating both blacks and whites, in Rhodesia the settlement agreement of 1980 allowed the white minority to retain ownership of the best lands. Having slept on the issue for over twenty years, the government of Robert Mugabe is now using the land issue as a way of remaining in power, encouraging landless peasants to occupy rich, white-owned plantations. Without denying the justice of the cause of the African peasants, it is now seriously doubted whether Mugabe's actions are motivated by the interests of the majority.

Looking back to my student days and thereafter, when the Labor government of Harold Wilson betrayed the rights of the African majority and hence its own principles, I cannot help wondering whether it is ever possible for human beings to act in the name of principle when their self-interest is at stake. I will have occasion to address this question in another chapter. For now, suffice it to say that the preponderance of evidence seems to show that quite often principles are used as a screen for personal interests. All too often, the maintenance of one's self and party's interest override cherished principles in the name of which liberation wars are fought.

The Indomitable Sylvia Pankhurst

One British citizen stood out as a friend of the underdog, and was an advocate of Ethiopia since the days of Mussolini's invasion. That person was Sylvia Pankhurst, a member of the famous family of suffragettes who made history in the years during and after the First World War by agitating for women's rights. Women in Britain did not have the right to vote before that time, and the suffragette movement was crucial in their struggle to attain it.

Sylvia, the youngest daughter of Mrs. Mary Pankhurst, was drawn to radical causes, so much so that Bernard Shaw, in a letter he wrote to her, said that her politics represented the "infra-red end of the revolutionary spectrum." In 1935, when Mussolini invaded Ethiopia, Sylvia took up the cause of Ethiopia and its exiled Emperor, Haile Selassie. I had heard about her from my English teachers at the Wingate School in late 1947 or early 1948. None of their remarks were favorable; in fact they painted a picture of her as an angry troublemaker who had no understanding of Ethiopia. The most critical was my English teacher, the venerable Mr. Stephen Wright, who interspersed his literary lessons with current affairs. To him, Sylvia Pankhurst was a bully and sycophant of the Emperor.

Then I met the indomitable Sylvia – first at a meeting organized on the occasion of the Emperor's birthday at the Ethiopian Embassy, then at her home in Woodford Green in the suburbs of London. Her son, Richard Pankhurst, was a Ph.D. student at the London School of Economics (LSE) and was responsible for inviting us to their home. I remember the first time I went there as if it were yesterday. The center of her attention among my friends was the poet Mengistu Lemma. (She had a weakness for poets, as her project of translation of the poem of the Rumanian revolutionary poet, Mchael Eminescu, "Emperor and Proletariat" illustrates). Mengistu also had befriended her son Richard at LSE. Sylvia dominated all conversation but also asked pointed questions, as I recall. At that time, I was politically a neophyte, so I deferred to my elders, Mengistu and Habteab Bairu. Sylvia also paid much attention to Habteab who was a younger brother to the emerging Eritrean leader, Tedla Bairu.

I do not remember much food at the dinner table, probably because things were still rationed. But I do remember the pot of tea and the biscuits that Richard kept passing to us.

Ms. Pankhurst's ally in the British Parliament was Mr. Fenner Brokway. Mr. Brokway acted as a spokesman on behalf of Africans, and was particularly helpful in Ms. Pankhurst's efforts on behalf of Ethiopia. He never failed to raise issues concerning Africa in the House of Commons.

Toward African Liberation

In 1957, Ghana became independent. Sudan had become independent a year earlier, and Tunisia and other North African countries had gained independence before Ghana. But Ghana, as sub-Saharan Africa's first independent country, held a symbolic power and had a mobilizing emotional impact on Africans. The events that led to Ghana's independence—the agitation of Nkrumah, Ghana's first President, and other political leaders, their detention by British colonial authorities and the massive support they received from their people, as well as sympathy and support worldwide—had a galvanizing effect on us, the African students in England. The West African Students Union, perhaps the best organized African student body, organized support meetings and demanded the release of the detainees.

Nkrumah and his comrades were released and called to Ghana's Government House to form an interim African government, pending a proper election and transfer of power. The official summons from the prison and the invitation to form an interim government earned Nkrumah and his comrades the sobriquet of "Prison Graduates" (PGs). Some of them, like Kojo Botsio, wrote "PG" after their names, stating tongue-in-cheek that it was their degree! I personally heard Mr. Botsio say this with a straight face in Accra at the All African Peoples Conference convened by Nkrumah in December 1958. The All African Peoples' Conference took place only two years after my graduation from law school; at age twenty-six, I was in an idealistic mood and attended that historic meeting as a starry-eyed believer in African liberation and eventual unity as advocated by Nkrumah. A word on the conference at this point will, therefore, be in order, in anticipation of a more detailed account of that historic event.

Ghana with its illustrious first President, Kwame Nkrumah, had become a symbol of Africa's liberation and hope. His writings on Pan-Africanism and the need for African unity inspired movements that are still struggling today in a continent that is divided, impoverished and marginalized in world affairs, despite its enormous resources. At the time Nkrumah convened the All African Peoples Conference, the vast majority of African countries were still under colonial rule. Nkrumah had convened a meeting of African heads of state earlier, in the spring of 1958, to set the stage for this meeting of political parties, labor unions, student and women's organizations. His strategy was to use these political and social forces to bring pressure to bear on governments, both independent and colonial.

The idea was to persuade the governments of independent countries to contribute toward the liberation of the territories still under colonial rule, as well as to lay the foundation for a future agreement on African unity. In addition, his plan was to increase the pressure on the colonial governments of Britain, France, Belgium and Portugal, so that these powers would speed up the process of transfer of power to Africans. According to Nkrumah's strategy, the peoples of the colonial territories would be more amenable to his vision of a united continent if the idea was preached vigorously before their independence; that is to say, before their leaders began to enjoy power for its own sake. In this he was to be bitterly disappointed. At the creation of the OAU in 1963, the idea of a United States of Africa was rejected in favor of a loose relation among sovereign states. I will say more on this, because I was present at the creation of the OAU.

In my student days in England, the Algerian liberation war captured the imagination of Africans as well as all who were sympathetic to African liberation. It was more written and talked about in France than anywhere else in Europe, of course; and it was due to my frequent visits to Paris to study French that I was able to learn more about that war. Before I graduated from law school in 1956 and left England to go back to Ethiopia, I was able to sensitize African students in England about that war. The French atrocities committed against civilian supporters of the FLN (*Front de la Liberation Nationale*) were front-page news and horrified world opinion. But it took another eight years of a bloody war before the French agreed to transfer power to the Algerians, despite the fact that they had already suffered a humiliating defeat at the hands of Vietnamese guerrillas at Dien Bien Phu.

I was able to hear first-hand reports from Algerian freedom fighters at the All African Peoples Conference. Franz Fanon (who led the Algerian delegation to the conference), gave a graphic description of the tactics and methods of the French occupation army to an attentive audience, several years before he became a world-renowned figure as the author of *The Wretched of the Earth* and other works. To the Africans and their guests from Europe and America, assembled at the Conference in Accra in December 1958, Fanon's penetrating account made Algeria another symbol of African liberation, in this case of northern Africa, and created a sense of continental solidarity transcending regional and racial differences.

The Western Powers' diplomatic policy of lumping North Africa with the Middle East and separating it from the rest of Africa was hotly contested, and Nkrumah used the sentiments generated to insist on the need for continental unity including North Africa. Perhaps in order to drive this point home at a personal level, he later married an Egyptian woman, presumably with the facilitation of his friend, Egyptian President Gamal Abdel Nasser.

Eritrea under the British, and its Disposal

In 1941, the British replaced the Italians as Eritrea's rulers. When I crossed the Eritrea-Ethiopia border as a thirteen-year-old boy four years later, Eritrea was occupied by the British Military Administration. This was changed to British Civilian or caretaker Administration later, at the end of World War II. When I was studying in England, the question of the future of Eritrea and the two other former Italian colonies was the subject of debate at the United Nations. The peace treaty signed in Paris in 1947 between Italy and the Allies stipulated on the disposal of the former Italian colonies—Eritrea, Libya and Somalia. Under that stipulation, the Allied Powers (the U.S., U.S.S.R., U.K., and France) were to determine the disposal by agreement. In the event of disagreement among them, they would submit the matter to the newly established United Nations.

The Four Powers could not agree, so the United Nations was asked to intervene. Libya and Somalia were easily disposed of, but Eritrea's case proved difficult. Emperor Haile Selassie used his considerable prestige and status as a world statesman to press his claim on Eritrea. He played astutely on the sense of guilt of the Western Powers, who had abandoned him to Mussolini's aggression in 1935. He based his claim on historical, economic and strategic grounds.

According to the Ethiopian contention, Eritrea was part of Ethiopia from time immemorial until Italy carved it off and colonized it. Economically, the contention went on, Ethiopia needed access to the sea, which would not be possible without the Eritrean Red Sea coast. Strategically, the Emperor argued, Ethiopia had always been attacked by foreign invaders from the north, using Eritrea as the launching pad.

While Emperor Haile Selassie pressed his claims using means both fair and foul, Eritreans were divided between those who wanted independence and those who favored some form of union with Ethiopia. The United Nations dispatched a Commission of Inquiry composed of representatives of five member nations—Burma, Guatemala, Norway, Pakistan and South Africa. The Commission submitted a divided report, with a majority of three (Burma, Norway and South Africa) recommending union with Ethiopia, while the minority of two recommended Eritrean independence. The U.N. General Assembly accepted the majority's report and, with American pressure, passed a Resolution in 1950 in favor of a compromise solution—federation of Eritrea with Ethiopia "under the sovereignty of the Ethiopian Crown."

This happened during my scholastic hiatus, before I started my legal studies. I therefore had the time and inclination to follow events from afar. I read news of events in Eritrea and Ethiopia and talked to people who were knowledgeable on the subject. One of the people who wrote extensively on Eritrea, generally supporting Ethiopia's claim on Eritrea, was the suffragette, Miss Sylvia Pankhurst. Using her weekly publication, *New Times and Ethiopia News*, Miss Pankhurst launched an attack on colonial rule in general and British policies on Eritrea in particular. Her reports and comments on events, backed by inside information from Ethiopian sources, proved extremely useful to Ethiopia's claim. British public sympathy with the Emperor and his government was also helpful, going back to the days when he lived in exile at Bath, following his famous, if unsuccessful, plea at the League of Nations in Geneva in 1936.

Mr. Tedla Bairu, who would later become the first Chief Executive of Eritrea under the U.N.-arranged federation, passed through London on his way to New York to attend the U.N. General Assembly debate on Eritrea. As head of the Unionist Party, he favored union with Ethiopia. I would later learn that members of the Opposition who favored Eritrean independence did also attend the U.N. General Assembly session, seeking support for their position.

The most prominent of these was Sheikh Ibrahim Sultan Ali, leader of *Al Rab Ta'l Isamia* (Moslem League) who attended in his capacity as President of the Independence Bloc. His friend and colleague in the Independence Bloc was Woldeab Woldemariam, the headmaster of my Geza Kenisha School and one of the most eloquent spokesmen for Eritrean independence. Tsegai Iassu, my former teacher at Geza Kenisha, who was one of Woldeab's former students and later his disciple, played a decisive role in influencing me and many Eritrean students at the Wingate to be supporters of the movement for Eritrean independence. He was later expelled from the Wingate as an "agitator," went to Eritrea and after a spell with the British Caretaker Administration, became a prominent lawyer. The two of us would later be involved in the armed struggle of Eritrea.

The attitude of Ethiopian students in England toward Eritrea and its future was colored by their indoctrination at school in their government's version of history. According to that version, Eritrea formed a central part of Ethiopia's "Three Thousand Year" history, and despite Italy's colonization of the territory, was an integral part of Ethiopia. Some of the more farsighted students, like Mengistu Lemma (a well-known poet and humorist), considered the federal solution and the democratic content of the Eritrean constitution as useful to Ethiopia itself. When the federation came into force in September 1952, a party was held at the Ethiopian embassy in London to celebrate the event and Mengistu Lemma composed and performed a song and dance act that was hilarious.

Eritra Picola, Eritra Picola...

MenTolia lebsesh, Yenetsanet wetet Techi besqatola.

Little Eritrea, Little Eritrea...Come forward, clothed in a cloak and drink the milk of freedom.

The use of "picola" (Italian for little) suggested a propaganda picture used by one of Ethiopia's newspapers showing a mother on a river bank stretching her arms toward a little girl on the other side of the river. The picture's caption in Ge'ez, Ethiopia's classical language, reads, *Zati atsm im atsmiye* (That bone is a flint from my own bone). An iconoclast by temperament, Mengistu was at once satirizing the image and suggesting that the little girl might teach the mother a thing or two. I gathered this when a group of us left the embassy party and went to a nearby pub to discuss the implications of the federation for the future of democracy in Ethiopia.

Nor did he spare the promising "child" any of the caustic comments. The *menTolia* with which he cloaked the child was a reference to the Italian style cape, which was widely worn by Eritreans over their cotton clothes (as I did when I was about ten). Mengistu, who had lived under Italian occupation in his native Harar city and attended Italian school there, was familiar with colonialism and its effects. Some of his poems written during the anti-imperialist and socialist phase of his sojourn in England were scathing in their attack on blind adoption of European ways. Indeed, the most pleasant and memorable experiences that I and most of the Ethiopian students in England had were his poetry readings at the student gatherings.

Mengistu Lemma had a significant influence in my political awakening and my leaning toward Left politics. He also aroused my appreciation of Amharic language and literature, as well as a revival of my interest in Ge'ez, which he had studied under his scholar father, Aleka Lemma.

The Incomparable Ojetunji Aboyade

My friends were not limited to Ethiopians and Eritreans. I was also exposed to the wider world of African student politics. After my return from forced repatriation, I spent two productive years at Hull University from which I obtained my LL.B degree. Our educational attaché had enrolled me at Hull following my return from my forced repatriation to Ethiopia, as I will describe later. As a result I obtained two LL.B's in 1956, one from Hull and one from London University where I had earlier finished one year course of law study.

At Hull I struck a life-long friendship with Ojetunji Aboyade, a Nigerian student of economics. Now Ethiopian student politics was narrowly focused on Ethiopia. It was, therefore, refreshing for me to be exposed to African politics in general and Nigerian politics in particular as a result of my friendship with Aboyade and, through him, with many other Nigerians, a few Ghanaians and other Africans. Ojetunji Aboyade whom we called Oje for short, was a brilliant student of economics; he obtained a first class honors at Hull and went on to receive a Ph.D. at Cambridge University. He would eventually become Nigeria's chief economic advisor and Vice Chancellor (President) of Ife University in western Nigeria.

Our friendship was close and abiding. When, in 1994, I started the process of selecting my foreign board of advisors to advise us on other countries' experiences of constitution making, Oje was among the fifteen experts I called upon to be members. I was waiting for his response to a letter I had sent to Nigeria, care of the ambassador of a neighboring country. A few weeks after we started the process of constitution making, I happened to be in Addis Ababa when I ran into the very ambassador who had volunteered to act as my emissary. Not suspecting that I was ignorant of what had happened, he began expressing his regret at the sudden death of "my friend," who'd had a state funeral. "I was present at the funeral," he said, "and it was very impressive; the president of Nigeria spoke at the funeral."

The man must have noticed the expression of utter consternation on my face and realized that he had made the wrong assumption. I had not heard of my friend's death of a heart attack until that moment.

Four years after Oje's death, in December 1998, I drove from Lagos to Ibadan with our mutual friend, Wole Soyinka, to pay my respects and perform a traditional duty of formal commiseration with his widow, Bimpe, and their children. Wole was kind enough to volunteer to take me to the Aboyade residence in Ibadan. In fact it was Oje who had introduced me to Wole, in the late 1970s, in Washington DC. Oje had insisted on our meeting, exclaiming in his inimitable way, "You must meet Wole; it is an experience to hear him speak and to see him think." "I know you two will hit it off because you are both crazies and two of my favorite crazy people."

A year or so after my visit, a memorial center was inaugurated in his name and a special book was published to commemorate his life. I was asked to contribute a short piece. In order to give a sense of what kind of man Oje was and the significance of our friendship, I reproduce here a portion of what I wrote in that piece.

> "Miss Rigby…" Oje would say, with an impassive face, "Miss Rigby, Mr. Selassie told Mr. Shelton to tell Mr. Ives to tell me to tell you that he wants his dinner kept."
> Miss Rigby, the bursar of Needler Hall, would be utterly confused, and her confusion, reflected in her frequently blushing face, was a source of impish delight for Oje who would burst out into a roar of laughter as she asked him to repeat what he said. She could hardly make out whose dinner was to be kept.
> Oje loved teasing people, and poor Miss Rigby was frequently his target because he liked her innocence and earnest, matron-like way of going about the business of organizing meals and sundry matters at Needler Hall. Oje's teasing was his way of expressing his feelings of human solidarity. He teased people whom he liked. But his

teasing could become sharp and turn into withering ridicule when confronted with stupid or condescending remarks, particularly by some of the arrogant or ignorant types among the English students of whom there were a few at Needler Hall.

I remember one Sunday morning we were lounging in the Junior Common Room, reading newspapers, when one English student asked Oje why African teeth were so white. I was not sure why but Oje's usually calm face stiffened, turning jet black (not livid!) with anger. Perhaps it was the tone of the question, or maybe he did not like the boy for some reason, but Oje said: "You mean you don't know? You see, when we are babies our mothers let us loose to roam in the jungle, and we go about biting the bark of the trees. That is why our teeth are white."

I expected the boy either to laugh at the absurdity of the story, or express annoyance at being patronized. But no, he fell for it and swallowed the story hook line and sinker.

"Really? " he said. "And aren't there snakes to bite the children as they roam in the jungle?"

"Oh no," Oje said with a straight face. "We get inoculated with the snake venom immediately after birth. So snake bites have no effect on African bodies."

Again the boy fell for it, and asked "What about lions?"

"What about them?" Oje growled, throwing a wicked look at me.

"Well, don't they attack you, especially at night?"

"Well, you see, at night we sleep on the tree tops where they cannot reach us." This time Oje turned full face towards me with a naughty smile, and I knew something else was coming. He asked the boy, "Do you know how we climb to the tree tops?"

"No," the boy said.

"We use lifts," Oje said and shook the house with his infectious laughter taking the assembled students with him. For everybody who had been listening joined in the mirth, except the poor wretch of a boy who left the room quietly, utterly embarrassed.

Oje was also a man of courage, both physical and moral. I will cite an example of an experience we shared to illustrate his courage. This too was part of the piece I wrote in the memorial book

> Needler Hall was the most comfortable residence for students at Hull University in the 1950s. It was comfortable compared to "Camp Hall," which was where the "plebs" lived. The fact that Needler Hall residents referred to Camp Hallers as plebs was an indication that they did consider themselves as privileged. I had no idea how we were selected to live at a comparatively better place. But I do remember that there was a lot of resentment among some Camp Hall residents.
>
> I remember Oje and I were involved in a fracas with some rowdy Camp Hallers on our way from a party one evening, while traveling in a bus. Oje and I were escorting two French girls who were our girl

friends—Christiane was Oje's girl friend and Monique was mine. The rowdy types had seen them dancing with us all evening at the party and seemed now to be determined to convert their envy into a vulgar show, fueled by alcohol and testosterone. Most of them were drunk but quiet. Suddenly, someone made an insulting remark to the girls and some from the group shouted, "Vive la France! Vive la France! Vive la France!"

One of these, who was obviously drunk approached Monique and touched her hair.

"Keep your dirty hands off her," I told him.

He cussed and lunged towards me and fell flat on his face as I stepped aside and tripped him. By that time the driver had stopped the bus, and pandemonium had broken loose. The pack had begun making a beeline towards me as I waited for the worst to happen. I would have been beaten to pulp by the whole gang had it not been for Oje's intervention. He rose to confront two of them who had rushed to attack me. He shouted at the top of his voice asking for calm:

"Listen everybody. There will be no fighting here. There is no reason to get excited. We all had a wonderful time tonight. We are all going to our places. My friend and I are taking these ladies who are our guests to their residence, after which we will go back to our residence for a good night's sleep...."

Miraculously, the rowdy group fell back, each going to his seat. And that was the end of what might have otherwise been a nasty encounter. From that day onwards, Oje and I became close friends. He was my best friend throughout the two years I was at Hull University.

Those who knew Ojetunji Aboyade knew that behind the good humor and folksy manner lay one of Africa's brilliant minds. He was a unique human being, a great scholar and practitioner as well as a noble humanist. He was one whom I was proud to call my friend. Hanging in a special place of honor in my house is an ***agbada*** that his wife Bimpe said he wanted me to have as a token of our friendship and of the good old days that we shared.

Chapter 6

LAW SCHOOL AND THE START OF MY PROBLEMS: MY FIRST TASTE OF SHOAN INTRIGUE

One fine morning, the dreaded Mrs. Holland, the liason officer for Ethiopian students, called to tell me the good news that that I could go ahead with legal studies. For reasons best known to her and to the Ethiopian Ambassador of the time, Ato Abebe Retta (whom she no doubt consulted), Mrs. Holland had dropped her previous opposition to my decision to study law. Ambassador Abebe told me one day that Ethiopians generally consider law as their natural domain and see no need for students to waste time studying it when they could be learning subjects more useful to Ethiopia, like engineering or medicine. In his own subtle way, he was telling me to expect trouble at some point in the future. That trouble would come soon enough, as I will relate presently.

Mrs. Holland enrolled Zewde and me in evening lectures and arranged for tutorials with a private lawyer who happened to be a Quaker, whose name escapes me. The lectures were in Roman Law, Constitutional Law, Contract and English Legal History. The tutorials were held at the Friends House near Euston Square, while the evening classes were held in a preparatory school in north London. I remember being quite excited listening to the lectures and reading the assigned chapters. The tutorial was not as enjoyable as the lectures. For one thing, we could not speak loudly at the Friends House; for another, the tutor was not very good. We soon complained to Mrs. Holland and stopped using his service. We depended on our own reading and lecture notes.

We were then enrolled in the Law Department of University College London at Gower Street. Zewde and I became close, studying together and exchanging views on a range of issues, not limited to law study. One such extra-mural activity was our holiday in Paris. After my decision to discontinue medical studies but before legal studies, we spent an adventurous time in Paris. I remember Zewde excitedly telling me that His Royal Highness, the Crown Prince Asfaw Wesen, Haile Selassie's eldest son, was in Paris and that if we hurried there we could meet him and ask for money. Zewde, who had palace connections, knew the Crown Prince and was certain that we would be well received. And so, we obtained French visas and set out for Paris.

Zewde's promise was fulfilled; no sooner had we arrived at the hotel where the Crown Prince was staying and told his valet of our arrival, than we were received and warmly greeted. At the end of the audience, lasting about half an hour, we were given twenty pounds sterling each, which was a fortune to two young students eager to paint the town red! We also used a portion of the money to enroll in the Berlitz language school. That decision to study French became for me the beginning of a life-long appreciation of French language, history and culture.

Meanwhile, our legal studies continued. At the end of our first year, we took the examination and I passed in all subjects, whereas Zewde failed. Things changed after that dramatically; our relationship deteriorated. I forget the details of what he did next because our communication was not as smooth and open as before. Zewde became secretive and we drifted apart. He attended classes the following year, but dropped out the year after. As for me, I took the second-year law examination in the summer of 1952, but failed to make the required grades. The reason for my failure was that I was involved in too much political activity, and did not concentrate on my studies.

That was when my troubles started with the authorities. One day, as I was preparing to take the exam again, Mrs. Holland summoned me to her office at the Ethiopian Embassy, at number 6 Princes Gate, and told me that I must hand over my passport. I was completely taken aback and asked her why. She simply said an order had come from "higher authorities" telling her to send me back to Ethiopia. I protested that this was an unreasonable order and told her that I would think about it before I handed over my passport. I added that I had my legal rights as a "loyal subject of His Majesty." She laughed at this last remark and said that before one can speak of one's legal rights, first one must pass one's exams. I was so incensed by this response that I told her something to the effect that I would one day make her eat her words, after which she ended the meeting with her face getting more and more red, all the way down to her neck.

So ended my first rough encounter with Mrs. Holland in the matter of my repatriation, but it was not to be the last. She reported the matter to the ambassador, who summoned me to his office a few days later. Although I liked the ambassador, I remembered that a couple of years earlier, he had been involved in a tussle with Chanyalew Gugsa, an old friend of mine, whom he asked to hand over his passport. Chanyalew was carrying his passport with him, and when he refused to hand it over, the ambassador ordered his chauffeur to tackle Chanyalew, who was heavily built, and managed to wrest himself from the chauffeur's hold, and ran out of the office before the ambassador could have him blocked. He never returned to the embassy; in fact he relocated to France immediately after that incident, and he would be most helpful in finding me lodging and other facilities whenever I went to Paris.

The lesson learned from the Chanyalew incident was not to carry my passport with me when I went to meet the ambassador. Ambassador Abebe received me in his office very cordially, starting with complimentary remarks about my good record as a student. He then said that it was his unpleasant duty to enforce the orders of "higher authorities."

"Do those orders include repatriation," I asked him point-blank.

"Yes," he replied with a noticeable sadness on his face.

"Why should I be singled out for repatriation when there are many other Ethiopian students with worse records than mine?" I asked.

"I can't answer that question; all I know is that they have decided for you to continue your studies in Addis Ababa at the newly established University College."

I then asked him if "they" included His Majesty. He was visibly annoyed and shifted on his chair. He turned his gaze away from me, waited a few seconds before answering and, in a solemn voice, said, "Put yourself in my place, and remember that we are talking about Ethiopia at the present stage of development. Even if His Majesty was involved in the decision on your repatriation, would anyone in his right mind say that he was?"

There was no need for me to answer, and in any case the ambassador was soon pleading with me to accept the order instead of forcing him to ask the Home Office of Her Majesty's government to expel me. He then added, "I will write to the concerned authorities that you are a good student, in fact better than most, and that it was unfair to single you out for repatriation."

On that amicable note and with a heavy heart, I agreed to go back to Ethiopia. Ambassador Abebe informed Mrs. Holland about my agreement to go back willingly, in which case there was no need for me to hand over my passport. Apparently, she said that I was tricky and pretending to agree as a delaying tactic. She therefore advised the good ambassador to authorize her to contact the Home Office. A person who was present at that meeting told me, years later, that he had never seen Abebe Retta so angry. He told her to mind her own business and leave diplomatic matters to him. When I met her a few days later, she was sweet reasonableness itself. She even complimented me on a one act play I had written, titled "The Angels of Death," and said that she was convinced that I would do well as a lawyer. This was a far cry from her derisive dismissal at our previous encounter, but after I learned of her rebuke by the ambassador, I understood the reason for her change of tone.

The ambassador was helpful. He said that my best course of action would be to go back and try to gain access to the Emperor. In this connection, he mentioned the famous humanitarian prince, Ras Imru, whose only son, Michael, had finished his studies at Oxford and was a friend of mine. "Use any means you can find to gain access," the ambassador said. "As you know, that is where matters are decided." I thanked him and left to deal with the details of my travel back to Addis Ababa, including selecting books and music records to take just in case I was not able to return.

As for finding a way to return to England, I was not satisfied with leaving matters to chance; I could not afford to wait until I arrived in Addis Ababa. I decided to start the ball rolling while still in London. To that end, I turned to two special people I had befriended over the years. These were two important young Ethiopian women who turned out to be crucial in my struggle to continue my studies: Alemseghed F. Hiruy and Imebet Seble Desta; respectively, the granddaughter of the great Ras Imru, and the granddaughter of Emperor Haile Selassie.

Although I had been friendly with Seble, it was Alemseghed who convinced Seble to write to her mother about my case, telling her about my good scholastic record and that I had become the victim of some secret and twisted conspiracy to frustrate my educational pursuits. There was no shortage of theories as to why I was singled out for this raw deal. One theory popular among my friends was that I had been shadowed by the Emperor's secret agents, who probably included the education liason officer, and that they had reported on my political activities. Then there was the theory favored by my Eritrean friends that speculated on the Shoan Amhara fear of Eritrean domination in the professional fields, particularly in view of the fact that the Vice Minister of Education was a well-known anti-Eritrean Shoan Amhara. We shall see which one of these theories proved to be valid.

Seble telephoned her mother, Princess Tenagnework, who was living in Asmara at the time, as the wife of the Emperor's Representative. She also wrote her a letter about me; Alemseghed told me this the day before my departure. There are things you do in your life that you regret the rest of your days. I will relate a story by way of example that I have regretted all my life. It concerns a ring Alemsghed gave me before I left for Addis Ababa. The evening before my departure, we had spent the evening together and as we were about to say goodbye, Alemseghed pulled out a specially made ring from her finger and gave it to me as a token of our friendship and good luck. The ring had the initials of the family and could be disassembled and required special skill to assemble it. I am ashamed to say that I lost that ring and would not dare tell her. My gratitude and fondness for Alemseghed is beyond words, enhanced by the fact that I always had a high regard for her mother, Woizero Yemisrach Imru, who was the wife of the great Eritrean, Lorenzo Taezaz. Yemisrach was a gentle lady of the finest character, a paragon of decency and good sense. Alas! She passed away before I could express these sentiments of gratitude and fraternal love.

As for Seble, the fact that she was the Emperor's granddaughter had been a barrier that I could not erase in my mind, even as she encouraged me to get closer to her and her royal family. Indeed, the family and especially her mother, Princess Tenagnework, the Emperor's oldest daughter (who was principally responsible for helping me to gain access to the Emperor in my hour of need), often complained to people who knew me that I had shunned her family and preferred the Imru family over them. As it happens, the complaint is not far-fetched; I felt more at home with the Imru family, in its liberal and humane atmosphere. The ambience at the home of the Princess was oppressive, and despite the fact that I liked Seble very much and was grateful for her invaluable help, I never could fit in the royal circle—even when they wanted me.

My reluctance to associate with royalty was known to some of the Eritrean dignitaries; Bitwoded Asfaha Woldemichael, the second Chief Executive of Eritrea, told me that I was a fool to shun royalty when others would give their right arm to be favored by it. What he did not understand was that apart from my sense of autonomy, I was also by conviction a social democrat and, therefore, opposed in principle to royalty. Tactical considerations may at times force one to deal with those in power diplomatically. Some people may even be forced by personal or family obligations to seek close association with royalty, as Mr. Seyoum Haregot did in marrying one of Princess Tenagnes's daughters, years later. Seyoum asked me to be one of his best men at his wedding, which he admitted was motivated by political concerns. I resisted at first, warning him that he was getting close to a doomed system, but I could not persuade him. I don't know if Seyoum reported this exchange to them or not, but my relation to the royal family was always a rocky one.

Forcibly Repatriated

It was a cloudy and drizzly London day in October 1953 when I boarded the plane bound for Paris, where I took another flight to Ethiopia, via Asmara. The journey was long and miserable, a night flight that took us over Europe, the Mediterranean and the Sahara. We stopped once for refueling. When I asked the hostess, a taciturn Armenian, where we were, she said Port Sudan, looking at me with disdain. When I arrived in Asmara, I was so disoriented that I decided I needed a couple of days to recover and so took a taxi to a hotel.

After five years in England, I was struck by the stark difference—the thinly spread population of the city, the poverty, and the smaller scale of the buildings. The cathedral that had seemed a giant structure in my childhood now appeared a tiny local church in comparison to the cathedrals in Europe. My hotel seemed like a tiny motel with small rooms and inadequate amenities. After a couple of nights, I checked out and took a taxi to my sister Bissrat's house. As soon as word spread that I was back, the house became a beehive of activity, with people coming and greeting me and women ululating and congratulating my sister. I visited my village, where I stayed one night while childhood friends and relatives came crowding our country house, eating and drinking whatever my mother could offer them. Then my mother and I returned to Asmara to stay at my sister's.

Before proceeding to Addis Ababa, I remembered the ambassador's counsel of trying every means to get access to the Emperor. His daughter, Princess Tenagne, was in Asmara, so I considered trying to meet with her; her daughter Seble had telephoned her, so why not use that connection to open this special door to plead my case? First I decided to see Tsegai Iassu and ask for his advice on the matter. Being a strong Eritrean nationalist, who had been expelled from school because of his views, Tsegai bristled with anger as soon as I broached the subject of meeting the Princess. How could I solicit the services of these exploiters of our people, he asked, when it was even possible that they were responsible for my present predicament? He argued that I would be better off without their help.

I was torn between two positions: one a counsel of the wise, coming from the ambassador who knew Ethiopian society and politics; the other coming from an Eritrean nationalist who thought that any dealing with the members of the system was compromising one's principle. It was a dilemma that I would face in my future career working in the Emperor's government. And although I respected Tsegai, I did not entirely agree with him. I knew that some of the government officials (like Ambassador Abebe Retta) were decent and fair-minded, and that it was unfair to generalize and condemn a whole people. So, I decided to follow the counsel of the wise.

My hesitant attempts to gain access to the palace of the Princess proved futile. The office-holders were Amhara hardliners who looked down on and mistreated Eritreans. These included the principal assistant to the Emperor's representative, one Kumlachew, and his Eritrean cronies. I later mentioned my attempt to my father's best friend, pastor Abraha Ristu, who was one of the leading lights of those favoring union with Ethiopia (like my father). The good pastor told me I was backing the wrong horse, citing his own experience with Kumlachew and his arrogant treatment of Eritrean elders even the veterans of the unionist party. He said that my father was lucky to have departed from this Earth before he saw the perfidy and dishonesty of the Ethiopian administration. "Your father proved he was truly a righteous man, by being spared our plight," he said.

After a couple of failed attempts, I decided to leave Asmara and try my luck in Addis Ababa. Meanwhile, I enjoyed the company of my relatives and a few close childhood friends. I was showered with questions on why I had returned, to which I responded with a white lie, telling them that I was on an extended vacation. I also met with Mr. Tedla Bairu, Eritrea's Chief Executive, and sought his assistance. I briefed him about my situation and asked if he could use his good offices to facilitate access to the palace of the Emperor's Representative and his wife, Princess Tenagne. He told me he could not do anything to help me in Asmara; he advised rather that my best option was to go to Addis Ababa and find people who could present me directly to His Majesty. He said the best person to approach would be Mr. Amdemichael Dessalegne, the Ethiopian liason officer to Eritrea during the British Administration. He told me that Amdemichael had been a good friend and admirer of my father.

I had expected Tedla to intervene on my behalf directly, either in Asmara or Addis Ababa; after all, as Eritrea's leader, he represented my interests. Little did I know that, even as early as the autumn of 1953, he was on a collision course with the Emperor's representative and his cronies, like Asfaha Woldemicael, who eventually replaced him.

On the whole, I was not impressed by what I saw and heard in Eritrea. As early as 1953, a year after the federation was installed with Eritrea's autonomy supposedly guaranteed by the United Nations, there were already signs of Ethiopian encroachments. It later transpired that Tedla put up a belated fight to maintain Eritrea's autonomy, but it was a losing battle. After nine years of gradually whittling away at Eritrea's autonomous status, the Emperor could be confident enough to abolish the federation, changing Eritrea to a simple province, the fourteenth of the empire. And as we shall see in more detail, that would lead to a thirty-year long armed struggle.

My frustrations and disappointments in Asmara convinced me to follow the "counsel of the wise" and try any and every means to achieve the aim of returning to England to finish my studies. I had been singled out for unfair treatment, and I was determined to go to the highest authorities to demand equal treatment with the rest of students, some of whom were not even studying. I could mention several to back up my case, many of them children of the nobility. Were we not equal in the eyes of the Emperor, as his loyal subjects?

So off I went to Addis Ababa. Upon disembarking from the Ethiopian Airlines plane, I was again impressed with the diminished scale of everything. The Addis Ababa airport from which I had flown to England five years earlier, had appeared huge; now it looked tiny. But it was still bigger than the Asmara airport.

The Iteghe Hotel—Base and Platform

After the usual customs clearance, I claimed my luggage and took a taxi to the Iteghe Hotel in central Addis Ababa. There, I ran into some old friends and acquaintances. The Iteghe had become the meeting place of returnees from foreign education and their friends and relatives who visited them. The returnees stayed at the hotel, where all their expenses were paid by the Ministry of Education until a proper job was found for them by the government. Foreign-educated students were soon to be known as BAs (Been Abroads), a phrase coined by the poet Mengistu Lemma. Some who did not come back with a degree attached BA to their names, at first in a humorous vein but perhaps also to confuse would-be employers. Mengistu himself added BA to his name, not to claim what he did not have, I am certain, but to amuse his friends and confound his detractors, who were many in the government. He also added HMLS (His Majesty's Loyal Subject) to his name. Given the critical views and sentiments expressed in his poems and other statements, that must have raised ministerial eyebrows.

On the eve of my departure from London, Mengistu and I and a few other members of the radical wing of the Ethiopian student body in Britain had discussed my future. Mengistu in particular was deeply interested to know if there were reform movements in Ethiopia among the students and the slowly-emerging intellectual class. I agreed to scout the situation upon my arrival in Addis and report back to them. The Iteghe Hotel seemed to me to be the perfect venue for my scouting work, and I started looking out for potential allies for the political struggle ahead.

My daily activities following my arrival combined two objectives: spending time with close friends and relatives; and contacting people who could help me gain access to the Emperor. One person whose advice and companionship was valuable was Isaac Abraha, my childhood friend and fellow traveler to Harar in 1945. Isaac had been sent to study medicine at Makerere College in Uganda, together with another Eritrean, Asmerom Legesse. Unfortunately, as a result of a student revolt at the college, they were both repatriated. Isaac eventually received a scholarship to study medicine at Beirut University, while Asmerom went on to study anthropology. But in 1953, they were both living in Addis Ababa and had definite anti-establishment views, though it was hard to pin them down in terms of organized activity.

In the evenings, I spent time with friends and at the same time looked out for students returning from the United States and Britain. From time to time, in between the flurry of these activities, I was invited to the homes of old friends and classmates. One such invitation would prove a turning point in my life. One day, I ran into a former classmate, Tilahun Kassaye, at the piazza, and he invited me to lunch at his house the following Sunday. That lunch was the first of many; Tilahun and his wife Tsighe Menkir apparently liked my company. It was on one of those occasions that I met Koki, Tsighe's younger sister and my future wife, as I will write in more detail below.

The Ministry of Education

Since the Ministry of Education was responsible for all student affairs, that was the first place I went to find out why I had been singled out for forced repatriation before completing my studies. In Ethiopia, as elsewhere, it was important to know who was who and how to access the decision makers. The main decision maker in this case was the Vice Minister of Education, Akalework Habtewold; (the Emperor was the titular Minister). Next to the Vice Minister was the Director-General, who at the time was Belete Gebretsadik. No one was allowed direct access to either of these high-ranking officials, so people either used go-betweens or waited in the corridors outside their offices, begging for attention as the officials came and went. Sometimes people stood in the corridors for days on end before any attention was given to them or their cases.

One day, Petros Bekhit, an Eritrean who was a member of the Evangelical Church in Asmara and married to a distant cousin, was surprised to see me standing in the corridor. Petros worked in the accounts department of the Ministry and took me away to his office. After I told him about my forced repatriation, he expressed great sadness to see me reduced to an ordinary suitor—"standing with the rabble," as he put it. He said that there were better ways of handling my case. First of all, I had to go through the bureaucratic ladder and not jump the queue; I had to see the Director-General before I could see the Vice Minister. Secondly, we had to find a person who could talk to the Director-General, and he knew just such a person. Thirdly, it was important to have inside information as to who decided to have me repatriated and why. He took me to see a man by the name of Aleme-Selassie Golla (Aleme to many), who acted as Secretary-General of the Ministry, a superfluous function, but one that was a repository of information. What I found out later was that Aleme, who was a kindly and spiritual man, acted as guide and unofficial therapist to many frustrated young students who passed through his office. The top Ministry officials must have appreciated this unofficial "counseling service," for they kept him in his post for many years.

Petros was on very good terms with Aleme, and he told me to spend my time listening to him and seeking his advice before taking any steps with regard to my case. Meanwhile he would try to find out why I was repatriated. It did not take Petros long to learn the real reason for my forced repatriation. A well-connected source in the Ministry, who had access to the archives, told Petros that it was the Vice Minster who had made the decision on the basis of an informer's story. I had been betrayed by someone in England who wrote to the Ministry that I was engaged in political activities. The most damaging piece of the information was a story that I had traveled to East Berlin and met with Communist Party officials. This was a lie—the first time I ever traveled to Berlin was in 1997, as a guest of the German government. But that lie, damaging though it was, gave me a clue as to who the informer was.

This damaging lie gave the Vice Minister, who made the decision on my repatriation, a good excuse in case he was challenged. In terms of logic and common sense, a student could not be forced to interrupt his studies even if he failed his exams, especially if he was allowed to take them again. In view of the investment made on a student's behalf, it did not make economic sense to interrupt his education for any reason—except a political one. The Vice Minister of Education, who was never favorable to Tigrigna-speaking people in general and Eritreans in particular, was thus provided a golden opportunity by the London informant who told him that I was engaged in communist activities. However, when I met him, the Vice Minister did not even hint at this political slander; he simply told me that I could continue my studies at the newly opened University College in Addis Ababa. If I ever had any doubts about Shoan perfidy, this was to put such doubts to rest. Akalework said he had asked Dr. Lucien Matte, the Jesuit head of the college, to find me a place. When I pointed out that there was no Law School at the new college and that, even if there were one, I would be set back at least two years, he said Dr. Matte would find a solution and dismissed me from his office, after telling me in no uncertain terms that I should forget going back to England to complete my studies.

There and then I vowed to myself to prove him wrong.

Ras Imru's Intervention

I did not waste any time looking for Dr. Matte; instead I redoubled my efforts to find someone who could take me to see the Emperor. Isaac and other friends insisted that I see Ras Imru, the noble aristocrat who was well-disposed toward progressive causes. I was a friend of his son, Michael, and his granddaughter, Alemseghed, so I had no difficulty in gaining access to the Imru residence; nor did anyone else. In fact, when I went there the first time, I found a long line of people waiting to present their petitions to the good Ras. He had just been recalled from his ambassadorial position in the United States of America and was entrusted with the task of receiving petitions from the public on behalf of the Emperor. Hence the long line. I decided to join the line.

When my turn came, I began telling him about myself and my case. He told me to wait in the waiting room and told his chief valet to set an extra place at the lunch table. After the last petitioner was gone, I was invited to join him and the rest of the family for lunch. At the table were his three daughters, including the oldest, Yemisirach (Alemseghed's mother) and another guest whom I did not know. Ras Imru's wife, Her Highness, was away. Ras Imru asked me more personal questions and expressed political views that surprised me. One remark that has stuck in my mind was his distrust of Khrushchev, who had succeeded Stalin. He also spoke of his admiration of India's Prime Minister at the time, Pandit Nehru. He wanted to know where I stood in politics, and when I told him I favored social democracy, he seemed pleased.

After lunch he asked to be left alone with me and asked me more about my case. He made notes of the main issues, and told me that he would take up my case with the Emperor. He did not hide his opinion that Akalework, the Education Vice Minister, was probably prejudiced against Eritreans. His view was confirmed when he found out that it was indeed Akalework who had ordered my repatriation. I had to tell him about the informant and the Berlin lies so that in case Akalework brought it up before the Emperor, he would be prepared to refute it as the unwarranted story of a jealous person, and demand proof. I left it there, not knowing when Ras Imru would take up my case with the Emperor, or what the Emperor's response might be. Here it will be useful to say a few words about Ras Imru to explain his favorable disposition towards me and my case.

Ras Imru was a cousin of Emperor Haile Selassie, and they grew up together in Harar. They had an interesting love-hate relationship from childhood on. Imru was one of Haile Selassie's trusted lieutenants and a principal supporter in his life-and-death struggle with Emperor Menelik's successor, Lij Yasu, in 1914-1916. With Imru's help, and that of other supporters, Haile Selassie (then known as Ras Teferi) was able to depose Lij Yasu in 1916 and eventually replace him. Imru stood solidly behind Haile Selassie throughout his earlier stormy career as a reformer and modernizer, when the traditional feudal forces were stacked against him.

When Italy invaded Ethiopia in 1935, Imru led a regiment that fought valiantly until it was defeated by the superior Italian forces. Long before I met him or his children—long before I ventured into Ethiopia—my father spoke of Ras Imru with admiration. I remember a story my father repeated to his friends about Ras Imru's noble behavior. As a prisoner of war (POW), Ras Imru was offered special treatment in exchange for his defection and denunciation of his Emperor. He refused, insisting that he was a prisoner-of-war, not a traitor or turn-coat.

He and several other like-minded members of the nobility were then taken to Italy and held as POWs for the five years of Italian occupation of Ethiopia. Berhe Assegahegne, an Ethiopian who met him during those years, told me that Imru was favorably impressed by Eritreans living in Italy who were a source of encouragement and moral support.

One such was Zerai Deres, an Eritrean living in Rome, who had been taken by his Italian mentors to Italy. One day Zerai was dressed in his traditional African costume, with a sword dangling from his side, standing on the step around the Axum obelisk that the Fascists took as war booty from Ethiopia. As he stood there proudly displaying his costume, a group of Fascists provoked him, making fun of his costume and insulting the "Lion of Judah," symbol of Ethiopian royalty. Zerai drew his sword and hacked several of them before he was overpowered and taken prisoner. Today, the scene of that extraordinary event is called Piazza di Axum.

Another Eritrean was the learned lawyer and diplomat, Lorenzo Taezaz, who was married to Imru's daughter, Yemisrach, and whom Ras Imru loved like his own son. Lorenzo served the Emperor in many important capacities, including briefly as the first Foreign Minister immediately following liberation from Italian occupation. For all his loyal and capable service he was "rewarded" by banishment to Moscow as Ambassador to the U.S.S.R. Because he was seriously ill at the time, his wife had tearfully begged the Emperor to spare him, but to no avail. He died a few months later aged 47, and Ras Imru is reported to have wept bitterly when he heard of his death. Many times during our conversation, the Ras mentioned Lorenzo fondly, remembering what he said and did.

There is a fascinating story about Ras Imru related in the memoirs of Ethiopian writer-statesman, Hadis Alemayehu (Tizta, 1993). Hadis had been a close aide and confidant of Ras Imru's during the Italo-Ethiopian war of 1935-1936, from the start of the campaign in the Shire front in northern Ethiopia to the Illubabor front in south-western Ethiopia, until they were encircled by the victorious Italian army, captured and sent into captivity in Italy. The story illustrates an aspect of Imru's character, revealing his nobility.

Hadis Alemayehu records in his memoirs that on the eve of their surrender, Ras Imru's troops were encircled by the Italian forces, and a messenger was dispatched by the commanding officer of the Italian forces asking the Ras to surrender. The Ras asked the messenger, "What if we do not surrender?" The messenger answered by stating that the Ethiopians were completely surrounded and that if they did not surrender there would be an unnecessary massacre. The messenger added that the Italians had high regard for the Ras for putting up a brave fight and that it would be a pity if he were to be killed in a pointless fight.

Ras Imru then convened a meeting of his high command, which decided unanimously that it would be better to surrender. Hadis records that Ras Imru made three conditions for surrender: first, that the Eritreans who had defected from the Italian army and joined to fight on the side of their Ethiopian brothers be spared any punishment; second, that there would be no punishment against the Holeta officers who had burned an Italian aircraft killing Italian airmen in Bunia, Wollega; and third, that the members of his regiment would be allowed to go back to their respective villages to live unmolested.

After consulting with his superiors back in Rome, including Mussolini, the commanding officer said he agreed to all three conditions. Hadis also records that the Eritreans, though grateful to Ras Imru for his concern, did not trust the word of the Italians and so they decided to escape, slipping through the encirclements at night and eventually crossing over to the Sudan.

Another incident that illustrates Ras Imru's character occurred while he was living as a POW on the Italian island of Panza. According to Hadis, who was with the Ras throughout his captivity, Mussolini sent a high ranking official of the colonial office to tell Ras Imru that all his property would be restituted to him if he only renounced his loyalty to Emperor Haile Selassie, as other Ethiopian noblemen had been induced to do with bribery and high office. With a bitter smile and a voice full of sarcasm, Imru thanked Mussolini's emissary and told him that he lost all his property when he lost his country, and that his property means nothing to him without his country and the Italians could give it all to anybody they want. And that was the end of the matter. He remained a POW until the end of World War II, when Italy was liberated by Allied troops.

* * * * * *

Several weeks passed and there was no response from the Emperor. I approached Ras Imru on several occasions, and he always insisted that I come for lunch and have an after-lunch chat. It was not clear whether he had presented my case and the Emperor had rejected his plea, or whether the matter was under consideration. The good Ras did not explain, beyond telling me not to lose hope. I knew that he would not lie to me, and I also knew that he met the Emperor several times a week. So why didn't he tell me what was happening? One reason had to do with protocol: you didn't talk about what the Emperor did or did not do unless and until you received imperial permission. And although the Ras was progressively inclined, he was, after all, the product of a system. Another reason was that the Emperor might not have responded to the entreaty, preferring to be noncommittal. Yet another reason—one I dreaded—might have been that the Emperor had rejected the plea, but surely I would have detected that from the words and demeanor of the Ras.

After a decent interval, I decided to try other options. One was to see Amdemichael Dessalegne, former Ethiopian liason officer with the British Administration of Eritrea, who was also an admirer of my father. A friend took me to Amdemichael's house, where his wife told me to wait on the porch until he came back from work. Upon his arrival, Amdemichael met me in the salon and gave me warm reassurance that he would do everything in his power to help me. He remembered my father with fondness and respect. Alas! Amdemichael's power did not cut much ice. My second attempt to see him proved futile, and I drew the conclusion that I was backing the wrong horse.

Back to Asmara

While I was trying other avenues of access to the Emperor, I heard from contacts in Asmara that the Princess Tenagnework was asking about me. I decided to go back to Asmara and submit my case personally to the Princess. But I did not want to advertise my travel plans, not even to my best friend, Isaac. Very early one morning, I packed my bags and went to the bus station, bought a ticket to Asmara and quietly left Addis Ababa. I arrived the following day. My secrecy was designed to avoid being stopped by agents of the Education Ministry. I was not becoming paranoid, but in view of the circumstances in which my fate was decided by hidden powers, I thought I couldn't be too careful. Better to err on the side of caution, I thought, than be surprised and regret it afterwards.

I lost no time in going to the Palace, seeking access to Princess Tenagnework. The news that she had asked about my whereabouts emboldened me; I suspected the reason for her inquiries was Seble's letter and telephone call. But when I presented myself at the Palace gate, they would not let me in, so I went to the office of the Deputy Emperor's Representative, Asfaha Woldemichael. Asfaha knew that the Princess was asking about me and was curious to know why and confirmed my suspicion that Seble had written a letter to her mother on my behalf. He jokingly asked me what relation I had with the Princess's daughter. I will never forget his mischievous smile when he asked me in Italian, "*Avete relazione con la ragzza, e vero?*" I answered him with a noncommittal smile.

Asfaha made a few phone calls. Then he rang the bell and a man clad in khaki came in and said "*Abet Goitai*!" [Yes, sir]. He was the office messenger and Asfaha ordered him to take me to Kumlachew's office. Kumlachew was the arrogant Principal Assistant of the Emperor's Representative. As I rose to leave, Asfaha told me in Tigrigna to "loosen my back" and bow to Kumlachew. "He likes it and it won't hurt you," he said with an impish smile.

Presently, I found myself face to face with Kumlachew. His reception was cool but correct; he rose from his chair to greet me and pointed toward a chair, silently indicating for me to sit. He even asked if I would like coffee or tea. I thanked him and said no. After an awkward silence, he asked me how long it had been since I had left Asmara for studies abroad. I told him five years, and that I left for England from Addis Ababa where I was studying.

"No wonder; your Amharic is impeccable," he said.

"I have had good teachers," I replied and said no more.

Then he started making phone calls. In one of them, he asked if Her Highness was free to see visitors and mentioned my name. He waited for a few seconds; then suddenly he rose from his chair and said, "Good morning, Your Highness. I have here with me…" He did not finish the sentence; he saw that I was watching him attentively, and sat down. I could not hear what was said at the other end, but I noticed that Kumlachew was nervous, although he did his best to hide it.

Suddenly he straightened, sitting upright and holding the receiver closer to his ear. "Yes, Your Highness," he said, "I have been waiting holding the phone... Yes, Your Highness, I will send him right away." He put the phone down and turned to me this time with a broad smile. "Her Highness is ready to receive you now," he said rising. The stiff back was loosened, the face was softened, the smile was warm, and he came from behind his desk to see me off. I thanked him, we shook hands and he told his office messenger to take me to the residence of the Princess.

The Princess Intervenes

I thought of the Arabian Nights and the cry "Open sesame" as I followed the messenger to see Her Royal Highness, Princess Tenagnework. There I was, walking to see a Princess whom only the privileged few could visit. Without her daughter Seble's intervention, I could not have come near the gate of her residence, let alone gain access to her inner chambers. I have written above about the promise Alemseghed Hirui and Seble Desta made to me on the eve of my forced departure from England, bound for Addis Ababa, to an unknown fate. Well, evidently both Alemseghed and Seble had kept their word.

The Palace's office complex was an impressive building built by Ferdinando Martini, the Florentine scholar-statesman who was the first civilian governor of Eritrea. The office complex lies in a beautiful building on a high ground of the palace compound. A few meters down to the center of the compound lay the residence of the Princess. Kumlachew's messenger took me as far as the gate, where I was surprised to see Hailu Bahru, a fellow student at the Harar elementary school. Hailu was equally surprised, and when I told him I had an appointment with the Princess, he himself took me to her. I later found out that he was related to her husband. Hailu was one class ahead of me at the Haile Selassie I elementary School in Harar, and his younger brother, Kelemu Bahru, who was staying at the Mission School, was one class below me. Halu used to visit his brother at the Mission School and we got better acquainted because I used to help his brother with his homework.

As he walked me to the Princess's office, Hailu did his best to find out why I was visiting the Princess, and tried even harder after I came out of the meeting, offering to have me for lunch at his house. But my mouth was sealed. He presented me to the Princess's valet and left. The valet asked me to wait while he went in to announce my arrival. She must have warned him ahead, for he was all smiles.

And so I arrived at the office of Her Royal Highness, Princess Tenagnework Haile Selassie, the Emperor's eldest daughter and consort to His Excellency Andargachew Mesai, the Emperor's Representative to Eritrea. Her office was located inside her residence. How does one feel at the door of the most powerful woman in Eritrea, and probably of the whole of Ethiopia, at the time? I don't know how others might feel, but I felt elated, because that was to be the door that opened the Emperor's door for me, a feat that even the venerable Ras

Imru could not accomplish. I had spent nearly two frustrating months waiting and nothing had happened, whereas now with one simple call from the Princess everything might change.

I was ushered into the office of the Princess, which turned out to be relatively simple, contrary to my expectations. She was sitting on a large sofa holding the receiver of a telephone, listening and sometimes speaking loudly. She motioned me to sit down on a smaller sofa in front of her. That shocked me beyond words, for I had heard that one does not sit with royalty unless one is *of* royalty, and I knew I had not an iota of blue blood in my veins. Instead of doing as she asked, I stood. She then said, "hold on one second," into the receiver and told me firmly to sit down. I sat down. From scraps of the talk, I gathered that she was speaking to her son, Iskindir Desta, who was studying at a naval school in England.

At last she hung up the phone and, with a broad smile, said:

"You are a real *shifta*, aren't you?" She then told me she had expected to see me when I passed through Asmara. Apparently she had been informed that I would not go to Addis Ababa but would stay in Asmara until meeting with her. What she did not appreciate was how difficult it was to gain access to the Palace. With all the best will in the world, people in high places—the insiders, so to speak—find it hard to understand the problems faced by the outsiders. This is not limited to royalty; even commoners who have ascended to positions of power can easily forget where they came from. I told her of the difficulties I had faced trying to enter the Palace, and that I had traveled to Addis Ababa only after my failed attempts. She seemed to accept my explanation.

"Anyway, I am glad you made it back to Asmara," she said and began to tell me what Seble had written and told her on the phone. In silence, I blessed Seble and Alemseghed with all my heart.

The princess was in her late thirties or early forties at the time. I found this remarkable—she had given birth to six children from her first marriage to a Shoan nobleman who was killed by the Italians in 1936. Her oldest living daughter, Aida Desta, was aged twenty-six years at the time and had graduated from Cambridge University four years earlier. If the two of them were to stand side by side, nobody would think them mother and daughter, but two sisters.

Tenagne was on the stout side and of short stature; she thus wore high heels. She had her father's forehead, and her mother's lips and nose. There was nothing fashionable about her hair-do; in fact it was plain and ordinary. Her fair, copper-colored complexion and smooth skin made her look much younger than her age and reflected a life of ease and comfort. A double chin seemed to defy the round smiling face, challenging the life of ease, but nonetheless did not diminish her charm of which she had plenty. She showed much of that during our meeting. She had a quick wit and asked probing questions on a number of issues, jumping from one to the other before one had time to complete answering the preceding question. It must be the way of royalty, I thought.

After the preliminary talk full of banalities, the Princess spoke about her plan. She said she would telephone the Emperor and brief him about my case and assured me that I would be able to return to England to complete my studies. Just to hear her speak so confidently warmed my heart. Then she added a bit of political gossip that surprised me. She said that the decision of the Vice Minister of Education to repatriate me was an attack on their work in Eritrea (that is to say, the work of her husband as the Emperor's Representative). At the time, I did not fully understand the intricacies of Ethiopian politics—the rivalries and power struggles between and among the various factions of the ruling class. She made it quite clear to me that my case fell into a pattern of political sabotage aimed at her husband's work in Eritrea. In my heart, I cried "long live political factions!"

In what way my case could damage the work of the Emperor's Representative was not clear to me, but that didn't matter in the least. When I later shared this information with Tsegai Iasu, he offered his own interpretation. He explained it in terms of extensive business interests that the Princess and her husband were developing with a power base in Eritrea, which apparently were not favored by the Habtewold brothers, including the Vice Minister of Education. Whatever the explanation, the Princess vigorously intervened, telling her royal father that I must be returned to England or else an entire segment of Eritrean public opinion would be alienated. This much I was told by my father's friend Dejasmach Gebrehannis, who was close to Asfaha.

In a matter of days, I was ordered to return immediately to Addis Ababa and get ready to leave for England. To my surprise but immense delight, the order came from the Ministry of Education, conveyed through the office of the Emperor's Representative. The Princess saw to it that I got the message and advised me to leave for Addis Ababa immediately and present myself to the Emperor. "His Majesty has been informed about you; he knows everything," she said with a smile. I thanked her and said I would do so.

An Ethiopian Airline ticket to Addis Ababa was bought for me, courtesy of the office of the Emperor's Representative and paid for by the Ministry of Education. I was met at the Addis Ababa airport by a car and driver and taken to the office of the Vice Minister, who received me with all the courtesy that was totally absent in our last meeting. The Vice Minister told me that it had been decided to send me back to England and that he had ordered arrangements to be made for me to leave soon. (Note: he said *"it* has been decided," without revealing who it was that decided). As I was talking to him, a phone call came from the Palace: I was to see His majesty, immediately! The Vice Minister took me there himself, but when we arrived at the Palace and approached the Emperor's office, the Emperor's aide-de-camp said firmly that His Majesty wanted to see me alone! That must have come as a shock to the Vice Minister; it was a source of immense jubilation for me.

I was face-to-face with the Emperor, which was to be the first of many such meetings in the future. The first question he asked was whose son I was. I said nonchalantly that he did not know my father, but he ignored my answer and repeated the question with a note of irritation. I mentioned my father's name and he said that he knew my father and his service as a member of the Unionist Party. "So, don't presume too much," he said in a mild rebuke. He had obviously been briefed well in advance, which he always was, as I would find out years later when I joined his government's service.

He then asked me what I was studying, and I told him I was studying law. He asked why I had changed from medicine. I told him I couldn't stand the sight of blood. He smiled and said that I would have made a bad soldier. He said he heard good things about me and remembered my academic record in school. Finally, he wished me well and dismissed me.

The Vice Minister waiting outside wanted to know what had happened. We left the palace compound and his driver took us back to the Ministry of Education, where he made phone calls ordering people to take care of the logistical details concerning my travel. He assured me that I could leave any time I wanted, and I noticed that he could not look me straight in the eye. What a turnaround, and what a difference an Emperor's word makes!

I thanked the Vice Minister as I left his office, paying him the perfunctory respect due an elder, and he ordered his driver to take me wherever I wished.

I asked the driver to take me to the home of Ras Imru. As a matter of courtesy and respect, I went to thank him for all his help, although I knew that the Emperor's order was made in response to the representations of the Princess. The good Ras received me with his customary gentle hospitality and congratulated me on succeeding. He also gave me the usual elder's counsel to do well in my studies, to come back to serve the nation, etc. From Ras Imru's house, I went to the home of Amdemichael Dessalegne for the same reason and thanked him profusely. To his credit, he did not claim any credit for what had happened. He simply said that he was glad things had turned out well for me.

Some three months after arriving from England, looking glum but determined to succeed, I was now on my way back to resume my interrupted studies. I was extremely pleased with the way things had turned out. But there was one more important matter I had to attend to before I left for England.

Engagement to Koki Menkir

I was in love.

She was seventeen, a student at the Commercial School of Addis Ababa. Her full name was Gohatsebah Menkir, but her family called her Koki. It was a chance meeting with my old school mate, Tilahun Kassaye that had started it all; some would say it was providential.

The chance meeting started a chain of happenings. I came. I saw. I wooed and waited. And in the end, I won the hand of a lovely girl.

It happened like this: On the third day of my lunch invitation to the home of Tilahun and Tsige Menkir (Koki's older sister), I arrived at their home earlier than expected. It was about one on Saturday afternoon in late October. Both husband and wife were late in returning from work. Tsighe worked in the Commercial Bank of Ethiopia and Tilahun worked at some government institution. Their house was in central Addis Ababa, near the Church of the Holy Saint Mary, and I had walked from the Iteghe Hotel half an hour away.

Because it was Saturday, Koki did not go to school and was helping with kitchen chores, as she normally did, when she was not studying. She received me graciously, bowing in the respectful manner that Amharas are known for, and told me that Tilahun and Tsighe would be home soon. She then went to the inner part of the house and brought me a glassful of *tella* (home-made local beer). This act of hospitality, though normal practice, is usually done on the order of the lady of the house. But Koki obviously considered me to be no mean guest and took it upon herself to act as the lady of the house would act.

From the first day I saw Koki, I was impressed by her quiet dignity and serious manner of speech. Even at the young age of seventeen, she exuded maturity and grace. I did not see her say or do anything frivolous; she walked and talked straight and did not engage in humorous banter with any of the other members of the family. Even her older sister, who was well-known for her wit, did not joke with her. I thought that the absence of levity in their relationship was because of the deference due to an elder, reinforced by the fact that Tsighe acted in *loco parentis*, as the mother substitute, because their parents were separated. I must also say that, in addition to her character, Koki was good looking and I was drawn to her at first sight; but she grew on me (to use a prosaic expression) as I saw more of her and as her physical beauty combined with a beauty of character to impress me even more.

Marriage was the last thing on my mind when I was forcibly repatriated in October 1953. I was only twenty-one years old, my education had been interrupted, and I could have no income to support a family before I got a decent job. Marriage was out of the question, for it would mean abandoning my educational ambitions and thus forfeiting my future prospects. Yet there I was—head-over-heels in love with this beautiful young woman, and at the same time desperate to go to England. What was I to do?

Before Koki, I had "dated" a few European girls (French, German, Italian, Swedish). None of these were serious relationships; with none of them was I in love as I was with Koki. This is serious stuff, I told myself, and said so to my friend, Isaac. I also informed Tilahun, Koki's brother-in-law. Tilahun expressed great surprise, but warmly accepted the news and encouraged me to come more often to their house to get to know all the members of the family. The elder sister suspected that I was deeply interested; Koki herself knew instinctively that I was falling in love. I felt that she, too, was falling in love, judging from the way she looked at me and got nervous when I got near her and touched her. But nothing was said.

All became urgent as my day of departure drew near. I had not discussed with Koki or any members of her family my predicament or the reason for my return to Ethiopia. As far as they knew, I was on a long leave. After I was told by the Vice Minister that I must leave soon, it was critical that I find out Koki's response to my sentiments. In those days, people who knew they were in love with each other did one of two things: either they eloped or they got engaged for a long time. Elopement implied or was accompanied by a consummation of the relationship, and that presented hazards, like an irate father with a shot gun. In my case, it would have made no sense, since I did not intend to get married at the time. I certainly was not anxious to be a shooting target for any of Koki's relatives from Menz or Jirru.

The other, more polite way was for the man to write the woman a letter declaring his love and asking for her hand. That was my preferred option, so I wrote a letter to Koki declaring my love and asking for her hand in marriage after a long engagement. She read the letter and, after consultation with Tsighe, told me that she was happy to accept but that I needed to observe the proper formalities. I knew that first, I needed to ask an elder to approach the family of the girl on my behalf and make a formal request for her hand. I asked Bereket Manna, an Eritrean elder whose wife, Eritra Gebre-Amlak, happened to be a close friend of Tsighe's. Bereket Manna kindly agreed to act as the go-between, and a meeting was arranged with the members of Koki's family at which Koki's father, Ato Menkir, was present. At that meeting Ato Menkir grilled me pointedly about my background and future job prospects, among other questions. After he was satisfied, he gave his consent and I rose to bow my respect, and that ended the formality.

The next step was to hold a formal engagement ceremony. It was important for the family to understand that the engagement was going to be a long one, lasting until I completed my education. Koki was willing to wait as my fiancé until I completed my studies—roughly two to three years, depending on when I resumed my studies, and her family went along with her wishes. Accordingly, a small engagement party was held at the home of Tilahun and Tsighe; photographs of Koki wearing her engagement dress were taken and we exchanged silent vows. I asked Girma Belew, an old acquaintance from Harar, and head of the Addis Ababa Y.M.C.A., to act as my best man. Very soon after that, I left for England. I left with mixed feelings: glad that my ordeal was over, but sad at leaving my beloved behind. I took to England with me a picture of Koki, which I had by my bedside throughout my studies until I returned in August 1956.

Chapter 7

AN EMPEROR MEETS THE FUTURE

❖❖❖❖❖❖❖❖❖❖❖❖❖❖❖

How time changes things—the healing hand of time. The last time I entered Addis Ababa, I did not know how long I would stay, or even whether I would ever get to leave it, given the mysterious circumstances under which I was recalled. No one was at the airport to meet me or give me a welcome hug. In contrast, on my way back to England five months later, I was ensconced in a warm cocoon. Friends and relatives cheerfully bid me goodbye, wishing me well. At the airport, I was surrounded by a coterie of people, some weeping as one by one they enfolded me in their warm embrace, their cheeks brushing mine; some of them tearfully, like my cousin Maria Bahlibi; others laughing and patting me on the back, like Tilahun Kassye and Isaac Abraha. The central figure in this drama, the person I was leaving behind with deep emotion, was of course my fiancé, Koki, who smiled shyly, trying to hide her feelings like a true Ethiopian. I too did my best to hide my emotion. No kissing on the lips (oh no—not in public!), no squeezing and embracing—that was contrary to accepted custom of the time. Just a simple farewell kiss on the cheeks with muffled emotions, which only the eyes might betray.

The Ethiopian Airlines flight took off and I settled in for a long flight back to England and began reflecting on my experiences of the past five months. But the past few months became just a launching pad; I began swimming on a sea of memories, mostly of the events of the previous few years leading to the moment of my forcible repatriation. Through most of the journey back to England, I tried to piece together fragments from my past student life and make sense of them.

I arrived in England from Africa in the middle of the winter. At four o'clock it was already getting dark. A crisp wind blew from the north as I got off the underground and stood hailing for a taxicab. It was the cold wind from the North Sea, which reminded me of a neighbor, an ex-colonial civil servant who had served in Uganda, and who used to complain of the north wind that brought on his lumbago. The taxicab arrived at number 15 Porchester Terrace, my old digs where I had lived together with my friends Habtegiorgis Indrias and Hailu Alemayehu. My landlady, an ever-smiling pleasant grey-haired woman, had kept my room for me because I had promised I would return. When my other friends heard of my return, they started coming to visit one by one during the weekends. The first weekend after my arrival, we all went to our favorite local pub and celebrated. I briefed them on what had happened during my stay in Addis Ababa and on the general political and social situation in Ethiopia.

After a few days, I reported to the ambassador, who was very pleased to see me back. "I knew you would pull it off," he said.

As I was leaving his office, I saw Tutu Imru coming in and greeted her. When I told her I was going to Mrs. Holland's office and that I couldn't wait to see the expression on her face when she saw me, Tutu exploded with her famous giggle and said she will wait to hear the outcome of my encounter with "that horrid woman." Obviously, Mrs. Holland was not her favorite person.

Before I walked towards Mrs. Holland's office, I said to Tutu that I did not know if Alemseghed had heard about my return and that I was anxious to be in touch with her as well as with Seble Desta. I explained to Tutu that the two of them had been instrumental in helping me gain access to Princess Tenagne and, through her, the Emperor.

I then went to Mrs. Holland's office. I knocked at the door of her office and entered when I heard her say, "come in." As she lifted her eyes and saw me, she went livid, as if she saw a ghost. I don't mind confessing that I enjoyed and savored the scene as I watched her sitting there speechless. When she recovered, Mrs. Holland managed to find face-saving words.

"Bereket!" she said, "what a nice surprise. When did you come back?"

"I am sure you mean how did I manage to come back."

"Yes, that too, of course" she said and added with exquisite hypocrisy, "any way, welcome back."

I sat down and asked her if she would find me a place to continue my law studies. She would be happy to do, she assured me, and asked me to give her a few days to make the necessary inquiries. She reminded me, as if I needed reminding, that we were midway in the academic calendar and that it might not be possible to be enrolled until later in the year. I agreed and left her, hardly able to hide my triumph.

Tutu was waiting eagerly to hear about the encounter.

"How was she," she asked.

"Stunned," I said, "Absolutely stunned." More giggles, this time prolonged.

I left the embassy elated, and with the thought of surprising one more person. I wanted to confront the one I suspected of writing the letter that led to my forced repatriation. I just wanted to see his face and observe his behavior on seeing me back. But, alas, he had disappeared from the scene upon hearing of my return. I never revealed his identity to any one: first because I did not have proof in my possession; secondly, because it would have been counterproductive. During the two and a half years that I remained in England, finishing my legal education, I saw him only once, and on that occasion, he avoided me like the plague. In later years when we both lived in Addis Ababa, working for the government in different ministries, we would meet on social occasions like weddings or funerals; he made sure never to come near me or talk to me. He held minor posts in the Emperor's government and was intensely disliked by most of those who worked with him.

Breaking Bread with Fellow Travelers

Between February and October, when I resumed my law studies, I had eight months of free time during which I read plays, novels, essays and literary criticism, and engaged in endless discussions and debates with student fellow travelers. Additionally, I traveled to Italy and France to further my language studies. I enjoyed reading Shaw's plays, Dante's *Divina Comedia* and Victor Hugo's novels and poems. I used to recite from memory (to the delight of fellow French enthusiasts), Victor Hugo's *Retraite de la Russie*, about Napoleon's fateful Russian campaign. Of Bernard Shaw's plays, I liked Saint Joan best maybe because I'd had a minor role in it at the Wingate. But the Shaw passage that I liked best was the long speech of the main character in "Man and Superman," which begins, "Marriage is to me apostasy...the profanation of the sanctuary of my soul..." Indeed a fellow Ethiopian student and I used to compete as to how much of the passage either of us could remember.

I also read, with great pleasure, the prefaces to Shaw's plays published in two volumes: *Plays Pleasant and Plays Unpleasant*. Other favorite British writers were Charles Dickens, H.G. Wells, and J.B. Priestly.

Occasionally, I went to London theaters and arts exhibitions with friends. Among the friends whose company I enjoyed three stand out: the Ethiopian poet/dramatist Mengistu Lemma; the artist Afewerk Tekle; and Habteab Bairu, the economics student turned art connoisseur and dilettante. There were others, of course, who shared with me their thoughts and ideas about issues and events back home. Hailelul Tebike was one; Assefa Berhaneselassie was another. But those with whom I broke bread, so to speak, and had closer interaction, were the first three listed above.

I will start with Habteab, who had a sharp analytical mind and a very warm personality. When I first arrived in London in the autumn of 1948, Habteab was very helpful in acquainting me with the intricacies of London student life. As a fellow Eritrean, he was also mindful of our common background and family connections in the Protestant fraternity of Eritrea. Habteab and Mengistu became my mentors on political matters and recommended books that eventually led me toward Left politics. But Habteab eventually drifted away from politics, particularly after his older brother, Tedla Bairu, became the first Chief Executive of Eritrea in 1952. Habteab's friendship with Afewrerk Tekle drove him to becoming an art connoisseur as well as a late-blooming *bon vivant* with an eye for the ladies.

Next I will say a few words about the great artist, Afewerk Tekle. Afewerk studied at the Slades School of Art at University College London, at the time I was studying law there. We became good friends and I learned a lot about art from him. Afewerk was a good companion, always joking and telling funny stories. He had a charming manner that attracted the ladies. However, at times he could be oversensitive and difficult to deal with. If he felt that people crossed him, he would pretend that they didn't exist, ignoring their presence entirely. This happened to Mengistu, who could be caustic at times and offend people, especially sensitive types. Afewerk was living near the Lancaster Gate area of London, sharing an apartment with Habteab, where Mengistu and I frequently visited. During one such visit, Mengistu said something to Afewerk; and when the latter did not respond, I was puzzled and asked him why, Afewerk surprised me by saying he didn't see anyone else in the room apart from me. Whereupon Mengistu moved close to Afewerk and shouted "hello!" into his ear. Afewerk did not even flinch; he just walked away, ignoring Mengistu and his shout. After several failed attempts to make his presence literally felt, Mengistu gave up and left the premises laughing. It took several years before Mengistu made his peace with Afewerk and the two started communicating directly with each other.

Mengistu Lemma was my mentor in Amharic language and literature (and Geez), as well as my close comrade in student politics during much of our sojourn in England. Together with Assefa Demise, Bekele Getahun and other progressive students, we framed critical political issues, pushing Ethiopian student politics from a mere annual social gathering to becoming a forum for serious debates. Mengistu and Assefa initiated the slogan, "Land to the Tiller," which was adopted and refined by students of later generations. Mengistu's poetry inspired many Ethiopian students, challenging them to appreciate their own culture. His slogan with regard to culture, adapted from his readings of Chinese political literature, was: "Nationalist in Form, Progressive in Content."

After he and Habteab dropped out of the London School of Economics, Mengistu concentrated on his literary work as well as political organizing, whereas Habteab turned to the leisurely life of aesthetic appreciation combined with the pursuit of the company of women. Of course, since they had interrupted their educational pursuits, it was a matter of time before both Mengistu and Habteab were returned to Ethiopia. They were placed in government departments that had no relevance to their educational background or inclination. Mengistu was placed in the Civil Aviation Administration, and Habteab in the Ministry of Education. Those of us who remained in England, continuing our education, heard with great interest, the fates of these and other friends.

The frustrations faced by our friends back home, combined with our readings in Marxist and other socialist literature confirmed for us the evils of the "feudal system." The news of the fate of our friends became the testing ground for our revolutionary rhetoric; it engaged our minds, confronting our theories with the reality of the facts of life back home. This confrontation of theory and practice would be a recurring theme in future struggles. At the time of our friends' return to Ethiopia in the first years of the 1950s, their fate confirmed us in our desire to work at fighting or at least reforming the system, instead of discouraging us. Reform and revolution became topics of debate among students, with the majority supporting reform rather than revolution. We organized meetings during vacation times and held many such debates, following the format of British parliamentary procedures.

Those were the halcyon days, years of innocence and idealism, when we thought and spoke of how we could reshape society back home. I feel no regret for our youthful passions and blind support of causes, for it is the privilege of youth to dream, to revolt against prevailing reality, and try to change it, even against all odds. The odds were clear—we were up against an established order led by an internationally-known Emperor and his powerful, wealthy, land-owning kinsmen who were not ready to give up their privileges. Our assumption that the oppressed would revolt in favor of the revolution would be put to the test less than a decade later, in 1960, when a *coup d'etat* led by Germame Neway, a Columbia University educated returnee, and his brother failed, as I shall describe later. We were to find out that our irresistible ideas of progress would crash on the reality of an immovable object.

By the time of the attempted coup d'etat of 1960, I had completed my legal studies and had been back in Ethiopia for over four years, working in the Ministry of Justice—popularly referred to as the Ministry of Injustice. Such sarcasm extended to two other ministries: Interior and Finance. I remember that when I joined the ministry, I noticed the vehicles registered under the ministry carried on their license plates the Amharic initial F. M. (*Fird Minstere*, Amharic for Ministry of Justice). But the people called it "*Yefidda Minstere* (Ministry of Injustice). The vehicles registered under the Ministry of Interior had on their license plates the initials, AGMI. When read, the initials gave the meaning of "Stinker" and people wanting to go over there from the nearby Ministry of Justice loudly said, "I am going to AGMI." And the plates on vehicles belonging to the Ministry of Finance carried the initials GEMI, which in Amharic meant "Stinking." To a newcomer like me, these mild expressions of grievance were clear indications of popular discontent with the government in general.

Ministry of Injustice

How did I end up in the Ministry of Justice? I must preface the story of my placement in that Ministry with a brief account of the Emperor's interest and role in education.

In those days, it was standard practice for students returning from abroad to be presented to the Emperor. The Emperor took special interest in all the university-educated youth, who by the time I returned were more than a hundred. From his earlier years, when he fought to gain and maintain imperial power, he put a high premium on education and the educated. The young and enlightened members of Ethiopian society looked up to him for support and encouragement. He chose to be Minister of Education precisely in order to exercise control over the process and the products of education. His frequent visits to the two first secondary schools and close interaction with school officials and students showed this interest at a more intimate level, as I saw when I was a student at the Wingate School.

When I was presented to the Emperor, the first question he asked me, as he did all others, was what I had studied. He asked me with a broad smile, "*Mindin-new yedekemkibet?*" [What was your endeavor on?]. I said "Law" and his smile disappeared. After a momentary pause, the Emperor ordered that I be placed in the Ministry of Justice. My preference was to be allowed to practice law, but that was of no account; I was placed in the Ministry of Justice by order of His Majesty. The order, signed by the Minister of the Pen, who acted as the Emperor's Principal aide, was in the form of a letter called "*qalaTye*" [Literally, word of the Emperor]. No ministry or government institution could act before the arrival of the *qalaTye*, which in my case meant that I had to await the dispatch of the letter and its arrival at the Ministry of Justice. In the meantime, I was still the "guest" of the Ministry of Education.

I was thus back to my old friend the Vice Minister of Education who had repatriated me three years earlier. This time his reception was friendly; not only had I the ace card, having been allowed to complete my education thanks to the Emperor's intervention, I now had my degree. In those days there were only a handful of people with degrees; so tremendous prestige was attached to a degree. The Ministry office that all returnees frequented was the one occupied by Alemeselassie Golla, a very warm and decent man who made everybody feel at home. Alemselassie acted as an unofficial psychological counselor as well as source of practical information on the inner workings of the government. He thus proved to be most helpful and very popular among the student returnees. Unlike many in the government, who told you what to do, Alemselassie simply offered his advice and left the decision to you.

Accordingly, we named him 'Tsebelu" [the healer, or literally, healing water].

One of his techniques of "healing" was to tell hilarious stories about people who had passed through his office, without revealing names. One that stuck in my mind was about the newly-arrived student who was so stuck-up about his degree that he expected everybody to bow to him with the respect due to a feudal lord. His words and gestures (which Alemeselassie reproduced with the accuracy of an accomplished stage actor), reflected his arrogant character and expectations. From the very first day of his arrival at the ministry, he addressed everybody with contempt. He demanded to see the Minister of Education. When some one told him the Minister was in the Imperial Palace, he did not understand that he was being ridiculed about his ignorance that the Emperor Himself was the Minister. He accused his informer of being a liar; he said he had seen the Minister go in to his office.

"I assure you, he is in the Palace," the informant said, to the delight of the onlookers, who enjoyed the tragic-comedy of the situation.

Finally, a kindly soul took pity on our would-be feudal lord and enlightened him that the Minister of Education was actually His Imperial Majesty, and that the person he had seen was the Vice Minister, whereupon our would-be feudal lord stormed out of the place. Alemeselassie then continued his story of the progressive humbling of the man, illustrating it with physical gestures. He said that whereas at first the man moved fast, held his head high and stared down people around him, in the end he moved slowly and with a bowed head. Using dramatic gestures that had us in fits of laughter, Alemeselassie ended the story thus: "Even when he waved the flies away from his face, as he stood in the sun outside waiting for his turn with the rest of the petitioners, the movements of his hands gradually became slow and lethargic. He got used to the flies."

I was listening to one of Alemeselassie's stories when I was told that the letter of my appointment to the Ministry of Justice had been delivered, with a copy to the Ministry of Education. The following day I walked from the Iteghe Hotel, where I was staying, to the Ministry of Justice. Walking down Churchill Road, I was sighted by Germame Neway, the Columbia University-educated revolutionary who would lead the failed coup of 1960. He stopped his car and gave me a lift to the ministry, which at the time was facing the square where the Ethiopia Hotel is located today. Outside the ministry, Germame and I remained in his car, chatting for quite a while. He did most of the talking, which consisted of his analysis of the feudal system and the inefficient and outmoded bureaucracy. His parting words still ring in my ears today. He said, "Do not speak more than you need. Listen more and study the situation. Beware of the *debteras* in the ministry; they can destroy you. I am sure you don't need any advice; I just thought I should give you the benefit of my two years of advanced learning in this place."

Squeezing my hand in a firm handshake, he said, *Berta!* [Be brave]. He spoke without a smile. In fact, as long as I knew him, I never saw Germame smile.

I was now in the Ministry of Justice. The first person I went to see was the U.S.-educated lawyer, Nerayo Isaias, whom I had met at the Iteghe Hotel. Nerayo, the first modern-educated lawyer of my generation to come back from study abroad, struck me as a genial man with a generous heart. I was to revise my view on that later. At any rate, Nerayo took me to the Secretary General of the ministry, introduced me to him, and left.

Encounter with Members of the Political Class

Astatke Tassew was the Secretary General of the ministry. It did not take me long to discover that both the man and his office were redundant. The office of Secretary General was a relic of the past; originally designed as a center for controlling the flow of information, it was once a powerful position. Its origin, in legal/institutional terms, was the Imperial proclamation establishing the ministerial system in 1943. The architect of the system and (next to the Emperor) the most powerful man in Ethiopia, until his fall in 1955, was the then Minister of the Pen, Woldegiorgis Woldeyohannes (WW). I was told by people who knew about these things that the Secretaries General of the key ministries had all been "WW Men."

The function of the Secretary General included receiving and filing incoming correspondence, and stamping and dispatching out-going correspondence, which made him the overall supervisor of the ministry's archives. Due to its redundancy, the post of Secretary General had fallen in disuse in modern public administration, even before the computer age revolutionized information flow and control.

Astatke Tassew was a good-looking and immaculately dressed man in his late thirties. He had courtly manners, never uttered an unkind word about anybody and never lost his temper under any circumstances all the years I knew him. In short he was a living example of the proverbial silken-tongued Shoan Amhara. He belonged to the middle level of bureaucrats also known as *mehal sefari* [middle men] who lay between the ministerial class and the army of lowly bureaucrats. At the time of my entry into the ministry, the middle bureaucrats were people with elementary education, a smattering of French, and a little English learned in night classes. Generally in their late thirties or early forties, some of them had also learned Italian during the Italian occupation of the country (1936-1941). This was also true of some of the Ministers, many of whom also spoke French and a little English, but hid the fact that they knew Italian. They need not have worried, for the Emperor followed Machiavelli's advice to the Prince—that those who had served the enemy become the most pliable and obedient servants. The Emperor had no qualms in appointing former "enemy collaborators," generally known as *Bandas,* to key positions. He did this to balance the powerful and popular guerrilla leaders known as *Arbegnas,* like the famous Ras Abebe Aregai, who looked down on the *bandas.*

Ethiopian politics at the time was further complicated by the fact that lying between the *arbegnas* and the *bandas* were the *sidetegnas*—the men who fled the Italian occupation and lived in exile in neighboring countries and in Europe. As the Emperor was himself the arch-*sidetegna,* they found favor with him and helped in mediating the contest between the *arbegnas* and *bandas.* It was all a question of power and control, and the Emperor was a master of manipulation, playing off one group against another. Those of us who were newcomers, with little knowledge of these complexities, had to walk a fine line in this political and social minefield.

In the first decade following his restoration to his throne (1941-1950), the Emperor feared the *arbegnas* the most, and dealt with them in different ways. These included material rewards such as land grants and villas built by the Italians seized as enemy property. He also appointed the guerrilla war chiefs to high government positions, such as governors of provinces and other posts, depending on their rank and local following.

Some disgruntled guerrilla war chiefs felt they did not receive the position and rank they deserved. The best-known case was that of Belai Zeleke, the *arbegna* from Gojam Province, was denied the appointment as governor of

Gojam, where he had proven his valor. He was captured while fleeing to Gojam, was tried for treason and executed, together with the son of Ras Hailu, another Gojam grandee. The ultimate penalty meted out against a famous *Arbegna* was seen as sending a clear message to other would-be rebels. In fact, it created more bitterness among the people of Gojam and even non-*Gojamyes* (people of Gojam origin) who admired Belai Zeleke. Before he organized his ill-fated coup attempt against the Emperor, Germame Neway told me of his admiration for Belai Zeleke and of this grudge against the Emperor for executing him. He had witnessed the hanging when he was a student at the Kotebe Secondary School.

By its very nature, the government of Emperor Haile Selassie involved an uneasy coexistence of modern ideas with traditional institutions. This was the main challenge facing my generation of educated people in Ethiopia at the time. The few educated elites made several attempts to address this issue. Germame Neway used his brother, General Mengistu Neway's position as commander of the elite Imperial Body Guard to garner support for his ideas of change. As he came from a wealthy family belonging to the Moja clan, he used the resources at his disposal to convene meetings and create a hard core of followers. Some of these meetings were held in premises offered by the Ras Imru family, until the Emperor heard about it through his special agents. No more meetings were held in those premises. Although no one was privy to what went on between the Emperor and his cousin Ras Imru, it was assumed that the Emperor was furious and told Ras Imru to stop it. Indeed, Ras Imru, who had returned from his ambassadorial position in Washington, was then shipped off to India, as ambassador. His liberal leanings (some say radical) were never appreciated by the Emperor, but made him an object of veneration among the educated elite and the mass of Ethiopian people. Germame later made him Prime Minister in his attempted coup, which, as we shall see, was to be the briefest premiership in history!

Germame also was banished to the governorship of Wolamo (Welaita) for a year or so, and thence to distant Jijiga in eastern Ethiopia. All this created a legend around his name and increased his popularity. Another member of the educated elite who was banished to India was my old friend and best man at my wedding, the poet Mingistu Lemma. As I said before, Mengistu and I belonged to the same group dedicated to progressive change in the country, beginning from our student days in England. As he was seen as the moving spirit of the group, the Emperor and his advisors thought his banishment would frighten us into silence or inactivity. But the activities continued in haphazard ways with more and more groups forming professional associations and debating clubs. The central YMCA provided a convenient forum for these activities.

Meanwhile I was appointed as Adjunct Lecturer at the University College of Addis Ababa. The first two years (1956-1958) I taught a class in jurisprudence, offered to judges, advocates and police officers in the evening. Later I taught a political science class on Ethiopian Constitution and Government. Teaching allowed me, and others, like me, an opportunity to reach out to the youth of the nation and sow the seeds of ideas for progressive change. I spoke unabashedly of the need for the rule of law, popular sovereignty and accountability. To teach these notions in a country ruled by an absolute monarch, was considered by some to be an invitation to disaster, and many feared for my safety. Indeed, I found out later that there had been intelligence officers planted in my classes who reported exaggerated versions of what I said. I must tell the story of how I found out, because it reflects the complexity and contradictions inherent in the system at a time of transition when the proverbial irresistible idea of progress was contending with the immovable object of reaction.

A few months before the attempted coup of December 1960, Workineh Gebeyehu, the Intelligence Chief and trusted member of the Emperor's private cabinet (who would also be one of the coup makers), phoned me in my office at the Ministry of Justice. We had met a few times before and discussed matters of justice, corruption and how to combat it and so forth. He asked me to meet him in his office. He was a suave and amiable man from Gondar (my favorite region of Ethiopia), and apologized for asking me to come to him. "I would have gladly come to your office, but I want to show you something here in my office," he said.

I went to his office where he received me with a quizzical smile, handing me a fat file. On the cover of the file my name was written in large letters in good handwriting. "I am glad you came as fast as you could, because after I talked to you, His Majesty called me and wants me at his office. I'll be back soon. Meanwhile enjoy your reading," he said and left.

I started reading the file immediately and found out about myself from the day of my birth: my background, my education, my political views, my friends and relatives, my likes and dislikes. Somebody had done a thorough job of compiling facts about me, some relevant, many irrelevant. The dossier was full of gossip and many untruths about what I had said in class. The dossier also recorded meetings of groups considered dangerous to the system. The names of Germame, Mengistu Lemma and others were mentioned as potential troublemakers. I was also considered a potential troublemaker, with the difference, it was noted, that I tended to speak my mind and therefore was less of a threat than the others.

I was still reading when Workineh returned, apologizing for taking so long. He smiled and sat down to look for my reaction. He was a bright and charming man; no wonder the Emperor chose him soon after he graduated at the head of his class, as a member of the elite body guard officer training course, taught by Swedish officers.

"So, what do you think of our intelligence service?" he asked with a chuckle.

"Impressive, but a lot of untruths and exaggerations."

"Exactly. That is why I called you. Do you see how easily it could be used by unscrupulous men interested only in advancing their careers?"

He then told me about his high regard for people like me who were trying to impart modern ideas of progress often at risk to themselves.

"It would be sad to see you harmed. Be careful what you say, where you say it, and how you say it."

He then proceeded to do an incredible thing. He rose and locked the door of his office, looked at me seriously for a while and then picked up the file. He struck a match and put the flame on a whole sheaf of pages he had taken out of the file. As the papers started burning slowly, he tipped the burning papers onto a metal wastepaper container, holding it until it burned out completely. I thus saw my security file go up in smoke and disappear, leaving a skeleton of a file for the archives. I thanked him and went back to my office, considerably chastened. I felt deeply indebted to Workineh. I was saddened to learn that he was killed in the aftermath of the failed coup. Actually, he commited suicide.

Tradition and Modernity in Contest

The new generation of University-educated youngsters was seen by the bulk of the lower bureaucracy, as well as the *mehal sefari*, as an alien, invading horde. We were placed in different institutions not always in accordance with our training, and were often caught "in the crossfire" of bureaucratic fights.

When I arrived at the Ministry of Justice in the autumn of 1956, there was only one other law graduate at the ministry, Nerayo Isaias. The two of us, later joined by several others, found ourselves in the midst of scores of *debteras*. These were the products of traditional Ethiopian Church education and formed the backbone of the administration at the time. The notion of modernization was anathema to them, not only for ideological reasons but especially because they understood its long-term implications—their replacement by the new educated elite.

The world of the Ministry of Justice in 1956 was a dense forest of old rules and archaic procedures, with Departments ands sections occupied for the most part by *debteras* who were masters of obscurantist thought and obfuscation. Efficiency was not in their vocabulary and when any one in a hurry requested a letter or a file presto, they would invent names and adjectives to describe him designed to frustrate him into acceptance of their rules of the game. As students of traditional Church education, most of the debteras knew Ge'ez, the Latin of Ethiopia, and would use it to communicate with one another. Now, I happened to have been given lessons in Ge'ez, first by my father, then at school, and eventually by my friend Mengistu Lemma. One particular day, when frustrated by a section head in the ministry, I heard a *debtera* utter a Ge'ez quote. I chimed in, responding in kind and went on to say more, in Ge'ez. He was thunderstruck; never had he dreamed that I, a member of the "alien hordes" might know Ge'ez. That became like "Open Sesame" for me, and from then on, I was pronounced as "one of us"—that is, them.

Very soon after my arrival in the Ministry of Justice, I attracted the attention of the then Vice Minister of Justice, Taddese Negash, because of a lengthy report that I wrote suggesting improvements in the administration of justice.

I had written the report after several weeks of close observation of the court system, which I did by attending, as a member of the public, several sittings of both civil and criminal divisions of the High Court and the Awraja (Provincial) Courts, and taking extensive notes. Taddese Negash, who also had the special title of *"Liquemequas"* [favored Palace official], liked my report and showed it to the Emperor, who apparently was suitably impressed and had me summoned to the palace together with the Vice Minister. When we were ushered in to the office of the Emperor, his expression changed from frown to smile, and he looked at Taddese Negash as if to say, "why didn't you tell me it was him." The poor Vice Minister was confused and simply said that I had only been in the Ministry a few months. He did not know (how could he?) that I had gone through a trial by fire in order to resume my interrupted legal education, which the Emperor knew.

The Emperor asked me how old I was, and when I said I was twenty-six, he turned to the Minister of the Pen and his assistants and asked, "Have you read his report on the justice system?" The Minister of the Pen said he had not, and was told to read it, which sent him scrambling, with a noticeable frown, to ask the Vice Minister for a copy. I doubt very much if he ever read the report or even if a copy was made available to him. His urgency was a mere formality designed to communicate the message that all the Emperor's commands are instantly obeyed. The Emperor made some complimentary remarks about the report, and then he went on to reprimand me for my earlier request to be allowed to practice my profession as a private attorney. Those were the days when he still was in command of his mental faculty, including a phenomenal memory, before advanced age diminished it. He asked the Vice Minister if he knew about my earlier request, and when the latter answered in the negative, the Emperor typically proceeded to reprimand him for not knowing all the things he needed to know.

You just couldn't win with the Emperor.

I need to give some more details on the top echelons of the ministry, the engine that drove the administration. At the top were the Minister and Vice Minister. The Minister of Justice in 1956 was Blatta Ayele Gebre, a French-educated Catholic who spent most of his time in the Imperial Palace, as did most of the other ministers. Daily attendance at the Palace was a requirement of protocol for all high-ranking officials.

I remember the Minister of Justice as a man who was vain but congenial, who left details to the Vice Minster. The Secretary General arranged for me to see him one day. His reception was dignified and grave, befitting a Minister of the Emperor. But he became all smiles when the Secretary General informed him that I could speak French. He immediately began speaking to me in French and I reciprocated. He welcomed me to the ministry which he said needed educated young people like me—the now familiar mantra which I had heard more times than I cared to remember.

It did not take me long to find out that the real power in the Ministry of Justice was the Vice Minister, who had the ear not only of the Emperor but of the then powerful Minster Mekonen Habtewold. I was informed by people in the loop that Taddese Negash, the Vice Minster, belonged to the powerful Mekonen faction, whereas Ayele Gebre, the Minister, did not. Taddese had suffered banishment under the former powerful Minister of the Pen, Woldegiorgis, whose downfall in 1955 was engineered by Mekonen—who then had the exiles called back and elevated to positions of power. Mekonen had become the Emperor's closest advisor and *eminence grise*, and he saw to it that the former top aides of Woldegiorgis, such as the Showan *arbegna*, Tsehayu Inqueselasse, were demoted or sent to distant places in the empire.

The cause of Woldegiorgis' disgrace was a matter of considerable debate. The most likely one accepted by most knowledgeable people, was the Emperor's fear of a *coup d'etat*. When, in 1954, the Emperor paid official visits to the United States and the United Kingdom, Woldegiorgis accompanied him and foreign journalists commented on the power of Woldegiorgis. This was just after an army group had overthrown King Farouk of Egypt, and commentators were quick to draw parallels, which must have alarmed the Emperor. It was also suggested by some insiders that Mekonen used the opportunity opened by these commentaries to whisper in the Emperor's ears about the undue power and influence of Woldegiorgis.

Whatever the real cause, the most powerful man in the Empire, next to the Emperor, was stripped of his power and sent to govern a small region, without the right to leave his post, unless approved by the Emperor. The only time he came to Addis Ababa without such permission was when the Emperor's second, and favorite, son was killed in a car accident (some say killed by a cuckolded husband). On that occasion he made his way to the Palace and flung himself at the feet of the Emperor, wailing in grief according to custom. He only stayed in Addis overnight.

Taddese Negash was a striking man in his early forties, intelligent and articulate. By virtue of these qualities, as well as by his suffering under Woldegiorgis, Taddese commanded general respect and admiration. After the report I wrote on the administration of justice, Taddese gave me more assignments covering different fields that had previously been handled by others, including Nerayo. The attention that he focused on me, and his occasional laudatory remarks, inevitably created jealousies and even some animosities. I respectfully asked to be given a definite line of work instead of being a trouble shooter or a jack-of-all-trades.

As a temporary diversion, the Vice Minister decided to give me the office of head of judicial statistics and Advocates Roll, in addition to acting as his advisor, both ministerial appointments. It was clear to me that this was a stopgap arrangement and that greater things awaited me. Before the end of my second year in the ministry, I was appointed Inspector General of the Ministry of Justice, which was an imperial appointment. The person who had held the office of Inspector

General, a man by the name of Hailegabriel Negero, had been a well-known Protestant preacher in his earlier life and was not the most efficient in his post at the ministry. I also suspected, judging from the occasional negative remarks the Vice Minister made, that he might have been a Woldegiorgis sympathizer, and that therefore Taddese had been waiting for an opportunity to replace him.

As a matter of courtesy, I paid Hailegabriel a visit and asked for his advice on the challenges of the work of Inspector General. I had found him friendly and earthy on previous meetings. In the spring of 1957, a few days before my marriage, I remember sitting in his office sipping tea when he volunteered the secret of a working marriage. "Money is the main source of all marital problems," he said, "If you hand over your entire salary to the wife, taking only pocket money, she will have no reason to suspect you of hanky-panky."

It was useful advice.

The Inspector General and the Administration of Justice

What does the Inspector General inspect? This question, which was posed in Gogol's satirical novel, *The Inspector General,* was one that I asked when I took up the function of the office. There was no written rule regulating the work of the Inspector General of Justice, and I remember consulting with Sir Charles Mathew, who was employed as expert on the codification project. Sir Charles, a former Attorney General of Tanganyika (today's mainland Tanzania) and Chief Justice of Malaya (Malaysia of today), was not very helpful. He had acted as judicial advisor to the Emperor's government for a brief period following the Emperor's return from exile in 1941. His view on the work of the Inspector General was colored by his specific experience and knowledge of Ethiopian conditions. He knew that in an imperial system, even one wishing to appear to uphold the rule of law guaranteed by an independent judiciary, it is not feasible to expect executive power to bow down to judicial power to the point of forswearing intervention. Thus everything depended on the subjective judgment of whoever held that office, or of the Minister or Vice Minister. Although he did not say so in so many words, that was the gist of Sir Charles Mathew's view, which I characterized as British pragmatism.

When I started examining the files of the department, I found records of many judges summoned to the Ministry to defend their actions, including their decisions; and when I started my work, several of the inspectors, including the Deputy Inspector General, did not seem to subscribe to the doctrine of judicial independence, although they had some vague sense of its importance. Their view of judges being summoned or court files brought for "inspection" was more than pragmatic; they enjoyed the power of making judges squirm by holding the threat of "inspection" over their heads. In other words, it was a question of power, not principle, and this was particularly true with respect to the Ministers.

The Deputy Inspector General, however, an intelligent man by the name of Mogues Wube, was concerned with the problem of ministerial intervention in the work of the courts of law, even though he did not articulate it in so many words. His concern became clear to me as we met more often and as he saw that I too was gravely concerned with the problem. He expressed sentiments of respect for judges who dared to defy ministerial orders, and disdain for those who complied with them.

The issue of executive intervention in judicial matters became critical and occasioned a great deal of controversy. I found several files brought from the archives of regional courts awaiting "inspection and disposal." Many of these files contained cases that were *sub judice*, so in theory no one in the Ministry had a right to order them brought out of the court archives. How, then, and why did they find themselves in the Ministry of Justice? What right does any officer of the Executive branch have to intervene in the work of the judiciary? This was the first question that occurred to me, and one that I raised with the officials in the department, starting with the Deputy Inspector General.

It was a question that haunted the corridors of judicial power and its relationship with the executive branch of government. It was also one of the questions on which my future relation with the powers-that-be, and my continuance in government, would be tested. The office of the Inspector General became the litmus test as to whether the government of His Imperial Majesty subscribed to the principle of judicial independence, as provided for under the Revised Constitution of 1955. If it did, then on what basis could the Inspector General inspect any work of the judges, or order court files to be brought to the Ministry?

Clearly, it was necessary to make a distinction between legitimate cases warranting intervention and those that must be out of bounds for any member of the Ministry, be he inspector or minister. I wrote a long memorandum to the Vice Minister outlining my views on the matter and requesting his support. In the memorandum, I stated that it is contrary to the constitution to intervene in judicial matters, and I defined the term judicial. I also outlined cases in which the ministry could intervene, cases of corruption or abuse of power not falling within proper judicial function. Even in such cases, I submitted, intervention should be the task of a properly-formed Judicial Service Commission, but pending the establishment of such a commission, the Ministry's Inspectorate could do the job.

Vice Minister Taddese was intrigued by the memo. He did not wish to reject my views and appear to be against the principle of judicial independence, but I could tell by the queries he raised as well as by body language that he was uncomfortable. He framed his arguments in terms of stages of development and the conditions in which the country found itself. When the judiciary is filled by educated people like you, he said, we can demand absolute adherence to the principle of judicial independence. Until then, we may have to be flexible and hold the threat of investigation over their heads, whether we investigate them or not. It was a nuanced argument, but I stuck to the points of my proposal and convened an in-house seminar of the inspectors and other personnel of the Department. Not surprisingly, many of the inspectors were not happy and during the following days, the ministry was abuzz with rumors of my undue influence with the Vice Minister: that I was convincing him to adopt a policy amounting to executive abdication of responsibility "in the face of a corrupt judiciary."

In order to counteract these rumors as well as to create an environment of general understanding between the ministry officials and the judiciary, I advised the Vice Minister to convene a meeting of all judges and judicial personnel, to be held at the High Court. At first he resisted but was eventually convinced of the wisdom of creating a better environment, which can happen without sacrificing "ministerial dignity." Indeed, such a meeting was overdue and when I consulted the President of the High Court and a few of the prominent judges, they welcomed it. The meeting took place with good results, inducing the Vice Minister to make complimentary comments to me and two other young law graduates who were becoming the backbone of the Ministry, Nerayo Isaias and Belachew Asrat.

Others joined the Ministry later, after graduation from McGill Law School, but these two were the most prominent. Let me say a few words about Nerayo and Belachew. Nerayo Isaias was some five years older than me and held a place of honor as the first law graduate of my generation to return from study abroad and take a position in the Ministry of Justice. He received both his LL.B and LL.M from the University of Illinois. From some of his views and attitudes, I could tell that his Protestant upbringing created a sharp sense of right and wrong. I could see this in most of his dealings as Deputy Attorney General. At the same time, he had a sort of "inner city" guile (*Yarada BilTet* in Amharic), which, combined with a wry sense of humor, helped him negotiate the maze of the *debtera*-filled ministry. He came from a mixed marital background; his father was from the Adwa city of Tigray, and his mother was of Eritrean lineage. She was the elder sister of Woldeab Woldemariam, one of the founding fathers of modern Eritrean nationalism and hero of the Eritrean liberation struggle.

Nerayo expressed to me, on several occasions, his disappointment at the way Eritreans of an earlier generation treated his uncle Woldeab. My rejoinder was that I was not answerable for the faults of another generation, but that my generation of Eritreans, and I in particular, loved and revered Woldeab. I even risked telling him that I had a secret meeting with Woldeab in Cairo in July 1956, on my way back from study abroad and that he was one of my mentors in my childhood. Nerayo and I remained friends until he died of leukemia in 1969. I was in "preventive banishment" in Harar at the time of his death, and had to beg the governor to allow me to travel for the funeral. Nerayo's cousin, the reverend Dr. Ezra, officiated at the burial ground at the Peter-Paul cemetery in Addis Ababa.

Belachew Asrat, who began work as an assistant in the Attorney General's office, was a dynamic and bright man who took his work very seriously. In fact he took his work so seriously that Nerayo and I used to joke about it, wondering whether he had a sense of humor. We both appreciated Belachew's char-

acter; so our jokes were made in fondness. The Vice Minister, who also liked Belachew, told me once in appreciation that he was good but inflexible. I am sure he meant this as a compliment, because in the world of royal governance, inflexibility is equated with strength of character. Belachew came from Shoan nobility on his father's side. His grandfather, Dejasmach Woldegabriel, was one of Emperor Menelik's high and mighty. And his maternal grandmother came from a Tigrean aristocratic family. Although Belachew professed equality as a modern democratic principle, his background did show from time to time.

I got on very well with Belachew, barring occasional controversy. On one particular occasion, I took exception to a remark made by him in my office. He and I and others, used to take a coffee break at Enrico's. One morning at about eleven o'clock, I was talking to a man who had come all the way from Tigray to appeal a decision made by the local magistrate. Since he did not know much Amharic, the official language, I was speaking to him in Tigrigna when Belachew entered. He saw I had a matter pending, so he sat and waited until the man left.

Then, as we left my office to go to Enrico's, Belachew turned to me and said, "Bereket, let me give you a word of advice. I know you meant well, but you should always speak in Amharic in a government office." I told him that the man did not speak Amharic; his native tongue was the same as mine and I did not see the necessity of using an interpreter. Belachew was not persuaded by my argument. Was this an expression of his "inflexibility?" I did not wish to impute any chauvinism to Belachew; after all he had Tigrayan blood flowing in his veins. I had no doubt that Belachew was sincere in his concern to forestall any accusation of favoritism for Tigrigna-speaking people leveled at me. But I doubt that he appreciated the depth of feeling I, and most speakers of "minority" tongues, have about their language.

The issue of language has proven crucial in Ethiopia, as elsewhere in the world. Years later, long after the imperial regime was overthrown, this issue would become a cornerstone of the newly-established post-imperial Ethiopian state. Language is a basic factor of politics in a multi-ethnic society, and any ruling group ignores or underestimates the importance of language at its peril.

To return to the topic of my work as Inspector General: from that time onward, until I commenced work at the Attorney General's office in December 1962, I walked a fine line in my work, between respecting the independence of judges and carefully monitoring cases of corruption and abuse of power. My inspectors had to walk the same fine line, occasionally using the bludgeon instead of the scalpel in dissecting cases involving corruption and abuse of power. I had the inestimable assistance of Mr. Mogues Wube, my deputy, in streamlining the work of the Department and in holding the various inspectors to the guidelines I had established. It is worth emphasizing that there were many corrupt judges who needed to be held accountable; the question was, what mechanism of accountability to employ. One day in the future, I hoped then, a proper Judicial Service Commission would be instituted to do the job.

Associate Justice of the Supreme Court

One fine morning in January 1959, I was summoned to the Emperor's Palace. The usher took me to the office of Ato Gebrewold Ingidawork, Deputy Minister of Pen. Ato Gebrewold, a soft-spoken man in his mid-fifties, received me gracefully and took me to the Emperor's chambers. He walked a few steps toward the Emperor's desk and whispered in his ear. He then moved a few steps away and solemnly announced to me and the assembled entourage that it had pleased His Imperial Majesty to appoint me Associate Justice of the Federal Supreme Court.

The federal court system was envisaged under the Federal Act, the international instrument establishing the federation between Eritrea and Ethiopia in 1950. The Federal Act was based on United Nations General Assembly Resolution 390 A(V) of 1950, which provided for an autonomous Eritrean entity with its own legislative, executive and judicial bodies as well as its own police and power of taxation. The federal judiciary was separate both from the local (Eritrean) judiciary and the national (Ethiopian) judiciary. But since under Resolution 390, Eritrea was an autonomous unit "under the sovereignty of the Ethiopian Crown," the Emperor had ultimate say on all matters, including the appointment of federal judges.

Pursuant to the U.N.-arranged federal structure, the Federal Supreme Court was established by the Federal Judiciary Proclamation of 1952 (Proc. No. 130/52). The Supreme Imperial Court was authorized by another law to sit as the Federal Supreme Court, but when sitting as such its composition would comprise the President of the Supreme Court (the *Afenegus*), a citizen of Eritrea, and a person "of proven judicial experience in another land." (Proc. No. 135/53). It had original jurisdiction in matters involving disputes between the two governments (Ethiopia and of Eritrea), in actions against ministers and government officials. Its appellate jurisdiction lay in reviewing decisions of the High Court sitting as the Federal High Court; in decisions of the highest court of Eritrea where the case involved the Constitution of Eritrea, Federal Act, international law and treaties; in matters where the validity of an Eritrean law was called into question as unconstitutional; or where the case involved federal laws designed to ensure the enjoyment of human rights and fundamental liberties. The Federal Supreme Court, sitting in Addis Ababa, heard cases on appeal from the Federal High Court. The majority of cases involved matters of finance and interstate commerce and communication. During the time I sat as a Justice of the Federal Supreme Court, the presiding judges were: *Afenegus* Takele Woldehawariat, and then *Afenegus* Taddesse Mengesha. The third justice was Dr. Buhagiar, who was also President of the High Court. Buhagiar was Maltese with a British educational background, a good sense of humor and an amiable disposition. He got on very well with me and the rest of the members of the Ministry of Justice, as well as with most of the judges of the High Court. In the late 1950s, Belachew Asrat and I sat with him as judges in a temporary appointment designed to clear outstanding judicial work left by judges of the old school who found it difficult to deal with the new commercial cases.

Afenegus Takele was a highly esteemed *arbegna* who had been imprisoned twice for alleged conspiracy to overthrow the Emperor. When I worked with him at the Federal Supreme Court, which sat once a week on Saturdays, he would insist that I join him for lunch after work. His house was the center of *arbegna* meetings, and I came to know many former *arbegnas* who were under his command during the Italian occupation. Takele was a colorful character, very eloquent and charismatic, upright and generous. Every one of the former *arbegnas* who frequented his house revered him. He reminded me of my father and we became very close. In 1969 he was killed in a shoot-out after imperial forces surrounded his house. He was allegedly involved in a plot to overthrow the Emperor. I was in Harar under a banishment order when he was killed.

My work as Justice of the Federal Supreme Court came to an end when the Emperor abolished the federation in November 1962.

Chapter 8

A Shaken Emperor Makes Concessions

December 15, 1960 marks a watershed in modern Ethiopian political life. That was the day when a Columbia University educated intellectual named Germame Neway and his older brother, General Mengistu, head of the Imperial Body Guard, made an attempt to overthrow Emperor Haile Selassie, in a military coup. The coup attempt failed but it shook the imperial system with far-reaching implications for the future. While imperial apologists and supporters were shaken by the event, those of us who stood for progress were emboldened. Thus, as a prelude to the challenges and dilemma I faced serving as a lawyer and high-ranking official of an imperial government it will be helpful to relate the events surrounding the coup and put it and its impact in perspective.

A Nation's Wake-up Call

It was a fine morning in mid-December 1960. Emperor Haile Selassie had travled on a week's state visit to Brazil. A couple of days after his departure, we had a death in the family; my wife's second niece, Amsale, had died and we were sitting in mourning as was required by custom. It was a sudden death and the funeral had been a tumultuous affair; everyone who knew Amsale wept bitterly, lamenting her untimely death. For family members and friends and everyone in her neighborhood, her death was the event of the month, until it was eclipsed by a political earthquake.

On the second day after the funeral, we had risen early and driven to the mourning place in the section of the city known as Aware. The cool morning air was invigorating as we drove the short distance from our house and joined the other mourners. The women were dressed in black; the men wore black ties or came in open shirts. Outside the house of the deceased, neighbors had pitched a tent and several close relatives had spent the night keeping vigil. As we arrived at the place, the mourners were preparing for breakfast, and we had hardly sat down to eat when news came to us about unusual troop movements—reports of military trucks rushing to and fro on the main arteries of the city, carrying soldiers from place to place. And, as more news started coming in by word of mouth of in-coming mourners, we were told that tanks were deployed at strategic positions of the city. When we opened the radio, we heard martial music sounding, instead of the usual songs. Suddenly a voice came on the radio with the news that there would be an important announcement of historic significance and asked the public to stay tuned. The assembled mourners were perplexed. Some whispered to each other; others simply waited in silence. Belete Gebre, Amsale'e uncle and I looked at each other, inquiringly. It was a moment pregnant with great expectations; but few, if any, guessed what we would learn later.

The expected moment came in the form of the tired voice of His Imperial Highness, Crown Prince Asfaw Wesen Haile Selassie, the Emperor's older son and heir to the throne. Everyone was shocked to hear the Crown Prince denounce the regime presided over by his father and which he had been patiently waiting to inherit. The speech, which as later turned out, was written by Germame Neway, the brain behind the coup, was an indictment of the "oppressive feudal system." It promised a better system under which the Crown Prince would be a constitutional Monarch.

I felt I had to go. Something extraordinary was happening and I could not sit there doing nothing. Even at the risk of offending some of the close relatives, I decided to leave and extracted myself from the group and left the tent. First I went to my friend Araia Ogbazghi's house seeking further clarification. Araia was not in. Then I went to my office, where I found two-day old messages waiting for me, written by the secretary and left on my desk. The messages were phone calls from people close to Germame and they simply said, "we will call again" adding, "It is urgent." I marveled at the twist of fate; Amsale's death probably saved my life. Given my previous conversation with Gemame, I suspected that had I been present in my office, I would have gone to the rebels' headquarters at the palace in Sidist Kilo, from which Germame and company were directing the rebellion.

The rebels—the Emperor's Body Guard led by Mengistu Neway and the Head of the Emperor's Intelligence Service, Colonel Workineh Gebeyehu, had ordered the arrest of almost all the Cabinet Ministers and other dignitaries close to the Imperial Throne, and kept them in the Palace. Germame had also summoned people whom he considered fellow revolutionaries or fellow travelers. I later found out from some of the survivors of the failed coup that Germame and Workineh had been looking for me. Conceivably, I would have been among those killed in the aftermath of the failed coup had I been in my office that day and answered the call.*

*[Colonel Kalekristos Abai, an officer of the Imperial Body Guard who was implicated in the coup, has recently written a highly informative book in which he gives a list of names of people that the coup makers had drawn up as future members of the Cabinet. My name was among the twenty-one names in the list. See Y-1953 *Yemengistu Gilbeta Mukera*, Col. Kalekristos Abai. 2005; pages

160-161. The book is in Amharic and the title means *The 1960 Coup Attempt of Mengistu*]

The December revolt, as it became known for many years, was the first direct challenge the Emperor had faced in over thirty years. The fact that the rebellion came from his most trusted and pampered Body Guard added poignancy to the event. The reaction to the event was mixed. The Crown Prince's speech was greeted with confusion and suspicion by almost everybody. How could he rise up in rebellion against his father? Surely, he was being used as puppet by other forces. It soon turned out that this was indeed the case. And diehard supporters of the system, which included most of the higher echelons of the government as well as the absentee landowners and the Emperor's kinsmen, were outraged.

On the other hand those who welcomed the coup belonged to my generation of Ethiopians and a few disgruntled older people. Judging from conversations I had with several members of my generation of educated Ethiopians, it was a welcome event. Some were naturally anxious about their civil rights, considering the bad record of military regimes in the area of human rights and the rule of law. But the general view was that nothing could be worse than what we had and that a military regime guided by radical individuals like Germame would clear the way for a better republic. It was a view unschooled in the disappointments that would come later. Certainly, on one point the outcome of the failed coup proved a step forward to progress. It had effected a loosening of the bonds that held the feudal system.

The coup failed because the bulk of the imperial army and the Air Force remained loyal to the Emperor and fought and defeated the rebellious Emperor's Body Guard. When they knew their coup had failed the Neway brothers decided to take the top members of the imperial regime with them. There was a horrendous massacre of Ministers and other dignitaries in the Emperor's Palace in Sidist Kilo. Incidentally, my Boss, Taddese Negash and the former Minister of Justice, Ayele Gebre, were among those killed. Taddese was related to the Neway brothers on his mother's side.

Clearly, Germame was an equal opportunity revolutionary; he did not spare his blood relatives; nor did he consider the past service of some of Ethiopia's heroes like Ras Abebe Aregai. It was later reported that when Ras Abebe challeneged Germame's right to treat him the way he did (denying him water for instance), Germame first brought water and gave it to him and then responded by reminding Ras Abebe of the guerilla fighters that made him a hero and whom he had forgotten. The exact words related to me by a survivor were: "Did you ever think of the peasants who sold their oxen and followed you, and who made you Ras?" [Ras is the highest title, after the King].

The Loosening of the Bonds

The coup failed but, despite its failure, had an impact on government and society with implications for future changes. Its impact on government was first felt in the shape and behavior of the executive. The massacre of most of the

Cabinet members left the government truncated, the whole government system was shaken and the bureaucracy was left dithering for a long time. As veteran journalist, David Talbot, put it referring to the decimation of the Cabinet of Ministers, "The Departments without heads have been filled with acting heads." Talbot, a Caribbean-born journalist, became the butt end of jokes for many weeks thereafter. Indeed, Talbot's pedantic style of writing used to provoke ridicule among my English teachers at the Wingate School. My English grammar teacher used to cite examples of grammatical errors from Talbot's writings. One example I remember was a report of the Emperor's visit to the Wingate, which Talbot was covering for The Ethiopian Herald, of which he was the editor. Describing the Emperor's tour of some part of the school's classrooms, Talbot had written, "Walking along the corridor, a door was opened that led to the science laboratory." "Find the mistake," Mr. Wright would command us, and provide the clue himself by asking, "Who is walking along the corridor, the door or His Majesty?"

The vacuum left in the Emperor's government was not a joking matter. Nor did the Emperor feel inclined to reoccupy his palace. Instead, he decided to donate it to the University; the blood of his Ministers spilled on the palace ground proved too much for his sensibilities. The contents of the palace—furniture and other valuable articles—had been looted by the mob. According to one report, during the ride from the airport the day of his return, he heard the welcoming crowd cry *Haile Slessie, Dires Lenebsie* (roughly, hearty welcome, Haile Selassie), he is reported to have remarked: "These were the same people who looted our palace."

Perhaps a more profound effect of the coup was in releasing the suppressed energy of the public, and emboldening the progressive voices. A significant and promising manifestation of this was that of student activities, which was the most threatening to the imperial regime. Students began to organize poetry festivals in which budding poets like Yohanes Admasu and Melaku Bekele, showed their talents. Most of the content of the poems was revolutionary, lamenting the condition of the oppressed peasants. In the poems and in other forms of popular expression of resistance, Germame and his fellow coup makers acquired the status of martyrs.

Then there was the African connection. Students from other African countries who were beneficiaries of the Haile Selassie I scholarship fund, also contributed to the gradual radicalization of the university students, and introduced the concept of Pan Africanism advocated by Ghana's President, Kwame Nkrumah. Refugees from southern Africa found themselves in Addis Ababa. Even before the December revolt, emerging African leaders like the Kenyan Tom Mboya, Tanzania's Nyerere and Zambia's Kaunda, had been frequenting the Ethiopian capital, requesting assistance from the Emperor and his government in their struggle for independence for their respective nations. Their public speeches and meetings with students and other groups had given further impetus to thinking in terms of organized popular movements. I helped organize the first public appearance of Tom Mboya delivered at the National Library. I had also met both Tanzanian leader Nyerere and Zambian leader Kaundu at private dinners given in their honor. The frequent visits of these leaders encouraged the progressive movement in Ethiopia spearheaded by the students and intellectuals.

My involvement in African affairs had started earlier, first in England, as I have already written, and later in the late 1950s. About 1958, a group of us had formed an Africa support committee, which was, however, soon co-opted and emasculated by the government. As I will explain in more detail below, my interest in African affairs, and friendship with people like Tom Mboya probably contributed to my selection to attend the All African Peoples Conference convened by Nkrumah in Accra, December 1958. A few months earlier Nkrumah had convened a meeting of African Heads of State and Government. The Emperor sent his youngest son, Prince Sahle Selassie, to represent him. He would eventually take African affairs more seriously, particularly in view of the fact that Nkrumah was upstaging him as Africa's premier leader, as more and more newly independent African nations were taking up their rightful place in the family of nations. It impelled him and his government to decide in favor of playing a more active role in African affairs, which culminated in his hosting of the founding conference of the Organization of African Unity in May 1963 about which I will say more.

The students were not the only segment of society affected by the coup. The military and the labor unions were also aroused. The military would eventually play a crucial role in bringing about drastic changes. Labor unions, with the assistance of university students and teachers started organizing clandestinely and demanding better wages and conditions of work, threatening strikes. Together with University of Addis Ababa Professors Mesfin Woldemariam (Geography) and Seyoum Gebreigziabher (Public Administration), I would play a role in helping labor unions to organize themselves. Labor unions continued organizing their members at first clandestinely and then openly, forcing the government to pass legislation permitting them to organize.

According to Seyoum Haregot, Minster in charge of legislative matters at the Prime Minster's office, the Emperor became an advocate for full union rights. The Emperor's reign was characterized by this kind of adaptability. Some would call it opportunism; I call it survival strategy. Thus strange as it might appear, the Emperor ordered his Prime Minister to prepare legislation protecting union rights. The result was the Labor Relations Proclamation of 1963, which, while giving labor unions hitherto unknown rights, created mechanisms of control for the government. Nonetheless, it represents progress in that there was change from the jungle of lawlessness to a situation of mutual accommodation between unions on the one hand and employers and the government on the other. Up to then, companies had their own arbitrary rule of hiring and firing with no legal redress, leading to periodic confrontation and violence.

As can be seen from this brief account, the attempted coup of December 1960 left behind it a host of challenges, the security issue being the most important. During the first few months to a year, the Emperor and his principal advisors were principally concerned with survival. After all, it was his most trusted aides who revolted against him. He was particularly stung by Workineh's "betrayal." He was in a state of denial often remarking that Workineh must have been compelled to go along with Germame's scheme, under duress. Not only did he have complete trust in Workineh, he was very fond of him. In fact part of Workineh's task had been to spy on all the top military brass, including General Mengistu. The Emperor did not trust even his close kinsmen; to the contrary, he followed the Machiavellian principle of elevating children of the underprivileged to top positions to watch over the privileged inner circle—"Take care of my friends, (or relatives), I can take care of my enemies."

What about the heads of the armed forces who remained loyal and foiled the attempted coup? Who were they and why did they remain loyal?

There were five principal actors in the drama. They were: General Merid Mengesh, Chief of Staff of the Armed Forces, who was the Emperor's relative; General Kebede Gebre, Chief of the Ground Forces; General Assefa Ayana, Chief of the Air Force; General Isaias Gebre-Selassie, Deputy Commander of the Ground Forces, who was an Eritrean; and Dejasmatch Kebede Tessema, Head of the Militia, a wily member of the Old Guard known for his loyal service to the Emperor from the days before he was Crown Prince.

Before the outbreak of hostilities between the rebel forces of General Mengistu and the loyal forces, efforts were undertaken to mediate between the two sides. General Isaias Gebreselassie and Dejasmatch Kebede were sent to speak to General Mengistu and Germame.

I happened to know General Isaias rather well; during his childhood, before he went over to Ethiopia, my father had been his mentor in the Asmara Protestant Mission. I talked to him at length after the coup was foiled and part of this story is based on our conversation then. According to General Isaias, he and Dejasmatch Kebede, noticed signs of tension between Germame and Workineh. The Police Chief, General Tsighe Dibu had also been forced to go along under duress. It may well be that the Emperor's claim that Workineh was forced was well founded. But when I asked General Isaias later whether the Emperor's claim was based on the mediator's assessment of tension, he told me that this was not reported to the Emperor, not by him any way. The Emperor, he said, was completely disoriented for several months and even asked for Workineh at times long after Workineh's death.

A matter of great significance confronting the post-coup situation was the disposal of hundreds of officers and enlisted men and some civilians who took part in the rebellion. This obviously raised security as well as legal issues. The security issues involved police matters and General Isaias was appointed Acting Police Chief in which capacity I met with him on several occasions. This is before I became Attorney General. The vacuum created by the decimation of the Cabinet and the dissolution of the Imperial Body Guard had thrown the government system into turmoil, and willful people like Ras Asrate Kasa, another kinsman of the Emperor, filled in the vacuum. Asrate Kasa had himself appointed Head of a Commission overseeing the disposal of cases of the rebellious officers.

The principal coup leaders were either killed or captured a few days after their coup failed. Germame was killed resisting arrest some fifty miles south of the capital. Workineh committed suicide, and General Mengistu was wounded and captured. His trial thus became the object of great curiosity and a bellwether of what would happen to the other rebel officers.

My Real Test Begins

I was shocked to learn that I was appointed judge to try the case of General Mengistu Neway, the leader of the attempted coup. It was one of the worst moments of my life, one that tested me in every way. The man responsible for my appointment was Asrate Kassa, presumably at the suggestion of Blata Kitaw, the person appointed to preside over the trial. Blata Kitaw was a respected judge with whom I had sat as a high Court judge to try some criminal cases a few years earlier. He was a Catholic mission-educated man and fearless in his judgments. The other judge was Solomon Abraham, a man with close connections to the imperial family. Though he was a fellow Eritrean, we never saw eye to eye on many issues.

To say that I was in a quandary would be an understatement. There I was; a supporter of the attempted coup, an admirer of Germame whom I respected. Was I to judge a popular hero—the leader of a historic deed with which I agreed? Hell, no! I said to myself, and I was determined not to be part of it. Within my family and close friends, we held council. I was against involvement and my wife Koki and my close friends, especially Arefaine Abraham, were decidedly against my being involved. The question was how to wriggle out of it.

We agreed on a plan: I must feign illness and get out of town and hide. Arefaine drove me to Ambo, and Koki was to hold the fort at home and answer all questions saying she did not know where I went—I had just disappeared. Ambo is the resort town about a hundred miles west of Addis Ababa and people who knew me and saw me would report to the authorities about my whereabouts. It was a desperate and unrealistic plan.

Meanwhile they were looking for me at the Ministry of Justice. Asrate Kassa's office would not let go; the phones kept ringing. We agreed on another plan: I must get into a hospital and report with illness. I checked into the Ras Desta Hospital, where I became the patient of Dr. Alexander Dimitrov, a Yugoslav physician. Dr. Dimitrov asked me to describe my symptoms. I told him how I was affected by the hanging of Workineh and Germame's dead bodies, which were displayed on one of the city squares. Some of my friends had researched about Dr. Dimitrov and his close friends. Two of these happened to be friends of mine; in fact one of these, General Aman Andom, was not only a friend, but also a relative of mine. The other, Girma Atnafseghed, was a friend from

Wingate and later England days. Girma agreed to speak to Dr. Dimitrov asking him as a favor to take care of me.

To this day, I do not know what exactly Girma told Dimitrov. He later told me that he confided in him that I did not want to be a judge in Mengisitu's case, which would have presented the good doctor with an ethical dilemma. There I was telling him in earnest that I had suffered a nervous breakdown brought on by a shocking experience and he believed me. He prescribed a number of vitamin and other injections to help me recover! But I did not want to "recover"—at least not for some time. And if Girma told him the truth, Dr. Dimitrov would stop the prescriptions; but far from stopping them he kept ordering them until I decided it was time to leave the hospital and disappear, two weeks later.

The Asrate crowd would not let go. While I was at the Ras Desta hospital, a woman by the name of Zeleka, reputed to be a special agent of the Emperor, visited me. I was puzzled and suspicious. It was generally believed among informed circles that Zeleka was connected to the Special Intelligence Branch of the Emperor's grandson, Iskindir Desta. I never had any connection with this woman before, be it socially or professionally. Nor did my wife. So we knew that they were watching me closely and probably trying to find out about my condition from the doctor.

It was time to leave the hospital, but where to go—that was the question. That was when I entertained ideas of escape from the country, maybe through Harar into Somalia, which had just become independent. After all, I thought, didn't another Eritrean, Idris Suleiman, escape using that route? We did not have children at the time and leaving the country for a while would not be hard on Koki. She could join me later. All kinds of wild ideas came to mind; so determined was I not to sit in judgment of General Mengistu that I was ready to do anything to escape.

Then I thought of my old friend Haile Selassie Belai, Dean of the School of Agriculture at Alemaya, Harar. Why don't I go there and wait it out, I thought, which was what I ended up doing. Dr. Haile Selassie Belai, a noble human being whom I had known since the Wingate days, received me with enthusiasm and complete understanding of my dilemma. In fact he agreed with my decision not to be involved in General Mengistu's judgment. He and his wife, Itsegenet, who was expecting a baby, were generous hosts to me for some three weeks. I stayed inside the house during the day, reading books, and we would sometimes venture out to Dire Dawa, in the evening. It was while I was there that the tragic death of Patrice Lumumba was announced and I remember being stricken with sadness. I explained to my hosts that I had met Lumumba a year earlier at the All African Peoples Conference in Accra. More on this later.

One fine morning we heard on the radio that the judicial panel appointed to try General Mengistu had commenced its work. I was glad to hear this piece of news but remained cautious just in case it was a trick designed to draw me out of my hiding. A week later we heard that the case had indeed started. Obviously the Asrate crowd had given up on me and selected a substitute, Colonel Abebe Teferi, an army officer. I decided to leave for Addis Ababa, but before I left I wanted to meet General Aman in Harar, where he was Commanding Officer of the Third Division. He was appointed to that post just before the December events. I told Aman my story and he agreed to write a letter to Dr. Dimitrov.

Armed with the letter I returned to Addis Ababa and reported at the Ras Desta Hospital with my wife. Dr. Dimitrov wrote a medial report about my "nervous condition" and gave me a copy of the report. I went to the Ministry of Justice and met Colonel Tamrat Yigezu, Acting Minister of Justice. He told me about some wild rumors that I had defected to Somalia. After I showed him the medical report he told me not to worry and that he would show the doctor's report to Ras Astate Kasa as well as the Emperor. He added that otherwise, I risked being arrested and tried for disobedience of the Emperor's order. Tamrat was a good man and was very helpful to me at that critical moment.

But I was not out of the woods yet. I was summoned to the office of Asrate Kassa and interrogated. Asrat threatened me with arrest and prosecution. At the same time he wanted my cooperation in his scheme of things. One of those schemes was the prosecution of the rebels. Clearly, he was looking for allies in his bid for power, which he thought was within his grasp while the Emperor was still weak and disoriented. Evidently, he was backing the wrong horse; intimidation did not work with this particular horse.

Then all of a sudden, I became seriously ill. I suffered the most excruciating pain and I was taken to the Dejach Balcha Hospital run by Russians. I was in no position to have a say, and my wife and friends were not satisfied with the reception by the hospital staff, so they took me to the Haile Selassie Hospital at Sidist Kilo. There, a German doctor examined me and had my kidneys X-rayed. He told us with as much drama as he could muster that one of my kidneys had collapsed ("She is dead" is what he said). He said that the "dead" kidney must be removed at once before it affected other parts of my vital organs.

I am writing about this medical episode in some detail because it came at the right time to save me from the arrest and prosecution hanging over my head. This illness, which people confused with my previously reported "illness," had the miraculous effect of confirming my story that my disappearance was indeed caused by real illness. What clinched the story was the German doctor's prescription of removing my kidney. But I was in no mood to have any doctor remove my kidney. My wife and her older sister Tsige, saw to it that I would go abroad for treatment. Someone suggested Israel as the closest and we all agreed on that. I flew to Israel via Athens disembarking at Tel Aviv airport. From there I was taken by car to Jerusalem where I reported at the Hadasa Hospital, the following day.

Surprise! Surprise! The X-ray taken at the Hadasa Hospital showed my kidney actually functioning. It is true, the doctor said, that there was a large kidney stone lodged in the kidney but the blocking had improved so that my kidney would be okay. And the prescription?

Drink liquid, lots and lots of liquid.

"Including beer, if you like beer," added the good doctor with a smile. I noticed his British accent, so I asked the inevitable question. Yes, he said, he was born and brought up in London and went to school at University College, London. "My Alma Mater," I cried.

We didn't exactly establish a Benthamite Society but we had a very cordial relationship. My hosts were Tekletsadik Mekuria, the Ethiopian Ambassador, and Yoftahe Dimetros, who had just completed his study at Hebrew University.

I Attend the Eichman Trial

There was an unexpected bonus to my medical visit to Israel. The Eichman trial was underway and Tekletsadik, with the historian's keen eye, suggested that I might be interested in attending the trial, which I gladly accepted. My Israeli hosts made all the necessary arrangements for me to find a seat in the courtroom.

I was present when the Attorney General of Israel, Gideon Hausner, opened the case with a prolonged cry, weeping in the name of the victims of the Holocaust. I was more impressed by the equanimity of the judges especially the President of the tribunal, Judge Landau. Day after day, survivors of that tragic episode in European history gave incredible accounts of how they were separated from their loved ones who perished in the fires of the Holocaust.

After a couple of weeks, I had enough. I came away from the Eichman trial disheartened about human nature but with a new insight into the creation of the state of Isarael and the related question of the persecution of Jews, historically. The German-born American philosopher, Hannah Arendt, who was present at the trial, as I later learned, wrote a controversial article. She coined the memorable phrase, *The Banality of Evil* to describe the whole experience of the Nazi bureaucracy overseeing the horrific machinery of death, in which people like Eichman, and all the little bureaucrats, were inured to any human feeling. Evil had so triumphed that what should shock no longer shocked, and was instead subsumed in routine. Watching Eichman sitting impassively in the bullet-proof glass cage which served as the prisoner's bar, I wondered how such an ordinary-looking man could be responsible for the horror that the survivors described. What did the Nazi ideology and practice do to turn such a man into a monster? Questions, and more questions for which I had no answers.

At the hotel where I was staying, there were several journalists from Europe, including a young German journalist from *Frankfurter Algemeine*. At our hotel also stayed a couple of police officers who supervised the guards watching over Eichman, including the food he ate. One morning at breakfast, one of these officers told us about Eichman's behavior towards the food they served him. Each time they served him, he would finish everything they gave him, so they kept increasing the size of the food, until one day he mournfully, but dutifully asked if he could be given less. The officer said with a laugh, "The man could have just left

A Shaken Emperor Makes Concessions

what he could not finish. Instead he thought it was his duty to finish whatever he was given. What kind of mentality is that?"

As I reflect on this today, one question that I ask myself and for which I have so far found no answer is: how Israelis and Jews in general feel about the fate of Palestinians who have been dispossessed of their land and rendered homeless. I know that this is a question for which scholars and statesmen of different political stripes have tried–so far in vain—to find an answer. I also know that people with conscience, both inside Israel and among world Jewry, grapple with this question—and certainly should—especially during Passover, when the traditional admonition is, "Remember, you too were a slave."

Before I returned to Ethiopia, I wanted to visit the Holy Places in the eastern part of Jerusalem, which at the time was part of Jordan. It would have taken only minutes to cross over from the Israeli side of West Jerusalem. But it was not possible. Nor did the Israeli embassy in Addis Ababa stamp my passport to give me an entry permit. The permit was issued on a separate *laissez-passer* because I would not be able to enter any Arab state with a stamp of the Israeli government on my passport. I therefore had to travel to Cyprus and from there cross by boat to Beirut, thence proceed to Damascus and Aman, Jordan, before I could go to East Jerusalem. I visited the Holy Places in Jerusalem as well as Bethlehem and Jericho. I then flew back to Ethiopia via Athens.

I returned from Israel in full health and good spirit, to the relief of my wife and other relatives and friends. I went to thank Michael Imru for all the help he rendered to facilitate my speedy trip for medical treatment. I have said this before, but I will say it again: it is not possible for me to express adequately the gratitude I owe to the Imru family as a whole for their friendship and for helping me in times of need. I want especially to single out Michael and his niece Alemseghed Hiruy, each in his or her way for coming to the rescue.

One Monday morning, a few months after my return, Nathan Marein called me to his office. A Dutch-born Israeli lawyer and Attorney General of Ethiopia for several years, Marein was sitting at his office in the Ministry of Justice. Soon after I returned from my medical trip to Israel I had spoken to him about the Eichman trial and my impression of the proceedings of the case. He wanted to know more about the case, but this morning he said he wanted to share with me some recent conversation he had with Colonel Tamrat Yigezu, Acting Minister of Justice. Nathan was a man with a great sense of humor and had hundreds of jokes, mostly Jewish, which he could tell at a moment's notice. As he offered me coffee he said that he was not going to waste my time; he was going to go straight to the point of why he wanted to see me.

He began by relating to me a story of how he came to know Colonel Tamrat and other Ethiopian dignitaries. "It was during the exile years in Jerusalem," he began and told me how he was retained by the Ethiopian Consulate in Jerusalem to represent Ethiopia in the dispute about "Deir Sultan," the portion in the Holy Place over which Ethiopia and Egypt were contenders.

That was how it started, but he soon grew to like Ethiopians and became a close friend with most of the dignitaries, including Col. Tamrat and his family. He decided to come to Ethiopia with the returning refugees in 1941. He told me how on the way back to Ethiopia from the Sudan, he carried on his back a small girl called Alemseghed Hiruy, my good friend and the daughter of Woizero Ymisrach Imru, Colonel Tamrat's sister-in-law. He smiled with nostalgia as he related that piece of story.

He was telling me this, he said, because he had a long-term and enduring friendship with Tamrat. He then dropped the bombshell. "I told Tamrat," he said, "that I intend to retire from my position of Attorney General soon. And when Tamrat asked him who should be his successor, Nathan Marein told him that of the available trained lawyers he thought I would fit the bill.

"So, get ready to take over from me," he concluded with a smile

"I just escaped from one noose and now you are putting another noose round my neck," I told him, and I explained to him about my tribulations with regard to the General Mengistu case and how I escaped arrest and prosecution by the Asrat Kassa camp. At this he exploded into a hearty laugh and said, "You mean your diplomatic illness."

"Why would I go all the way to Israel if it was only a diplomatic illness?" I asked.

"I know you had a serious case of kidney illness. But that was not what you complained of when you registered at the Ras Desta Hospital. Come on Bereket, I know and you know you were bluffing." He went on to say that he sympathized with my sentiments and reason for wanting to avoid being involved. But now things are changing. The Asrate Kassa Camp has lost out to the modern progressive faction. Asrate has been kicked upstairs and Aklilu Habtewold and his faction are back in the driver's seat. There is now a program of reform on many areas, and I and my generation must be part of this effort. This position would give me a wonderful opportunity to make a valuable contribution.

He was quite excited as he made these remarks. He stopped for air and rose from his chair. He looked at me and said, "Bereket, I love this country and would go on serving, but I am getting old and tired. I wish I were your age." He concluded that I had no choice but to accept but that he wanted me to accept the appointment with enthusiasm. He also asked me to come down from my "High Horse" and see the Acting Minister more often. He was referring to my attitude towards the High and Mighty of the regime, which he gleaned from my frequent remarks about my refusal to show my face at the Palace. In fact, I was not the only one with this attitude; neither of my other colleagues—Nerayo and Belachew—stooped or fawned on the "Big Guys", nor frequented the Palace grounds like some of the other educated returnees.

Marein said the Acting Minister is in desperate need of assistance from us. He also said that he knew about me through his brother-in-law, Michael Imru and his sisters, who were well disposed towards me. Tamrat has his eyes on me, Marein said and he reinforced his view. You have no choice, he repeated. Marein

 A Shaken Emperor Makes Concessions

was right: I had no choice. You can only bluff your way around imperial power once. The appointment came in November 1961 in the form of Deputy Attorney General, deputy to Marein that is. But this was to end soon; Marein retired in February 1962, and I became Acting Attorney General.

Law and Justice in a Traditional Polity

At the time of my appointment, Ethiopia was in the process of introducing new codes of law, mostly modeled on European codes. In fact the new, Swiss-based Penal Code had been in force since 1957, drafted by the eminent Swiss scholar Professor Jean Gravin, Dean of the Law School of Geneve University. The Civil Code, drafted by Professor Rene David, French Professor of Civil Law, had just come into force, followed by the Commercial and Maritime Codes. These were followed by the Penal Procedure Code and Civil Procedure Code. The Penal Procedure Code was drafted under the guiding hands of the Englishman, Sir Charles Mathew and the Swiss, Phillippe Graven, son of Jean Graven and his successor as Dean at the Geneve Law School. Phillippe and I spent many hours discussing legal issues and, over the years, we became good friends.

The Civil Procedure Code was drafted with Nerayo Isaias in charge as the main draftsman. Before Nerayo, Mohamed Abdurahman acted as advisor to the Codification Committee, which worked as an autonomous unit within the Ministry of Justice. Nerayo was Deputy Attorney General before me and was appointed Assistant Minster in the Codification Department of the Ministry of Justice. Neayo's Common Law background (He was educated in the United States) and knowledge of comparative law led him to look into the Indian Civil Procedure Code as a model. Sir Charles Mathew also was inclined in that direction.

As can be seen from this brief account, the Ethiopian legal scene was fast becoming a potpourri of the laws of different nations. For legal scholars it was a heavenly gift. That was how Professor Jean Gravin put it to me one day during lunch at his son Philippe's house. For those of us engaged in the application of the new laws and the administration of justice in general it was a challenge, at times approaching a nightmare. These laws, all drafted by some of the best legal minds of the world, were superimposed on a traditional society and a semi-feudal polity with an absolute monarch at the helm.

There are two significant facts related to this historic codification agenda. The first is that it was the Emperor himself who was driving the process. The other is that, although the original decision for wholesale codification was made by the Emperor, the practical work of finding the best draftsmen and managing the process from the top was done by Aklilu Habtewold, the Emperor's Sorbonne-educated Prime Minister. The Prime Minster, a man of humble origin, represented the modern educated elite. The Emperor himself, though of royal blood and mindful of the interests of his class, was a monarch with modernizing proclivities. It will be helpful to give a brief account of the Emperor's background in order to put his contribution in context.

Emperor Haile Selassie liked to compare himself to the Roman Emperor Justinian. He considered his Revised Constitution of 1955, and the codification program, as his prime achievements. The contradiction inherent in this program of modernization and the semi-feudal structure of the Ethiopian polity over which he presided is seen in the promise of the 1955 Constitution and the unfulfilled provisions of that Constitution. The Constitution promised cabinet and parliamentary government with an independent judiciary as guardian of a Bill of Rights. At the same time, as I have already said, it proclaimed the sanctity of the Emperor's person and the primacy of his power. In other words, the Emperor was a traditional ruler with modern pretensions. The tension between his modernizing agenda, with its wrenching demands, and the resistance of traditional concepts and vested interests marked the Emperor's fifty-eight-year rule, first as regent (1916-1930), then as Emperor, until his fall in 1974.

The origin of Haile Selassie's modernizing zeal is a French Catholic missionary education as a young man. This earlier contact with European ways was reinforced by contacts he had with the world of business and modern finance when he was a young governor of his father's province, Harar. These contacts with Europeans also helped him in garnering support in his bid for power against his kinsman, Lij Yasu, who had become a Muslim. This fact outraged the Established Church leaders and the feudal lords.

In 1936, Haile Selassie attained world fame when Italy conquered Ethiopia and he appeared before the League of Nations to appeal for help. His appeal fell on deaf ears but established him as a world statesman of great fascination. Four years later, Mussolini's fateful alliance with Hitler came as a boon for the Emperor, enabling him to return home and be restored to his throne with Allied assistance.

Five years of Italian rule had left him with an impressive infrastructure and the rudiments of industrial and commercial enterprises. The Emperor lost no time in exploiting these resources to his benefit and to those of his loyal followers. Meanwhile, he also acquired Eritrea with United States support. His imperial appetite overreached itself, however, when in 1962 he unilaterally abolished the UN-arranged federation, as I have already discussed. This historic mistake was rooted as much in territorial ambition, as in considerations of power. An Eritrea with a democratic Constitution and a democratically elected government constituted a threat to his absolute power, a "destabilizing" element in the feudal scheme. Indeed, the panel of jurists who drafted the UN-sanctioned Constitution of Eritrea worried about such a conflict between a democratic Eritrea joined with a feudal Ethiopia. Yet the guarantee they prescribed to deter Imperial Ethiopian encroachment in Eritrean affairs, i.e. that in the event of any dispute the UN General Assembly could be seized of the matter, no voice was raised in defense of Eritrea when the Emperor abolished the federation, occupied Eritrea and declared it a simple province of the empire.

My conclusion that the Emperor's action was actuated as much by territorial aggrandizement as by the power imperative is based on my own encounter with the Emperor. One encounter in particular will help illuminate the matter. A couple of weeks before he issued a proclamation dissolving the federation, the Emperor summoned me to his palace. He was curious to know my reaction to what he had already decided to do. After I was ushered into his chambers, he dismissed the entourage, stood up and, pacing back and forth behind his huge mahogany desk, turned his gaze toward me and looked at me with those penetrating eyes of his before he sprang a question. The question was, what was my view on the federation, and he resumed pacing to and fro. I answered by reminding him that the Ethiopia-Eritrea federation was established under international law.

He stopped pacing and, before I could continue, he cut me off and asked what would happen if it were to be dissolved. I said that dissolving it would have serious repercussions at the international level. He dismissed this with a wry smile. And went on to ask what I thought would happen in Eritrea. By that time he had stopped pacing. My answer was as rash as it was wishful thinking. I remember the exact words I used in response.

"Your Majesty," I said, "that would be akin to awakening the sleeping lions."

This snap answer was meant, perhaps unconsciously, to caution him against any rash step; little did I know that the lawyers at the Prime Minister's Office had already prepared a Dissolution Proclamation.

That day and for a few days thereafter, I expected the worst. I waited anxiously for the police to knock at my door any time, pick me up and take me to an unknown destination. At the time I gave the Emperor that answer, I had not thought of the consequences to me.

The Emperor's reaction to my rash response can be expressed as a flaming fury. To simply say that he was angry would be a gross understatement. His royal countenance was aflame, a body language more eloquent than any words. His normally inscrutable face spoke volumes.

With a wave of the hand, the equivalent of "**dismissed**" in military language, and without any further word he dismissed me. I left not knowing what would happen to me.

But nothing happened to me, and I have often told the story, comparing the Emperor's style with that of his military successors. This must be said for the record: if it were Mengistu Haile Mariam instead of Haile Sleassie, I would have been summarily shot.

In this respect his modernizing programs—the Constitution with its Bill of Rights and the new Civil Codes—and his felt need to be well regarded by the rest of the world probably had a restraining effect on his actions. They certainly reflect the complexity of the man and of Ethiopia under his rule. There can be no doubt that, from his first ascent to supreme power, he was determined to bring Ethiopia from its "medieval" backwardness to join the modern world. His record of modernization programs shows this beyond doubt and the codification was the last phase of that agenda. This inevitably posed a serious challenge to those of us who wanted the abolition of the feudal system and yet worked within the confines of the system. And the European-based legal codes dramatically illustrate this challenge. The Emperor himself faced dilemmas from time to time, forcing him to negotiate his way carefully between the views of the old guard and the new generation of modernizing elite who were his principal agents of rule. The following examples illustrate this dilemma.

At the time of my return from completing my law studies in 1956, the Codification Committee at the Ministry of Justice was engaged in reviewing and commenting on several draft codes, the main one being the draft Civil Code. And soon after I was assigned to work in the Ministry of Justice and for a couple of years thereafter, I made a point of attending meetings of the Codification Committee as well as the Parliament when it was debating the draft Civil Code. The parliamentary debate was the more interesting because of the conflicting views emerging during the debate. The Parliament was composed of two Chambers; The Chamber of Deputies and the Senate. The members of the Senate were former governors, Ministers and other dignitaries who had served the empire with distinction and some with no distinction.

The first day I attended the Senate meeting I was surprised to find that the former Minister of Justice Blata Ayele Gebre was addressing the assembled body. The item on the agenda that day was the section of the draft Civil Code dealing with the age of consent in marriage. He was arguing in favor of accepting the age of consent for marriage as proposed in the draft, which was eighteen. He was constantly interrupted by other members of the Senate; one of them kept yelling, "Old Maids." That member represented the majority view that eighteen is too old and that a girl would be an old maid if she has to wait until eighteen before she can marry.

The arguments went back and forth on this issue the entire session. Indeed, this became one of the most contentious issues in the debate on the draft code. The protagonists may be divided roughly into two groups: the traditionalists and the modernists. The former wanted to maintain the traditional law under which a girl can be married at an early age, as early as five. Under such an arranged marriage, it is the families that are being joined as well as the man and the woman. Betrothed (technically joined in marriage) at age five, a girl might stay with her parents or might be taken under the tutelage of her in-laws who raise her like their daughter. When she reaches the age of puberty, her husband would take over full responsibility, but the family and a *Wass* (guarantor) become responsible for her fair treatment in the marriage. Traditionally, the *Wass* occupied a central place in the marriage in such a system.

The implications of underage marriage are many. First and foremost, the girl had no say in the whole matter. Secondly, she may suffer physically as well as mentally, should the husband wish to consummate the marriage before she is physically ready. There is a limit to what the *Wass* or the parents could do to avoid or minimize such a suffering. Many divorces were caused by such problems. The third implication of such a marriage goes beyond the individual suffering of the girl and concerns her civil and human rights, including her right to education.

The modernists argued strenuously that Ethiopia must move apace with the rest of the civilized world in the matter of human rights, including women's rights. They also argued that the development imperative in modern times required that a girl's marriage must be raised and fixed by law, i.e. taken away from the private realm of the arranged marriage. In between the traditionalists and modernists, were compromisers who agreed that the age of consent might be fixed by law, but that eighteen was too high. This pointed towards a compromise solution and, in that respect, some of the traditionalists insisted that the most they could accept by way a fixed age limit was thirteen. But the diehard conservatives persisted in maintaining their view of no fixed age of consent.

The Emperor followed the proceedings through the periodic briefings he received from his Prime Minister and other sources. As was typical with him, he expressed no views publicly, but people interested in this and other controversial issues contained in the code, had ways of finding out the Emperor's views. To begin with, there was the chief draftsman of the code, Professor Rene David. An idiosyncratic man, David carried a light movable chair with him and held court for his admirers and other interested People; I was one of the latter. The Emperor sounded Professor David's view on the raging controversy. David, in typical Gallic melodrama, asked the Emperor to imagine a future of liberated Ethiopian womanhood—millions of them—taking their rightful place proudly in society. Educated professional women serving their nation side by side with their men folk! Who do you think they will be thankful for such liberation? And before the Emperor could answer the rhetorical question, Rene David said with a dramatic gesture: "Your Majesty, with a stroke of the pen you will liberate Ethiopian women from age-old subjugation. Generations will be indebted to you and bless you."

That did it. Who could resist such inspired counsel delivered with Gallic logic and panache? The Emperor was for a fixed age of consent; what remained was convincing his Senators and Deputies to come to a reasonable compromise on the age. The modernists had to go down; they said sixteen. Objection! Okay then,... fifteen! And it was agreed. The result is Article 581(1) of the Ethiopian Civil Code, which provides that marriage may be contracted between a man, aged eighteen and a woman aged fifteen. But Sub-Article (2) of Article 581 adds an interesting proviso; it gives the Emperor or a person appointed for such a purpose by him the right to reduce the ages by two years, in cases of urgency.

His Majesty was nothing if not astute. This clever proviso created an illusion of imperial control over the future legal process in these matters, thus mollifying the arch-conservatives.

During my work in the Ministry of Justice, I never heard of a case in which either the Emperor or a person or persons appointed by him intervened to reduce the age of marriage because of compelling circumstances, foreseen under Article 581(2). But the office of Attorney General as well as the prosecutors working under its supervision throughout the country handled cases involving disputes concerning marriage. Cases arising out of marriage without parental consent were the majority in the main cities, while in the rural areas, the problem concerned lack of knowledge of the law.

The following section will further elucidate this matter.

Caught Between Tradition and Modernity

The office of the Attorney General was, among other things, the testing ground between the contending forces of tradition and modernity, between progress and reaction. By and large, knowledgeable and progressively inclined individuals understood and even supported the proper functioning of the Attorney General's office, as of all law enforcement agencies. By proper functioning I mean working strictly in accordance with the law, which assumes knowledge and appreciation of the law, that is to say, the new laws.

During my tenure of the office of Attorney General and for some three years before I assumed the office, the principal new law was the Penal Code promulgated in 1957. The Criminal Procedure Code had also just come into force. The Attorney General, his prosecutors and the police were charged to use these laws in their work. One of the critical changes in the penal system introduced by these new laws was the centralization of criminal prosecution in the hand of the state. Many conservatives resented this development, because it took away an important instrument from their hand, the power to punish or prosecute in private capacity.

The new codes created a sense of insecurity and confusion among people with material interest like landlords. To conservatives and generally people with vested interest, a law is a good law and a person enforcing it is a good person, only to the extent that the law and its enforcer protect or advance their vested interest. Thus an Attorney General who does not satisfy this conservative imperative is bad. One particular conservative, a big land owner from the central region of Showa, once told me that I had usurped the Emperor's crown because I rejected his request to prosecute a neighboring small landowner, which he could do under the old system. When he asked to lodge a private prosecutor's suit I told him he could not because all initiative and all decisions to prosecute were the jurisdiction of the Attorney General's office. That was when he accused me of usurpation of the imperial crown. It is a dramatic illustration of the tension arising out of changing laws in a traditional society.

At this point it is necessary to describe the function of the Attorney General.

As it was constituted at the time I assumed the function of the office, and for some fifteen years before that, the office was modeled on the English system. Before that, except for the five years of Italian occupation, the office of Attorney General (or Advocate General) was unknown in Ethiopia. The Italians introduced the office of the *Procuratore Generale,* which British legal advisors of the Emperor did not adopt when they helped establish the judicial system post 1941. Instead they introduced their own system under which the Attorney General is the preeminent legal advisor of the government, principally dealing with criminal prosecution on behalf of the State. In considering the function of the Attorney General, what cannot be overstressed is his independence from any pressure in performing his duties. He must be insulated from politics in deciding whether to prosecute a case or not; he must not be used as an instrument for any political or personal interests of powerful forces in society.

There was one crucial difference between the English system and the one adopted in Ethiopia. Under the English system, in addition to the Attorney General's office, there is the office of the Director of Public Prosecution. In Ethiopia the two were merged; there were prosecutors working under the command of the Attorney General. At the same time, there was the Minister of Justice who acts as the political head of the entire Department and was answerable to the Cabinet and the Emperor. The coexistence of the two, presumably designed to ensure the autonomy of the prosecutorial function of the office of the Attorney General, could at times lead to friction and conflict, which happened a few times during my tenure of office. Unlike the system in the United States, the Attorney General in Ethiopia was not a member of the Cabinet of Ministers. And as I noted above, such non-membership operated as an asset shielding the office from undue political pressures. Nonetheless, subtle attempts at influencing the decision of the Attorney General were not unknown, originating from Ministerial colleagues, friends or other "persons of substance."

During my tenure, the Emperor himself rarely intervened directly in the work of the Attorney General's office. But if he wanted to intervene, he had indirect ways to do so, an obvious one being through his Prime Minister. But then the Prime Minster, a trained lawyer, did not intervene directly either. The Emperor could also intervene through the Minster of Justice, bypassing the Prime Minister. After all, the Prime Minster and all Ministers were appointed and dismissible by him; they all worked at his pleasure.

If the Prime Minister wanted to intervene, his main avenue would be through the Minister of Justice. During my tenure, the Prime Minister never intervened, and one Minister of Justice tried to interfere. When I told him to mind his own store, he reported the incident to the Emperor; I never knew whether he did it through the Prime Minister. The case concerned matters of security, which was usually the area on which conflict occurred between the Attorney General and the Security Branch of the government. Now it might be reasonably expected of the office of the Attorney General to cooperate with the Security Branch in the apprehension of persons posing a threat to the security of the state. The Ministry of Interior had security matters under its jurisdiction, including oversight over the police and regulatory powers over their administration. But in criminal matters—in the investigation, apprehension and prosecution of crimes—the Attorney General had oversight powers over the police. These two separate functions clashed from time to time, especially where the Police Commissioner had direct access to the Emperor or the Prime Minister or both.

The tension between the two offices was dramatically illustrated in the case of the officers of the Imperial Body Guard who had been involved in the December 1960 rebellion. After the trial and execution of General Mengistu, their leader, several hundred officers and enlisted men were detained and the disposal of their case posed interesting legal issues. Their case was straightforward; however, the trial of hundreds of them and the type of punishment they should receive became problematic. The men who had "saved" the Emperor's throne, Asrate Kassa, being the leading light, were in charge of deciding the fate of the rebel officers. Presumably, Asrate Kassa and his group did not trust the lawyers at the Ministry of Justice to handle the case of these rebels. Nathan Marein, the Attorney General of the time, was consulted on legal issues but he was expected to rubber stamp decisions already made by the Asrate Group. When he insisted on due process, a special prosecutor was appointed to deal with the case of the rebel officers. That man was Colonel Teferra Gebremariam, a retired police officer who had some experience in prosecution work. It was he who conducted the prosecution of General Mengistu.

Before Col. Teferra's appointment, I had run-ins with the security people over a number of cases, involving questions of security. A constant issue of contention between the security people and the prosecutors in my Department was whether the case did indeed involve national security. The security people almost always defined cases in terms of national security and where we disagreed they would run to the Emperor and complain. A typical line of complaint was that "these lawyers" are undermining national security with their insistence on the rights of "criminals."

The only case in which the Emperor and the Prime Minister intervened that I can remember was one that involved a charge of treason against people who allegedly supplied to the embassy of Somalia in Addis Ababa classified information. The case involved one Ethiopian from the central region (an Amhara) who worked in the central archives of the Ministry of Interior, and three Ethiopian Somalis. The former supplied the information from his vantage point as an archivist, while the others acted as couriers and links with the Somali embassy. The Prime Minister's intervention was in the form of a call asking me to conduct the prosecution myself, which was not objectionable in any sense.

The Emperor's intervention came later after the prosecution had been completed and the accused were convicted. It turned out that the security people had complained that I was not severe enough in my prosecution and as a result the accused did not get the punishment they deserved, i.e. the death sentence. The security had even ingratiated themselves, somehow or other, to the judges trying the case—at least to one of them. That judge had asked me to go to his chambers the day of the arraignment of the accused. He wanted to know from me why I cited the articles of the penal code which did not carry the death penalty with it. I was courteous and explained to him the technicalities involved in citing articles, an explanation that I was to make to the Emperor later. When he knew that I would not budge on the point, he made a remark that is hard to forget: "You could have at least added the appropriate article that calls for flogging."

I thought discreet silence was the better part of valor and quietly left his chambers.

The Minister of Interior had appealed to the Emperor to reprimand me and order retrial. The Emperor then summoned me to the Palace and wanted to know the details of the case and why the accused were not sentenced to death. I explained to the Emperor the nature of the crimes of which the accused were charged and the evidence available to the prosecution. I further explained to him that the charges are based on the evidence, which determines the specific article of the Penal Code to be cited. According to the available evidence, the information supplied to the Somali Embassy was information dispatched from the Ethiopian Embassy in Mogadishu, describing the arrival of ships in the port of Mogadishu carrying arms shipments. Now supplying such information—or any information—to the Somali government by an Ethiopian official is prohibited and any official committing such act is answerable in law. But the nature of the information was not such as to jeopardize the security of Ethiopia. Consequently, the article of the Penal Code applicable to the prosecution was not one that demands the penalty of death but maximum imprisonment of fifteen years.

The Emperor listened with keen interest, asked a few technical questions and then told the Minister of Interior who was present that I did the right thing and dismissed us. But as I turned around and began to walk out, he called me back and asked me if the fifteen years imprisonment was with hard labor; I said that it was and he made an interesting comment that stayed with me, an indication of his attitude toward crime and punishment. He said, "Isn't that worse than death!" It was a statement in the form of a question, which was his usual style.

Years later when I was an exiled Mayor of Harar (see below), the Emperor was visiting a regional hospital. As he walked slowly along the corridor of the hospital ward, looking at the patients lying in their beds, I saw an elderly and scantily dressed patient rise from his bed and approach the Governor asking him to give a written petition to the Emperor. According to tradition, and the Revised Constitution of 1955, everyone had the right to petition the Emperor. I doubt if the Emperor knew the man but I recognized him; he was the principal defendant in the case I just described. The Emperor's *Aide de Camp* took the paper from the governor's hand, and I never knew whether the man was granted amnesty or not.

After the "Case of the Somalis," as it became known, I had more hassle from the security branch; and the Minister of Justice was intimidated by their constant complaints. Col. Teferra was appointed Deputy Attorney General a few weeks after the "Case of the Somalis." Just before his appointment I had a serious argument and falling out with the then Minister of Justice, Bitwoded Asfaha Woldemichael. Obviously, the security people must have convinced the powers-that-be that I was "beyond control." The city was abuzz with rumors that I was partial to the Somalis because I was Eritrean and supported the

Somali claim over the Ogaden region which had been the cause of war between the two countries.

Almost immediately after his appointment, Col. Teferra was informed by the Minister that all cases involving security matters would henceforth be handled by him and by him alone. Remember him? He was the special prosecutor who handled the case against General Mengistu Neway. When I told him that this was unacceptable, he told me calmly that he was following orders and asked me to go and check with the Minister.

Colonel Teferra was a soft-spoken, courteous man with serpentine guile. He would put you at ease at all times, but you never knew what he might do behind your back.

When I went to see the Minister, he told me that the order came form the highest authority. He called the Secretary General of the Ministry and briefed him about my complaint and asked him to corroborate the reason that he had given me. The Secretary General said that there was indeed a letter from the Ministry of the Pen (i.e. from His Majesty) to that effect. After the Secretary General left, the Minister said to me that more things were done behind the scene in Ethiopia than I could ever know. He said that he knew and understood Ethiopia better than I did and warned me in an avuncular spirit to tread carefully if I knew what was good for me. I thanked him for his concern and advice and went to my office to write a letter of resignation.

The following day, I showed the letter to the Minister. He was beside himself; he was utterly shocked as well as appalled at my "ignorance" of the Ethiopian reality. You cannot resign from an imperial appointment, he said, and pleaded with me to cool down and think it over. The Minister was a recent appointee, having been recently transferred from his position as Chief Administrator of Eritrea. He was an Eritrean who had known and respected my father as I said in a previous chapter and he invoked my father's name in pleading with me not to be rash. He told me to forget any idea of resignation from the Emperor's service. It is not possible; it simply is not done. Didn't I know, for Heaven's sake?! Since he played the role of an elder and invoked my father's name, I decided to respect his wish and seek other ways of leaving the Emperor's government. In any case I had been considering an exit route ever since the Emperor dissolved the federation of Eritrea and Ethiopia. But I could not use that as reason for leaving his government. As a close friend whose views I had sounded had put it to me, it would amount to knocking at the prison door and asking for admission there. I certainly had no wish to join prisoners, some of whom I had prosecuted!

My exit route had to be via the Law School, which had just been established and in the creation of which I had a hand. But I am running ahead of my story of that period.

PART III
INSIDE AN EMPIRE

Chapter 9

BETWEEN LAW AND CLANDESTINE POLITICS

As a high-ranking government official involved in the administration of justice, my first business was to oversee the application of the law in my daily work. Among lawyers and policy makers, the question of separating law from politics has always been a matter of controversy, and in an ideal situation, there should be no mixing of the two. A minor philosopher friend of mine once said, law is the frozen politics of yesterday; yet, once enacted or otherwise brought into force, the law occupies a higher place and should command all politics. But we were not living in an ideal situation when I was engaged in the administration of justice in those days; far from it. Moreover, insistence on a strict application of the law frequently pitted those of us engaged in the business of law in direct conflict with powerful interests that were directly or indirectly backed by the Emperor and some members of his government.

And why get involved in clandestine politics?

In the preceding chapters, I have more than hinted that my life in the government of Emperor Haile Selassie was a complicated one. I was torn between serving in a system that I did not really support, while at the same time deeply interested in and working toward change. Working for change from within the system was not possible, contrary to what some of my friends and I imagined in our student days, before we were rudely confronted with the reality—an imperial regime that was like the proverbial immovable object. Suddenly, the "immovable object" was shaken by the events of December 1960. Those historic events infused in the progressively inclined elites of the time—all those who desired change—a sense of empowerment, intimating the possibility of change. The question became: what kind of change and by what means? It was a historical irony that the very social forces and institutions created by the Emperor's programs of modernization became the agents of change. Principal among these were the armed forces, the labor unions, and the students and their teachers.

In a novel published in 1993, "*Riding the Whirlwind*," (Red Sea Press), I give an insider's view of another, and more momentous, event in Ethiopian history that overthrew Emperor Haile Selassie's government. I will come back to that event and its consequences in a later chapter, but I must stress here what is often forgotten: that the seed of that event was sown in the December 1960 coup attempt. Whereas Germame's attempted coup remained exactly that, a failed attempt, the events of 1974 were transformed into a revolution, albeit one that eventually degenerated into a reign of terror, as we shall see.

There were both internal and external forces interested in change following the Germame coup. The internal forces were the military, labor unions, students and teachers and the left wing of the intellectual elite. The external forces were the Americans and their Western allies, on the one hand, and the Soviets on the other.

Emboldened by what they saw in the wake of the Germame coup—a shaken Emperor willing to accept change and a government in disarray, at least for the first few months—the forces of change began making demands on the government. These were organized demands that could not have been imagined before, and if made, would have been dismissed out of hand. The armed forces began demanding higher pay and better conditions of service; the labor unions went beyond their previous practice of writing polite petitions to the Emperor, and demanded legal recognition. They went on strike in several industries to make their demands credible. The students and their teachers spearheaded a revolutionary movement calling for land reform. Their slogan, "Land to the Tiller," reverberated throughout the empire. Their earlier, more timid attempts at challenging the government were replaced by more aggressive posture and language. Their periodic poetry and essay contests became direct attacks on the Emperor and his principal aides and kinsmen like Asrate Kassa.

As the organized demands on the regime multiplied, various elite groups quickly formed underground movements seeking to harness them into a cohesive movement for change. Equally quickly, foreign powers began redoubling their efforts to understand and influence these new forces. Naturally, the protagonists of the Cold War, the United States of America and the Soviet Union, started sending feelers and contacting people they considered to be potential leaders. The Americans had a huge advantage over their adversary because of the combined material and cultural resources at their disposal. They had infinitely more financial and other material resources. They were also beneficiaries of the fact that English was the language of instruction in the institutions of higher learning in Ethiopia, as well as the language of communication in diplomatic and commercial circles. Thousands of Ethiopians went to English-speaking schools and hundreds (later thousands) studied in American and British Universities.

The American Ambassador (Richards) had been allegedly involved in the 1960 coup attempt. But the matter never became a bone of contention, because the Emperor could not afford to be at loggerheads with the Americans, from whom he received considerable military and economic assistance. Beginning in the aftermath of World War II and continuing through the end of the 1940s, the

United States, in pursuit of its strategic and geopolitical interests in the Horn of Africa, forged an alliance with Ethiopia, which it regarded as the most important state in the region. The convergence of US interests with the social and political interests of the Emperor and his regime was epitomized in the 25-year treaty concluded in 1953, under which the United States was granted naval and air facilities and a communications base in Asmara, the capital of Eritrea.

Between 1953 and the overthrow of the Emperor and his regime in 1974, Ethiopia received some $279 million in US military aid and more than 3,500 Ethiopian military personnel were trained in the United States. Moreover, beginning in the mid-1950s, an increasing amount of US economic and financial aid was given to Ethiopia.

Thus it is understandable that the Emperor accepted the quiet withdrawal of the American Ambassador who allegedly had contacts with Germame and his co-rebels during the short-lived rebellion. He was replaced by Edward Korry, a Kennedy appointee.

Ambassador Korry did not show any interest in changing the imperial regime into a progressive republic created in the image of the United States, contrary to the expectations of some naïve people among the educated elite. Instead, he developed a sophisticated program of reforming the system gradually. Korry was assiduous in cultivating contacts with young bureaucrats at the cabinet and sub-cabinet levels, organizing seminars on a range of issues, and unofficially hosting meetings of future decision makers, maintaining all the while an active official dialogue with the Emperor and his Prime Minister. Yet the clamor for change was taking on more radical overtones throughout the country, outside Korry's cautious "development diplomacy."

The United States tried to straddle the fence—both supporting the Emperor's government, and trying to distance itself from his politics. While trying to identify and control the forces of change, it continued to defend the imperial regime from alleged "communist" subversion. The contradictions of US policy were sharpened by growing numbers of Peace Corps volunteers in Ethiopia, who frequently aligned themselves with the aspirations of the emergent social forces. Some of them were even expelled from the country for helping student protestors.

Dangerous Liasons: Walking a Fine Line

I was one of Ed Korry's targeted "potential leaders" and was invited to his house and numerous embassy receptions, often together with others of my generation, mostly American-educated. And on a few occasions, I was the sole invitee, during which Korry would grill me with endless questions about what needed to be done. A former journalist, he had an instinct for the jugular in asking questions, and as a trained lawyer, I was the artful dodger. But on one occasion, at least, I let my defenses down…

What would you say, I asked him, if your government were to use its good offices and enormous power to suggest to the Nobel Committee that they offer the Emperor the Nobel Peace Prize in exchange for his declaring Ethiopia a constitutional monarchy and handing over power to his Prime Minister, as well as preparing the Crown Prince to step into his shoes soon? He was stunned by the suggestion; he took a deep breath and a generous helping of the Scotch he had in his hands as I went on to argue, "The Crown Prince has been waiting all his life and the Emperor is not getting any younger. Unless there is change soon, things could go out of control." After a momentary reflection, Korry said, with a smile, "I can't buy that." Note his words (and those were his exact words): he did not say, "We Americans cannot order the Nobel Committee." He only said, "I can't buy that." And that was that; my fancy idea was dead.

Korry's most famous effort became known as Awassa I and Awassa II, a series of seminars he convened at the lake side resort town of Awassa in southern Ethiopia. He invited the leading lights in government and business for weekend workshops on development. A range of issues was discussed, covering economic growth and social change as well as the requisite modern administrative structures. Social science research methods and personnel were employed in preparing the seminars, and the ambassador took infinite care not to appear to be undermining the Emperor's government. The Emperor himself had been persuaded, after recovering from the shock of the Germame coup, to launch his own reform projects in many fields, including judicial, administrative and land tenure.

In the end, these reforms proved illusory; in any case they were undertaken to steal the thunder from the demands for reform being voiced by the various forces of change. In the field of judicial reform, some of my colleagues in the Ministry of Justice and I were appointed members of committees. Nothing came of it. Public administration professionals were appointed to administrative reform committees. Some promising drafts eventually came out of these committees, aimed at rationalizing the system of government administration. The land reform project took many more years to complete but the final draft that came out of it did not satisfy anybody. On the contrary, it fueled more radical demands on the part of reformers, while the landed gentry were adamantly against any change. The Emperor was caught in a double bind.

While all this was going on, I was involved in some underground activities. My associates were for the most part old friends with whom I had shared ideas and ideology during my student days in England. Some of them have since passed away, like the poet Mengistu Lemma and the economist Assefa Demisse. Our underground network eventually crystallized into a core group of reformers, led by the great Arbegna Takele Woldehawariat, about whom I have already written in connection with my work as a Federal Supreme Court Justice.

It will serve no useful purpose to list the names of the others. To begin with, some of them dropped out of the group without any explanation, putting the rest of us in a quandary. The existence of our group was later discovered by the Emperor's secret service, leading to Takele's banishment to a distant province, and the rest of us were put under surveillance. This inevitably created suspicions and mistrust among the members of the group, crippling the nascent underground movement. In at least one case, there was suspicion of betrayal. There was no hard evidence, but there was circumstantial evidence to suggest that a character weakness had induced one person to leak secrets which were picked up by the Emperor's extensive intelligence service. That, Takele believed, was the cause of his arrest and banishment, as he indicated in a rhyming couplet adorned with Amharic "wax and gold" (double entendre). He sent this verse to me as a warning to avoid the person suspected as weak link. With Takele's banishment, we stopped meeting regularly as a group; doubts and suspicions were beginning to have a corrosive effect on our relationships as comrades committed to the cause and to one another.

Despite this suspicion, some of us continued our underground work, making contacts with key persons in forces with potential for change. My assignment was the most critical and also the most dangerous, namely, developing contacts with the military and university students. Labor was assigned to another person but I also helped in that area due to the close contacts I had developed with labor union leaders. Two colleagues in the university—Professors Mesfin Woldemariam and Seyoum Gebreigziabher—and I encouraged some of the best students in our classes to help educate and organize labor unions. This turned out to be one of the most important strategic decisions on our part. Four prominent university students answered the call to help organize labor unions; they were: Fissehatsion (Fisseha) Tekie, Gebreselassie Gebremariam, Mesfin Gebremichael and Tesfa Gebremariam. With the help of the International Confederation of Free Trade Unions (ICFTU), these "Four Musketeers," (as Seyoum called them), were destined to play a prominent role in the organization of the labor union movement in Ethiopia and Eritrea by occupying critical positions in the Confederation of Ethiopian Labor Unions (CELU). Fisseha became the Secretary General of CELU, while the other three also held key positions.

CELU's President, Beyene Solomon, was my earliest and most important contact during the underground phase of the organization. Beyene's keen intelligence, indefatigable energy and ingratiating personality more than made up for his limited (third grade) education. Another of our earliest contacts, principally cultivated by Professor Mesfin, was Abraham Mekonnen, leader of the Wonji sugar plantations workers. Abraham ended up being co-opted by the government, becoming a minor bureaucrat, salaried and superannuated. Others took up his mantle at Wonji and as he became head of the Ethiopian labor unions at the national level. In all our contacts we sometimes used code names. Mesfin gave Abraham the code name Maru (sugary) and he used that code in phone conversations until the movement came out of the shadows into the light of legal recognition. Abraham was articulate but tended to prefer demagogy to reasoned appeal, unlike Tsegaye, his successor at Wonji.

My contact with labor unions began a few years before the establishment of CELU. Almost immediately after my return from England, I made efforts to know more about the labor situation, based on a firm conviction of the need to help organize unions and link them to a more politicized student movement.

The most important unions, in numerical terms, were concentrated in the textile industry; followed by the Wonji and Metahara Sugar Workers Union. My most serious contact came in late 1957 when I was commissioned by the government to examine the complaints of railway workers. Since it will help explain my association with and close contacts with unions in general, I will give a brief account of this special commission.

Historically, the Ethiopian Railroad Workers' Syndicate was the pioneer of unionism. Formed in Dire Dawa in 1947 as an employee welfare organization, not as a labor union proper, its leadership was paternalistic and cooperated with the government as well as with the French management. This condition would end as unions became more and more radicalized. In contrast, the Syndicate of the Union of Free Workers in Eritrea, co-founded by Woldeab Woldemariam and Tsegai KaHsai in 1952, was more radical in its demands, owing to the different historical conditions in Eritrea at the time.

My investigation was concerned with complaints of the Ethiopian Syndicate, with a special focus on working conditions and the management's right to dismiss workers. I had enough leeway to examine all aspects of the workers' complaints, which ranged from low salaries to harsh working conditions, and especially the management's arbitrary rule and power of dismissal without any right of appeal or other legal remedies. One clause in the government-approved statute of the company stated that the company was the sole judge in matters of hiring and firing (*La compagnie est le seul juge*).

I visited every railway station from Addis Ababa, through Dire Dawa, to as far as Dewelle, on the Djibouti border, interviewing as many workers as time allowed. Before I set out, I met the General Manger, a M. Auriot, who presented the company's side by dismissing the workers complaints as immaterial. When I began asking some hard questions, he realized that I was not impressed and shifted ground. In a word, he made a subtle offer of a bribe. I remember saying "*Monsier le directeur, je suis vraiment surpris de vous entendre dire cela.*" (Sir, I am really surprised to hear you say that). I then got up, shook his hand and left briskly.

My investigation enabled me to learn a great deal about the problems facing Ethiopian workers and to gain a valuable insight into the unholy alliance between government and employers. Employer arrogance was derived from their financial power and the patronage that such power could buy. Government ministers took the employers' side in all disputes, as I would find out by the fate of my report. My report described the bad working conditions and miserable wages and criticized the company's unchallenged practice of dismissing workers at will. It recommended a change of policy and the introduction of regulations establishing a balanced worker-employer relationship. The report was submitted to the Minister of Public Works (the official in charge of these matters) and then completely ignored—buried in the archives of the Ministry. Its recommendations awaited the rise of a radical labor union movement.

My First Encounter with the Military

Of my two assigned areas of contact, the military was by far the most difficult. Our group leader, Takele, assigned me the military because I was friendly with a few high-ranking army officers who took my course on government and constitution in the evening classes at University College of Addis Ababa. One of these officers was General Aman Andom, perhaps the most popular and one of the few highly trained military officers. We shall see below what role he played as leader in the revolution of 1974.

General Aman and I were not only friends, but also relatives and fellow Protestants. I knew him when I was a teenager in high school and he was a popular army captain, long before he joined my class at the university; and we met often socially in our respective houses. At the time he was attending my class, around 1958, he was in charge of Operations in the office of the Chief of Staff of the Ethiopian Armed Forces. He was transferred to Harar as commander of the Third Division early in 1960, a few months before the Germame coup attempt. Many of his friends and supporters believed that the Emperor transferred him to Harar because he was afraid of him. Some even argued that there was a rivalry between him and General Mengistu Neway, and that the latter, who had the Emperor's ear, was instrumental in Aman's transfer in order to get him out of the way in time for the December 1960 coup.

Aman and I used to meet often, and we invariably talked about politics, including the role of the military, and more specifically, the possibility of using the army to bring about changes in Ethiopia. This was in the late 1950's, a year or so before Germame's coup of December 1960, but a few years before several civilian governments were overthrown in quick succession in several African countries.

After my evening class on constitution and government, Aman and I habitually drove to a nearby coffee shop and continued our discussion over coffee, sitting in my car or his. Occasionally, we met at his house, where he would invite a select few young officers who were his followers. They all admired General Mulugeta Bulli (who was one of those killed by Germame). Apparently, Mulugeta had a long-term coup plan, patterned after Gamal Abdel Nasser's 1952 coup in Egypt, and had intimated his plan to Aman and a couple of other trusted officers. Some of them were at the meetings in Aman's house.

A question frequently asked in my class and elsewhere at that time, was: should the military intervene in politics, or be concerned only with the defense of the nation from external threat? In my class and in conversations, I always made my position clear on this issue. Shorn of all technical terms of political science, it was this: civilian government rests on authority, legitimated by various mechanisms that secure habitual obedience. Whether the government is a monarchy governing through prescriptive right, or a presidential regime based on popular mandate, it commands authority because there is a general acceptance of its legitimacy.

When a serious break occurs in the habit of obedience, resulting in revolt, the mechanisms of peaceful persuasion give way to physical coercion. But a government that loses popular mandate cannot indefinitely use armed forces to maintain itself in office, for this condition invites armed intervention in politics. When a government becomes too dependent on the armed forces and makes use of them too much or too frequently, the armed forces tend to end by seizing power on their own behalf.

Aman's view of the role of the military in politics was a nuanced one. He did not like the Emperor's regime with its incubus of corruption and inefficiency; he preferred a constitutional monarchy and thought that a military coup should aim at transition toward such a system, with the military acting as guardian of the change. In fact, it was after an exchange of views with Aman that I proposed to U.S. Ambassador Korry to dangle the Nobel Peace Prize to the Emperor in exchange for a genuine transition to a constitutional monarchy. It was generally known that the Emperor would have loved to receive the Prize, and that Korry's negative reaction reflected either a genuine fear of not being able to deliver the Prize, or a lack of appreciation of the Emperor's desire. Perhaps we imputed too much diplomatic power to the Americans even to the point of influencing the decision of the Nobel Committee.

The relationship that I had with Aman was a peculiar one. On the one hand I informed him about the existence of an underground movement dedicated to bring about change in the country. I told him that the group considered the armed forces and especially himself as a popular leader, as indispensable factors for change. At the same time, I could not go any further; I could not reveal the identity of the members of the group. Nor did he insist in knowing such details. By the same token, I did not ask for details of the movement in the army's side, beyond making sure that there was mutual understanding of the need for cooperation. I made it clear that if the army wished to go it alone and rely on brute force only, it would result in failure. I gave examples of cases where such a mistake led to defeat. In fact, after the failure of the Germame coup, there was no need to belabor the point.

Throughout my underground activities, especially when dealing with the military, two questions confronted me. The first was: as a lawyer dedicated to the rule of law and human rights, how could I justify the involvement of the military, that is to say the use of force to bring about change, which my underground group and I were seeking? The second was: how does one make sure that the military return to their barracks after they help bring down the imperial regime? My answer to the first question was that the imperial regime was built on violence and used violence to maintain itself in power. Peaceful change was out of the question, as the charades of the Emperor's "reforms" demonstrated. The second question was not so easy to answer. Experience in other countries, and in Ethiopia later, would show that the military almost always ended up ruling in their own name, excluding any possibility of installing a civilian government or even sharing power with civilians. Aman and I discussed this on many occasions; he declared himself to be a democrat not interested in power for its own sake, but as an instrument of change. "That is what they all say until they occupy the seat of power," I would tease him. "That will not happen on my watch," he would respond. His fate after the 1974 revolution, about which I will say more, may have been partly linked to this philosophy. Indeed, he was described as the reluctant hero, summoned by history to play a role that ended up consuming him.

The African Connection

The challenges to the Emperor's rule reached a decisive point after the December 1960 coup attempt. And the forces that led the challenge were creatures of his modernization programs, like the university and high school students. The University of Addis Ababa was founded in 1950, under the Emperor's order and close watch. The university provided an opportunity for students from different parts of the country to live and study together, share ideas and common dreams about the future of the country. To this common experience was added another factor that operated to speed up the revolutionary process that would eventually engulf the country. This factor was the arrival of students from other African countries.

The process of decolonization of Africa, starting with the independence of Ghana in 1957, played an important role in the political awakening of Ethiopian university students. Emperor Haile Selassie established a scholarship in his name inviting the influx of many African students. These developments provided opportunities for progressive forces in Ethiopia to utilize the African connection to their own ends. In addition to the scholarship, the Emperor's government started taking initiatives in inviting leaders of African liberation movements, encouraging them and providing some assistance. Consequently, young African leaders from the political as well as the labor union movements began frequenting the Ethiopian capital. For the first time, the Ethiopian media began publishing news accounts and writing editorials on African liberation movements in positive terms.

I became a good friend with some of these young leaders, including Tom Mboya of Kenya and Felix Moumie of Cameroon. Mboya ended up becoming the second most important political figure in Kenya until he was assassinated, presumably by jealous rivals of the Kenya African National Union (KANU) Party in 1968. Felix Moumie was assassinated in Switzerland in 1960, victim of poisoning by an agent of the French Secret Service. I became close to both these leaders; Mboya visited Addis Ababa several times before Kenya's independence in 1963, while Moumie came twice and was planning to make his third visit when he was killed. These and other African leaders, like Nyerere and Kaunda, enriched the political experience of young Ethiopians by the speeches they delivered at public meetings as well as at private gatherings that my friends and I arranged.

These developments reinforced the Pan-African connection in Ethiopia, which contributed toward an awareness of Ethiopians of their Africanness, enhancing their desire for change. Some of the guest students regularly received newspapers from political parties in their homelands. Ethiopian students who were never exposed to a free press had access to these newspapers. More importantly, the daily interaction of the students started free discussion and questioning of the status quo. This was reflected in debating events that I took part in, where students fearlessly challenged official government policies and hitherto unquestioned dogmas.

An example of the growing awareness among Ethiopia's students of their Africanness was the song "*Africa Ahgurachun*" (Africa Our Homeland), a student continental anthem that marks a break from the past insularity of Ethiopians. In that respect, if there is one thing on which I feel proud in having made a modest contribution, it is in helping facilitate meetings of African leaders with members of the Ethiopian elite, including some important ministers who were sympathetic to the idea of Ethiopian involvement in African affairs.

I was appointed a delegate to the All African Peoples Conference convened by Ghana's Kwame Nkrumah, held in Accra, December 1958. I was told by Petros Sahlou, head of the African Department at the Ministry of Foreign Affairs, that I was put on the list of delegates, in recognition of my involvement in activities concerning Africa and Africans. The choice of the delegates was made by the Ministry of Foreign Affairs, in consultation with the then-reigning gray eminence of the regime, Mekonnen Habtewold, Minister of Commerce and Industry. In addition to his ministerial portfolio, Mekonnen was also in charge of cultural affairs as well as head of a special intelligence network. Those who selected the delegation could not have chosen a more diverse and interesting group of people. The person chosen to lead the delegation was Getachew Mekasha, a conservative royalist who, at the time, was Director General of the Ministry of Interior.

Getachew did not hide his inordinate pride in his class and ethnic origin (Amhara) and his chauvinism vis-à-vis other Africans. Throughout our mission in Ghana, he never tired of downgrading the other Africans and making fun of some of their names. One delegate who was the source of his uncontrollable mirth was a Nigerian delegate by the name of Gohoho, who apparently approached Getachew seeking assistance from the Emperor. We never heard what he got in response to his requests; all we heard was Getachew's boastful claim that "they were all" approaching him for assistance. Getachew's chauvinism was not limited to other Africans; he was also contemptuous of other ethnic groups of Ethiopia. I remember him once boastfully imitating a war cry uttered by Meneliks's warriors during the conquest of the Somali-inhabited Ogaden region. He informed me in all seriousness that the conquerors scattered the highland staple, Teff, into the Shebelli and Juba rivers flowing from Ethiopia toward Somalia. Why? It was an expression of highland superiority over the lowland Somali, who did not rise high enough in "civilization" to make *injera*!

Surely—I thought and told him—surely, there were better ways of undertaking the "civilizing mission."

Getachew was chosen to head the delegation because of his loyalty to the imperial regime and his membership in the ruling class. The rest of us were selected on the basis of some merit, because the regime wanted to impress the rest of Africa. The other members of the delegation were: Ms. Hirut Imru, Dr. Aklilu Habte, and Mr. Tedla Tebeje. Hirut was the daughter of Ras Imru and, like her father, a very gentle and progressive humanitarian. She was educated in social studies in the United States and, for many years, was head of a UNESCO-supported community development program at Majete, in northern Shoa province. She was revered by the community she served, and respected by her peers.

Dr. Aklilu Habte was a graduate of Ohio State University who later became President of Haile Selassie University. Aklilu was a thoughtful, soft-spoken and generally decent man, who was also shrewd and focused on advancing his own career. The last but not least member of our delegation was Mr. Tedla Tebeje, educated in India with a degree in social science. Tedla was influenced by Indian socialism of the Nehru variety and was very much opposed to Getachew's chauvinism and arrogance. Aklilu and Hirut were also shocked at Getachew's style of dealing with people and concerned that his behavior would send the wrong signal about Ethiopia and Ethiopians to the rest of Africa. I agreed with them. In one particular strategy meeting, we tried to impress upon him the fact that the elite of future African leaders were assembled at that historic conference and that we should respect them and conduct ourselves accordingly. Getachew did not seem to object to this reasoning, but continued to behave as before, with disdainful arrogance.

Who were the delegates and why the All African Peoples Conference?

Nkrumah convened the All African Peoples Conference eight months after the meeting of independent African heads of state and government, which he convened in the spring of 1958. Whereas the spring 1958 meeting involved government leaders only, the All African Peoples Conference was a meeting of political parties, liberation movements, labor unions, women's organizations and student and youth organizations. At that time there were very few independent African states; there were many independence movements led by emerging political parties. These came from all over Africa, from Algeria to Southern Africa, and from Zanzibar to the Gambia. The Algerian delegation was led by the late Franz Fanon, of *The Wretched of the Earth* fame. We stayed in the same hotel with the Algerian delegation, so I had occasion to chat with some of them. I must say, I did not find Fanon as warm and communicative as the other members of the Algerian delegation. .

Because of our knowledge of French, Aklilu and I ended up spending much time with the Algerians, the Tunisians, and other French-speaking delegates, acting as interpreters for them when they wished to interact with other English-speaking delegates. The Tunisian delegation, representing the Neo-Destour Party, which included two women, was more outgoing than the Algerians.

The thing that impressed me most was how much the sub-Saharan Africans respected and became friendly with the North African delegates. The Algerians and their *Front de la Liberation Algerienne*, (FLN) had become household words among literate Africans, and when Franz Fanon stood on the platform to address the Conference, there was a standing ovation. We were all taken by the heroism and sacrifice of the Algerians.

The leaders of other political parties, liberation movements and mass organizations took their turn to address the Conference, which included several observer delegations. For instance the Labor Party of Great Britain sent an observer delegation; I happened to be seated near two of them and had opportunities to chat with them during the break. They followed British parliamentary practice, shouting "Hear! Hear!" whenever some one said something they liked.

It is not possible to describe all the main events of the Conference, but a reference to some significant events and delegation will give an idea of its historical significance. There were plenary sessions and several committees assigned the task of fleshing out the aims of the Conference program. The committee meetings enabled people to meet informally and exchange ideas and views. The plenary sessions were solemn affairs at which almost all the participating delegations spoke, including some well known personalities from different parts of Africa.

There were some amusing speeches and witty remarks. Of these I will cite two. One was a speech by the leader of the Afro-Shirazi party of Zanzibar who complained that when they demanded independence, the Colonial Office responded by telling them they were not yet ripe for in dependence. "As if we were bananas," he said to prolonged laughter. Another was a speech by a certain Akpata, leader of the Dynamic Party of Nigeria. He was a follower of Nkrumah and a proponent of the "African Personality," which Nkrumah stressed in some of his writings. In the course of his speech, Akpata waxed eloquent on polygamy as an important expression of our potency as Africans. "If the Europeans are not able to practice polygamy, can we help it?!" Prolonged laughter and "Hear! Hear!"

The Conference was presided over by Nkrumah himself, but because he had to attend to government business, the day-to-day running of the meeting was delegated to the Secretary of the Conference, the Kenyan labor leader, Mr. Tom Mboya, who carried it out with efficiency and good humor. Another Kenyan, Dr. Kiano, spoke in the name of the Kenyan delegation. Before delivering his speech, he surprised the Conference by unfurling a huge banner on which was written, "Release Kenyatta Now!" He waved the banner and the hall went wild with excitement and applause. Mboya seemed as surprised as the rest of us, which led to speculation that there was a rift in the Kenya delegation. It later turned out that there was indeed a rift and a rivalry between the brilliant and charismatic Mboya and the scholarly but not physically imposing Kiano.

It is hard to describe the enthusiasm and sense of optimism about Africa's future we felt at the All African Peoples Conference in 1958. Nkrumah's strategy was to mobilize the political and social forces of the African continent and set them to work for African liberation and eventual unity. He had not been able to mobilize the government leaders, who made rhetorically pleasing statement about Africa's liberation, but were not willing or able to commit their treasure and manpower to achieve that end. And as for African unity, which Nkrumah preached as a fundamental goal, not only were they divided along ideological grounds—some siding with the West, while others had Soviet leanings—but they were ensconced in their newly acquired power and too comfortable to risk losing it. Clearly other forces had to be mobilized to put pressure to bear on the independent governments to adopt Nkrumah's agenda of liberation and unity. This was the main reason that prompted Nkrumah to convene the All African Peoples Conference.

What kind of forces took part, and from which countries did they come?

Over one hundred organizations, from some thirty countries, representing different political parties and mass organizations were invited to the Conference. Although the convenor was Nkrumah's own Convention Peoples Party (CPP), the record shows thirty-five original sponsoring organizations, from some twenty countries. Of these countries, only eight were independent in December 1958: Egypt, Ethiopia, Ghana, Guinea, Liberia, Morocco, Sudan and Tunisia. All the others that sent delegates were still under colonial occupation, albeit in the final phase of their progress toward independence. The host country, Ghana presented three organizations, two political parties and the Ghana Trade Union Congress. An impressive number of organizations were invited from southern Africa, including the historic African National Congress (ANC) from South Africa, Basutoland (Lesotho), Bechuanaland (Botswana), and South West Africa (Namibia). Similarly, several organizations were invited from eastern and western Africa, including some from French-speaking Africa. Of the latter, none was given a warmer reception by the conferees than the delegation from Guinea, which consisted of the one ruling party, the *Parti Democratique de Guinee*.

Many who were destined to lead their respective nations to independence in the 1960s and become household words in Africa, participated. But one man captured the African imagination; of all the participants, one delegate who came alone was to make history and become a martyr, barely two years after the Conference. That man was Patrice Lumumba of the Congo. And the conference record doesn't even list him as a delegate from that country.

The political landscape of the Congo was confused at best in those days, with the Belgian colonial authorities discouraging the emergence of independent minded leaders and encouraging and supporting those who were beholden to them. Lumumba was a fiercely independent nationalist whom the Belgians and their American allies marked for elimination on a false charge of being a "communist."

What is not generally known is that Lumumba would not have taken part in the Conference at all, but for a fortuitous event involving the delegation from

Zanzibar. According to the account reported to me at the time of the Conference and thereafter by Mr. Abdulrahman Babu, the Zanzibari delegation (led by Babu) was stranded in the Congo capital, Leopoldville, (Kinshasa), because it missed its connecting flight to Accra. Babu was so impressed by Lumumba as a fellow revolutionary and leader that he included him as a member of the Zanzibari delegation. They flew to Accra together, where I met them. Babu and I hit it off immediately and became good friends. In 1964 Babu engineered a revolution in Zanzibar overthrowing the Sultanate. After Zanzibar and Tanganyika became independent and united as Tanzania, Babu held several cabinet positions, including Minister of Foreign Affairs. Babu later fell out with Nyerere, who incarcerated him, and I joined in a widely supported movement of friends of Africa imploring Nyerere to release him. He was released in 1977 and came to the United States, where we met again. I helped persuade him to support the Eritrean cause of independence, which he did to the very end.

Lumumba was a man with a personality very different from that of Babu. The few occasions that I met him during the Conference, I was impressed by his keen intelligence and quiet, non-confrontational manner. He had a cold logic and quiet confidence, and an almost messianic belief in his destiny as a leader. I never saw him deliver a public speech; indeed, I doubt very much if he was given platform at the Conference. But people who heard him report a fiery speaker. He was a tall and imposing presence, probably six feet two inches in height.

Lumumba's martyrdom came as suddenly as his meteoric rise to power. His martyrdom symbolized the suffering and oppression of the still colonized people of Africa and his name became revered. When the Russians opened a university in his name, many young African students left for Moscow to study at Lumumba University.

From Accra to Addis Ababa, via Asmara

The mood of the participants of the All African Peoples Conference was upbeat. The Conference created such enthusiasm, that to many the millennium seemed to be around the corner. The songs, the drumming, the dances and demonstrations, the speeches, the resolutions and slogans reflected this spirit of optimism. The moving spirit of this new African awakening was President Nkrumah whom the Conference saluted and many made a commitment to emulate. We all left enthused and with a firm commitment to work for the cause that was the theme of the Conference—African liberation and African unity.

At the end of the Conference, we traveled home via Rome, because there were no direct flights from east to west Africa, a fact that underscored Africa's dependence on Europe. We were welcomed in Rome by the Ethiopian Ambassador, Girmachew Tekle-Hawariat, who was also a popular author of the Amharic novel, *Araya*. He received us at the embassy and quizzed us about the Accra meeting. He did not seem to be particularly interested in African affairs. Although progressively inclined in his political views, he was a typical Ethiopian patriot imbued with ideas of Ethiopia's uniqueness.

In later years I was to deal with Girmachew when he was the Emperor's Minister of Information, a post that often landed him in dispute and royal reprimand. My respect for him grew after I heard him declare to the Emperor that he did not believe in news monopoly. He said this in defense of his attempts at liberalization of the news media, which naturally landed him in trouble with the Emperor. When he made that bold declaration, those of us who were present feared for his fate. But he only received a severe warning from the Emperor, who told him that he had crossed the line, and must be careful and remember to whom he was talking. The words of the Emperor still ring in my ears: "*Hulettegna,tirf qal attinagher*! ("Don't make unnecessary remarks again).

Girmachew was removed from the ministry not long after the incident.

We left Rome, taking Ethiopian Airlines to Addis Ababa with a stopover in Asmara, my hometown. I decided to spend a few days in Asmara, and so disembarked at the airport. The following is a digression from my main narrative, but it illustrates the complications of my underground work even as I continued in government service. My Eritrean origin and connection is an important part of my story, as I will explain.

I found more interest among Eritreans in African affairs than I had expected, especially among the young. Many people wanted to know about the Accra conference, so I spent a great deal of time talking to people in informal meetings, in coffee shops and in private homes. I even gave a semi official talk to a group of government officials and a few young business men at the Officers' Club.

I also made a courtesy call on the Emperor's Representative, Andargachew Mesai. I dreaded visits to his office and those of his ilk, so my visit was brief; I hated all the palace formalities and the stupid ushers who reveled in them. But I did use the occasion to visit his spouse, my erstwhile benefactor, the Princess Tenagne, who lived a few minutes walk from his office. The Princess gently scolded me for not visiting her and her family. It is a scolding that she and her daughters made whenever we met, and for which I could give no satisfactory answer except to say that I was too busy. That answer never satisfied them and I knew it. As I said before, I did not feel comfortable in their company, and could not bear the tension of befriending them while at the same time being engaged in revolutionary activities.

More to the point, I knew that the Princess and her husband were ruling over my people, who were living a wretched existence at the time. I felt the pain of the people as I listened to them and watched their deteriorating situation—and a pang of guilt for serving in the government that was responsible for their condition. It was a wrenching experience. The clash of values and conflicting commitments that I experienced from the day I entered government service became more acute as my involvement in clandestine politics deepened. And whenever I visited my home town, this feeling became intolerable. My involvement in underground activities was one way of releasing the tension.

The All African Peoples Conference at Accra had the effect of sharpening this contradiction as my commitment to African liberation and African unity was added to the already cluttered schedule of my underground activities, over and above my burdensome duties at the Ministry of Justice. At that time I was Inspector General of Justice, and was not yet involved in decisions on the prosecution of cases; that would come some four years later; meanwhile there was a deteriorating political situation in Eritrea. The Emperor's Representative was encroaching on internal Eritrean matters, over the objection of many prominent Eritreans both in government and the public. Courageous newspaper editors and commentators, who criticized this illegal encroachment, citing Eritrea's autonomous status under the UN-arranged federation, were being persecuted by the puppet government in Eritrea. Some were banished to distant provinces in Ethiopia. There was also a deteriorating economic situation caused by the punitive policies of the Emperor's government. Friends and relatives, speaking in hushed tones, gave me detailed accounts of what was happening.

Matters came to a head in early spring of 1958.

Chapter 10

AS THE SUN KING BECOMES "AFRICA'S FATHER"

❖❖❖❖❖❖❖❖❖❖❖❖❖❖❖❖

It was a bright morning in early March. Asmara was astir with rumors of a popular uprising. Amid a general excitement among the city dwellers, police vehicles hurtled to and fro, moving from one end of the city to the other. Curious onlookers seemed puzzled by the unusual movement; some of them whispered the word *shobero*. Soon the word was heard practically everywhere. *Shobero* is a corruption of the Italian *sciopero* which means strike.

It was a time of economic depression. On top of the political crisis caused by the interference of the Emperor's Representative in Eritrean affairs, the poor harvest of that year and the diminishing purchasing power of the population led to hunger and distress. People did not have enough to eat and were angry but helpless. They would follow any protest movement at the slightest provocation. The nationwide general strike paralyzed the city and all other major cities, like the two ports of Massawa and Asab. The population came out in support of the strikers by organizing demonstrations.

The demonstrators assembled at the main market place and began marching toward the government quarters. Their line of march was orderly and disciplined. They carried placards with slogans on freedom and the right of unions to organize. As they passed the main streets on their way to their intended destination, their ranks swelled. They had just crossed what was popularly called the "38th parallel" (the dividing line between the poorer and richer sections of the city) when shots were heard. The police had opened fire on the demonstrators, on the order of the officer in command who later claimed that he was given the order by the Eritrean Chief Executive. Several people lay dead and wounded in the street.

I was in Addis Ababa when I heard the news and was stunned and saddened. In government circles, opinion was divided between the die-hard empire apologists, who welcomed the action taken by the police, (who thought that the strikers had to be taught a lesson lest the matter should get out of hand and lead to copy cat strikes by workers in Ethiopia proper), and the more liberal minority who held that the use of excessive force to the point of killing demonstrators is counterproductive and leads to further public disaffection in an already disaffected population.

My immediate boss at the time, Taddese Negash, who did not approve of the shooting, told me about a conversation he overheard at the imperial palace, a few days after the shooting incident. The Eritrean Chief Executive, who had been summoned to Addis Ababa, had just come out of an audience with the Emperor. Interested people wanted to know, who authorized the shooting? Did the order come from the Emperor? Taddese Negash quoted to me the reply of the Eritrean Chief Executive verbatim, imitating his peculiarly slow manner of speaking. "I can hear an order of His Majesty," he had said boastfully, "from the inflexion of his voice, and I can read it from his facial expression."

1958 was indeed an eventful year; for in addition to the strike and the shooting that followed, there were student demonstrations. These protested government decisions aimed at crushing the autonomous sentiment of Eritreans, including the removal of the Eritrean flag from government buildings (replacing it with the Ethiopian flag), and the imposition of Amharic on Eritrean schools as the language of instruction, replacing Tigrigna and Arabic. High school students organized demonstrations, school boycotts and other acts of resistance in protest over these actions. Several students were detained and treated roughly by the police.

These events spawned a general resistance movement, starting with a peaceful underground organization and ending in armed struggle that would change the history of Eritrea and of the region. The peaceful underground movement was known as *MaHber ShewAte* (Cell of Seven) in the highlands of Eritrea and among Eritreans living in Ethiopia, and as *Haraka* in the western lowlands of Eritrea. *Haraka (*Arabic for movement) was conceived and first organized by Eritreans living in the Sudan who had strong links with the Sudanese Communist Party. When I became associated with *MaHber Shewate* in Addis Ababa in the early 1960s, I had no knowledge of this fact; only that the underground movement aimed at organizing Eritreans in order to protect their rights that were being steadily eroded by Ethiopian government authorities and their allies in the Eritrean government.

There was a connection between the strike of the spring of 1958 and the creation of Haraka. The Sudanese labor unions, which were dominated by the Sudanese Communist Party, encouraged the establishment and growth of a strong labor movement in Eritrea. When I was in Accra I was approached by an aide to President Sekou Toure of Guinea, who asked me about the Eritrean Syndicate of workers: why didn't they send a delegate, was I aware that they were invited, etc. He was curious to know more and also anxious for me to meet Sekou Toure. I met Sekou Toure who revealed to me that he was aware of the developments in Eritrea through his contacts in the Sudanese labor unions. Indeed, the Syndicate of Eritrean Workers was on the list of invited organizations. Curiously, enough, their Sudanese counterparts and sponsors were not in the list of invited organizations. When I pointed this out to Sekou Toure, asking why they were not invited, he simply said, "*Oui, ca c'est drole*" (Yes, this is strange) and we left the matter there. But I did have occasion in Addis Ababa in May 1963, to remind him of that among other things, as I will explain below.

The Plot Thickens

I was straddling two contradictory worlds—the one of high government office, the other of a secret underground movement—and it was only a matter of time before the tension simmering below the surface would seek release, and my secret life as an underground organizer would catch up with me. I was a high government official engaged in the administration of justice, at the same time involved in activities that were against the law and thus potentially disastrous to me and my family. I justified this by telling myself that a revolutionary sets out to right some wrong, and must take the risks that go with the undertaking. No great deed can be accomplished by being cautious; or as George Bernard Shaw once said, nothing was ever achieved by "a reasonable man." And so on and so forth—justifications are not hard to come by once you make up your mind to do something.

A powerful force lies behind the impulse to right wrongs, an invisible, unfathomable force the source of which philosophers and psychologists have tried to trace and explain. All the great religious and political movements in history can be traced to it. Looking back to those years, I can't help feeling that we were in the grip of such a force. I marvel at the passion with which we flung ourselves headlong into the unknown, unmindful of the risks involved, aware only of our desire to change things. As Desta, a character in my semi-autobiographical novel *Riding the Whirlwind* puts it, we considered ourselves the midwives of history:

> Every sign of decay in the empire, every excess in the sprawling bureaucracy with its decrepit command structure and frustrating bottlenecks, seemed to validate Melaku's vision of our historic mission. My comrades and I organized our lives with that vision as our guiding light. It defined our attitudes toward practically everything, including our relations with people around us at home and in the workplace. It dominated our thoughts. It permeated our consciousness.

The character goes on to confess that those exciting days remain an important part of his make-up, and describes himself as an unrepentant revolutionary—"unlike some who have 'graduated' to a more 'pragmatic' view of life, and others who shudder at the thought of their past, which they try to forget."

Am I making a similar "confession" now? Well, I know that I write in the tradition of Rousseau's *Confessions*, if not from the same exalted pedestal. My "confessions" are cerebral as much as visceral; they come from the head as well as from the heart. Looking back on what we did and could not do, my account is that of an aging revolutionary, lamenting the passing of a romantic era and, as subsequent pages will show, also responding to the primordial urge to record. I will chronicle some of the excesses of revolutions, some of the misdeeds of revolutionaries that I have known. That sensitive monitoring instrument called conscience, instilled by a Protestant upbringing and backed by a critical mind honed in the skeptical sciences, will not rest until it records these excesses. Unlike the good Catholic to whom the confessional is available, the Protestant or agnostic has to do his own "confessions" in writing.

But first I must summarize the development of some events that had a decisive impact on my own life. The six year period between the All African Peoples Conference held in December 1958 ,and my resignation from the post of Attorney General in 1964, saw the liberation of the majority of African countries from European colonial rule, with some interesting consequences. Several among them opened embassies in Addis Ababa, and some of the young African diplomats expressed sympathies with the Ethiopian students and others who were making demands for change in the country.

This coming of Africa into Ethiopian life created a heightened sense of political and social awareness, especially among students and other young people. One event, above all else, epitomized this process—the establishment of the Organization of African Unity (OAU) in May 1963. The founding Conference was held in Addis Ababa, with Emperor Haile Selassie as the host.

The Organization of African Unity (OAU)

Before the establishment of the OAU, African states were divided into two groups, known as the Monrovia and Casablanca groups, the first generally understood to represent pro-Western countries, while the second was said to be less so, Egypt and Ghana being the prime representatives. One of the aims of the OAU was to put to rest the division by creating a continental body to speak with one voice on behalf of all Africans. This objective has not yet been reached even today, despite several attempts.

Ever since the Accra Conference of December 1958, I watched with great interest the movement toward the establishment of a continental unifying body. I did this in an academic sense by reading and researching the subject, and actively through my involvement in helping finalize the draft OAU Charter, on the eve of the May 1963 meeting.

Being involved in finalizing a draft charter was not a decisive role by any stretch of the imagination. For one thing, the political decisions were arrived at by the heads of state; the role of lawyers was merely to provide coherence and give form to the political decisions. For another, the draft that Ethiopia was requested to write was based on an earlier Nigerian draft that had provoked division. Ethiopia, as the prospective host of the meeting, was asked to prepare a final compromise draft. The Ethiopian government appointed a drafting committee to be chaired by Getachew Kibret, head of legal affairs at the Ministry of Foreign Affairs. I joined the committee, ex officio, in my capacity as Attorney General. Other members were Seyoum Haregot, from the Prime Minister's Office, and Teshome Gebre-Mariam. Getachew made available to the committee the original draft, on which he had done commendable work. The committee, which met at the Prime Minister's office, then went over the draft, article by article and presented a final draft to the government, which circulated it to other African governments, before submitting it to the Founding Conference of the OAU on May 20, 1963.

All preparations having been completed, African leaders began to arrive in Addis Ababa, and were received at the newly constructed Bole Airport by Prime Minister Aklilu Habtewold and some of his colleagues. As the festivities began it was as though the city was on edge with political excitement: Africa had indeed come to Addis Ababa. Most of the leaders traveled by air; only one came by ship, all the way from west Africa—the President of the Ivory Coast, Houpghet Boigny, who had air travel phobia.

Two remarkable incidents come to mind. One is that when Kwame Nkrumah of Ghana arrived, an advance guard that was waiting for him slaughtered a sheep and had him step ceremonially over the blood. I was reminded of the occasion of my marriage, when one of my best men suggested that I make a similar crossing over a slaughtered goat before the wedding. I objected strenuously and persuaded my friends not to do it; and I wondered if Nkrumah's people had arranged it because he wrote and spoke about African culture. I suppose the practice, which dies hard, is meant to chase evil spirits away. I also remember that when Emperor Haile Selassie visited the Sudan, some tribesmen of an area he visited, slaughtered a bull just as he arrived at a site, and the blood came gushing out the severed neck; he was horrified, but kept his horror to himself.

The other remarkable event was the arrival of Egyptian President, Gamal Abdel Nasser. I went to the airport earlier, with some of my friends, and we found that the airport was filled with literally hundreds of thousands of people. Most of them were turbaned country folks, so it was obvious that they were Ethiopian Muslims who had come from from Harar, Jimma, Arsi, Sidamo and other distant provinces. This was not "in the books" of the government, and was an immense surprise. It was an emphatic demonstration of solidarity with the Muslim/Arab world at a time when Muslims felt excluded from government affairs in a country ruled by a Christian king.

If any one had any doubts as to the reason for this massive presence of Muslim multitudes at Bole airport, it became clear when Nasser appeared at the door of the airplane; no sooner had his tall figure appeared than the multitude voiced their feelings, shouting "NASSER! NASSER! NASSER!" I could feel the ground shaking. Nasser waved with supreme pleasure, as I could see from his smiling, charismatic face. It was a sobering experience to all who witnessed it. As the Ethiopian Prime Minister led Nasser toward the VIP reception lounge, I could see from his furrowed brow that he could not hide his displeasure.

After Nasser's arrival, other leaders came, and in each case, the orchestra played the appropriate national anthem. The dramatic high point of the arrival ceremony was Nasser; and I am sure that Nkrumah, who had expected no less a reception, was disappointed. On the other hand, in all the photos of the assembled leaders, with the host, Emperor Haile Selassie, holding the central place of honor, Nkrumah was second only to the Emperor. Nasser came next and was always urged by his colleagues to move to the center. As one group assembled, I noticed that Nasser had found himself on the left of Ben Bella of Algeria, farther away from the center whereupon, Ben Bella moved to Nasser's left and nudged Nasser toward the center.

The conference was opened with much pomp and ceremony, at the newly-built Africa Hall. To put the event in historical context, it was opened when the Pan-Africanist idea of continental unity had become popular and the period was marked by changes in international relations. The end of the European colonial rule and the rise of the Non-Aligned Movement occurred against the backdrop of an East-West rivalry for global influence and control. The United Nations, which was created to act as a harmonizing center of nations, had instead become an ideological battleground between East and West with the emergence of competing blocs in which Third World countries began to play a significant role. Their votes were sought and their friendship was cultivated by the rival global powers—the United States of America and its Western allies on the one hand, and the Soviet Bloc on the other.

All eyes were thus focused on the meeting held at Africa Hall, May 20-25, 1963; practically all governments had their diplomatic representatives or special envoys participating as observers at the conference. The gallery of the hall was filled to capacity by the international press and other observers. From the comments I heard and my readings of the press reports, it was clear to me that the media did not expect the conference to succeed in establishing the OAU, believing that African leaders were too divided to agree on creating such continental body. And who can blame them for such doubts?

How did this happen: how was Africa able to surprise the world?

First and foremost, there was the need of a common effort felt by all thoughtful Africans at a time when the continent felt the adverse effects of colonial rule and was vulnerable to the manipulation of outside forces. Even beyond Africa, Afro-Asian cooperation was sought as evidenced by the meeting held in Bandung, Indonesia, in 1959, and the concept of Third World cooperation.

Apart from such general awareness of the need for unity and cooperation, much of the success for the creation of the OAU must be attributed to personal diplomacy and leadership. In this respect, Emperor Haile Selassie occupies a central place. His elder statesman status and prestige gave him great advantage, of course, as those of us who were close enough could observe the deference with which some of the younger leaders approached his person and addressed him.

I will cite an example of the interplay of African culture and diplomacy when the Emperor employed these combined resources in the service of African unity. Nkrumah threatened to walk out of the conference when he discovered to his dismay, that his plea for a strong union of African States was rejected by the others. The conference reached a moment of crisis, one that the outside press had anticipated and perhaps hoped for—at least some of them. Several caucuses were held to resolve the crisis, but Nkrumah was adamant. When all were about to give up, the Emperor approached Sekou Toure and, holding his hand and looking him in the eye, pleaded with him to bring his brother Nkrumah back to the fold. The Emperor addressed Sekou Toure as an African father: "*Mon fils, je vous prie.*" (My son, I implore you). Sekou Toure responded as an African son, and replied: "*Oui pere, je vais essayer.*" (Yes father, I will try).

And try he did—and succeeded. He brought Nkrumah back to the fold. No one knows what the exchange was between the two leaders as they talked behind closed doors; we can only imagine. But when we consider Sekou Toure's success in bringing Nkrumah back to the fold, one reason may be that they were of the same ideological persuasion; after all, didn't Nkrumah come to Guinea's rescue with generous financial aid when the French destroyed everything as they left Guinea? Another reason had to do with Sekou Toure's powerful personality and incredible ability, as I can testify, having met him four times: once in Accra in 1958, at the 1963 conferences, and then in 1980 in Freetown during the OAU annual meeting, and lastly at Howard University when he came to visit during my academic tenure there.

Nkrumah's decision to play along and be part of the creation of the OAU was a source of much jubilation among Africans, especially my generation, which regarded African unity as a historical imperative if Africa was to progress. This sentiment was also shared widely among older generations, as I found out talking to some of the Ethiopian ministers and military officers. I remember General Isaias Gebre-Selassie telling me at a chance meeting how happy he was that Nkrumah didn't walk out. To my surprise, the general said he thought that Nkrumah's was "the only way" for Africa.

Nkrumah kept quiet through much of the Conference until the closing session, when he came back with his usual eloquence and harangued the meeting with poetic flourish. He began his closing address by reminding us that to the ancient Greeks the name Ethiopia referred to all of sub-Saharan Africa. He then waxed poetic, paying tribute to the conference host, Emperor Haile Selassie, and his people; he started by saying, "I leave you with these thoughts", and then, paraphrasing biblical passages he ended intoning, "Ethiopia shall rise/Ethiopia, beacon of African freedom/ Land of the wise, Ethiopia shall rise..." This was received with prolonged cheering and applause.

That day, I was sitting in the gallery next to a British journalist who remarked, "Nkrumah is incredible; he is now on a charm offensive." There was no love lost between Nkrumah and the British, who considered him to be a communist sympathizer and therefore inimical to their interests.

The conference was marked with some great oratory, punctuated with humor and laughter. But there were a few embarrassing moments. One such moment was when Congolese President Joseph Kasabubu referred to Emperor Haile Selassie, as "*Son Excellence, President* Haite (sic) Selassie." No sooner had he said that than a participant was heard quipping, "Kasabubu made a booboo

Another, more serious, incident that rocked the conference was when Somalia's President Aden Abdalla unexpectedly raised the Ogaden question, accusing Ethiopia as an occupying imperial power. Aklilu, the Ethiopian Prime Minister, rose to respond and as he climbed the podium one could feel the tension rising much to the joy of the international press; some were seen rushing out to send the news back to their headquarters. The Chair appealed for calm and sought ways to mediate the conflict. It was then that President Modibo Keita of Mali, the gentle giant, rose to suggest a solution; he asked for a break and the chair gratefully accepted. Modibo Keita and a couple of others, whose identities escape me, mediated a solution and the conference resumed its business.

There were many eloquent speeches. There were moments of serious challenge to the moral and intellectual sense of Africans. Ahmed Ben Bella's speech caught the African imagination by urging his brethren to speak less of banks and development and more of creating a "blood bank" to be used for the liberation of the territories still under colonial rule. He made his impassioned appeal "in the name of the one million Algerian martyrs of the revolution waged to liberate Algeria," and became an instant hero among the Addis Ababa population. The girls referred to him affectionately as *Ben Belliyye* (Darling Ben Bella). Nyerere of Tanzania, eager to impress upon the participants, said: "It shall not be written in history that the Addis Ababa meeting failed because Tanzania did not sign the proposed Charter."

In the midst of the serious business of state there was much laughter and jokes. The President of Madagascar (Malagasy) was long-winded in his address, which he punctuated with ad lib digressions that always began with "*Et ici, je fais un parenthese...* (And here, I would like to say in parenthesis)—earning himself the sobriquet of "parenthetical president" among the African literati.

There were also mutual compliments and peace-making among sworn enemies. Leopold Sedar Senghor of Senegal, who was not on speaking terms with Hophuet Boigny of Cote d'Ivoire, suddenly found himself complimented by his erstwhile adversary, who showered Senghor with compliments and offered an olive branch to the "*poete extraordinaire de la poesie francaise.*" Senghor accepted the olive branch graciously. The mood of reconciliation even affected the Ethiopian and Somali leaders.

Perhaps the most hilarious occasion occurred during the closing session of the conference. The conference organizers agreed that the closing address should be made by the newest member of the African states, which happened to be Uganda. It fell on the young Prime Minister, Milton Obote to deliver the closing address. Obote, in his eagerness to please the host government, overstepped his bounds and thanked the Ethiopian government for "looking after us day and night." The hall exploded in prolonged laughter, as some in the gallery exchanged glances seeking an explanation. But among the participating heads of state, one had been caught slumbering and was rudely awakened by the laughter. It was President Habib Bourguiba of Tunisia, and he turned to his laughing Foreign Minister Said Slim who between uncontrollable giggles whispered into

Bourguiba's ears; the latter roared with laughter again provoking another milder laughter from the rest of the audience in Africa Hall.

Why the laughter?

The Ethiopian government had indeed looked after the guests day and night. The mirth was due to the fact that the female population of the "Red Light District" in Addis Ababa had been mobilized to serve their country and Emperor under the able hand of one Aseghedech Alamiro, chief madam of the district. Nocturnal arrangements were made by which African leaders and their entourages would not feel lonely and cold at night. Quite the contrary; Africa was grateful for Ethiopia's sensitive hospitality, as food and drink flowed and all concerned had happy nights.

I cannot swear to the truth of this, but I was told by an unimpeachable source that Asegedech Alamiro and a few of her nocturnal comrades were awarded medals by His Majesty, who commended them for their service. Indeed, such service continued long after the Emperor left this Earth to join His maker in 1975. Addis Ababa and the nocturnal ladies have proven an inestimable asset in foiling any attempts to move the OAU (now the AU) to other African capitals. The complaints, whispered by attending leaders during such attempts is, "Why are they trying to deprive us of the pleasures of this hospitable city?"

The AIDs epidemic may have somewhat tempered this sentiment.

Now let me summarize the achievements of the OAU as well as its weaknesses. The draft Charter was approved with little change. The OAU adopted the UN principle of sovereignty—governments, not people, are represented by the organization. Moreover, the modern African state system, shaped by colonial history, was accepted. Thus the prohibition, by the OAU Charter, of interference in the internal affairs of a nation meant tension building up along the colonial dividing lines.

Nkrumah had advocated the creation of a United States of Africa that would transcend the colonial (and pre-colonial) legacy and transform the fragmented state system created by European intervention. He argued that the post-colonial state system would be politically divisive and economically wasteful, a contention that proved prophetic. The tension between the Pan-Africanist ideas and the fragmented state system is implicit in the compromise solution embedded in Article II of the OAU Charter, which advocates "the promotion of solidarity and cooperation" among African states, as well as the defense of their territorial integrity.

The OAU was thus a creature of compromise, reflecting the realities of an ideologically and geographically divided continent. This was in itself no mean achievement. But as a creature of compromise, the OAU tended to be all things to all governments, and its resolutions by and large have been ineffectual. Controversial issues were continually postponed for fear of a split in the organization, a condition that denied it the opportunity to exert moral authority to censure errant leaders or governments, even those engaged in grave violations of human rights, such as Idi Amin of Uganda, Mengistu of Ethiopia and Siyad Barre of Somalia.

On the credit side, the OAU could boast of some successful mediations of conflicts. The first such mediation concerned a territorial dispute between Algeria and Morocco. It was followed by other efforts in the Congo in the mid-1960s and in Nigeria in the late 1960s. In all cases the issues were clear-cut and the debates focused and coherent. "OAU Principles" of sovereignty and territorial integrity were applied with clarity and consistency, since they provided a comfort zone for African presidents and prime ministers who were ensconced in the power structures of their respective countries, which none of them wished to abandon. Poor Nkrumah! He did not appreciate this fact, engrossed as he was in his admirable ideal of African unity. Some of the African leaders even accused him of inordinate ambition to become "the first George Washington of Africa."

In Southern Africa the OAU's role was commendable. The decolonization of the former Portuguese territories of Angola, Mozambique and Guinea Bissau, saw African leaders using the OAU machinery and moral authority to good advantage. The OAU established the Liberation Committee through which financial and military assistance was channeled to the freedom fighters of those territories, while at the same time diplomatic campaigns were conducted in support of their respective causes.

The OAU fell far short of its stated objectives and periodic rhetorical commitments when it took on more complex interstate and intrastate conflicts. Its inability (or unwillingness) to mediate between Ethiopia and Somalia, or to confront the challenges posed by the developments in Eritrea and southern Sudan, are among its signal failures. On the other hand, it occasionally met challenges head-on, as it did, for example, in the Chad dispute by seating the Habre delegation to the exclusion of the Goukouni delegation in 1987. Again the divisive question of Western Sahara ended with the admission of the Sahrawi Arab Democratic Republic to OAU membership. That decision cost the OAU Morocco's membership, underscoring the risks which have caused the OAU to postpone the resolution of contentious issues for fear of a split.

I have attended a few annual meetings of the OAU. I have also studied the role of the organization in an academic context, from a detached perspective. My overall conclusion of its performance is thus viewed in a larger historical perspective. The OAU played its role against a background of a fragmented postcolonial state system with a troubled economy, famine, war and political unrest. All of these factors have undermined Africa's confidence and dampened the earlier enthusiasm. In almost all states, perceived national or domestic needs have dictated harmful policies, including costly militarization. Such conditions do not foster bold moves in the settlement of disputes, but instead induce caution and inaction.

The OAU was changed into the African Union (AU) in 2002, with a new Charter. It is too early to tell whether the new organization will fare better than its predecessor; but it surely cannot do worse. The success or failure of the new organization will hinge on its response to the popular demands for democratic change being made against a backdrop of the global economic revolution, which undermines the very sovereignty principle on which the state system is based.

Moving Toward a Critical Moment

While the drama of continental African politics was being played out with the OAU as the harmonizing center for common policies, the effect of the dramatic developments was felt in Ethiopia, particularly in student politics and among the intellectual elite. Meanwhile, my own life was getting more complicated as I continued in my work at the Ministry of Justice and at the same time was involved in the underground movement. I continued in helping the labor movement and kept my contacts with military officers. With Takele's detention and banishment to distant Jimma, the group of "conspirators" formed under his leadership, of which I was a member, had been dealt a devastating blow. I had broken any association with the Eritrean underground (Cell of Seven) following the arrest of its leader and many members in Addis Ababa.

Fortunately for me, none of the members of the cell with which I was associated were arrested. But one of the arrested Eritreans was an older man with whom I had exchanged some confidences and who I knew to be the person responsible for purchasing arms to be dispatched to would-be freedom fighters in Eritrea. The man's name was Fitawrari Manna Adhanom. This was around the time when stories were heard about Hamid Idris Awate leading a new armed organization called the Eritrean Liberation Front (ELF). The civil resistance was being transformed into an armed struggle, and the arrest of the Cell of Seven members drove some of the remaining members into the arms of the ELF. As it turned out later, Fitawrari Manna was tortured severely by the police but did not reveal any name of his associates. I had been spared the humiliation of arrest and torture, thanks to the heroic resistance of Fitawrari Manna, for nothing could have spared me that fate, had I been exposed by him. Indeed, the fact that I occupied a high government post would have made things worse for me.

In September 1963, I traveled to Dar-es-Salaam, Tanzania, to attend a conference on African customary law. I had also been invited by the British Council to visit Britain as guest of the government. The visit followed the Dar-es-Salaam conference, so I made arrangements to continue to London. While I was in England, labor unrest occurred in Ethiopia and one of the leaders with whom I had met on several occasions, committed suicide, thus infusing more drama into an already dramatic situation. When government inspectors and the police began investigating the causes of the unrest and the circumstances of the suicide, my name came up as one of the people clandestinely helping the labor movement. An inside informant told this to Teshome Gebremariam, a lawyer who was well-disposed toward me. Teshome informed my wife, Koki, and advised that I should stay abroad until matters cooled off. In the absence of today's instant communication system, there was no way Koki could relay the message to me. But even if she had, I would not have heeded the counsel but would have instead returned to face the music.

By the time I returned to Addis Ababa, two weeks had passed and the labor unrest had been resolved. Koki told me of Teshome's information and I immediately contacted Colonel Dawit Gebru, Assistant Minister of Social Affairs, in charge of labor matters. Colonel Dawit did not tell me the whole story; he indicated that my name had indeed come up, but that he himself had investigated the matter and found no evidence to suggest that I had instigated the labor unrest. He did, however, ominously hint (with typical Amharic ambiguity) that "Higher Powers" were interested in the story and that I should be careful. That, coming from an experienced police officer and a decent man, was enough warning. "Higher Powers" meant, of course, His Imperial Majesty, and I knew I would be shadowed by his special security. I therefore made a decision to keep my head down and lie low. As far as labor was concerned, the four college students had taken over and were doing a good job helping the labor movement to stand on its own feet; I did not need to meet any of the labor leaders at night, as I used to. I also stopped meeting military officers.

As for the rump of the "conspiratorial committee," which remained headless and disoriented after Takele's arrest, I only met a few members selectively and individually. One of them, a businessman and former diplomat, kept the link with Takele through personal couriers. It was one of these couriers who brought me a short letter from Takele marked "Top Secret. To be opened only by His Excellency, the Attorney General." This was, as I have already said, the letter in which Takele used the ambiguous Amharic literary style known as *Semnna Work* (Wax and Gold) to inform me that we had been betrayed by one of the members. His intention was to warn me and, through me, the others to lie low. And lie low I did, having duly conveyed his message to the others.

Meanwhile, the arrest and detention of the members of the Cell of Seven had the effect of cutting my contacts with any members of the Eritrean underground. Our attention was now focused on finding ways to spare the detainees any torture. To that end a task force was formed, headed by young women who knew their way in police circles, to carry bottles of whisky to the main investigators as an incentive to go easy on the detainees. Naturally, a part of me hoped this would work, not only to save the poor young detainees from torture, but also to prevent my own exposure. I confess that I had no qualms about spirits being smuggled in to the police officers. Whether some of the young women did something extra in addition to the "spiritual" incentive, I will never know, but I wouldn't be surprised if they did, knowing the character of some of the investigating officers.

A couple of Eritrean elders approached me with the idea of organizing a committee of elders to petition His Majesty to grant amnesty to the detainees. The leader of the group was Bashai Tedla Zewoldi, who was always in the forefront at social occasions such as funerals and weddings. He convinced me that a properly written petition hand-carried by General Isaias Gebre-Selassie, would

result in the release of the detainees, because the Emperor was always looking for occasions that would show him at his most magnanimous, especially now that he was being called "Africa's Father." I agreed to draft the petition and to talk to General Isaias, all of which I did. When General Isaias saw the petition, he teased me about my becoming a real *debtera* and agreed to talk to the Emperor and present the petition. Meanwhile, Bashai Tedla organized a committee of Eritrean elders, composed of both Christian and Muslim leaders. And just as he had predicted, the Emperor responded to the petition and amnestied the detainees.

Meanwhile, my life at the ministry of justice had reached a critical point. As I said before, I had discussed an academic future teaching at the newly established law school. I approached Professor James C. N. Paul and he was very eager to have me join his faculty, provided that I obtain release from the government, which was the sticky wicket.

I then approached Bitwoded Asfaha, the Minister of Justice. I had earlier tried to resign because of the obstacles placed in my way as Attorney General, but he had persuaded me to rethink my decision. Now I explained to him that I had been offered a teaching position at the new law school, on the condition that I obtain a release from the government. Is it not better to help prepare future judges and lawyers than to be confined in an office, however important the office? I asked him rhetorically.

I remember his eyes lighting up, at that point. "That's it," he said, "that's the route we should take." He asked me to write a short application addressed to the Emperor making the same argument, and he promised to submit the letter himself.

Weeks passed, then months, and no response came from the Emperor. When I asked Bitwoded Asfaha about it, he was evasive and eventually started avoiding me. So I concluded that I would never get a response. The dean of the law school had meanwhile obtained a fellowship for me to spend a year doing research at the University of California at Los Angeles (UCLA). The fellowship was awarded annually by the Beverly Hills Bar Association to an African scholar to research on a subject of his choice. I decided to accept the offer and asked Dean Paul to go ahead and take care of all the necessary arrangements. When I mentioned the matter to Bitwoded Asfaha, at first he was inclined to go against accepting the offer before I got my release from the government. But when I urged him further, he came up with an interesting idea. He said he would grant me temporary leave from the ministry to accept the fellowship, if we had a "gentleman's agreement" that I would return to my position if and when ordered to do so by the government. He said he would continue asking His Majesty for the necessary release, but that unless and until I obtained it I must consider myself under an obligation to return to my government post.

Thus Bitwoded Asfaha put me under an obligation. He gambled on the strength of his knowledge of my family and my own history that I would not break my word. As I said before, he knew and respected my father. Bitwoded

Asfaha was taking a risk, but I also knew that because the Emperor liked and trusted him, nothing would happen to him. After all, he had delivered Eritrea to the empire on a silver platter and was awarded the high honor of acquiring the royal title of Bitwoded (The Beloved One). In fact our relationship was a complex one: as an elder, I paid him due respect, but as one who was instrumental in ending Eritrea's autonomous status under the federation, I had difficulty in dealing with him. Our difficult relationship was softened by his tremendous sense of humor as well as his unfailing kindness to ordinary people, which I observed during our brief work together.

What remained for me to do then was to plan my exit carefully, without arousing suspicion or drawing the attention of what we called the *Kerkedions*— the imperial security service. At last, I was getting out of a phase of my life that was too intense and too overcrowded to afford me any quiet haven of reflection. I was now getting ready to move on to a more leisurely life in which there was a promise of fulfillment. Academic life had always appealed to me, and now I was taking the first steps toward its realization.

The prospect of going to the United States of America on a fellowship excited me and I looked forward to my journey. True to his promise, Jim Paul, the quintessential "fixer of things," had made all the necessary arrangements. It was not for nothing that his old friend, Professor Murray Schwartz of the UCLA Law School, described Jim Paul as "the greatest salesman in the world." It did not take him long to persuade the appropriate personnel at the United States Information Agency (USIA) to invite me as an honored guest and thus pay for my transportation. I was therefore able to go ahead of my family, on an official visit, before settling in Los Angeles and starting my fellowship at UCLA.

The soft-spoken and amiable Jim Paul took care of everything, including tickets for my wife Koki and our two-year old son, Asgede. Everything was arranged, but anything could happen to wreck our plan. The Emperor could, without advance notice, send me packing to a distant province as governor or appoint me as ambassador to the USSR, which was where he sent those who fell out with him (e.g., fellow Eritrean lawyer, Dr Lorenzo Taezaz in 1946). I warned Jim Paul to be prepared for surprises: that anything could happen in Abyssinia (a pejorative term for Ethiopia, which we used in a spirit of self-deprecation). But Jim was impervious to doubt or pessimism; he was convinced that nothing would happen. He told me that he had spoken to the Justice Minister, Bitwoded Asfaha who was favorable to the idea of my joining the Law Faculty. It is not Asfaha I am worried about, I said to him. I know, he said, but even *up there*, there will be no objection, he reassured me.

"These Americans," I thought. "They are ever optimistic; no wonder they are leading (misleading?) the world in all things." I remained cautious; what did Jim Paul know about the inner working of Habesha politics?

I waited until the Emperor was out of the country attending the second OAU summit in Cairo in July 1964. Then, one fine day in July, I packed my bags and headed for Bole airport.

Chapter 11

FROM GOVERNMENT TO ACADEMIA... AND MORE POLITICS

Very few people knew I was leaving. I had decided not to reveal the date of my depature even to Bitwoded Asfaha; the less he knew, I throught, the better for him, in the event the Emperor inquired into the matter. Asfaha had been considerate to me despite the fact that he knew the Emperor was not well-disposed toward me, for reasons he kept close to his chest. I doubt if Asfaha was aware of my underground activities, but I suspected that the Emperor knew, at the very least of my involvement in Takele's group. There was a love-hate relationship between the Emperor and Takele, going back to the Italian occupation era and Takele's fame as a guerilla leader (*Arbegna*). At the time I left Addis Ababa, Takele was living in banishment in distant Jimma. There was no way I could contact him and bid him goodbye, much as I wished to.

A couple of trusted friends took me by car to the airport. Once we were at the airport, I insisted that they leave me at the departure gate without any fuss or ceremony. I did not want any friends or relatives to come crowding to see me off noisily and tearfully and thus arouse curiosity among the ubiquitous and invisible government security agents. But once in the departure lounge, I was caught by one Graham Tyer, a correspondent for the British Broadcasting Corporation (BBC), an inquisitive man whom I had known when he was a teacher in one of the local high schools. Graham wanted to interview me on a controversial subject of criminal procedure called the *Afersata*, the traditional method of crime detection, sometimes also referred to as *Awchachigne*.

I showed reluctance to being interviewed on a subject that I was leaving for a long time, especially at an airport while I was waiting for my flight. Graham never took no for an answer. "It will only take ten minutes of your time. Come on, be a sport, old boy." He would not let me go, and I rather liked him, so I agreed to do the interview. I explained to Graham the origin, use and abuse of this traditional procedure of crime detection, a communal method of investigation in which the entire village where a crime is alleged to have been committed is called to assemble, by the governor, then forced to remain in one place, deprived of food and rest, until they ferret out the offender.

"This is an outmoded method and has now been superceded by the new Criminal Procedure Code. Why are you interested in it?" I asked Graham. He said that an uncle of one of his former students was a victim of the procedure and was in jail awaiting trial. The governor of the district used the *afersata* to victimize the boy's uncle, and Graham in fact had advised him to go to my office and petition.

"Well, good luck to him, because I will be away for quite sometime," I informed Graham. He wanted to know where I was going and I told him I was a guest of the USIS, which had the effect of stopping the conversation. Graham, a left-wing intellectual was averse to anything American. Soon, my flight was announced, and I boarded the Ethiopian Airlines flight to Nairobi.

I decided to spend some time in East Africa, on my way to the United States. My principal reason was to have a clear sense of the emerging post-colonial reality in my part of the world. I wanted to deepen my knowledge of African politics and law with a view to getting a graduate degree before I settled down to a teaching career. I was also in need of rest after years of ceaseless work at the Ministry of Justice, which gave me no respite.

In Nairobi I was guest of Tom Mboya, Minister of Constitutional Affairs, who introduced me to some of his colleagues in the Cabinet of President Jomo Kenyatta. One of these was Mr. Charles Njonjo, the Attorney General, who was known among his peers as the black Englishman. Educated at Fort Hare, South Africa, he revered all things British and wore pin stripes and carried a rolled umbrella all the time. He was so stiff that I felt a draft of the north winds hitting me. Tom sensed my dislike of the Njonjo and, as soon as we left his office, Tom told me that despite his affectations and English mannerisms, he was not a bad man at heart. Nonetheless, I did not wish to see him again. I was told later that Njonjo never flew in an airplane piloted by an African. This could be an exaggeration, but my informant swore to its veracity.

I did see other Ministers and political leaders, notably the colorful and charismatic Oginga Odinga. Odinga was the number-two man in the ruling party, the Kenya African National Union (KANU), and a presumptive heir to the presidency. Ironically, it was my friend Mboya (a fellow Luo), who was seen as the real successor to that exalted office, which was why he was eventually assassinated, presumably by jealous rivals in the KANU hierarchy. Mboya was a brilliant speaker as well as indefatigable organizer, and a favorite of western powers. Odinga was suspected of harboring communist leanings, and of being favorable to China. When I raised this point to Mboya once, he dismissed it as the propaganda of Odinga's enemies. He did not reveal the names of these "enemies"; nor did he give any inkling of his own rivalry with Odinga. Mboya was nothing if not shrewd.

I would again encounter Odinga two years later, in London, where he came to promote the publication of his book, *Not Yet Uhuru*. The South African writer and anti-apartheid activist, Ruth First, then living in exile in London, who was helping him in writing the book, arranged our meeting. I had become good friends with Ruth and her husband, Joe Slovo, who was one of the ANC leaders, and they both suggested that I should meet Odinga whom they respected.

Odinga was a delightful man—a hearty type who spoke his mind and was not afraid to say he was on the side of the people. I was impressed by his commitment to social justice and democracy in Kenya and the rest of the continent. *Not Yet Uhuru*, the title of his book, was also the theme of our conversation in which he decried the corruption and abuse of power of African governments. He did not mince his words, even when he talked about his leader, Kenyatta, and his coterie of sycophants and supporters, who were for the most part Kikuyu.

An unexpected meeting occurred in Kenya that would cause a detour in my travel itinerary. I ran into Haileab Tseggai and his Yugoslav bride-to-be, Biba, at the Ethiopian Embassy, Nairobi. A manager of Shell Oil in Dar-es-Salaam at the time, Haileab is a distant relative and one of my favorite Eritreans. He introduced me to Biba and then demanded (no less) that I be his best man. I had to comply—tribal custom and all that! After the wedding, we drove to Tanzania and spent the night at Moshi, listening to African music practically all night. We then headed to Lake Maniara and Ngorongoro Crater. We stayed at the Lake Maniara Hotel where we ran into Mr. Charlie Chaplin and his large family. Chaplin looked the picture of contentment, lying on a deck chair and reading a novel. He returned my greeting and invited us to join him and his family for tea, which we respectfully declined.

After spending a few magical days in this tourist paradise, we were on our way to Dar-es-Salaam, where I spent a few more days, swimming at the beach and in the evenings meeting old friends and making new ones, including the young, newly appointed Tanzanian Attorney General and members of the law faculty. Haileab mixed with the social elite, both Tanzanian and foreign, and he entertained many of these in his house where I met them. I asked to see President Nyerere, whom I had met before, but I was told he was out of town.

From Dar I flew to Uganda, by way of Nairobi. I was interested to meet people at Makerere College and also see old friends. Among them was Professor Colin Leys, with whom I became a life-long friend, although we did not see each other for many years. I also met my class mate from England, Freddie Mpanga, who was special legal counsel of the Kabaka (King) of Buganda, Frederick Mutesa II. Mpanga took me to the hotel where all the elites socialized, including the then Prime Minister (later President) Milton Obote. Those were the good old days when politics was a gentlemanly affair and politicians were approachable and popular, before the advent of the ugly political era, epitomized by Idi Amin.

Freddie introduced me to Obote, who was engaged in a chat with one Okello. He asked us to join him, and after we were through with the banalities of African mutual greetings, I reminded him of the closing speech he had delivered at the founding conference of the OAU in Addis Ababa, whereupon his face lit up and he forgot his chat with Okello and started telling the story of his "day and night" remarks. When he finished telling his story, everyone roared with laughter, except Okello.

Okello was the illiterate soldier of fortune who led the uprising that had overthrown the Sultan of Zanzibar a few months earlier. Tanzanian statesman, Mohamed Abdulrahman Babu, who was one of the organizers of the revolution, told me later that the Americans suspected that the Chinese had been involved in the revolution in Zanzibar and were doing all they could to counter them. According to Babu, a native of Zanzibar, who was pro-China, all the assistance lavished on Tanzania from US-AID and the World Bank was actuated by this strategy.

Kampala completed the circle of my East African tour. I had been aware of the British colonial policy of encouraging a regional cooperation, with a common currency and common market. Even in social services, there was a regional distribution of services. Under this policy, for instance, Makerere College in Kampala took care of medical education. This policy was inherited by the new independent governments of Kenya, Tanzania and Uganda and was still being followed when I visited the region in the summer of 1964. It would change later due to personality clashes as well as resentment of Kenya's disproportionate share of the resources.

I left Kampala reluctantly, but I was expected by my hosts to be in the United States by mid-August. I had spent a fruitful and enjoyable time in Kampala, considered by many to be the pearl of Africa. I had exchanged ideas about my future research with scholars like Colin Leys and Freddie Mpanga. I also picked up useful material on law and politics. I did the same on my next leg of the trip—Ghana and Senegal—on my way to the United States.

New York—My First Encounter with America

I arrived at the recently renamed John F. Kennedy International Airport, on a warm, sunny August day. I had seen busy airports before, but this one was in a class all its own. I cleared immigration easily, with nobody asking me why I came to the United States. The young immigration officer perusing my Ethiopian passport simply said, "You are from the land of Abebe Bikila. Welcome to the United States."

What a wonderful discovery, I thought—an athlete eclipsing a world-famous Emperor and displacing him in the pantheon of celebrities! Long live the Olympiads!

Once past the immigration zone, I saw hundreds of people, some standing with eager faces looking for arriving passengers, others milling around the arrival corridor. As a guest of the United States Information Agency, I knew I would be met; and sure enough, I saw a man carrying a placard, with my name written in large letters. Seeing me walking toward him, he greeted me with a smile.

"Would you be Mr. Bereket?" he asked.

"I would," I said, and off we went.

After a little under an hour, I was deposited in a nice hotel in Manhattan, where I was given a couple of messages and a sealed envelope, along with the key to my room. Once I was settled, I opened the envelope. There was a note of welcome written by the appropriate official of my host agency, attached to a copy of the itinerary of my US tour. After a couple of hours' sleep, I climbed down the carpeted stairs leading to the restaurant, before I went out to experience my first night in New York. At the entrance of the restaurant a young black waiter dressed in a smart hotel uniform welcomed me with a broad smile, and ushered me toward a table. He gave me a menu and launched on a gastronomic sermon about the day's special. I told him I'd prefer choosing from the menu. I reviewed the menu and settled on a New York steak.

Some remarks are so striking that one remembers the exact words. Upon hearing my Afro-British accent, the waiter said, "you talk quaint, where you from?"

"Ethiopia," I said. Judging from the vacant expression on his face and lack of response, I gathered that the name did not ring a bell

After I finished eating my dinner, topping it with a delicious apple pie, the waiter came with the check and I gave him a fifty-dollar bill. He came back with the change, which included a silver dollar that he slowly placed on the table, separate from the rest of the change. When I pocketed the silver dollar with the rest of the change, he looked at me and, in mock disappointment, said, "Well, I gambled and lost, didn't I?"

"No you didn't," I said and tipped him with two dollar bills. "I want the silver dollar as a memento, that's all." He took the tip, smiling broadly and I stepped out into the streets of New York City. New York is indescribable, especially at night. It is trite to say that there is nothing else like it in the whole world. My hotel was five blocks from Times Square and, after a few minutes' walk I was overwhelmed by the glittering neon lights, and by the motley crowd walking and talking excitedly, against a background of incessant traffic. I was awed by the buildings that seemed to touch the sky; no wonder they call them skyscrapers! Not since I first stepped inside the Cathedral of Santa Maria del Fiore of Florence (The Dome) in 1954, had I felt this feeling of insignificance at the sight of human creation.

I walked for miles, enjoying the sights and sounds, absorbing the magic of my first night in New York, strolling along wide avenues that were teeming with people. I have no recollection of how long I walked, or how far, but I do remember that I had to take a taxi to get back to my hotel long after midnight. According to my itinerary, I was to be picked up early the next morning, by a guide commissioned by the host agency to take me to some historic landmark. I was deeply conscious of the fact that in mixing pleasure with duty, I should be aware of the need to be punctual and alert the following day, which would be the first day of my tour.

A Bird's Eye View of America

The itinerary was well-conceived, stretching over four weeks and covering different parts of the United States. There was a delicate balance between visiting historic sights and important institutions as well as meeting important people. Starting in New York, I visited the Ford Foundation and the African-American Institute and met with people involved in them. Jim Paul joined me in some of these visits, especially the Ford Foundation. He had made an arrangement with the USIA to converge his visit with mine. He was interested in building a law library for the newly opened Addis Ababa Law School, of which he was Dean, and he thought that our joint visit to some of these institutions like the Ford Foundation would be helpful. Wherever we went, he began by introducing me as the "youngest Attorney General in the world." I then remembered how his friend, Murray Schwartz, had characterized him as the best salesman in the world. It was my first view of the world of foundations and institutes, of how they operate and how fund-raising is done by the likes of Jim Paul.

Jim was committed to raising funds for the new Addis Law School, especially the library. Indeed, as a result of Jim's persuasion, Judge Charles Weizanski, a member of the Board of Governors of the Foundation, had already traveled to Addis Ababa to study the "absorption capacity" of the institution seeking the funding. I had met Weizanski at the home of Jim Paul during his visit a few months earlier. He was an urbane man who, upon learning that I had studied law in England, engaged me in long anecdotes about English judges. He particularly liked to talk about the legendary Lord Denning, hero of all students of English law.

Another person I remember who was helpful during these visits was Wayne Frederick whom I had also met in Adds Ababa. I thought he was an official of the State Department in Washington, but for some reason he was in New York and helped facilitate contacts with funding sources. Then there was Harris Wofford who must have persuaded my hosts to carve up a portion of my tour to introduce me to a different aspect of America—the world of politics. The organizers of my tour had included a visit to the Democratic Party Convention, in Atlantic City, New Jersey. Harris met me at the Convention and introduced me to many of the principal actors in the Party. There Harris introduced me to some of the principal players, including Bobby Kennedy, United States Attorney General, who was having a reception. From our Addis Ababa days, Harris knew me not to like VIP receptions. He thought I would raise objections to attending Kennedy's, and was pleasantly surprised to find me receptive to the idea. In fact I was enthusiastic, because I admired the Kennedy family for their position on the race issue. He had argued that I was still Ethiopia's Attorney General and it would be interesting for him to meet me and vice versa.

"Say no more," I had told him, "I would be happy to meet him."

Our meeting with Bobby Kennedy was brief, because it seemed as though the whole world was there, lining up to greet Kennedy and his wife, Ethel. I couldn't help comparing the occasion to a reception at Buckingham Palace, or the Emperor's Gibbi in Ethiopia. There the Kennedy couple stood, like a royal couple, receiving homage from their subjects; the only thing missing was a crown. Our turn came; Bobby said "Hello Harris." Harris pointed to me and said, "Mr. Attorney General, I would like you to meet Bereket Habte Selassie, Attorney General of Ethiopia"

"So glad to meet you, sir," Bobby said, shaking my hand with a broad smile, then turned to his wife: "Ethel, the Attorney General of Ethiopia." Ethel smiled graciously and shook my hand. Harris said, "I would like to bring him to meet you at your convenience."

"Sure, Harris, any time. I would be very glad to do that. Call my secretary to arrange a meeting."

Meanwhile, the pressure from the people behind us was becoming unbearable; people literally breathing down our necks and pushing us. We moved forward and the ceremony continued.

The 1964 Democratic Convention was really a coronation. Lyndon Johnson had been President for nine months, following John F. Kennedy's assassination in November 1963. The country was not as yet against the Vietnam War. The Kennedy magic had rubbed off on Johnson, and the Democratic Party was scaling the heights in the opinion polls. There was no question but that the Convention would choose Johnson to be the candidate for the 1964 election. The drama really centered on the question of who would be his running mate, and Johnson had kept the suspense up to the last moment. The announcement came toward the end, with characteristic flourish; the running mate was Hubert Humphrey.

Outside the convention hall, demonstrators held up placards, saying "Bobby Go Home." The demonstrators were supporters of Jimmy Hoffa, President of the Teamsters Union, whom Bobby Kennedy had investigated for alleged Mafia connections. I was curious to know why they were telling him to "go home," and Harris gave me a long explanation about the "carpetbaggers" in the past, who came from New England to the South and were not welcome.

1964 was an election year, and we saw posters of Barry Goldwater, the senator from Arizona who was the Republican Party candidate for the presidency. Under the picture of Goldwater, a caption read:

"*In your heart, you know he is right.*" And under the caption, someone had scrawled:

"*Yes, extreme Right.*" I pointed to the poster and Harris said, "Welcome to American election politics."

In Chicago, I stayed at the home of my friend Don Levine and his wife, Joanna. The couple took me to musical events and Don introduced me to some of his colleagues at the University of Chicago, including Lloyd Fallers, whose book, "*Bantu Bureaucracy,*" I would read later with great interest. Don and Joanna hosted a dinner in my honor, to which they invited academics such as Edward Shils, the renowned political theorist. I also visited the law school and discussed constitutional law, including aspects of civil rights. Don and Joanna then drove me from Chicago to Detroit, where Joanna's parents lived. It was a memorable ride, my first tour by car to any part of the United States, which gave me an idea of the wealth of the country. I remember in particular the lunch we had at Kalamazoo, Michigan, an area where agriculture experts experimented with the Ethiopian native grain, *teff.*

Back in Washington, I visited the Department of State, as well as the Attorney General's office and the Supreme Court. At the Justice Department, Jim Paul and I were received by Burke Marshall, the Assistant Attorney General for Civil Rights, who apologized on behalf of Robert Kennedy who was traveling. Marshall was very courteous and warm. We then saw Charles Runyon of the Office of the Legal Advisor at State. At the Supreme Court, Jim, who had clerked for one of the Supreme Court justices and was familiar with the place, took me to meet Chief Justice Earl Warren. Warren, whom I had met in Addis Ababa during his short visit a couple of years earlier, was a gracious man. He invited us to attend a reception held a few days later, and it was there that I first met the Sudanese lawyer and scholar, Dr. Zaki Mustapha. Zaki was the 1963 Visiting Fellow at UCLA Law School, just before me. He and I would become life-long friends, and I would later ask him to be a member of the External Advisory Board of the Constitutional Commission of Eritrea.

Most of the memories of my visit were pleasant, but there were a couple of unpleasant incidents. One occurred at a dinner party at the home of a friend of Jim Paul's who will remain nameless. My wife and I were guests together with Jim, at the dinner party of this very good couple. They had two children—a boy and a girl—aged about sixteen and seventeen respectively whom the parents introduced to us. Dinner was served and we had sat down for coffee and chat when the boy started launching into verbal attacks on his mother. Every time the mother spoke, he would make fun of her. He would turn to his sister and laughing, ask, "Did you hear her?" The sister would answer, "Yes, I did; she thinks she is intellectual" or words to that effect, and they would roar with laughter.

My wife and I looked at each other in shock and amazement. Everyone except the parents was embarrassed. Apparently, the poor parents were used to it. On our way back to the hotel, Jim said something to the effect that these were the products of Dr. Spock's doctrine of leaving children free to do whatever they liked. Jim was obviously embarrassed. It was our first view of a part of American social life that I would see more often in later years, a dysfunctional family.

Years later, I met the father who had since retired from government service and asked him about his family. He said they were all doing well. The son had taken up some vocational work and was happy with his work. So, it seems it all worked out in the end.

The other incident had to do with an obnoxious man at Harvard. I don't remember his name or exact title at the university, but he had something to do with receiving visitors. I had been at the office of the Attorney General of Massachusetts the late Edward Brooke who later became a United States senator. My next appointment was with the obnoxious type, but I was delayed at the Attorney

General's office and was about twenty minutes late. As I was entering his office and before I could apologize and explain my absence, the man exploded into an angry tirade. First off, as I was ushered in by his secretary, he bellowed, "You are late!" at the top of his voice. I was so stunned that I did not even respond. He called his secretary and told her to make another appointment.

The poor secretary was embarrassed and made excuses for his behavior. Quite frankly, I don't remember what his excuse was, and I didn't care. Perhaps he had an irate wife waiting for him at home, or had a stomach ulcer. At any rate, I kept calm and said to her not to worry, but I was boiling inside. I couldn't wait till I got out to the open air.

On the day that I was supposed to see him, I gave him a taste of his own medicine—I decided to ignore him; to keep him waiting one more time, visualizing him stewing in his own gall and fulminating. I am generally well disposed to people and forgiving of their weaknesses; but not this time. I had heard of racist behavior in the South; I did not expect it from a man in the top University in New England, the place of enlightenment. It became a talk of Harvard Square, Cambridge, Mass., at least among the circles that heard about the incident, including the community of Ethiopian students. Among the latter, opinion was divided between those who said, I did the right thing—"the bastard deserved what he got"—and those, a minority and probably a wise minority, who thought I should have honored the second appointment.

According to the minority opinion, typified by my old friend Dr Abraha Tedla, I did not need to go down to his level, and I did just that by staying away and probably made him happy. If I had kept the appointment, he would have been shamed into admitting his bad behavior. What this counsel of the wise missed was my own feeling at the time and the temper of the times. We are talking about a time when racial prejudice was the norm in America and I was not prepared to stomach any of that. If it was a mistake on my part, all I can say now is that everyone has a right to make a mistake, if not to repeat it!

In Cambridge, Mass. I was invited by Ethiopian student leader, Ephrem Isaac, now professor at Princeton, to address the Ethiopian students, which I did. I spoke about the administration of justice in Ethiopia. Ephrem Isaac and his friends would pursue me later after I settled at UCLA asking for a repeat performance. In fact it was the start of my involvement in student politics that would last for many years. Ethiopian students in North America (ESUNA) would ask me to chair their annual meeting in Cambridge the following year and it would be one of the charges leveled at me by the Emperor's government later. ESUNA was spearheading the Ethiopian student movement at the time, which became more and more radical.

Between Research and Student Politics in America

My tour of the United States lasted four weeks, from August 9 to September 7. Now it was time to begin my one-year fellowship at the UCLA Law School.

Jim Paul, who had returned to Addis Ababa, brought my wife and two-year old son to the USA with him. My friend General Aman Andom, whom Emperor Haile Selassie had exiled as a military attaché in Washington, took me to Dulles airport to meet them. Jim's father was also there to meet us. Jim had told his parents of our coming and they wanted us to spend a weekend at their retirement home in Easton on the Maryland shore. Before my family's arrival, I had spent some time with Aman and his family in Washington DC. But the day after my family's arrival, Jim insisted that we go to his parents' home, where we spent a memorable time, swimming in the lake and talking about war and peace, among other things. Jim's father liked showing old pictures of his days as a soldier in Europe during World War I. I wondered if he became a Quaker because of the experience of that war; I never asked, and neither Jim Paul nor his parents volunteered. It was enough for me that they were among the kindest and most decent people I ever had the pleasure to meet. I am certain that Jim's amiable disposition and his passion for justice and peace were influenced by his Quaker upbringing.

A few days' later, I was off to Los Angeles with my wife Koki and our son Asgede. We were met at the airport by an agent of UCLA who took us to our residence, a two bedroom apartment in Santa Monica. It would be our home for a year. Public transportation being what it was in Los Angeles, I had to buy a car. A few days after our arrival, I bought a second hand 1958 Chevy. Next, I had to take a driving test, which I passed on my first attempt.

Thus settled more or less comfortably, I began my research fellowship at the UCLA Law School in September 1964. I was introduced to the faculty, which at the time was headed by Dean Maxwell. Three members of the faculty and their spouses became our very good friends. One was Murray Schwartz, a popular Professor of Criminal Law and an old friend of Jim Paul's. Murray and his gracious wife, Audrey, went out of their way to make me and my family feel welcome. Another couple was Leon and Alita Letwin, who also happened to be our neighbors. Alita was very helpful to Koki and we exchanged visits in each other's homes. Their three boys were a delight. Asgede was a couple of years younger than their youngest son and their eldest son looked after Asgede and played with him with patience. Another delightful couple, with whom we became very good friends, were David Mellinkoff and his wife, Ruth.

I also had good relationships with three other members of the faculty, although we did not become close. They were: Don Hagman, Herbert Morris and Norm Abrams. Don and Eileen Hagman hosted us in their home in the San Fernando Valley on one memorable occasion. And I used to enjoy frequent conversations with Herb and Norm. Our talk combined serious discussion with humorous jousting, with Herb and Norm frequently poking fun at each other.

I began my research on African customary law and the role of the judiciary in that respect. My fellowship did not require me to take any courses, but I attended Murray Schwartz's classes during part of the fall semester. I also attended seminars, including one given by Norm Abrams on criminal procedure, focused on post-conviction remedy. Otherwise, I was left to do pretty much what I wished with my fellowship time. I found out that I had made a false start with customary law and the judiciary, although the research and reading I did was useful for my future doctoral dissertation. By the time I enrolled in the Ph.D. program at the School of Oriental and African Studies (SOAS) of the University of London, in September 1965, I had decided to do research on constitutional development in Africa, with a focus on the Executive. I had shifted the focus of my research and reading to that subject, by mid-1965.

My year at UCLA, and in Los Angeles in general, gave me a welcome opportunity to explore many aspects of American life and culture. Admittedly, Los Angeles is not necessarily representative of the rest of America; but it does include Hollywood, and America is viewed by much of the world through the prism of Hollywood. To add irony to my own advent to the City of Angels, my fellowship funds came from the Beverly Hills Bar Association, a fact that was the source of much teasing by my friends since Beverly Hills is where many of Hollywood stars live. When my friends asked if I enjoyed Hollywood parties, I answered that I was never invited, adding that I was a happily married man, thank you very much.

The only people who did not tease me were David and Ruth Mellinkoff. David had been a successful attorney for some of the residents of Beverly Hills, and he thought that money from such a source was money well spent. And he added once, with a twinkle in his eyes, it is money well spent, provided the beneficiary is worthy of the fellowship. I became very close to David and Ruth and, on several occasions, several years later, stayed as their guest at their lovely home near the UCLA campus. David's book, *The Language of the Law* influenced my thinking on law and legal drafting, as it did a generation of legal practitioners.

While at UCLA, I corresponded with Jim Paul who kept me abreast of developments back at the Addis Ababa Law School. He also gave me tidbits of local gossip of Addis Ababa, including what was being said about me. For instance, in a letter written in October 1964, Jim mentioned a "short talk" with Bitwoded Asfafa, the Minister of Justice, who complained to him about my departure to America without bidding him farewell. Jim advised me to write to him and explain my hurried departure. Other news concerned the publication in the *Ethiopian Herald* of an article I had written. In March 5, 1965, Jim wrote:

> Your article in the UCLA paper was reprinted in the Herald here. You caused a stir in some quarters, for it was felt that you were critical of the codes, and since your identification with HSU (Haile Selassie University) was also published, we got some criticism here.

Jim then advised me to be cautious and to give the HSU Law School advance notice. Until the summer of 1966, I did not publish anything more. But the article I published in July 1966 in *the Journal of African Law* was to be one of the causes for my troubles later.

1965 was a year when the first protests against the Vietnam War were heard in the USA.

The early and mid-1960s were also the time when the Civil Rights movement was gathering momentum, with the Reverend Martin Luther King being recognized as the leader. It was while I lived in Los Angeles that the Watts Town Riots took place. Two incidents occurred affecting me in the wake of the Watts Town riots, which are of interest. The first was a chance meeting I had with the poet Langston Hughes at the home of an elderly African-American couple whose names escape me. I was invited to their home because the nephew of an Ethiopian friend of mine was living with them. The lady of the house added, presumably as an incentive that Langston Hughes, an old friend of theirs, had come to see the Watts Town area to write about it. Wouldn't I like to meet him? I had read some of his poems and heard many stories about the Harlem Renaissance, of which he was one of the leading lights, so I welcomed the opportunity, of course. It was a very enlightening moment; I learned a great deal about American politics in that one meeting. We toured the burnt-out areas of Watts together; he took many pictures as we did the tour, all the time talking about the history of the struggle in which he took part, including his earlier left wing leanings.

The other incident was not so pleasant. It happened while I was coming from work late in the evening one day. I had been doing research at the UCLA library and took the San Diego Freeway to go home, as usual. I had just turned onto Sawtelle Boulevard, when two policemen pulled me over. They were both white and carried guns. One of them approached me on the driver's side of the car walking slowly from behind, while the other came on the passenger side. The first then asked me for my driver's license, while the second flashed a torch inside my car. I handed over my license and asked what was the matter. Instead of answering, the second officer asked me where I was coming from and where I was heading, while the first officer scrutinized my license. I explained where I came from and where I was heading.

By that time, they knew I was not who they were looking for, the second officer said to his colleague, "Hey, I think he is African or something." I'll never forget the exact words and the manner in which they were uttered. Telling about the incident, I would joke to friends later that I was saved by my accent. But at the time I was under their control, it was no joking matter. I was scared to death, for I had heard hair-raising stories about police brutality and degrading treatment at the hands of jail inmates.

I also met many Ethiopian students who were studying at UCLA and other institutions of higher learning in the area. They had a branch of ESUNA in Los Angeles, and some of them were active in it. They were, by and large, well-read intellectuals and critical of the Emperor's government. One of them, with whom I became a close friend, was the poet, Yohannes Admasu. We met fairly regularly to exchange views and discuss the future of Ethiopia and Africa. On a couple of occasions, we met in my apartment, where Koki cooked Ethiopian food. At other times we met at the home of other Ethiopians or at a book shop/coffee shop in Westwood Village, as it was then called. The owner of the bookshop was an engaging middle-aged man who liked to debate about politics and culture and occasionally tease one of the group, Nigussay Ayele whose looks and manner of speech, he said, reminded him of Mussolini. We frequented the shop because we enjoyed the company of the owner, who had a gift for provoking healthy debate with a dose of good humor. We all had fun.

I found the UCLA group, on the whole, a more critical bunch than most of the leaders of ESUNA, who tended to be polemical. It was a time when Ethiopian students worldwide were questioning the status quo and searching for answers to many questions. The most important political questions were related to the change of regime and methods of change—was it going to be through revolution or evolution? The axis of division among Ethiopians in general and students in particular was based on the answer to these questions.

In late July 1965, the annual meeting of ESUNA was held in Cambridge, Mass. I was invited to attend; once there, the members elected me to chair the meeting. My seniority and experience in government may have been contributory factors. Some of the students had known me when I taught at the University College of Addis Ababa and were familiar with my political views. Campaigning for the student presidency were Hagos Gebreyesus and Shibiru Seifu. Hagos, who was of my generation and about my age, was the candidate of the emerging radical student movement. Shibiru, who was encouraged by the Ethiopian ambassador to challenge Hagos, was a conservative, albeit a well meaning and naïve one. Hagos and I would part company later, standing in opposed camps over the question of self-determination for Eritrea. Indeed, the Eritrean question would become the most divisive issue among Ethiopian students, as well as future liberation fronts and political parties, as I will discuss in a later chapter.

It was customary for the government to provide financial support to Ethiopian student organization to defray the expenses of conferences and other meetings such as the celebration of the Emperor's birthday. Ambassador Teshome gave money to help the meeting and it was rumored by the students that much of that money was directed toward securing Shibiru's election. Another rumor was that I had come all the way from Los Angeles to help get Hagos elected because we were of the same Tigrigna linguistic group. This was designed to pull the majority non-Tigrigna speaking students from supporting Hagos. What Teshome and many others in the Emperor's government at the time did not realize was that the emerging generation of radical students were thinking beyond linguistic loyalties and striving to develop a national agenda transcending ethnic divisions. The proof of this was the election of Hagos with an overwhelming majority by a majority, non-Tigrigna student body. Indeed, the 1965 election of Hagos and his allies marked a turning point in Ethiopian student politics in the United Sates and was emblematic of the emerging radical movement of Ethiopian students worldwide.

The evening following the election, Hagos invited me for coffee at a coffee shop in Cambridge and he thanked me for my contribution to his election, adding that had the meeting been chaired by another person, the forces of reaction, as he put it, might have had a chance, given the embassy's influence. Apparently, in the eyes of many, I provided a needed counterweight to Ambassador Teshome's influence. After all, we were both lawyers and of the same generation and had similar rank in government. It is of interest that Teshome had succeeded me as the Attorney General of Ethiopia three months after I left the office, but held the office only for five months. The Emperor, for reasons best known to himself—but which were all too obvious—appointed him ambassador of Ethiopia in the United States.

Before his five months' stint at the Ministry of Justice, Teshome had worked in the netherworld of the Emperor's "Private Cabinet." This was not the constitutionally sanctioned Cabinet of Ministers; it was an extra-constitutional entity created to help the Emperor monitor the activities of his government. Nobody knew what the appointees of the Emperor's Private Cabinet did. Thus I had no idea what Teshome did in that netherworld, but that he was in His Majesty's good books—that he was in the inner circle of imperial supporters—was made clear by his subsequent appointments.

Teshome's predecessor as ambassador to America, Mr. Berhanu Dinke, had fallen out with the Emperor and asked for political asylum in the United States. He had written some outstanding pieces on Ethiopian politics and culture, and had become popular among the radical students. Teshome was sent to America to offset Berhanu's influence, both in the policy circles in the United States and among the students. Hence his attempts to defeat Hagos' election to the presidency of ESUNA. After Teshome's failure in this mission, he was recalled to Addis and, as consolation prize, appointed Chief Justice of the Supreme Court.

The student movement was fast becoming more and more radical. By the time of Teshome's recall to Addis Ababa, student politics had gone beyond control everywhere. My role in this was practically negligible as I had no formal role in student activities. But that fateful meeting in Cambridge in the summer of 1965 contributed to my being perceived as a leading member of the student radical movement. Although my past involvement in the underground movement may have been a factor, it was generally believed that Teshome's report to Addis Ababa on the election of Hagos and my role in the conference was critical in the development of such perception on the part of the Emperor and his government, as I would find out a couple of years later.

In England—Doing Doctoral Research

It was time to move on. My fellowship ended; my stay in Los Angeles was over. At the conclusion of a very pleasant year at the UCLA Law School in the summer of 1965, I was headed for London. I had decided to apply for a doctoral program at my alma mater, the University of London. Starting in early 1965, I began corresponding with a number of people at the university, including Professors Anderson and Allott, respectively head of London University's Institute of Advanced Legal Studies, and head of the Legal Department of the School of Oriental and African Studies (SOAS). There was no problem of acceptance into the doctoral program in the department of law of SOAS. The problem was finding funding sources, and I obtained that principally from the British Council. My earlier contacts helped in this matter, especially Iain Murray of the British Embassy in Addis Ababa, who had arranged for my official visit to Britain in 1963, as a guest of the British Council. I received scholarship funds sufficient to see me through two years, so I girded myself for a rigorous regimen, vowing to finish my research and write my dissertation in that time.

As part of the enrollment formalities, Professor Anderson and I discussed my choice of topic for my doctoral thesis and the course of lectures I needed to attend. After I informed him that I had decided on a topic—a study of constitutional development in Africa with a focus on the executive branch of government—he counseled that the best person to act as my academic advisor was Professor A.N. Allott. I had met Allott twice before: once in Dar-es-Salaam in September 1963, at the Conference on African Customary Law, and a second time in London later that year, during my visit to England. During my visit he had asked me to give a lecture to his class on my work as Attorney General of Ethiopia; so we had formed a good relationship.

The title of my dissertation was "The Executive in African Government: A Comparative Constitutional Study." A revised version of the dissertation was published in 1974 by Heinemann as *The Executive in African Governments*. My decision to undertake the study was inspired by the political events in Africa that culminated in the creation of the OAU. Another motivation was perhaps expressed best by a comment made about the book, which stated that "Africa is the world's laboratory for the student of comparative government."

My research involved a comprehensive survey of the new African states, both Anglophone and Francophone. My comparative study of African constitutional systems began with a look at the formal constitutional texts, then I expanded it to cover the political and social context, which included the variety of political systems and the historical antecedents on which they were based, as well as the new realities that dictated divergence from the legacies of the colonial past. I became interested not only in the institutions of governance but in the dynamics of executive power in a larger context. My practical experience in government as well as my acquaintance with some of Africa's leaders spurred this wider interest.

The chapter outline of the book that came out in 1974 will give the reader an idea of the scope of the study. Here it is:

    Part One: The Constitutional Framework
    Chapter 1 African Neo-Presidential Systems
    Chapter 2 Dual-Executive Systems in Historical Perspective
    Chapter 3 Monarchical Systems

Part Two: The Dynamics of Neo-Presidential Power
Chapter 4 Pre-colonial and Colonial Sources of Style
Chapter 5 One Party in Relation to Neo-Presidentialism
Chapter 6 Role of the Civil Service in Neo-Presidentialism
Part Three: The Advent of Military Rule—Crisis of Neo-Presidentialism
Chapter 7 Structure of Military Intervention
Chapter 8 Problems of Military Neo-Presidentialism.

As the outline of the book shows, the central feature of the system is what I called neo-presidentialism. It is a system reflecting the emerging authoritarian government rule, grounded in the twin pillars of a one-party system and a pliant civil service.

The picture is complicated by the advent of military coups, in which many of the civilian governments of the new states were overthrown by army officers, some of them (like Nkrumah's overthrow in 1965) incited by foreign governments. In fact Part Three of the book on the military was not part of my original thesis but evolved out of the number of coups that occurred in quick succession. I remember my Sudanese friend, Kalafalla Rashid (later Chief Justice of Sudan), joking about this. Every time there was news of a coup, he would ask me, "How is the hunting?' "What hunting," I would say, and he would answer laughing: "The hunt for the disappearing African civilian governments." I did not blame him; my research project had become like a hunting exercise in which I was shooting at a moving object, and missing. But in the midst of my little "crisis of relevance," the idea of including the coup phenomenon in my thesis was born. Part Three was the outcome, and my thesis advisor was not only supportive, he was enthusiastic about it.

Thus, I was off to a good start on the academic front. I followed a course of lectures relevant to my research. I had the thesis outline and introductory chapter approved and the rest was a matter of applying my mind with vigor and concentration. Considering the fact that my research was a comparative constitutional study covering all of Africa, I needed to travel to countries in Europe that had colonial links with Africa. I traveled to Paris, Brussels and Rome to examine relevant data and to interview scholars and others with knowledge of countries that were the subject of my research. I added Geneva to the list for financial, political, and meteorological reasons.

Early in 1966, I had written a letter addressed to the Director of the Graduate Institute of International Studies (*Institut Universitaire de Hautes Etudes Internationales*) applying for funds for a research project to be conducted in Geneva in the summer of 1966. The director, M. Jean-Paul Chatelanat, responded by offering me "*a titre exceptionnel,*" a modest sum of Swiss Fr. 750 a month for the duration of my research period. I accepted the offer gladly, for it was a good addition to my British Council stipend, enabling me to pay for travel and hotels expenses as well as for the collection of data. Thus I used Geneva as my base when I traveled to Paris for research and interviews. It was also a welcome change from London's unpredictable weather.

The intellectual climate of Geneva was of a different sort, also. In London, I had confined myself to the arid zone of legal scholarly endeavor relieved by occasional fiery debates and fire-side chats with friends and fellow graduate students in the junior common rooms. The rigor of intellectual discussions in the classroom and in special seminars was important in helping to discipline me. Not only did I accumulate knowledge by reading the literature on my research subject; I went beyond the narrow discipline of law and read works on anthropology, history, and sociology, particularly as it was related to Africa. In Geneva, the intellectual milieu was enlivened by the presence of political activists among the African exiles, from places like the Congo (Zaire), Cameroon, Guinea, and especially Ethiopia.

Family, Friends and Politics

Being a married man with a three-year old child, unlike my earlier student days when I was single and carefree, I had to take care of the family. There was no way for me to concentrate on my doctoral program unless and until I took care of the family first. This meant, first and foremost, decent housing. I was thus comfortably settled with my wife and son in an apartment at 18A Broadway Parade, Crouch End, London, N.8. It was a two-bedroom apartment on a second floor with a window overlooking the street. The first day of our occupancy, after we moved from a hotel, I remember Koki uttering a rare ironic remark. Looking out of the window, she said, "Broadway Parade! I can't imagine a parade on such a narrow street." Yes, indeed, Broadway Parade was (perhaps still is) a narrow street, like most London streets; but it was a decent, quiet and safe neighborhood.

Crouch End was, at the time, a lower-middle-class neighborhood with a few black families. Our immediate neighbors were a couple from Guiana (formerly British Guiana), who had two children, one Asgede's age. Asgede was not of school age, so he did not yet speak English. When we lived in Los Angeles he was hardly exposed to English-speaking children of his age; and this was before the advent of *Sesame Street*. He spent his daytime with his mother and the evening with the two of us. This continued to be the case in London as well, until he started playing with the neighbors' children who spoke to him in English. He was fast becoming bilingual by the time Koki and he left for Ethiopia in the summer of 1966. Koki was pregnant and we agreed that it would be better for her to go home and be among her close relatives when she gave birth. She gave birth to a girl, Finot, on December 31st 1966. When we were reunited in August 1967, Asgede had practically lost the English that he had picked up in London. He spoke to me in perfect Amharic.

One question that had concerned me in London was that Koki, who had always been actively and gainfully employed, was homebound without something to occupy her. A good mother and wife, who gave her home life priority over everything else, she nonetheless missed being actively engaged outside the domestic environment. I was concerned that she might be frustrated being homebound all the time, so I found friends who recommended that she work at the office of the African National Congress (ANC), on a part time basis. There was no pay, just a small stipend to help defray cost of transportation. The important thing was that she kept herself busy, helping in a worthy cause.

Moreover, her work for the ANC led to my own contacts with some of the leaders running the ANC office at the time. One of them was Raymond (Mazizi) Kunene; the other was Joe Mathew, son of the famous professor Mathew, one of Mandela's early mentors. I also met another South African who was taking a course with me—Professor S. A. de Smith's class on the constitutions of the (British) Commonwealth. His name was Joe Slovo. Joe was critical of de Smith's book, *The New Commonwealth and its Constitutions*, which had just come out and was required reading for the class.

For reasons that will be clear later, I need to say something about Kunene and Slovo.

Mazizi Kunene, a Zulu intellectual and man of letters who later wrote an epic poem on Shaka, the Zulu king, was an affable man with a warm personality. He made the ANC office lively with his easy African laughter and gift of listening, more than speaking. When he spoke, in his baritone voice, he used African idioms and proverbs. Mazizi wore a red turtleneck vest and a black leather jacket nearly all the time, which made him stand out in any company. There were disagreements between him and some of the leadership in the London office that caused him to leave the ANC. Eventually he settled in America teaching African literature at UCLA.

Exile politics, as I would find out myself, can be bitter and fratricidal. Years later, after the fall of apartheid, I heard that Mazizi had retired from UCLA and gone back to South Africa to live in his native Durban. And so it was that during my stay in Cape Town in the fall of 2003, where I spent a semester at the University of Cape Town, leading some students as part of the Study Abroad Program of UNC- Chapel Hill, I asked our local coordinator, Dr. Vernon Rose, to help me trace my friend Mazizi Kunene. During our tour of Durban, where we stayed at the Tropicana Hotel, Vernon asked one of the hotel workers, an Indian with an impressive beard, if he knew of Mazizi Kunene. He said he had heard of him, but did not know where he lives but that he would find out and, in a matter of four hours, he traced Mazizi. I was not prepared for what I found out.

Our Indian hotel worker offered to take us to where Kunene was staying, a retirement home, which turned out to be not just a retirement home, one of those places where old people without relatives are lodged. We were led up the stairs to the lounge, where scores of gray-haired old men and women in their eighties and nineties—all white—were sitting, looking vacantly at you or past you. It was a terrible shock to find Mazizi among these people; I was mortified to find a once vigorous revolutionary reduced to a mumbling old man who uttered gibberish and did not recognize me.

I asked one of the nurses what was wrong with him. She said it was dementia, and that his wife had brought him there some eight months ago. He did not recognize me, but responded to my name when Vernon said, "Your friend Bereket is here to visit you. Do you remember Bereket." His eyes were half-closed and his head was hanging loose, when he said in his distinctive baritone, "Who could forget Bereket!" After which he went back to the merciful slumber from which the nurses had awakened him. It was one of the saddest moments of my life.

The other friend was Joe Slovo, a South African Jew of Lithuanian origin, as he liked to say. We met in class and became close friends. Joe invited me to his home and introduced me to his wife, the writer Ruth First, who had a razor sharp mind and a pen to match. Their house was in North London, not far from where I lived. I found out very soon that they were both members of the South African Communist Party (SACP), which was supported by the Soviet Union.

Joe Slovo and other members of the SACP were also members of the ANC at the same time, in accordance with a strategy of protracted struggle that the two organizations had worked out. Indeed, Joe, who became the head of the SACP also acted as the head of the military wing of the ANC until the fall of apartheid. The backing of the Soviet Union was crucial in the anti-apartheid struggle, which probably explains the ANC/SACP strategy of joint struggle.

One day, Joe and I were having a debate on the difference between the Soviet and Chinese approach to Third World liberation movements. As usual, Joe waxed eloquent, singing the praises of the Soviets, and I argued in favor of the Chinese, partly in earnest, and in part to tease him. There followed a horrific argument, almost a row. It was one of those rare moments when Ruth tried to mediate. They had an interesting relationship, as a couple and as comrades in a common struggle. It was a relationship marked by comradely loyalty and intermittent fights that were embarrassing to behold. When Ruth intervened to chide Joe for his excessive praise of the Soviets he cut her short by resorting to his customary humorous response. Instead of answering Ruth, he turned to me and asked me why the Chinese killed all their cats. I shrugged: why? "Because," he said with a chuckle, "the bloody things did not know how to say Mao; they kept saying meow, meow!" We all laughed. A brewing row was thus averted, and I: " Or as Louis Chat-orze said, *l'etat c'est meow*."* A delayed laughter was the result, and it was not as hearty as the first one. Never mind.

[* This is a play on words. Chatorze combines chat (cat) and quatorze (fourteen in French). And in place of moi, as in *l'etat c'est moi* (I am the State, as Louis the 14th declared), we have meow. No wonder the joke flopped!].

Joe Slovo, it turned out, was a close friend and confidant of Nelson Mandela and was his advisor during one of the treason trials. Throughout the period of our friendship in London, Joe never mentioned this. I only found out by reading Mandela's autobiography, *Long Walk to Freedom, in which* Mandela remembers him fondly and with great admiration. After the fall of apartheid, when Mandela formed South Africa's first democratic government, he appointed Slovo Minister of Housing. The few ANC members that I had the chance to talk to during my stay in South Africa in the fall of 2003, remember Joe Slovo with reverence. His wife Ruth was killed by a letter bomb in her office in Maputo, Mozambique in 1986. It was assumed that the South African security forces were responsible..

Joe Slovo died of cancer in 1997

But back to London, and the mid-1960s.

In those days, Ethiopian opposition political activity abroad was concentrated among university students. I spent much time discussing politics with many of the students who were studying in England, including: Herui Tedla, Taddese Tamrat, Gebeyehu Ferrisa, Haile (Bubamo) Arficio, and Gebresealassie Seyoum. Some student leaders who were studying in France and Germany also paid London visits. The most notable among them was Haile Fida, who later became head of the MEISON group destined to play a crucial role helping the military government of Mengistu Haile Mariam.

Chapter 12

Banished but Undefeated

In late August 1967, having obtained my Ph.D. degree in advanced legal studies, and having traveled to some European capitals to renew important contacts, I boarded an ALITALIA flight from Rome to Addis Ababa. It was a pleasant flight, but when I was about to land at the Bole Airport, I had a strange premonition mixed with a feeling of unease. It was as if I regretted deciding to come back, even as I looked forward to seeing my wife, my son, and my eight month old daughter whom I had not yet met. And as if to confirm the strange premonition, Addis Ababa received me with a frown—it was raining cats and dogs when we landed.

I was to face yet another turning point in my life. There have been a few turning points in my life, all marked by changes of place and circumstance. The last one was my exit from government service heading for graduate studies in America and England. Some among my friends and relatives regarded my resignation and decision to "go back to school" as an ignominious descent from an exalted position to inglorious anonymity. How can an Emperor's Minister voluntarily relinquish a position that others would give their right hand to attain? How can he descend to the level of the masses? True, by the sentiments of the time, I had followed an unusual trajectory. But what people did not appreciate was that I was yearning for freedom—the freedom of thought and action that in my situation at the time could only be attained by academic life. And to that end I "went down" to the life of a student and sweated hard to obtain a doctorate in law, and was now ready and eager to join the law faculty at Addis Ababa University.

Even when frowning, Addis had its inexplicable charm—a charm that has captivated all visitors, from its founding in Menelik's days at the turn of the century. Its modern infrastructure, struggled to provide its inhabitants the decent life promised by its rulers but couldn't catch up with the demands of changing times and a burgeoning population whom it attracts like a magnet.

I did not see any change since I had left three years before, except for some new facilities inside Bole Airport. Neither the buildings nor the people had changed. I saw the same baleful police in plain clothes, pretending not to see you, but watching you advance and studying your face and movements; the same khaki-clad airline ground hostesses and unsmiling customs officers, and assorted airport employees and travelers carrying their bags and trundling along the corridors of the airport.

After I cleared customs, I was met by a young immigration officer, holding a small boy by the hand. I recognized the boy as they came closer; it was my five-year old son, Asgede. The young officer told me that he had been persuaded by members of my family to bring the boy inside, past the immigration and customs lines. I thanked the young man and I picked up Asgede and kissed and hugged him. To this day, I feel the warmth that engulfed me as I hugged my son. On his part, he was eager to tell me about his prized possession. When I asked him how he was, he answered, "I have a dog at home!"

We walked out together to the section where families and friends wait. More kisses and hugs of my wife Koki and other family members followed, before we were carted off by friends to our rented house near the headquarters of the OAU. After a few days' rest, I went to see the new Addis Ababa Law School, where the all-American faculty had made all preparations in anticipation of my arrival, including an office and arrangements for me to teach two law classes. They also elected me, in absentia, member of the Faculty Council representing the Law School. Everything seemed fine and dandy, until all plans—theirs and mine—came crashing down.

I had actually moved to my office, shared with a young American, Bill Ewing, with whom I would become friends for life. I even taught one class. Then word came from the Dean of the Law School, Professor Quentin Johnston (on loan from Yale Law School) that I was prohibited from teaching.

Why, I asked—on whose orders?

He didn't know. He was utterly confused and frustrated. There he was, an American Dean of an all-American faculty, and he could not retain his first and only Ethiopian faculty member. All he knew was that the Vice President for Academic Affairs had informed him that there was a problem concerning my presence in the university. He advised me to see the Vice President for Academic Affairs, who was none other than my friend Jim Paul, former Dean of the Law School and the person responsible for my joining the faculty in the first place.

Ah, the wheels of fortune! I should have, of course, expected it.

Jim Paul's office was in an elegant building that used to be Emperor Haile Selassie's residence before the 1960 coup attempt, after which the Emperor donated the entire campus to the university. The high-ceilinged, beautifully furnished office was one of the largest on the campus, second only to that of the President. The effect of the large office and the big desk over which Jim Paul's slight frame was humped when I entered was to diminish his significance, instead of enhancing it. He seemed to be swallowed by it all.

We exchanged greetings, asking each other about our respective families. Then a long silence followed before I resumed the conversation. When I raised the issue at hand, Jim was practically tongue-tied; he would not tell me where the order came from. All he could say was that he didn't want to speculate. He was obviously embarrassed and could not look me straight in the eye. He shifted constantly in his chair, and mumbled almost tearfully that it was all beyond his competence; there was nothing he could do to change things. The "best salesman in the world," now appeared to be helpless, caught in the maze of Ethiopian intrigue. It was disconcerting to watch him squirming; I was almost sorry for the man. That amiable face of his, familiar to all who knew him, became a field of conflicting emotions, with nervous smiles flipping on and off like a dysfunctional blinking light.

In the end he gave me the obvious advice: the best thing for me to do, he said, was to see the president of the university. It was all so absurd that I, too, was tongue-tied; I could not find words to express my feelings. Instead, I found myself laughing, which made Jim more nervous. I decided to leave, and, as I rose to leave Jim Paul's office, I was assailed by a Kafkaesque sense of bureaucratic absurdity. The saddest part of the entire experience was the fact that Americans who were there to help build a rational system of government, of law, were acting as players in an absurd game. First a Law School Dean could not decide on a personnel matter that was within his job description, namely hiring and retaining a member of his faculty; he passed the buck to the next man in the ladder—the academic vice president. Then a vice president for academic affairs passed the buck to his superior, in a case in which he could, in a normal situation, simply pick up the phone and tell the Dean to do what he is supposed to do. But no, the "buck" had to be passed—to the highest authority of the University.

I gave up on Jim Paul; I stood up, shook his trembling hand, thanked him and left his office. Although I liked the man, and still do, it dawned on me that he had fallen prey to the affliction common to holders of high office. His appointment as academic vice president had gotten the better of him, of his advocacy of the rule of law. Evidently, ambition and a taste of power had affected his sense of integrity and freedom. He couldn't have had an easy conscience; in fact he did not, as I found out later. A couple of years after that meeting, he came to Harar during my exile and visited me in my office in the municipality building. The reason for his coming to the province was the occasion of the graduation ceremonies of the regional college of agriculture. He said he had to come to pay me a visit as an old friend. After offering him the customary coffee, I teased him about the danger of being seen visiting me, lest it lead to his expulsion. That hit him hard, as I could tell from the pained look on his face.

We changed the subject several times and finally, before he rose to leave, he asked, "Well, where do we go from here?" It was an absurd question, given my situation, which he knew. I answered, "We? I don't know about you, Jim, but I am not going anywhere from here until the powers-that-be decide otherwise."

He flashed an embarrassed smile and left without saying a word, with the pain visible on his face.

What price ambition! I thought.

President Kasa Woldemariam was an old Wingate school contemporary of mine. His secretary, Marie Tedros, whom I knew from my student days in England, arranged for me to see him. Marie, a London-born Eritrean who was straight as an arrow and very pleasant, did not see the intrigue brewing behind the scene, so she put me on the calendar to see him straightaway. I saw Kasa the day after I saw Jim Paul.

It was a strange meeting. To begin with, Kasa was not feeling well; when I was ushered into his office, he was coughing. Kasa and I had never been close friends at school but we had a mutual respect as we were both champion debaters and therefore rivals. But that was in the innocent days of youth. Since then a lot had happened, the most life-changing being his marriage into the royal family. Everyone who did not know the secret of Kasa's background, including myself, was surprised to learn about the marriage. It transpired that this tall, good-looking and well-spoken man came from a prominent Oromo family from south western Ethiopia. When he returned from study abroad and was presented to the Emperor, the Emperor lost no time in hatching a plan to entrap him in royal marriage. He commanded him to frequent the Palace; and not long thereafter, he was married to Seble Desta, one of the Emperor's granddaughters. (Seble was the one who wrote her mother on my behalf when I was forcibly repatriated from England, as I have related.)

I did not know whether to congratulate Kasa or commiserate with him. Kasa's marriage to Seble was a political one, designed by the Emperor to bind an important Oromo clan to the royal throne. Nor was it the first time this was done; arranged marriages were part and parcel of the old order, not only in royal circles but even among ordinary citizens. In the case of royal marriages, they were supposed to help cement dynastic rules and nation-building or, more accurately, state construction.

To his credit, Kasa did not flaunt his royal connection; yet the fact remained that without it, he would not have been appointed president of the university. I was now facing him and asking him to explain why I was not allowed to teach in the law school. Between intermittent coughs, he tried his best to dodge the question, simply saying that I knew enough about Ethiopian politics to guess who could make such a decision. He could not spell it out, because it simply was not done; no one attributed such controversial decisions to His Majesty, who, though all-powerful, had to be insulated from blame of any kind. It was that conventional wisdom that Kasa was invoking to protect himself from blame. But I did not let him get away with it; I challenged him in legal and rational terms, because I knew him to be a rational man with a sense of right and wrong. I reminded him of the fact that as president of the university, it was his duty to uphold academic freedom and the integrity of the process of hiring and firing of teaching faculty.

He burst out laughing and started coughing again. I saw the humor of the situation; we were playing a game with each other, both knowing who was to blame yet not saying it. Neither could point an accusing finger at the source of the problem and my (our) woes.

"You'd better take care of that cough," I said. "You need to be in good health to meet the challenges of your job."

"I know," he agreed.

Somewhat mischievously, I added: "You need to be healthy for the job; but the job does not guarantee you good health."

Another burst of laughter and coughing fits.

"I rest my case," I said, smiling wickedly.

"Stop it," he said still laughing. "Do you want to kill me?"

I stopped teasing him and he rose to say goodbye and wish me luck.

"You will need it, Bereket. Lots of it."

Those were his parting words as I left his office. We were never to see each other again. Seven years later, Kasa was among the Ministers and other dignitaries executed by the military dictatorship in a mid-night massacre on November 23rd, 1974.

Such are the hazards of royal connection!

Kasa's ominous statement about my needing lots of luck proved true. It was not long afterward that I was awakened by a knock on my bedroom window (as described in the Prologue), summoned to the Emperor's presence, and banished to the province.

On My Way to Exile

It was early evening in September 17, 1967, a week after I had been taken to the Emperor's august presence escorted by his Minister of Security, and curtly told that I would be sent to Harar. When you are under the power of an Emperor and told you were to go to a certain place, you don't ask questions. You just go.

So it was that I found myself boarding a train at the Addis Ababa-railway station. As I boarded, I had a feeling of déjà vu; the last time I traveled from Addis Ababa to Harar was as a thirteen-year old boy with my friend Isaac Abraha, over two decades before. As I sat waiting for the train to start, the scenes of that time came rushing to my mind, as though the whole thing happened the day before. I thought of the misadventure of losing Isaac's bag, of our grief and distress, as well as of the colorfully costumed man who sang and danced, moving from wagon to wagon. At the time, I had suspected that man to be a disguised government spy, and I expected him to materialize again, this time.

Then the whistle sounded, awakening me from my reveries. The train started slowly, huffing and puffing and gathering momentum as it rolled past familiar places. I saw a man in dark sunglasses standing by the window, and turning toward me from time to time. Could he be a member of the Emperor's spy network, assigned to be my invisible chaperon to ensure my arrival at my destination? Knowing the way the system worked, I couldn't put it above the Minister of Security.

My destination was Dire Dawa and I traveled all night, arriving there a little after daybreak

Built by French engineers as a hub of the Addis Ababa-Djibouti railway, Dire Dawa is one of Ethiopia's modern cities. The railway, originally known as *chemin de fer franco etiopien*, was the most important artery for the country's economy, connecting the capital with the port of Djibouti. And Dire Dawa was built to accommodate French railroad personnel and their families. Before long, it became a center of trade and commerce for expatriates as well as local merchants. At the time of my banishment to Harar, Dire Dawa was the second largest city in Ethiopia proper—third if we count Asmara.

In the imperial system, if you are the subject of banishment, as I was, you are not supposed to know why you are banished; nor the place and time of your dispatch. I was not naïve enough to expect that an exception would be made in my case. So when I asked the Minister about it, I did not expect an answer specifying details on my banishment. After all, keeping you in the dark was an important part of the punishment. The Minister smiled mischievously and simply said, "You will find out soon enough."

He did do me one small favor, however; he told me to get ready to travel to Harar within a week or so. He did this small favor probably considering my previous position or perhaps my youth (he was old enough to be my father). All that week before my departure to Harar, I noticed cars following me everywhere I went, including the last steps into the railway station. I expected someone was at the ticket office reporting on my arrival at the station and my boarding the train. My only question was: why not a police escort all the way? Why, after the "shock and awe" tactic of hauling me to the Security Minister's office and thence to the palace, did they modify and treat me with kid-gloves?

I could think of three reasons: first, my Eritrean origin; second, my reputation among most of my generation of educated Ethiopians; and third, the fact that I was known and generally liked among the diplomatic community. With respect to my origin, the Emperor handled all issues having to do with Eritrea and Eritreans with extra care, especially at a time when the war situation in Eritrea was going from bad to worse. With regard to my popularity among the Ethiopian educated elite, his policy was to be seen as a benevolent ruler. He treated my generation of the educated elite, all products of his education policy, as a father treats his children. He said as much to us students, in 1954 during his visit to England on his way back from the United States. As for the diplomatic community, the Emperor, in his advanced years, was particularly anxious to maintain a reputation as an enlightened monarch who governed in accordance with the rule of law. Being seen openly treating me otherwise would have amounted to losing face.

Yet he had to punish me in one way or another.

The solution was to sugarcoat my banishment in the form of an imperial appointment. That was why it was announced after I arrived in Harar that I was appointed as the legal advisor to the governor general of Harar. As an astute observer, a man by the name of Zegeye Mengesha, put it to me in confidence when the announcement was made: "You are a legal advisor in a lawless system, where the rule of law was displaced by martial law." Hence the cloak and dagger involved in that "appointment" and what happened to me in Harar, as "His Majesty's Guest," as I will explain shortly.

I arrived at the Dire Dawa train station, after a night's journey. As soon as I got off the train with my one bag, I saw a man walking toward me. He seemed to know me, for he smiled and called my name and offered to carry my bag, which I gratefully accepted. He was a tall and well-built man. His name was Mamo Habtewold; captain Mamo, he added immediately with a smile. Here we go again, a police captain, I thought, examining the left side of his waist for signs of a gun tucked in its holster. I followed him to his Volkswagen Beetle, and we were off to Harar.

Dire Dawa is a totally different world from Harar. Although Harar is the capital of the region, Dire Dawa is larger, more modern and the favorite place to visit, with its glitter and comfortable hotels, modern amenities and its tree-lined streets, emblazoned with jacaranda and flaming trees.

Then there is Dire Dawa's warm climate and lower elevation, which provides more oxygen and contributes to the general atmosphere of relaxation. During the rainy season in the highlands, people flock down to Dire Dawa. The variety of languages as well as the colorful dresses also makes it more attractive—colorfully dressed and slow moving Somali women, shuffling in their slippers and talking loudly among themselves; equally colorfully dressed Aderes, Oromos, mixing with Amharas in the *megala* (market).

The railway station which the locals call *leghar* (a corruption of the French *la gare*) is the nerve center of the city: in point of fact, it is where the city originated, with the first constructions built to house the French employees of the railway company. The rest of the city grew fast, radiating from this center and expanding further and further with impressive buildings built for business as well as residences of the rapidly increasing population. Ethiopian customs officials and their hangers-on were among the first proud inhabitants of Dire Dawa. As happened elsewhere in Africa, commercial or colonial adventure was accompanied or followed, and in some cases preceded, by Christian missionary activity. In Dire Dawa's case French Catholic missionaries established their missions with the start of the railway, an unwritten understanding between Church and State in the colonial enterprise. French Lazarist missionaries and Jesuits opened schools, hospitals and clinics side by side with their churches.

As soon as we were on our way to begin negotiating the winding road up Dengogo Mountain, Captain Mamo told me more about himself. He allayed my fears when he told me that he was one of the several hundred Imperial Body Guard officers who were detained after Germame's attempted coup in 1960. I heaved a sigh of relief; he must have noticed this, because he turned to me for a split second and smiled broadly.

"Were you at the Meshalokia detention camp when I came to visit," I asked.

"No, but other officers who were there told me later," he said, adding that I and my colleagues in the Ministry of Justice were known as the defenders of the rebels.

He then told me with a serious tone that he was the private secretary of the Governor General who had sent him with instructions that I was to see no one and talk to no one before I met him.

"So, are you taking me to see him?"

"Yes, those are my instructions." He did not say much else on the subject after that, changing topics and asking me about family and sundry matters. Did I have a family? Where were they? How many children did I have? I asked him similar questions. His wife was a nurse working in one of the regional hospitals, and he had two children.

We climbed to the highlands of Harar. This was familiar territory to me from my childhood, and also from having visited Harar several times thereafter. We drove along the eucalyptus tree-lined road, passing Amaressa, then Alemaya (Haremaya to the locals). We arrived in Harar with its cool and invigorating air, its streets lined with jacarandas, and the ubiquitous eucalyptus.

We pulled up at the residence of the Governor General. As he opened the door for me, Captain Mamo said softly, "The boss will tell you everything, but let me add my own word of advice in remembrance of your good deeds, of what you did for us." He then told me that the city was filled with eyes and ears that would follow me wherever I went. I should listen and observe, and say nothing. "If you do that, you should be okay."

"Thank you," I said, shaking his hand.

Unexpected Hospitality

Until I was ushered in to the living room of the house and saw him, I had no idea who the Governor was. I had refrained from asking Captain Mamo because I did not want to seem too inquisitive. I was pleasantly surprised to find that the man who would be my "jailor" was actually a man I had known during my years as Attorney General

Dejasmatch Workneh Woldeamanuel rose from his seat and greeted me, smiling. We shook hands and he pointed to a sofa to his right. He whispered something to Captain Mamo who nodded, bowed and left us.

"Captain Mamo will take your luggage to the Ras Hotel where a room has been reserved for you. You will be our guest for lunch and then you can go and rest. You must be exhausted." As he was speaking these words his wife, Woizero Bruke, came through the door leading to the kitchen and greeted me with a broad smile. That didn't surprise me because I knew Bruke to be his wife. I had met her in London during her visit for medical treatment a few months before, while I was in the last stages of writing my dissertation. I was introduced to her by her sister-in-law, Selamawit, the Governor's younger sister, who was with her most of the time. I knew Selamawit and her husband, Dr. Aklilu Habte, so I visited her in hospital a few times.

Bruke spoke of my visits when she was in hospital and the help I rendered her and Selamawit after she was released from the hospital. It seemed to me that what I did was blown out of proportion. It is possible that in her condition at the time, a visit such as mine, which might have been unexpected, was given a value beyond what I thought it deserved. In any case, out of courtesy I didn't think it wise to contradict her; my silence, signified agreement, but I felt ill at ease, as though I was claiming an undeserved credit.

The Governor supported his wife, saying that she had indeed told him about the help I and other Ethiopians had rendered. In a fleeting moment of crazy speculation, I began to wonder whether she might have had a hand in my coming to Harar. Perish the thought! I said silently, chiding myself for even thinking it. But in my heart, I felt a sense of calm, knowing that such gratitude coming from the Governor's wife—deserved or not—could do me no harm in my exile under her husband's watch. As I was to learn during my three years of exile in Harar, every expression of sympathy helps—every gesture of solidarity that I was to receive from students and some teachers; every sentiment of support subtly given to me by representatives of the captive nations of the region, such as the Somali, the Oromo and the Adere, as well as the few Eritreans who lived in Harar.

Bruke left us to go to supervise her kitchen staff, and as soon as we were alone, the Governor changed the mood of the meeting, assuming a serious tone.

"I suppose you have been wondering why you were sent here?" After he saw me nodding gravely, he said something that I remember as though it was yesterday:

"This is not a picnic; it is called *ghizot*," he said looking me straight in the eye and waiting to let his grave words sink in.

He needn't have bothered. I knew it was not a picnic; the question in my mind ever since that fateful morning when I was taken to the Emperor's palace, had been, what would it be like—what form would it take. Would it be chains and leg irons, or would it be a more lenient treatment? I knew it was *ghizot*, which is Amharic for banishment.

The Governor must have read from my face that I knew, for he changed his tone.

"The first thing I want you to know," he said, "is that no harm shall be done to you under my watch; none whatever."

But there were conditions: "You are to speak to no one," he said, "outside the circle of people in my office. Your movements will be from your house to your office and from your office to your house."

It could have been worse, was my silent reaction. And I acknowledged my consent by nodding affirmatively.

"If you need company and civilized conversation," he continued after a brief silence, "you can come to my house any time."

"I am most grateful," I said and kept quiet.

As if he fathomed my thoughts, he continued to assure me that if I did as he counseled (or rather subtly commanded), he would see to it that, in time, the conditions of my exile might be improved. He stressed the word "*might*", watching me with a smile that was inquisitive and affirmative at the same time. Again, I signaled acceptance by a nod, even though I was not sure whether he was playing his own game or was genuine.

Dressed in Ethiopian costume, Bruke came into the living room to announce that lunch was served and we moved to the large dining room. The Governor lived in a large, two-story house, enclosed by tall stone walls adorned with different varieties of bougainvillea. The dinner table was covered with white cotton cloth and laid for three people, by which I assumed that they did not expect another guest. The gleaming silverware attested to the care with which the mistress of the house selected her household possessions and supervised her domestic servants. The servants consisted of a butler, his woman assistant, a cook and a couple of odd-job assistants who did errands, including gardening. Ethiopians of the Governor's generation, and of his wife's, did not indulge in the bourgeois hobby of gardening; it was left to the next generation to adopt that delightful habit.

Woizero Bruke, a soft spoken and decent lady, dealt with her servants with a quiet authority that was firm but polite, unlike some high class ladies I had known who justified their status by the degree of humiliation they inflicted upon their servants. As I came to know the Governor and his spouse more closely during my three-years stay in Harar, I discovered that their decent behavior was actuated not by any expectation of payback, but by a social conscience ingrained in them, a function both of their Christian upbringing and of *noblesse oblige*. I would learn years later that Bruke exhibited the same decency and calm self-confidence that I observed in Harar during her years of imprisonment, when they were detained by the military government along with members of the royal family following the overthrow of the Emperor in 1974. Modest in appearance and demeanor, Bruke was not a beauty, but she was blessed with a rather pleasant face and a warm personality.

The lunch was sumptuous, with every variety of Ethiopian cuisine. As expected, the lady of the house continually urged me to eat more and more; and eat I did. In the end, after we were served with coffee, the Governor said he would go to have his siesta, presumably before confronting the world of suitors, petitioners and other supplicants to the most powerful man in the region. I thanked my hosts for their hospitality and asked if one of the servants could accompany me to the hotel, since I did not yet know my way. In response, the Governor told one of the servants to call his chauffeur and told him to take me to the Ras Hotel, which turned out to be not so far from the Governor's residence. The Governor told me that Captain Mamo would pick me up from the hotel and take me to the office the following morning. I thanked him and left.

After the chauffeur deposited me at the Ras Hotel, I went to the desk, and asked for the key to my room. As if on cue, the manager of the hotel, a very pleasant man in his mid-thirties, appeared and extended his hand to greet me. Actually, he extended both hands and bowed so deeply that I remember feeling embarrassed. His effusive welcome made it look as if I were a star guest, which I would have been in my earlier incarnation. But given my drastically changed status, his effusion puzzled me. A couple of the hotel employees looked on as their boss gave me the VIP treatment. At least one of these employees is an agent of the security, I presumed, and he or she will be reporting on me—the people I meet, the company I keep, what I say and what others say to me.

I remembered the Governor's admonition: "Speak to no one." Except, of course, to the chosen few.

I napped for a couple of hours, took a shower and came out of my room to sit at the front veranda, which was half full of people, including French visitors who had come from Djibouti. It was after six pm. The biggest hotel in the city, the Ras was the social center of the city's elites who met almost every night for gossip and chats over coffee or beer.

It lay at the intersection of two of the main streets of the city: one leading southwest to the Ogaden sub-region, the other leading to the historic city center and the headquarters of the government of the region. Midway along this street, between the hotel and the government headquarters, there was a square with an equestrian statue of Ras Mekonen, Emperor Haile Selassie's father. The face of the statue was turned toward the Ogaden, the vast Somali-inhabited area that Mekonen pacified and ruled over as Menelik's first Governor, following the conquest of the region.

Running parallel to the main street, at a lower elevation, is what the locals call *Botega,* corruption of the Italian *via delle botteghe* (shopping area street). Alas! Many of the "shops" in *Botega* were now patronized by members of the oldest profession, who catered to military officers and low ranking government officials.

Later that day, after work hours, Captain Mamo came to visit me in the hotel. He suggested that we take a ride around the city to get a bird's eye view of some of its features. He said, with a big smile, "Tonight is tourism night. Enjoy it while you can; you may not get another opportunity for some time."

I agreed and we left in his VW Beetle, first to an elevated bluff called *Aboker* where we had a good view of the modern part of the city. We then drove back to the city, into the western entrance of *Botega.* It was getting dark and the lights of the "shops" were being lit, and Ethiopian music was heard. The loudest music blaring from the most frequented place was a song called *"Aderech Arada,"* sung by the famous Mahmud. It was a popular tune at the time and seemed appropriate for the red light district, because in it, the singer laments the loss of his love who left him to join the "market" (*arada*).

There wasn't much else to see or hear, so I asked if we could go to see the walled city center. We entered the walled city through Showa Ber and drove along a narrow street passing many small shops before we reached the square that served as the bus terminal. The square was dominated by the Church of Medhane-Alem (Savior of the World) build by order of Emperor Menelik after the battle of Chelenko that led to the victory of his invading forces. The story, as told by a French adventurer and Menelik's admirer, Henri de Monfreid, (in *Menelik: Tel qu'l Fut*) goes as follows: On the eve of the battle, Abdullahi, Emir of Harar sent envoys to Menelik and his army with "gifts" of ropes with a message that if Menelik and his army surrendered their arms and converted to Islam, they would be spared; if not, they would be tied with the ropes and delivered to the Emir in Harar.

Menelik's response was a solemn vow that when (**not if**) the Good Lord gives him victory over the Emir's army, he would occupy Harar and build the Church of Medhane- Alem on the very spot where the mosque stood. Menelik was a man of his word; he did exactly that. De Monfreid adds that when Menelik entered Harar at the head of his victorious army, he climbed the minaret of the city's principal mosque and pissed from it to the ground below, before ordering the Mosque demolished. The construction of a Christian church inside the walled city was certainly a symbolic act of a conqueror, signaling the end of the Emirate and the start of the rule of a Christian Amhara king. Later during my sojourn in Harar, I would hear sentiments of resentment concerning this fact.

As we drove back out of the walled city, I mentioned this story to Captain Mamo and he expressed some negative views about the Harari (also called Adere), remarks that reflected ethnic and religious bigotry, typical of a conquering tribe. We passed a woman carrying a large pot on her head, going out of one of the gates. Captain Mamo pointed to her and expressed his feelings of contempt.

"Do you see that woman? Do you know what she is carrying in that pot?" he asked.

"Water?"

"No, she is carrying her husband's excrement—going to dump it on the dry river bed outside the wall."

I was intrigued by this piece of information and asked if there were no toilet facilities. He said there was no room in the crammed walled city, although some of the well-to-do residents have installed septic tanks. He added that they dry the excrement first, by putting it on the rooftops for the midday sun. A year or so later, I raised the question with an Oromo farmer, Grasmach Abdullahi Gelmo. I tried to put it delicately so as not to offend any sensibilities. I asked him to enlighten me on the matter of waste disposal in the city. He validated

Mamo's story and was equally contemptuous of the Adere, even though he was a fellow Muslim and, as an Oromo, did not belong to the ruling Amhara people. He put it into perspective by explaining why the men did not venture out of the city to answer Nature's call. That was, he said, because his people, the Oromo of the surrounding areas, from time to time revolted against the Emir's rule and attacked the Adere.

We reached the Ras Hotel. I thanked the captain, said good night and went straight to bed. The following morning, Captain Mamo came to the hotel where I was just finishing breakfast. When I offered him to have breakfast, or at least coffee, he declined politely and said that the Governor was already in his office, expecting me. Within minutes, we were at the office. The Governor rose to greet me with a broad smile, saying, "Welcome."

From the outset, Governor Workneh did not play games with me. He told me the truth about my condition, vowing to treat me with fairness and decency to the best of his ability. Naturally, I wondered about the limit of his ability in such matters. What instructions did he receive from the Emperor or the Minister of Security on how I was to be dealt with? From what I knew about the Emperor and his ways, he thrived on ambiguity, rarely giving a direct order in precise terms. Ambiguity seemed to be a governing principle—one among many—in the imperial system. It was convenient, because it left room for maneuver, allowing a more conscionable Governor like Workneh to spare me unpleasant treatment. That was my hope and, indeed, my expectation, in view of his kind reception the previous day.

While Awaiting His Majesty's Pleasure

Governor Workneh began our first conversation in his office by informing me that my official title was "Legal Advisor to the Governor General of Harar." He must have seen the smirk on my face, because he seemed to fumble for words. Legal advisor in a martial law regime! I was sure he felt the irony, which was why he could easily forgive my smirk. We just have to do what we can, he seemed to say, while awaiting his Majesty's pleasure.

Governor Workneh was a man with a sense of humor who enjoyed a good joke or story. He came from the Shoan nobility and this fact together with his Christian upbringing was reflected in his treatment of people. His favorite quotation was Christ's injunction, "When you do good to the least of these, you have done it for me." For all that, he had an acute sense of his position of power and privilege, evidenced in his behavior, including the way he walked and talked. He spoke calmly and slowly with measured words. I never knew him to raise his voice. That is not considered the behavior of a *Chewa Sew* (decent man), which he thought himself to be, and which I knew him to be through and through. He dealt with anger in a peculiarly aristocratic nonchalance, smiling it off, and never showing it. In rare instances, his smile might break and explode into a barking staccato of laughter. All of which was part of a defense mechanism, cultivated from childhood as part of the armory of a ruling class.

As in his speech, so in his walk—he moved in measured steps, never hurried. As he came out of his office, he would be greeted by suitors whom he would acknowledge, one by one, with a nod of the head and an ever-present smile. Whenever a suitor spoke about his or her case, he would tell his secretary to take down the name and remind him of the case later. He seemed to glide rather than walk until he reached his car where a chauffeur waited holding the door open. Naturally, the Governor sat in the back—not for him the pretense of new-fangled folksiness that some "Big People" adopted by sitting in the front seat beside their driver. Nor would he share his back seat with anyone below his rank.

The Governor had a team of aides who assisted him in the daily running of the region's government business, the principal one being the Deputy Governor, who at the time was Meharenna Minda. But he had the ultimate responsibility. He was anxious to make me feel at home in his domain, because he thought that I might help lighten that responsibility. This came out in our very first encounter, that morning in his office.

"You know, there is a lot that you can do to help me. A lot," he said.

"Name one thing," I challenged him in good humor.

He then went into a detailed explanation of the challenges facing his domain, particularly the Ogaden region, which was under martial law, with a military man as governor. He was anxious, he said, to govern in accordance with the rule of law, but that it was difficult. I asked him what I, a lawyer, could do to help in such a situation. There was a deliberate twist in the way I asked my question, and he acknowledged the irony with his famous smile.

"I know very well that the military have a way of handling matters that may not be in accordance with the law. But it is my duty to hold them to the standards of the law."

"Such as it is," I remember saying, referring to martial law.

He nodded his agreement and went on to explain to me the situation in the Ogaden, stressing two related facts. First, the rebellion in the Ogaden was supported by the government of Somalia, which claimed the Ogaden as its own. Second, the eyes of the world were focused on the situation; we could not, therefore, ignore international opinion.

"That is where your help comes in," he said.

I was given an office in the main building of the regional government, located directly opposite the Governor's office. It was a small office minimally furnished with a simple desk and three chairs. A couple of days after our meeting, Captain Mamo brought a pile of dossiers and deposited them on my desk. He said the Governor wanted me to review them and submit briefs on each of them. Most of them concerned land disputes between regional notables, which the Governor found it hard to resolve without offending one side or the other. I assumed that he needed my name and experience to back up whatever decisions he made, which assumption proved well founded. It was all nauseatingly dull and tedious work, but was not bad, considered against the alternative of being chained in some miserable prison. In my moments of loneliness and tedium, I made an effort not to forget that possible alternative. I also managed to find spare time to revise my Ph.D. dissertation in order to turn it into a book manuscript. It was later published by Heinemann of London.

For the better part of a year, I assisted the Governor in preparing memos or briefs on similar cases—all land-related cases. There were only two instances involving "international" issues. One was about American officers who were part of the US military presence. Some trigger-happy officers and NCOs who were on a hunting trip in the Ogaden region flew a helicopter and machine-gunned gazelles, thus angering the Chief of Police of the martial law administration, who complained to the Governor. The Governor was anxious not to upset the Emperor's delicate policy toward the United States; at the same time, he was outraged at the behavior of the American officers, mostly NCOs. The Chief of Police of the Ogaden, General Mesfin Embaye, was even more enraged and wanted justice done, because the Americans not only behaved cruelly but broke the law.

The Governor sought my advice and asked me to draft a letter of complaint in English, addressed to the commanding officer of the Americans, requesting appropriate sanctions, which I did. This did not satisfy General Mesfin Embaye, the chief of police. He wanted his day in court—in an Ethiopian court. The Governor inquired whether that were possible; I told him that according to the law of the country it was not only possible but an imperative—anyone who breaks the law must face the consequences. But I added from my experience as Attorney General that I had come to grief when I had tried to push that imperative to its logical conclusion in a hit-and-run case involving an American. If he wanted to do what I did as Attorney General, I would prepare the necessary papers, but he must realize that American power would weigh in ultimately, nullifying his efforts. The decision was his. He chose not to pursue the matter, beyond a strongly worded rebuke of the behavior of the officers and a plea not to repeat it.

How a similar case would be handled today is a question that every nation with pride in its sovereign rights should ponder, and that the invasion of Iraq and the scandal at Abu Ghraib makes poignant.

The other case involved a group of Ethiopian Somalis who were arrested on charges of forming an irredentist underground organization with the aim of separating Somali-speaking areas of Ethiopia and joining them with Somalia. The police arrested six of the alleged conspirators but not the presumed leader of the group. Ugaz (Chief) Hasen Hirsi was the spiritual leader of the Issa clan of the Somali people, and the higher authorities (presumably the Emperor and his Minister of Security) made a political decision not to arrest him. This angered the police investigating the case, who alleged that the Ugaz was in the conspiracy up to his neck. The Governor faced the pressure of the police who wanted the Ugaz arrested, but he could not order his arrest for fear that he would be reprimanded by his superiors. He asked my view and I counseled that he should seek the opinion of the Attorney General, who should be apprized of the matter anyway. The Attorney General at the time happened to be a fellow Eritrean, Amanuel Andemichael. As I had expected, Amanuel took charge of the case himself and came to Harar to conduct the prosecution. I sat in court and observed.

The evidence of the prosecution was not sufficient to convict the accused, and certainly not to arrest a revered man and thus create unnecessary political problems. Eventually, the case was withdrawn and the accused released, to the dismay of the chief investigating police officer, Colonel Muluwork. The colonel could not hide his displeasure and blamed me for masterminding the debacle of the case, thus denying him promotion.

Stories of my sympathy and support of Somali irredentism started with the rumor machine of the provincial police, and would haunt me till the day I left Harar, and even beyond. Muluwork and I knew each other during my tenure at the Ministry of Justice. He was known among police detainees as the torturer, who would forego torturing a detainee in exchange for favors by relatives or friends, including a bottle of Johnny Walker a week or the companionship of the fair sex. Indeed, one of the Somali accused claimed that he had threatened to torture him.

In the Thick of Things

After a year of "legal counseling," I was assigned an administrative job. One fine morning, Governor Workneh sprung a surprise; he called me to his office and quietly announced that His Imperial Majesty had been pleased to appoint me Mayor of Harar. By that time, my wife and our two children had joined me, and I had moved from the hotel to a rented house in a pleasant part of the city called Timkete-Bahr. The governor had even given me permission to travel to Addis Ababa to attend the funeral of my former colleague, Nerayo Essayas, who had died of cancer. This had been a surprise to me because earlier, he had not allowed me to travel to Addis to attend my brother Tewelde's wedding. So, things seemed to be changing. I wondered why.

And how had the mayoral appointment come about? The Governor anticipated my question and with that ever-present smile explained that he had told the Emperor of the good work I had done, with diligence and without complaint. He had represented to the Emperor that the historic city of Harar needed a new mayor, and that with my background and knowledge I would help to raise the profile of the city. The Emperor granted his request with a warning that I was to be watched with the same care as before. Therefore, the Governor said, with an embarrassed smile, that I was to be head of the city from which I could not exit without his permission.

A mayor who could not leave his city without permission! At least my banishment had acquired a sort of dignity, being linked with the historic city in which no less a voyager than French poet Rimbaud lived. When I jokingly made this point to a visiting friend, he thought I was being serious and angrily responded saying that I, who had been Attorney General of the whole country, was now Mayor of a small provincial town. Clearly, he did not see the humor of it.

Once installed in my new office, I set out to work as though it were a dream appointment of a lifetime. The optimism I assumed was part of my survival imperative; "They" wanted me to be depressed as punishment; I responded by providing "service with a smile." That smile and the underlying motto turned out to be infectious and transformed the working environment of the municipality of Harar.

The Mayor's office was built during the Italian occupation of Ethiopia (1936-1941), when it served as the headquarters of the regional government. The Mayor was assisted by an executive secretary who supervised the different departments, the main ones being technical services, social and health services and land registration and taxation. There was a municipal council, half elected and half appointed. The elected members were mostly Aderes from the walled city, whereas the appointed ones were ex officio representatives of different government services. The tension inherent in such composition was expressed from time to time in acrimonious exchanges between Muslim/Adere hardliners and Christian/Amhara hardliners. An example of this involved the relocation of the city's Christian cemetery. The proposal to relocate it near the Muslim cemetery was rejected by hardliners of the two sides, both arguing in favor of preserving the traditional insistence on maintaining distance between the two sites. I was reminded of this unity of views when the Pope agreed with Muslim clerics against birth control in a 1995 conference devoted to the subject.

Anyone involved in the life of a city in the throes of modernization against a background of a traditional society is plagued with conflicts of one kind or another. My own work as Mayor landed me in myriads of problems. The job involved programs of development —building new infrastructures such as water pipes, and new roads, cutting through lands belonging to well-connected individuals and families. Moreover, problems of enforcing payment of unpaid or evaded taxes or water bills owed by the imperial palace and the regional branch of the Ethiopian Orthodox Church often landed me in heated debates and angry diatribes.

But the problems associated with municipal administration were not, as such, my principal problems. These were related to student radical movements and my alleged association with them. The late 1960s and early 1970s were times of turbulence worldwide. The radical movement in Europe, the United States and elsewhere reverberated in the four corners of the earth. In Ethiopia, university students, teachers and high school students were in the forefront of radical movements, demanding drastic changes in the imperial system, including land reform and democratic change. The high school students in Harar, as well as the students of the Alemaya College of Agriculture, had caught the fever and had begun expressing their demands in class boycotts and demonstrations. By the time I had become Mayor of Harar, these movements had become the main problem of the government both in Addis Abba and in several of the regional capitals.

My contact with the Alemaya College students had started as a result of a tree planting project I designed for the Hakim Gara mountain lying to the south of the city, looming like a huge crescent. I asked the appropriate college teachers to help me in the project and they prepared a nursery of three or four different types of trees. I ordered the technical services of the municipality to divide the mountain into three segments for planting the trees. The idea was to create a competitive environment. The three segments were then divided among the civilian population of the city, to the military and the provincial police. It was one of the more successful projects undertaken by the city, one that is remembered to this day, as the trees have grown to become a pleasant feature of the city, attracting tourists. And the experience connected the city to the college community of teachers and students.

But neither this nor the other services that I rendered to the city helped me when the inevitable conflicts arose. Indeed my problems as an exiled "troublemaker" became compounded because of some of my decisions concerning the distribution of land. People who wanted to settle scores with me for decisions I had made as Mayor would combine to fabricate offences I had not committed. A common charge was that I was leading the students astray, inciting them to boycott classes. At first, the Governor dismissed everything they said as vindictive lies. But as the accusations multiplied and spread like wildfire, Governor Workneh could not ignore them without risking condemnation. He also knew that everything was reported to the Emperor by more than one source. The sources included the regional Police Chief and the commander of the region's army regiment, as well as the Deputy Governor. (Yes, the Deputy watched over his boss and reported on him to a higher authority!). His Majesty's ears did not discriminate when it came to information flowing towards the crown. As the Englishman, Sir Charles Mathew, one time judicial advisor of the Ethiopian government put it: "In Ethiopia, it is important to know not only who goes with whom, but also who goes on whom."

By the spring of 1969, some eighteen months after I became Mayor, things were beginning to get out of control. There were school boycotts and demonstrations, with riot police using water hoses to disperse demonstrators. Twelfth graders, being in contact with Addis Ababa University students, led the protests, much to the chagrin of government officials and parents. And it was widely believed by both parents and officials that I was behind these movements; I had become radioactive. Whereas at the start of my mayoral "career," people would greet me with warmth, expressing appreciation for the improvements in some of the city's services, now I was greeted with jeers and catcalls. The only ones who seemed immune from this were the Governor and his wife. (In fact, the Governor's wife confided in me one day that one of her sons, a twelfth grader, was involved in the demonstrations, and that she encouraged him not to oppose his friends vocally, even though she did not approve of the student activities. She was afraid he might be victimized by his peers).

What was amazing to me was the fact that even children began to call me names, as they passed me by in the street. Children being the mirror of society, I knew that what they said reflected the views and attitudes of their parents. A favorite epithet hurled at me was *agamido*, (bandit) which was also used at the time to describe Eritrean rebels who were in their eighth year of rebellion under the leadership of the Eritrean Liberation Front (ELF). My family was not spared the harassment, either. One afternoon, my seven-year-old son, Asgede, asked me what *agamido* meant. He told me that the children in his school had called him the son of *agamido*. I told him *agamido* meant a brave fighter, and he should be proud of it. That put his mind at ease and the next time someone called him by that name, he proudly repeated what I had told him; and that seemed to confuse them and end their harassment.

Toward the End of My Banishment

Matters came to a head with two events. The first was a fight that broke out at the Harar Teachers Training Institute (TTI), a government-run boarding school. The student body of TTI, totaling about six hundred, included some eighty Tigrigna-speaking students, with the rest being Amharas and others. Previously, there had been some instances of hostility occasionally resulting in individual fights, but this was the first time that it became a communal conflict. Those from Eritrea and Tigray were pitted against the rest. There were no clear issues of contention; just hate mails and anti-Eritrean and Tigrayan graffiti. One memorable hand-written slogan said, "Rather than pamper Tigreys (Eritreans and Tigrayans), we should kill them."

The Governor ordered that one sent to Addis Ababa for review by a handwriting expert, to be compared with the students' examination papers. Nothing came of the investigation, which added to the sense of isolation and peril felt by the Eritean and Tigrayan students. A critical moment was reached when someone gathered their clothes and dumped them into the waste pit. Then the Governor ordered that they be separated and put in different premises, amid their demand that they be shipped back home. The Governor was dead set against this because of its political repercussions, especially in Eritrea. He asked me and two Eritrean elders to plead with the Eritrean students not to insist on leaving.

The sense of peril was genuinely felt by the Eritreans, a feeling made palpable by the murder, near the Botega area, of Mekonen Hagos, a university service student of Eritrean origin, in whose sudden death the police were prime suspects. In the wake of Mekonen's murder, General Mesfin Embaye warned me to take extra precaution and issued me a Colt 45 with one hundred bullets. In addition I took out a rifle and ammunition from the municipality security department and took it home for protection of my family. The situation was becoming so chaotic that it had the atmosphere of the Wild West in an American movie.

Several attempts were made to resolve the conflict. In one such effort I addressed the assembled student body and tried to reason with them. One statement I made became a memorable quote, taken out of context by Harar residents. It was a reference to a local saying to the effect that when the nose is struck, the eyes weep. It was a warning to the students that if they harmed the minority among them, it would hurt them as well as others. This was later cited to suggest that I was biased in favor of the minority students.

The Governor decided to send me in the company of the region's head of the Orthodox Church (a bishop) to mediate. We expected a favorable response by the students out of respect for the high cleric, but as soon as the good bishop opened his mouth to speak, the students booed, to his utter shock and bewilderment. He was literally shaking when I escorted him out and he exclaimed, "Oh, Dear God! What have we come to?" We left the school grounds immediately and reported to the Governor, who was so angry that he ordered the police to arrest the culprits; (who were never identified). It was the only time when I saw the Governor lose his cool.

The other event that affected my relationship with the Governor concerned developments in the Eritrea liberation struggle and Arab support for that struggle. In 1968 and 1969, the Eritrean guerrillas of the ELF had begun to draw international attention with a series of spectacular actions—including sabotage and airplane highjackings. The Emperor's Representative in Eritrea, one Asrate Kassa, incited public opinion against Arab residents in Eritrea and his actions were copied in several Ethiopian cities. It looked as if Governors were vying with each other as to who could raise more anti-Arab protests. Meharenne Minda, Harar's Deputy Governor, a past master at intrigue, convinced Governor Workneh that Harar should not be left behind and must mobilize public protests against the Arabs.

The Governor asked for my advice; I told him it was a bad idea, and unfair to peaceful Arab residents of the country, who might be harassed or even killed. The Governor, under intense pressure from his Deputy, overruled me and authorized his Deputy to plan the protest march. He also told me to help in mobilizing the residents of the city for the protest march. I refused, but the march went ahead nonetheless. Judging from the catcalls I received from some of the demonstrators, I assumed that Meharenne must have told some of his minions about my refusal. Then the real strife began.

I became a target of slanders and abuse. To the laurels previously placed on my head like *agamido*, were added others like "Arab-lover," *yejemmala ashker* (servant of Arabs), "mercenary," etc. Every time I left my office, a contingent of city plebs assigned to harass me would shout these epithets loudly. I knew who was putting these poor souls up to it. One of them was the provincial Police Chief, General Gashaw Kebede, whose application to the municipality to give him a huge tract of land I had rejected, because there were prior claimants who happened to be poor residents. An additional rumor was that I was a communist and was distributing communist literature to students in the city. With regard to this charge, the Governor had questioned me in connection with a lecture I had delivered at the College of Agriculture. His main complaint was that I had given the lecture without his permission, which was true, and I pledged to him not to repeat it as long as I was under his watch. He then asked, as a side issue, if I had distributed any communist literature to the students. I said I had not, and that was the end of the matter.

In late December 1969, following the murder of the university leader Tilahun Gizaw, there were student boycotts and riots everywhere in the empire. The government and especially the regional police were agitated and did some crazy things. One day in late December, I was visited in my office by a young police officer who told me that his boss, General Gashaw, wanted me to come with him for questioning at the police headquarters. I was astounded by the gall of the general, who was using his police power to wreak revenge on me for my rejecting his request for a land grant. Crazy times make one do crazy things. I pulled my Colt 45, which was loaded, out of the desk drawer and, pointing the gun at him, said:

"Tell your boss to come and get me himself, if he is man enough."

I must have had a wild look on my face, for the officer turned deathly pale and he rushed out in fright. Immediately after he left, I phoned the Governor and informed him what had transpired and told him that I had had enough of this nonsense and would write him a letter.

Gashaw's tricks knew no bounds. Before sending the officer to "arrest" me, he had managed to force information out of three high school students, making them "confess" that I had been behind the student demonstrations and boycotts. One particular demonstration had happened during the TTI crisis and was called to express solidarity with the Eritrean and Tigrayan students. I found out later that that demonstration was organized by Mekonen Hagos, the murdered university student, which was why the police were prime suspects in his murder. The Governor told me later that he was shown the three students signed "confessions," but had asked to interview the students personally. However, Gashaw kept giving excuses for not bringing the students to the Governor. Sometime later, one of the students who was the nephew of a district governor, told his uncle that there was no truth to his signed statement, which was made under duress. Then the student himself told me, with profuse apologies, that the confessions were all fake and that he told his uncle in order that he would inform the Governor.

So Workneh knew Gashaw's story to be false but mentioned nothing to me about it at the time!

The letter that I wrote to the Governor was a two-page lamentation on my unjustified and unexplained exile. Written on the heat of the moment, it was not what one might call a calculated, lawyerly memorandum. It ended by requesting the Governor to find me a solution, either by securing my release from government service and allowed to live and work wherever I chose or failing that, let me have my day in court. Let them charge me or let me go! I was in my rebellious mood and damn the consequences!

I signed the letter, put it in an envelope, and told my secretary to deliver it by hand to the Governor. I had marked it "Urgent and Confidential."

The Governor's response was one of calm reproach. He phoned me and asked me politely to come to his office, which was just across the yard. He said that he would not take any of the steps I requested, and advised me to destroy all traces of the letter and tell nobody about it. He said it was an invitation to disaster and that he would consider the letter as if it had never been written.

Well, that was one piece of advice I did not accept. Indeed, I straightaway showed the letter to Ato Abebe Retta, the then Minister of Agriculture who had come on a visit. I knew and liked Ato Abebe from my student days in England when he was the ambassador of Ethiopia to the United Kingdom. He had always been kind to me and was not in agreement with the way I had been treated. But he too counseled caution. He said he would talk to the new Minister of Interior, Bitwoded Zewde Gebrehiwot, who was a good friend of his. Abebe Reta was a man who kept his word; a couple of weeks later, the Governor informed me by phone that the Minister of Interior had instructed him to send me to Addis Ababa for "consultations." I could not contain my delight and left for Addis immediately. The Minister met me a day after my arrival and told me that he was working something out for me; meanwhile I was to stay put in Addis, visit relatives and generally relax pending the outcome of his efforts. He did not specify the nature of his efforts but I could tell from his favorable reception that my days in exile were going to be over soon.

Back to Addis Ababa

Some ten days later, the Minister of Interior told me that I was going to be transferred back to Addis Ababa as his Legal Advisor. "If it comes to legal advice, why not be at the center of the action, instead of at the periphery?" he said jokingly. He was known for his humor.

I phoned my wife Koki from the home of my friend Asseghid Tessema, at whose house I was staying during the visit. Asseghid and his wife Sally decided that the situation called for a celebration, and by the end of the evening Asseghid and I were "in orbit," as he put it the following morning. We had finished half a bottle of Johnny Walker (black label), bought for the occasion. I will never forget Asseghid's friendship and solidarity throughout my time of exile. He visited me a few times and brought me books and magazine and sweets for my children. Another man whose solidarity I appreciated was Shimelis Adugna. It was indeed a time when one could tell who was a true friend and who was a fake friend of good times. Although eventually, differing views or opposed positions on the Eritrean question would send us our separate ways, I remember both Asseghid and Shimelis with fondness and gratitude.

The story of how Minister Zewde persuaded the Emperor to have me transferred from my place of banishment, as related to me by Abebe Reta, was an example of how his Ministers could manipulate the Emperor in his advanced age. He was nearly eighty at the time and there were unconfirmed reports that

Alzheimer's had begun to affect his memory. According to Abebe Reta, what Minister Zewde told the Emperor was that my presence in Harar had exposed His Majesty's government to adverse publicity and negative comments by foreign visitors. A common question asked by foreigners, Zewde told the Emperor, was: "what is a man like this doing as Mayor of a small provincial town?" Having thus carefully prepared the ground, and having read the Emperor's face, Zewde then proposed that if the subject of the controversy (that is, me) must be watched, he himself would do the watching, here in Addis, while at the same time making me work. The Emperor fell for it and agreed to my transfer to the Ministry, with the warning that I was to be watched closely.

My new position was Legal Advisor in the Ministry of Interior, a new position which the Minister said could mean whatever I wanted it to mean. I could begin, he said, by reviewing the laws concerning the Ministry and see if there were any that needed revision or amendment. A tall order. The Ministry oversaw the regional administration of the whole country, including Eritrea (since 1962), the police, immigration, and security in general. The Minister also told me that, with my background, I could act as his advisor on a number of issues having to do with law and development administration. His concluding words still ring in my ears. He said with a broad smile:

"*Ineho feres. Ineho meda. Ingdih megaleb newa*!" (Here is the horse, here is an open field; so ride on!)

I attacked my job (again, as if it were my dream job!), studying the laws relating to the Ministry, and seeking the views of officials on their respective departments or sections. I came to the conclusion that the sensible thing to do was to separate the administration side of the Ministry from the security side. I knew that the security side was untouchable; it would be a waste of time even to try to change anything having to do with security. So I focused on regional administration and found out that a study had already been made under the aegis of the Public Administration Institute, a semi-autonomous government entity headed by some of the best minds of the country. I also found in Kifle Hagos, an official of the ministry and a fellow Eritrean, an able and willing collaborator. Kifle had been part of the previous attempts at rationalizing regional administration and was enthusiastic in embracing my ideas but cautioned me not to expect too much. He said he was willing to help but was not optimistic that anything positive could come out of these kinds of efforts, in view of his frustrations in the past.

Together with Kifle and others, we tried to revive the earlier initiatives undertaken with the expert advice of the Public Administration Institute, with the goal of giving more autonomous power to the regions on a number of important issues. But it became clear to me that it was an uphill fight. Then, all of a sudden, Zewde was demoted and sent as Governor General of Sidamo and replaced by Getahun Tessema, a staid but decent man who did not wish to upset the apple cart. Getahun came from the generation of Ethiopians with some degree of education who had seen the best and worst of Haile Selassie's government and were getting old and tired. They regarded with benign indifference all attempts at change undertaken by the generation that came after them—my generation. But Getahun still retained a glimmer of hope and from time to time would reluctantly show that glimmer. His earlier reputation as a progressive reformer did not completely abandon him, which was why he did not stand in the way of any attempt to improve the country's administration. In all the meetings I had with him he never opposed any idea proposing change or improvement. But, whereas Zewde would pat you in the back and say, "go ahead or well done" to a piece of memorandum, Getahun would smile and utter a tired word of caution that might have a demoralizing effect on a timid subordinate. Caution and tiredness summed up his ministry and those of his generation.

Suddenly, a Family Problem

None of the initiatives I took with Kifle and others had born fruit when all of a sudden I was faced with a serious family problem, which caused me to shift focus, from work to family. At age three, my daughter Finot was not showing any signs of speaking and her movement was awkward. We kept hoping that she was just a slow starter and that she would speak soon enough. Well, it did not happen, so we took her to the Pediatric Section of Princess Tsehai Hospital for testing. A Swedish pediatrician and head of the section, and Dr. Nebiat Teferi, the noted Ethiopian pediatrician, examined her and heard from us her history of birth. Finot had a difficult birth and it turned out that she had suffered brain damage as a result of shortage of oxygen due to the delayed delivery.

The conclusion of the doctors was that she would never be able to speak. My wife and I were devastated by this piece of news. From then on, my daughter became the center of my attention. I began exploring job prospects abroad and finally landed on a job offer at the World Bank. But the question remained: how could I get release from the government. I could not repeat what I did the last time and leave without permission. Even if I did, I could not take my daughter with me. The solution was for me to convince Minister Getahun to secure my release by taking up my case with his friend, Prime Minister Aklilu. When I broached the subject with Getahun, at first, he was extremely reluctant but I pleaded with him at least to mention to the Prime Minister and arrange a meeting for me. Finally, he agreed to talk to the Prime Minister. However, there was no movement from the Prime Minister's side; I must have waited six or seven months before I gave up on Getahun. I later learned from the Prime Minister's private secretary, that he had indeed taken up my case with the Prime Minister. Getahun would not tell me why there was no outcome from the Prime Minister' side; so I presumed the Prime Minister either was afraid of authorizing my release himself or of telling the Emperor. Whatever the reason for Getahun's inaction, I concluded that the only way out was to find some one to take me to the Emperor. Some friends, Shimelis Adugna among them, advised me to speak to Abebe Kebede, administrator of the Emperor's private charitable empire (known as Bego Adragot). Shimelis Adugna not only recommended him but offered to talk to him, and he did, clearing the way for me to meet Abebe.

I knew Abebe to be a devout Christian who had a reputation for honesty and kindness. I was so desperate to give my daughter a chance that I agreed to go to Abebe. He received me with gentle courtesy and listened to the story of my daughter with great interest. At the end of it, he agreed to talk to the Emperor. He added that the Emperor liked children and that if he agreed to give me an audience, it would be a good idea to take my daughter to the palace with me. He said he had not seen my daughter, but from some who had seen her, she seemed to be a delightful child; all the more reason why I should take her with me when I see the Emperor.

It didn't take Abebe more than a week to get back to me with positive word; he even made an arrangement for me to see the Emperor. As soon as I heard from Abebe I informed Minister Getahun who was glad to know and offered a word of advice on what to say to the Emperor. He said that if I could secure from the Emperor permission to take my daughter out and release from my government employment, on his part he would see to it that the Prime Minister did not object. With that promise, I took my daughter to see the Emperor on the appointed day. Now no one who saw Finot, could resist liking her. As I waited in that familiar waiting room, many stopped to look at her and remark about her beauty. When we were ushered to the Emperor's presence, I held her by the hand, gently pulling her forward and the Emperor looked at her with a big smile. Suddenly, out of nowhere, Lulu, the Emperor's Chihuahua, came running towards her. Finot cried and wrapped her arms around my legs. The Emperor cried *"ayzosh lije, ayzosh,"* (don't be afraid, my child), confirming Abebe's point about his love of children. After sniffing her and me briefly, the dog left us. Finot was three and a half years old at the time; yet she remembers the incident to this day, and laughs when I remind her of it, saying, "that funny dog!"

What followed was typical of the Empror's handling of his subjects. First of all he behaved as if he did not know why we were there. Abebe who was standing to his right got close to him and whispered in his ears. Still the Emperor waited staring at me. The last time I had an audience with him was three years earlier in Dire Dawa where he was spending his annual three-week retreat during the St. Mary *Filseta* fasting time. One day, while I was in my office, Governor Workneh called me and told me that the Emperor wished to speak to me. From past experience, such a call meant trouble, so I thought of a number of things on which I might be questioned by the Emperor. The only matter on which I could be questioned by the Emperor, I thought, would be on the issue of the outstanding bills the palace owed the Municipality, which were overdue by two years. I had ordered the water and electricity to be cut from the palace premises, pending the payment of the bills. So I studied the files and took them with me, just in case.

I needn't have bothered. Immediately after I was ushered to the palace, the Emperor ordered everybody out and we were left alone. After his habitual walk back and forth behind his desk, he asked me how I was and how was the work. I said I was fine and the work was fine. Then he called my name (he always called me Berekete-Ab) and made a short speech about the way the university students were talking about socialism

"Haven't we brought socialism to our beloved people?" he wanted to know.

"Yes, Your Majesty," I chimed, ludicrous though it was. But, hey, I was an exiled "trouble maker", completely at his mercy. I was not going to contradict him, even though I knew it was laughable and I would tell the story to friends for years thereafter. Having secured my concurrence with his claim as a socialist innovator, he then asked me to elucidate on that claim. I was trapped and could not go back on my ready consent. So, I gave examples of the government owned entities like the Telecommunications, the Imperial Highway Authority, the National Bank etc, to prove to him that he had indeed brought socialism to his beloved people!

"That's right. Why can't these students accept the truth and stop their nonsense?"

"I don't know, Your Majesty."

"Yes you do. It is people like you whom we educated and raised to high places who should tell these students what you just told Us."

I just bowed my head and said nothing.

"Anyway, Workneh has told Us you have been doing a good job," he said and, with that famous flip of the wrist, he ended the audience. I left the palace with a sigh of relief..

That was three years before.

Now I was facing that fierce look again, not knowing what lay behind it.

Abebe, who probably thought I had lost my tongue, said, "*Nigerachew Inji*! (Come on, tell Him). I began by thanking the Emperor for granting me the opportunity of the audience. I said I brought the child so that His Majesty could see with his own eyes and find out if this lovely creature was not able to speak. I told him about the doctors' conclusion and that, according to their recommendations that I decided to seek medical help and that I should hurry and take her abroad where there may be better facilities to help her. I was not ready for what the Emperor said in response, cutting me short. I choose to believe that it was just a perfunctory remark uttered by him in order not to appear gullible. Addressing me, he asked:

"Do you seriously think that what God had willed human hand could correct?"

I was not about to engage in theological or philosophical dispute with an all-powerful Emperor when I needed his indulgence.

At that moment Minister Getahun's advice came to me in a flash. He had advised me to invoke Almighty God in asking the Emperor's help. So I said, "Your Majesty, All is possible to God. In his mysterious ways, God could use the hands of the doctors to make the necessary corrections. As a parent, it is my duty to do everything in my power to seek all possible medical help. And May it please God to grant my wish that Your Majesty give the necessary permission for me to take my daughter abroad."

He reflected for a moment and then looked at Finot. He asked her to tell him her name. She did not respond, but giggled.

The Emperor said, "*Ishi Yimoker*" (Allright, let it be tried). I was pleased and bowed appropriately and took my daughter home. On my way home I reflected on the words the Emperor used—"Let it be tried." Ambiguity, again. Could he be playing cat-and-mouse with me? Having taken Finot home, I rushed back to the office to see Minister Getahun. I decided not to speculate on the Emperor's words, but rather to give it a positive spin. I pleaded with my Minister that it was now up to him to persuade the Prime Minister to issue the necessary order releasing me from my job and allowing me to join the World Bank.

It took another three months before I could finally receive the release. Meanwhile, Mr. Iain Murray of the British Embassy had arranged for me to visit Britain, so I used the opportunity to do the interview by an employee of the World bank while on a visit in London. In all of these arrangements I had the inestimable help of Mr. Bulcha Demeksa, who at the time was an Executive Director at the bank. While I was in London I got a call from a man representing the Bank. His name was Hugh Scott, Assistant general Counsel of the bank. He came to my hotel and we had a lengthy conversation, which served as an interview. The letter of appointment came in the latter part of 1972, and I joined the Bank's Legal Department soon thereafter.

1968. I am giving a speech at a mayorial reception. Seated at the right hand corner of the picture is Koki.

With a group of Eritrean elders. The man with his back to the camera is Seyoum Haregot. Addis Ababa, circa 1971.

Addis Ababa 1972. With Colonel Belachew Jemaneh, after a meeting on Law and Regional Government Administration.

London, 1972, At a reception during my visit as guest of the British government. The man with the half visible face is Sir Duncan Cummings, the last British Adminstrator of Eritrea.

General Aman, after his quarrel with the Derg in November 1974

Aman, on the eve of his resignation from his position as Head of State and Chairman of the Derg

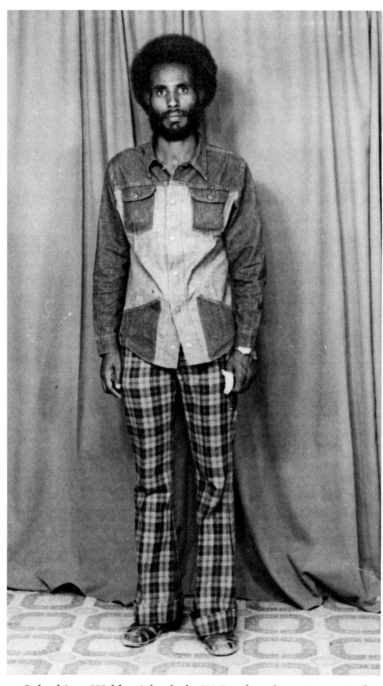

Gebrehiwet Woldemichael, the ELF cadre who got me out of Mekele and into safety in Eritrea, in November 1974. The picture was taken just before he left the Field in 1981.

Washington DC, 1974, My children: Asgede, Finot and Sebene.

Spring 1975. A group of ELF and EPLF fighters at a historic conciliation meeting at AmeSi. I am standing on a lower ground to the left of Isaias. To his right is Hirui Tedla and to Hirui's right is Ibrahim Totil. (photo by Redazghi Gebremedhin)

With my daughter Finot, after I returned to Washington from the Field in 1977.

With my mentor, the legendary Woldeab Woldemariam. Rome 1982.

Taken in 1993, with my brother Tewolde (since deceased).

My elder brother Tekeste, his daughter Tsion and myslef (Stockholm, 2003).

My brother Elias, my sister Bissrat, and a relative (Nairobi, 2005).

PART IV

WORLD BANK, REVOLUTION, AND "DIPLOMACY"

Chapter 13

AS FATE WOULD HAVE IT

At long last, I was ready to go. All the formalities for my exit from the government were finalized. Earlier, unbeknownst to me, Minister Getahun had submitted my name for the position of Minister of State in the Ministry of Interior (the number two position), but the Emperor rejected that, permitting instead the lower position of Vice Minister. That was the position I had assumed at the time I obtained the release from my government position. At the same time, the hiring formalities for joining the World Bank were completed courtesy of Mr. Finsas, the World Bank's representative in Addis Ababa. Thus, by the end of January 1973, I was out of Ethiopia on my way to Washington, D.C.

As I sat in the restaurant of the Rome airport, waiting for my connecting flight to Washington, the past five years of my life flashed back and forth in my mind like a nightmarish film—years of trials and tribulations, but also of exciting challenges. It was hard to absorb the fact of the changing reality; it all seemed unreal. I had much to be grateful for, especially for my family's integrity, thanks to the loyalty and pluck of my wife Koki. And I was thankful for the moral support and good will of a few friends, as well as the decent treatment I received at the hands of conscionable high government officials, especially Governor Workneh (my supposed jailor). In this connection, I must put on record what Workneh told me about somebody special. The Governor and I were walking in the Hakim Gara hills one Saturday afternoon, examining the trees we had planted some months earlier, when he confided in me that during a visit to Harar, accompanying the Emperor, the venerable Ras Imru had quietly urged him to treat me well. According to the Governor, the exact words Ras Imru used were, *"Bereketn Adera"* (I commend Bereket to your care). When I heard this, I remembered the good Ras's intervention in earlier times when I needed help. I also remembered that a few days before my wedding day, his wife and oldest daughter had deigned to come to my humble residence in the Casa Incis section of Addis Ababa to see what I needed for the wedding. They entered the kitchen and saw food being prepared for the small wedding by my domestic helper and some relatives.

The following day, I was astounded to find that a considerable amount of a variety of Ethiopian cuisine was delivered to my home by servants of the Ras Imru family. Ras Imru and his family were the finest representatives of the better side of Ethiopian nobility, with decency and a sense of honor and chivalry, amid a generally sordid company of tawdry "noblemen." What in the Left's literature is often consigned to the dustbin of history as feudal, contained within it certain values that the succeeding social order (the bourgeois order) has lost—a sense of honor and chivalry. I know that I will be demonized by some zealots for making this point, but I am past caring what such zealots say.

All these thoughts came back to me as I sipped the cappuccino served me by a talkative Italian waiter, just before my flight was announced. The waiter and I were engaged in an interesting conversation; he said he was a member of the Communist Party of Italy and inundated me with endless slogans when he discovered that I spoke Italian. I nearly missed my flight, engrossed as I was in the conversation. When I heard the last words of the announcements about my flight ("*imbarco immediato*"), I didn't wait to hear my loquacious Italian interlocutor finish his sentence; I sprang to my feet, grabbed my carry-on bag and rushed toward the gate, turning round and shouting, *"scusa, scusa!"* I boarded the plane just as they were about to close the door. I settled in my seat and relaxed, ready for departure. It was a pleasant flight taking me to a new phase of my life.

I Join the World Bank

It was an unseasonably warm and sunny day on February 1st, 1973. Washington was captivating, with its magnificent buildings, splendid parks, wide avenues and large monuments. Unlike my last visit, twelve years earlier, however, I did not have time to linger, savoring the city's beauty; this time I had an appointment to keep. I had arrived in Washington the previous day and spent a restful night in a small hotel in Georgetown. After a continental breakfast with a generous helping of good coffee, I decided to walk to the bank from the hotel. My appointment was with Hugh Scott, Assistant General Counsel for administrative matters, and the man who had interviewed me in London some four months earlier.

In the days that followed I was inducted into the IBRD (International Bank for Reconstruction and Development), the official name of the World Bank. Long before I joined it, the World Bank had become emblematic of international development aid, with employees numbering in the thousands, many of them from Third World countries. When I started work at the Bank, its professional staff numbered over 3,500. For most of these professionals, employment at the World Bank was like finding the Holy Grail; apart from the good salary and benefits, there was the prestige. As for me, the World Bank was just a way of finding the means to enable my daughter to get the best possible medical treatment. But, as it turned out, it also served as an education in the intricacies of development financing. In less than two years, I was to learn more economics than I had learned at the University of London.

I made it in time for my 9 a.m. appointment and was ushered into Hugh Scott's office. He rose to greet me. He was a lanky, slow moving and slow talking man with a long face and sharp features. After a few minutes' chat, he took me to meet the other members of the Legal Department, which numbered some thirty lawyers at the time. As he walked me down the corridors, I noticed a name posted on one closed door that was familiar—Christian Walser. I said to Hugh that a long time ago when I was in law school, I had a Swiss friend with the same name. "Well" he said, "Christian is Swiss and he may well be your friend." He was on a Bank mission abroad and would be back a week or so later.

A week later, I was in my office reading through the World Bank manuals, as part of my orientation, and lo and behold, a bearded man burst into my office and cried, "Bereket, my dear friend!" The voice was familiar; it was Christian's, but he had put on weight, and that long beard changed his face completely. I sprang up from my chair and we shook hands and hugged. He took me down to the cafeteria where we reminisced on the good old days, over coffee and cakes. We updated each other on our respective works and families. He had an eight-year old boy (Thomas) and a five-year old girl (Sabina). I told him about my children: Asgede, by then aged twelve, Finot, and the youngest, Sebene, aged two. I informed him about Finot's medical problem, and he emitted a prolonged cry of anguished commiseration—Ohhhh! Christian is one of the kindest and most loyal people I have had the good fortune of befriending.

We had not seen each other for some eighteen years, since our last meeting in Copenhagen when we attended a conference convened by the Liberal International. The conference occurred the year of my graduation from law school, but Christian had one more year. His English had improved considerably since then; he had spent a year at the Chicago Law School and then joined the World Bank where he had been for five years when I joined.

It was all serendipitous. Christian would be very helpful to me in negotiating the intricacies of the Bank's corporate maze, and his wife, Judith, assisted me in finding suitable accommodations. Until I found a house to rent, I lived first with friends (Terry and Jeannie Sidley) in Alexandria for about a month and, after that, I sublet an apartment, near Dupont Circle. The Walsers told me about a Mr. Williams, a British employee of the Bank who was living in a rented three-bedroom house with a basement, not far from where they lived in northwest Washington. It was in a pleasant middle-class neighborhood, within walking distance of an elementary school. Mr. Williams was retiring and relocating to his homeland in Britain, and the landlady's agent agreed to transfer the lease from him to me.

At that time, I was neither able nor willing to buy a home. I had already built a house in Addis Ababa, and buying a home abroad was not an option then; it never occurred to me that such a need would arise. It would take a highjacked revolution in Ethiopia and a betrayed liberation struggle in Eritrea to drive out hundreds of thousands of people in mass exodus seeking refuge in foreign lands. I will say something about the stolen revolution and the betrayed liberation a little later. I am making the point here that, at the time, I resisted all counsel and blandishments to buy a home, even when I was able to obtain financial assistance. Christian Walser, for one, did his best to persuade me that it would be a good investment; but I did not budge, much to my regret later.

The housing question thus settled, I called home to tell Koki. With the assistance of the World Bank office in Addis Ababa, my family was able to join me in mid-June, a little over four months after I left them. I had Asgede enrolled in Lafayette Elementary School for the 1973-1974 academic year. Sebene, at two, was too young to go to school; she stayed at home with her mother, her aunt Hirut and a domestic helper brought with the family. Finot's "schooling" was another story which I tell in the next section.

The head of the World Bank's Legal Department, or General Counsel, was Ronnie Broches who was Dutch-born. His deputy was Lester Nurick (American), and there were two Assistant General Counsels, Piero Sella (Italian) and Hugh Scott (American). The rest included a few senior attorneys and the majority of junior attorneys. Piero Sella, a mild mannered, low-key and sophisticated man who spoke both English and French in addition to his native Italian, was considered the conscience of the Department. All the junior attorneys adored him as an extremely kind and helpful supervisor. No similar sentiment was expressed in regard to the other supervisors. In time I also found Piero to be exactly as the others described him. He was calm and polite to a fault, entirely unaffected by the stress of the corporate environment.

I completed my orientation and was inducted into the routine of the Bank's work. According to Jean Webb, who orchestrated the initiation ritual of the Department's new employees, I was ready to "graduate" from trainee to a full-blown attorney of the World Bank "in record time." When I told Christian about this, he laughed it off, noting that Jean said that to everybody, "except maybe those who were not qualified to pass the interview. And he never came face-to-face with those anyway!" We had a good laugh, but I liked Jean Webb who, in his late fifties going on sixty, was obviously the odd man out in the department, sixty-two being the compulsory retirement age for all UN and UN-based employees, at the time. Jean could at times sound insensitive during the "training" sessions; his attempts at simplifying could appear condescending. I remember once when he was explaining to me the intricacies of the money markets. Imagining that I would grasp the issues better, he asked me to think of an African village market with sacks of grain, different fruits and vegetables and other things brought by farmers and displayed on the ground. Wall Street, he said, is a complicated kind of market of invisible commodities.

Now an African or Asian with a modicum of education can grasp abstract ideas without being reminded of simple village economic facts; and at least two "Third World" lawyers working in the Bank thought Jean Webb's exotic examples were condescending. My own view was that he was motivated by a desire to help, compounded with an eagerness to please. When overdone, such motives can easily end up being misunderstood. Nor was this limited to Jean Webb; as I would discover later, too many World Bank staff suffered from a sense of superiority vis-à-vis the people they go out to help. More often than not, missionary zeal may be a mask for a species of professional hubris.

A World Bank attorney plays a central role in the Bank's lending activities, if not in shaping its policies. He or she is involved in preparing loan documents, negotiating loan agreements with borrowing countries and to these ends, periodically traveling to countries under his/her area of responsibility. In my case, these included Burma, Greece, India, Iraq, Mauritania, Morocco, Upper Volta (Burkina Faso), and Yugoslavia. Much of the work was repetitive and boring, but the documents on the history and political economy provided a good deal of education, and there were occasional moments of excitement, especially during negotiations when knowledgeable negotiators challenged some of the Bank's terms and conditions. My own view on the Bank has been shaped not only as a result of my insider's look, but due to much reading and reflection on its role. The following is a summary overview on this topic.

The World Bank—Rich Uncle to the Poor?

Beginning in the late sixties, some serious criticisms began to be leveled at the World Bank. Even as it began to increase the volume of its development aid, the criticisms multiplied, coming from different quarters. The Bank was viewed differently by different people, depending on their perspectives, which may be reduced to two basic positions, divided along a Left/Center axis and a Center/Right axis. The Left critique argued that the Bank was an instrument of Western corporate capital and was useless to the mass of the Third World peoples, since only the ruling elites derived benefits from its lending activities. The argument also held that multinational corporations also benefited by selling goods that were not a matter of necessity to ordinary people.

The Centrist position was essentially supportive of the Bank's role as an important vehicle for transfer of resources, for development of the Third World, and as a facilitator of trade among nations. The numerous publications financed or sponsored by the Bank itself fell into this category. Their wealth of information provided an insight into the Bank's philosophy and into many aspects of its diverse activities. At the same time they could be considered as organizationally self-serving. In fact the first major work sponsored by the Bank, written by Mason and Asher (1974), came two years after Teresa Hayter's devastating critique, *Aid as Imperialism* (1972).

The Right critique, viewing foreign aid as wasteful, charged that the Bank's "soft" development aid (interest free and low interest credit) did not help in influencing the borrower countries to redirect their economies towards a market orientation. The Liberal/Center answered this critique by asserting that the Bank promoted economic growth, domestically by stimulating capital accumulation through savings and investment, and externally through export expansion and diversification. The claim that the Bank's role did not have the effect of redirecting economies toward a market orientation has been disproved by events.

To the above may be added what may be called a Third World perspective, which is not reducible to a single category because it is a composite of different ideologies. Its unifying theme is a sense of a historical wrong committed against the Third World, a wrong that has yet to be rectified. Movements toward rectification converged in a demand for a new international economic order (NIEO), which was given a stamp of legitimacy when the United Nations General Assembly passed a resolution adopting some of NIEO's demands in 1975. One aspect of the demand was that there should be equitable representation in the governance in the World Bank and its sister institution the International Monetary Fund (IMF).

Both the IBRD (World Bank) and the IMF were created at the close of World War II, at Bretton Woods, New Hampshire, by the dominant forces of the world economy, led by the United States of America. The IMF was mandated under its charter to provide short-term loans to help member countries facing balance of payment deficits, and to enforce financial discipline in the post-war international financial system. Its role has been cast as that of a policeman of the international financial order. The IBRD, on the other hand, was mandated to help finance reconstruction of Europe after World War II, and to foster development efforts through the transfer of resources world-wide.

The governance of the two Bretton Woods institutions has been and is still dominated by the United States and four or five of its Western allies, most of them represented in what has come to be known as the G-8. These economic powers and the other industrial nations are often referred to as "The North," and the less developed world is collectively known as "The South." The South's attempt, through NIEO and other initiatives, to redress the inequality of their trade relationship with the North proved unsuccessful. And the governance of the World Bank and the IMF have remained virtually unchanged.

In the present era of globalization, the prospects for a new, and fairer, global order are remote. The gap is widening: the rich get richer, the poor get poorer—and are heavily indebted as well. The recent annual protests at G-8 venues are an organized, if feeble, continuation of the failed attempts at rectification of the past thirty years. If history is any guide, it is doubtful whether such protests will succeed in securing a fair deal for the South, in terms of equitable distribution of resources and fair terms of trade.

The record of the World Bank after a half a century of lending and technical assistance is a mixed one. Its major achievements lie in infrastructure, a traditionally "safe" sector for lending with guaranteed financial returns. The Bank's record has also been noteworthy in the area of manpower development, principally centered in the education sector. In the more problematic area of agriculture, the Bank has grappled with contradictory policies, some flowing from its own philosophy, others stemming from those of its borrowing countries.

Clearly, the Bank's role cannot be viewed outside the context of the dominant economic and legal order in which it is not generally expected to act as an "honest broker," given its central position in that system. The lending policies and practices of the Bank have tended to reflect the ideology and interests of the dominant forces of the global system. Consequently, the benefits of its lending have not always accrued to the supposed beneficiaries—the great mass of the people of the Third World. Indeed, much of the benefits have accrued to the industrialized countries in the form of sales of goods and services, with some benefits trickling down to the developing countries. And even these trickled benefits have tended to be concentrated in the hands of urban and other local elites.

A recent example of Bank policy may serve to illustrate the persistence of this historic pattern. The World Bank's financing of projects involving the extractive industries such as oil, gas, coal and other minerals has barely advanced its declared policy and rhetoric of reducing poverty. In 2001, the President of the Bank, Mr. Wolfenson, commissioned a panel of experts to study the role of the Bank in the extractive industries. In 2004, following a three-year investigation, the panel recommended that the Bank should stop financing oil projects by 2008, and should immediately begin to support oil or gas extraction or mining in countries with a well-established rule of law and effective regulation. The panel's aim was not only the elimination of corruption but the fair distribution of the benefits derived from Bank-financed projects. Not surprisingly, the Bank management rejected the recommendations.

The appointment of the neo-conservative hard-liner and principal architect of the Iraq war, Mr. Paul Wolfowitz, is an indication of what we can expect in the future operation of the Bank. Funny, how they're all named "wolf!"

In view of the foregoing and the overall record of the Bank, I don't know how long I might have stayed as an employee. I know that I was conflicted even then, long before the onset of the current worldwide protest movement by anti-globalization forces. In my daily contacts at work, I occasionally expressed views that surprised some in the Bank. One morning, a little over a year after I had been in the Bank, Ronnie Broches, the General Counsel, called me to his office and told me that he had been informed by a reliable source about some "radical" views I had expressed, "unworthy of a professional man" like me with a promising future. He asked me what I thought of Teresa Hayter's work on the Bank; I said that she had made a critique that needed to be answered, which was as noncommittal as I could make it. He said, she will be answered.

He advised me to be careful of what I said. While I was free to express my views, he said, it would stand in the way of my bright prospects if those views did not tally with the policies of the Bank. He then informed me that he had spoken about me to some of his senior colleagues, and that I was being considered for the position of Secretary of the Bank, a post carrying the rank of Vice President. One day, he came to my office and asked me if I was too busy to have coffee; I said no. He then took me to the office of the Bank's then Secretary, a genial man from Pakistan. Broches introduced me to him and withdrew, leaving us alone.

The Secretary then made a long speech about his work and switched to the good old days at Oxford. He made several references to the works of P.G. Wodehouse and told a number of jokes, capping each joke with a hearty laugh, in which I joined out of sheer politeness. I felt as if I were in the Senior Common Room of Balliol College, Oxford!

Then in July 1974, just before I left for Ethiopia, Broches again mentioned the position of Secretary, informing me that it was to be vacated in a year, when current Secretary was retired. I thanked him for his confidence in me and for sharing the information. I then said that we would see what happened after my return from Ethiopia, in three or four months' time, not knowing that I was not destined for that kind of professional career.

Fnot's Fate Unfolds

The impact of my daughter Finot's condition on my life and the lives of the other members of my family has been momentous, as I will explain. To begin with, she was the reason why I came, and brought my family, to the United States. While it would be far-fetched to describe it as idyllic, my married life was a happy one. Ours was an ethnically mixed marriage; I am Eritrean, Koki is Amhara (Ethiopian). Although there were some expressions of dismay on both sides of the family, as was to be expected, this fact never posed a serious problem to us as a couple. The only potential problem was language when it came to my mother speaking with Koki, since neither spoke the language of the other. The few times they "spoke" to each other there was a lot of laughter as they used sign language and struggled with words; (the two languages being related as Semitic languages, there are many common words).

All our children were born in Addis Ababa, and Amharic was spoken at home. Finot was born December 31, 1966, four and a half years after Asgede. Koki and Asgede had left London for Addis Ababa in June of that year, leaving me behind to finish my doctoral work. I had some six months to go before Finot was born. I lived in anxiety for several weeks before the birth and was greatly relieved when I received a telegram announcing the good news. The telegram did not mention that it had been a difficult birth, a fact that I would learn upon my joining the family in July 1967. Yet there was no sign of the mental retardation that would emerge later.

Of all the vicissitudes of my life—and I have had several—none was more painful than the discovery that my little daughter, Finot, had suffered brain injury at birth, and that as a result of the injury she would never be able to speak. That was what Koki and I were told in a grave voice by Professor Bo Bahlquist, head of the Ethio-Swedish Pediatric Clinic at Addis Ababa, one gloomy afternoon. It was one of those moments when you feel as though the entire universe had conspired against you. It is darkness at noon, and you feel as if life is coming to an end. If you are religious, you either seek divine help, prostrating yourself, or perhaps go the other way and begin to entertain doubts about the basis of your religion. I, for one, was sorely tested in that score, and strayed from the path for many years.

After Finot's evaluation, two members of the clinic, Dr. Nebiat Teferi and Dr. Nerayo T. Michael (who happens to be a relative of mine), encouraged us to take Finot abroad and try our luck. As they made the suggestion, the words of Professor Bahlquist rang in my ears—"I am afraid she will never speak." Obviously, his two colleagues were not as certain, and each offered to write to clinics in the US and UK to see if anything might be done for her.

As it happened it was the efforts of other friends that produced results. Foremost among these was Harris Wofford, my old friend from the early 1960s who was head of the Peace Corps, Africa Office. Another was Ruth First. Between the two of them, these old friends (who did not know each other), were responsible for our choice of the Institute for the Advancement of Human Potential in Philadelphia. Ruth First, the late South African writer and anti-apartheid freedom fighter, upon hearing of our predicament, had written me a long letter explaining the case of the daughter of a friend of hers who had been successfully treated at the Institute. Ruth strongly recommended that we apply for a place at the Institute.

I wrote to Harris Wofford, who was then President of Bryn Mawr College, just outside Philadelphia. He wrote a strong letter to Dr. Glenn Doman, Director of the Institute, requesting Finot's admission for evaluation and treatment. Because he learned that there was a long waiting list and that we might have had to wait for over a year, Harris enlisted the support of his friend and former boss, Mr. Sargent Shriver, to help in the efforts. Dr. Doman's letter of acceptance, written to Harris, with a copy to me, is a classic—it is a study in the delicate balance struck between the old ethical imperative known as the Hippocratic Oath (admit all patients, and do no harm) on the one hand, and the bureaucratic imperative (first come, first served) on the other. In a letter written to me on August 31, 1972, Dr. Doman explains the decision he made admitting Finot to his Institute. The following excerpt from the letter illustrates the dilemma he faced.

> "...I learned of your daughter, Finot, through a phone call from Dr. Wofford asking us if we could accept your daughter for treatment. His very strong recommendation in favor of your daughter's acceptance has been a very strong factor in our setting aside an early appointment for her. Sargent Shriver has also spoken in her behalf....
> In the truest sense of the word...every child in the world who requires treatment (in the Institute) would have it. There is however a long waiting list for children to be seen and evaluated here at the Institute...Dr. Wofford's strong appeal in your daughter's behalf has induced us to add her name *in addition to* the children already scheduled and not *instead of* another child."

The Institute's rules required that both parents be present at the child's first two-day evaluation and orientation sessions. Since I did not as yet have the Ethiopian government's release, we persuaded the Institute management that one of us, Koki, would be present at the first session and that we would both be present in the follow-up sessions. Koki and Finot left Addis Ababa for Philadelphia and were met at the airport by aides of Harris Wofford, then taken to the home of Bill and Ann Ewing where they stayed throughout. I was able to join Koki and Finot for the second evaluation, by which time I was cleared to leave government work and join the World Bank.

We stayed with the Ewings throughout the process of Finot's second "treatment." At the time, their first daughter, Susanna, was a toddler. Their kind hospitality and friendship, in addition to that of Harris and Clare Wofford, helped us immeasurably in meeting the toughest challenge we had ever faced as a family. I remember our evening chats and political discussions with Bill and Ann. This was during the 1972 election, and Sargent Shriver was George McGovern's running mate. We spent many hours discussing a range of issues, including Vietnam. Bill had been a young law professor in the newly opened Law School in Addis Ababa and shared an office with me during the two or three weeks I was in the Law School before I was banished to Harar.

The Institute followed what came to be known as the Doman—Delacato Method of treatment. It is an unorthodox and controversial program for brain-injured children, premised on treating the cause, instead of the symptoms, of brain injury. To this end Glen Doman and Carl Delacato established the Institute for the Advancement of Human Potential, in which children are treated as outpatients. The treatment is carried out at home by the parents; and therein lay the problems. The Institute instructs parents in the methods to be used in each particular case, following diagnostic evaluation; patients return to the Institute every two or three months for reevaluation. The therapeutic programs are arduous, requiring the full attention of parents and often helpers for the greater part of each day.

Success, even when it occurs after months or years of efforts, is slow and not easily perceived. Judging by the success stories and the long waiting list, people keep hoping for good results and a few persevere even when there is no perceivable progress. One of the success stories was the daughter of a friend of Ruth First, who told me about the Institute. The method uses what they call "patterning," involving crawling and creeping and moving of the arms and legs in different positions for which at least two people must be engaged each time. The theory is that the patterning stimulates the brain, conceivably leading to the growth of new cells. Apart from being very controversial, the method is exhausting and frustrating particularly when no appreciable progress is achieved.

We tried it with Finot for a little under a year, during which time Koki and a domestic helper carried out the job. It was beginning to affect the family in more ways than one. For one thing, Sebene, our youngest daughter, felt neglected and wanted to be "treated" the same way. For another, since I had to go to work every day, the entire burden fell on Koki, and this began to affect our marriage. Above all, we did not see any progress; so in addition to the negative views we had heard expressed by some doctors on the Doman-Delacato Method, we felt that we were wasting time and energy as well as risking collateral damage to the family. We decided to change course.

With the help of our indefatigable and loyal friend, Harris Wofford, once again we enlisted the advice and help of Sargent Shriver who facilitated Finot's enrollment in the Kennedy Institute for Special Education in Washington, DC. It is a school for the "mentally challenged," as the affliction is known nowadays. The Kennedy Institute uses an Individualized Education Plan (IEP) with each child, taught by an individual expert. Finot's attendance of this school had mixed results. She established a loving relationship with some of her more caring teachers, and two or three of the nuns who ran the school. We felt justified in sending her there instead of the Philadelphia Institute, which would have destroyed our family.

Meanwhile, the Empire is Tottering...Will it Fall?

I had been in Washington for a little over a year, working in the World Bank, when the gathering storm of protests spearheaded by Ethiopian university students exploded in the face of the old Emperor and his government, becoming a full-blown, many-sided revolt. It started with a series of army revolts at the periphery of the empire—Eritrea in the north and in Sidamo in the south; in Harar in the east, and in Debre Zeit, among the elite air force officers, in the center. The revolts of the military were followed and, in some cases accompanied, by strikes called by teachers, taxi drivers, labor unions, etc.

It seemed as if the hopes and dreams of my generation for meaningful change were on the verge of fulfillment. Everyone wondered whether His Majesty's government would collapse. Will the tottering empire fall? If so, what would replace it? Those of us living in Washington met regularly and asked these questions; and the answers came as if in a slow motion movie. In mid-June 1974, some four months after the first army mutinies, the various units of the military elected representatives to meet in Addis Ababa, at the headquarters of the Fourth Division (Meshalokia), and established a committee to coordinate their disparate elements and to guide and control the course of the fast-moving events. It seemed to be only a matter of time before there would be some kind of change. But nobody was certain what kind of change it would be—reformist or radical?

By the time the military formed the Coordinating Committee of the armed forces, or Derg (Amharic for committee) , in late June, public pressure and military threats had forced the resignation of Prime Minister Aklilu's government. The all-powerful Emperor succumbed to the pressure, accepted Aklilu's resignation, and chose the Oxford-educated aristocrat, Endalkachew Mekonen, to form a government. Endalkachew's choice meant more of the same. Everyone wanted to know if the military would accept the choice. Would they give Endlkachew a chance to reform the system?

The answer came soon. Not only did the Derg members not want to give Endalkachew a chance, they demanded his resignation and, as soon as he resigned, arrested him. By that time, they had quietly and methodically removed the principal pillars of the empire, arresting the ex-Prime Minister Aklilu and all members of his cabinet as well as all high-ranking army officers, governors and other dignitaries—including my benefactor, Governor Workneh. In Endalkachew's place, they appointed Michael Imru, a popular liberal intellectual and son of Ras Imru. Before they did all this, they chose as their gray eminence and guide, my friend and fellow Eritrean, Lt. General Aman Andom, first as Chief of Staff of the Armed Forces, then as Minister of Defence, and finally as Head of state. Aman was given the last post following the deposition of the Emperor.

The Derg deposed the Emperor unceremoniously on September 12, 1974, after making sure that his base of support was safely removed. They sent a small delegation to the palace to inform him that from then on he would live in a place assigned to him by the Derg. When they ushered him out of his glorious palace and into the waiting Volkswagen Beetle, it is doubtful if the reality of his diminished status had sunk in to his consciousness, for he waved to the mobs who were shouting *"Leba! Leba!"* (Thief! Thief!). He was used to cheering all his life. **Sic transit gloria mundi**, I said to myself.

In 1970, two years before the revolutionary ferment began, the Emperor had celebrated his 80th birthday with much fanfare. All high-ranking members of the government had been summoned to witness the occasion. As we walked past him, paying obeisance, he stood as if in a trance. It was as if he had withdrawn from reality, a condition that seemed to be confirmed by the obscene spectacle in which he was seen feeding cows and dogs on the roadside, every week, while people starved. The empire was tottering, yet he seemed unaware of it, or unconcerned. Rebellions and protests raged everywhere, yet he presided over a government that forged on, unconcerned with what was happening. In Eritrea, the liberation war raged and the government kept defining it as the work of a handful of rebels. In a series of engagements between the government forces and the Eritrean Peoples Liberation Front (EPLF), the government forces suffered humiliating defeats in Eritrea's Sahel region, and no one in the government seemed to care about wounded soldiers and their families. This fact was one of the particulars of the offence in the bill of indictment the army used against the Emperor's government.

The protests, army mutinies, Eritrea's war and the Wollo famine converged to build a momentum that became what a British journalist called "a creeping coup." In addition to the dismissal and eventual arrest of Endalkachew and many members of the Emperor's Cabinet, the Derg also insisted on the formation of a Commission of Enquiry to investigate corruption and other wrong doings of the Emperor's government. The fifteen-member commission was composed of five members elected by Parliament, five representing the armed forces and five representing the professions. I was one of the five elected by the Parliament, in absentia, while I was in Washington. I can only guess that what impelled them to nominate me may have been the notoriety I had gained as critic of government even as I served as the Emperor's Attorney General. Indeed, I had earned the Emperor's wrath and suffered exile and banishment, as I have already related. Now, as I was enjoying a peaceful and fairly lucrative life, I accepted the nomination with great reluctance and for a fixed term.

Of all the events that gave momentum to the revolution, none was as important as the famine in the northern region of Wollo, and the hundreds of thousands of victims that the government could have helped but didn't. That famine attracted international attention due to a report by Jonathan Dimbleby, a BBC reporter. A fickle international press, which had hitherto yawned with disinterest, was now galvanized by the sight of emaciated bodies, the victims of the Wollo famine. Dimbleby's film shown on the BBC and elsewhere led to a public outcry the world over. The Emperor was shown to be without his clothes, so to speak—feeding animals while peasants dropped dead like flies. The work of the Commission of Enquiry thus started with the Wollo Famine.

At first, I did not accept my election to the Commission of Enquiry. Apart from the hazards of getting in the middle of an uncertain situation, there was my family, which needed my support. I would lose my income from the World Bank if I just up and left. Despite my objections, the pleas for my acceptance of the Commission's work continued coming from different people. Since the Commission was formed during Endalkachew's ministry, the Ethiopian envoy in Washington passed on the ill-fated new Prime Minister's pleas to me. Endalkachew even telephoned me one night. But I was not moved. Then, Lt. General Aman Andom sent his own envoy, Mr. Kifle Worku, a civilian Vice Minister at the Ministry of Defense, with a special personal plea to accept if only on a short-term basis, assuring me that the financial problem would be taken care of. In a letter and through Kifle, Aman reminded me of our common struggle in previous years and urged me to come to help him in the hour of need. Aman's request was not limited to membership in the Commission of Enquiry; so I made it clear to Kifle Worku that I was not interested in any ministerial or other position, but that I might consider going to Addis on a short-term appointment to help in the work of the commission, provided the World Bank gave me leave.

My wife was not in favor of the idea, but I persuaded her that a few months' work would help the new and inexperienced officers and their leader who, she knew, was my friend. I promised her that I would not leave unless there was a firm commitment from Aman and his fellow-revolutionaries that alternative pay was arranged. (This question of alternative pay would give rise to unexpected problems later). Having talked Koki into reluctantly accepting my short-term appointment, I then held consultations with my colleagues at the World Bank. Most were excited at the prospect of one of their colleagues being involved in a revolutionary process. One of them, an Argentine, said that he would give his right arm to be in my place. I am sure it was Latin hyperbole; could it have been the Che Guevara effect, the subliminal influence of his renowned compatriot?

One person who was enthusiastic in favor of my accepting the appointment—but only short term—was Ronnie Broches, the Bank's General Council. He assured me that there would be no problem with my position in the Bank. Broches told the Bank's then President Robert McNamara about it and made sure that I spoke to McNamara. So, my decision was made to accept the appointment as a member of the Commission of Enquiry for a maximum of six months. I saw MacNamara in his twelfth floor office a few days before my departure to Addis Ababa. His reception was warm and cordial. I had seen him many times before, chairing meetings of the Bank's Board of Directors and at various Bank functions. I had heard him speak tearfully about the world's poorest people and of the need to abolish what he called "absolute poverty." But I had never come this close to him or talked to him personally. His record as U.S. Secretary of Defense during the Vietnam War was highly controversial, and many regarded his rhetoric about the world's poor as a kind of expiation for those "sins." If so, leading the World Bank is hardly life in Purgatory. But, judged by the standard of official development politics, by what has come to be known as the Washington Consensus, his record at the Bank was one of the best, if not *the* best.

Our meeting lasted about twenty minutes. After the customary introductions, he began by asking me if I knew what I was getting into: did I know any of the principal actors of the revolution? I said I did and he smiled and reflected a little. I also gave him a brief account of the causes of the revolt. He had indeed heard about the Wollo famine and spoke movingly about the horror of it all. He had been to Ethiopia and visited the Bank-supported agricultural project in the district of Chilalo in Arsi province, known as CADU. Finally, he said something that amazes me now but which I did not consider relevant at the time. Making specific reference to the French Revolution, he told me to beware. Remember, he warned, that revolutions end up consuming their children. As I rose to leave, McNamara shook my hand and said gravely, "just be very careful." As I will describe below, the Ethiopian revolution did consume some of its children and nearly ended up consuming me. To this day, I wonder how a hard-boiled business executive like Robert McNamara, generally perceived as uncaring, could have such historical knowledge and insight as to make a remark that proved prophetic.

Where Angels Fear to Tread

When I arrived in Addis Ababa, in late July, the Commission of Enquiry had begun its preparatory work, including the election of its chairman. According to fellow Eritrean and Member of Parliament, Mewael Mebrahtu, he and many of the other commissioners had delayed the vote for over two weeks, with the aim of electing me chairman of the Commission. My lateness forced them, he said, to accept the chairmanship of geography professor, Mr. Mesfin Woldemariam. Personally, I was glad I had come late, for I did not wish to chair the Commission as it might delay my planned return to Washington.

My brother-in-law, Abate Menkir, met me at the airport and took me to his house, where I stayed for much of the turbulent four months that almost cost me my life. Koki's oldest brother, Yohannes Menkir, had suddenly died some four months before, so the first thing I did upon my arrival was to visit my mother-in-law to pay due homage and share condolences. Of Koki's many siblings, Yohannes was the closest to me; he was a fine human being, with unique insights expressed in acerbic wit. I missed him very much especially during those fateful months.

The following day, Abate took me to the home of General Aman, which was very close to his own house. Aman was away in a meeting but I left a note informing him that I was in town and where he could reach me. He called me in the evening and sent a car to pick me up. He was very happy to see me and grateful that I had decided to come. He also revealed to me that some in the Derg were not favorable to the Commission, which was formed during Endalkachew's short ministry. He said that I could do better work as a minister and that I could take any ministry I chose. I told him that I was not interested in any ministry; that I came to help for a few months and was due to return to Washington by the end of the year. He was not happy, but he could not persuade me. He knew why I had gone to America in the first place and that I had a family to look after. There have been reports that my work with the Derg was in a ministerial capacity. For instance, in one of his books, the British writer, Fred Halliday, wrote that I was the Attorney General of the Derg, obviously confusing my earlier position under the Emperor. The fact is that I was a member of a commission that was not appointed by the Derg, and was even intensely disliked by the Derg. And my work with the commission lasted some four months before I escaped to Eritrea, as I will explain in the next chapter.

I briefed Aman on the arrangement I made with the World Bank and explained to him that the World Bank had agreed to release me on the understanding that there would be an alternative source to substitute my salary. He readily agreed that he would tell the Derg member responsible for finance, and make an arrangement for me to speak to the person concerned. It turned out that the person responsible for this, as for much else, was Mengistu, and Aman made an arrangement for me to see Mengistu a few days later. Mengistu listened intently to what I had to say and said that there would be no problem. But there were problems, not from the Derg, but from Mesfin, chairman of the Commission of Enquiry, who complained that the amount of money I was to be paid was far in excess of the salary scale paid to any other Ethiopian. He would repeat this again and again for years, although he knew that the pay was not for me, but for the upkeep of my family, which was living in a city with a very high cost of living. In the end, I said, there was a simple alternative: I would go back to Washington to resume my World Bank work, if Mesfin persisted in his objections. And that took care of it.

A couple of days after my arrival, Abate took me to the office of the Commission of Enquiry, which was located on the second floor of a building near the Parliament. Mesfin received me in his office and introduced me to the other members of the Commission, some of whom I knew. Among the five military representatives, I only knew one, a graduate of the Harar Military Academy as well of the new Law School. They all seemed pleased to see me join them in the heady exercise of power; we were in uncharted territory, investigating the wrongdoings of the Emperor's government. There were public expectations of great things to come. But no one knew what would happen, and that uncertainty was itself part of the excitement.

The Derg dished out its daily menu of charges of power abuse and corruption of the imperial government on the radio, in newspapers and TV. The TV showed the Emperor feeding dogs while peasants starved. Each time these pictures were shown the public reaction was harsh in the extreme, many demanding that the Ministers be summarily shot and their bodies exhibited dangling from trees all over the city so that the people would see and feel vindicated. This public outrage was closely monitored and managed by the public relations department of the Derg.

In the Commission's meetings the first few days, I could see that some of the members, especially the military representatives, were affected by the public sentiment and the Derg's management of public anger. I remember raising this point and asserting that the Commission was a legally constituted body, autonomous in its function and duty-bound not to be swayed by mob action and reaction. There was a stunned silence. Then Mesfin spoke in support of my sentiments, and inquired if there were any objections; there were none. This point would later become one of the bones of contention between the Derg and the Commission. I also raised the question with General Aman, who was in favor of applying due process principles in the conduct of the Commission's inquiry. He assured me that he would raise this point among his Derg colleagues so that there would be no misunderstanding.

With the exception of Mewael, who had experience in pleading and parliamentary questioning, none of the other Commissioners had experience in criminal investigation of the magnitude involved in the Wollo disaster. There was also a police officer with some experience in simple criminal investigation. Consequently, the task of masterminding the strategy and mechanics of the process fell on our meager shoulders. So where and how to begin? Mesfin was in favor of starting with the Wollo famine, having been involved in fund raising (as well as consciousness-raising) for the victims. I agreed wholeheartedly and we went about designing the strategy for the investigation.

Issues Concerning the Wollo Famine

We first had to frame the issues by answering some questions. What was the cause of the catastrophic famine? Was drought the only or even the main cause, or was there a way in which government policies and politics contributed to the disaster? If so, in what way, and who in the government was responsible? Why was the government caught unaware of such a disaster in a central region of the country, where there had been instances of drought a decade earlier? How did such a pattern escape government ministries such as the Ministry of Agriculture? Or were the responsible government departments aware and did not take the necessary steps to avert the famine? What could they have done in that respect? Was there a cover-up of the disaster before and after Jonathan Dimbleby's film exposed it to the rest of the world?

There were lengthy debates and exchange of views on these questions. Having agreed on the answers, the Commission then prepared a list of documents to review and of people to summon for questioning in its plenary sessions. Target ministries and responsible personnel were identified. Standard procedure of legal discovery was followed. Documents in concerned ministries, such as Interior, Information and Agriculture were identified, tagged and flagged. Summons of concerned personnel were also issued.

A question that caused some heated debate was the responsibility of the Emperor in the matter under investigation. Some of us anticipated that the Prime Minister would shelter under the imperial cloak, arguing that he was following orders. Apart from the fine legal issue of whether the command of a superior can be a defense in criminal prosecution, the Commission faced the question of whether the Emperor could be prosecuted under existing law. It became an emotional issue; a couple of the members even ridiculed the very idea of raising the issue. In this respect, the law was on their side since the Commission was following strict legality in its undertaking and the Constitution of Ethiopia rendered the Emperor immune from any legal responsibility. The Emperor was the Derg's prisoner; so whether he was legally responsible or not, politically he was made helpless, which was more important from the perspective of those in power.

As was expected, Prime Minister Aklilu invoked the Emperor's order and his indisputable power in his defense. I remember asking the Prime Minister whether he thought the Emperor was above the law, or the law was above the Emperor. His answer was that the law was above everybody. But then the law (the Constitution of the time) made the Emperor's power indisputable. The law was thus on the side of Aklilu. Whether he could use that defense in the case under investigation—in criminal negligence and dereliction of duty in the matter of the Wollo famine—was another matter. The Commission's findings were that Aklilu and some of his underlings were responsible for dereliction of duty and for cover-up of the famine.

The Commission's proceedings became an educational undertaking of unexpected significance. The Commission decided to make its proceedings public, broadcasting the process on the national radio in a strategy that worked wonders. It galvanized public opinion, like a kind of "soap opera," as some of the principal personalities of the imperial regime were questioned on their role in the making of the Wollo disaster and held to account for their actions and omissions. There had been nothing like it in Ethiopian history. Since I asked most of the questions, a close friend joked that, in a matter of four months, I had become more famous than in all my years of legal work.

The Commission became so popular that the Derg began to get worried, seeing it as another power center. Eventually, some of the top Derg members began to harass us, threatening to kill the Ministers if the Commission did not deliver quickly. There were repeated complaints that the process was taking too long. What the members of the Derg meant, of course, was that the quasi-legal investigative process was getting in the way of their ambition to be done with the remnants of the previous government and rule the country in their own name, which they eventually did. They feared that a continuation of the Commission's process would lead to public validation and thus undermine their authority.

All this raised an interesting question about the relationship betwee law and revolution, or more specifically, legal process and revolutionary process. I remember raising this question both with Aman and Prime Minister Michael Imru. To my surprise, I found Aman favoring the primacy of legal process, even though he was acutely aware that there were elements in the Derg demanding summary execution of all the detainees. This troubled him greatly and was one of the causes of the eventual break between him and the Derg. Prime Minister Imru, on the other hand, had no qualms about letting the Derg use revolutionary methods. He told me that in a meeting he had with the political committee of the Derg, he offered to resign and let them take whatever revolutionary measures they needed to take. Indeed, before long they accepted his resignation and, after the overthrow of the Emperor, made Aman head of state and government. This would not last more than three months.

Meanwhile, the Commission continued questioning individuals who had been involved in the Wollo famine in one way or another. These included: former Prime Minster Aklilu; three former Ministers of Agriculture; former Ministers of Interior, including my two benefactors, (Zewde Gebrehiwot and Getahun Tessema); former governors of Wollo; former Minister and Vice Minister of Information; newspaper editors and radio managers. As the Ministers were brought to the Commission, a throng of city mobs shouted "*leba! leba!*" (thief! thief!) and this was duly reported in the media. It served to whet the appetite of the radical elements in the Derg who began to complain that our handling of those who appeared before us during the questioning sessions was too soft and respectful.

These elements were clearly after blood. They ordered the entire Commission to appear at their headquarters one night and subjected us to a series of intimidating comments and questions. This was designed to compel us to do their bidding. We held fast to the principle of due process and insisted that they give us time to complete the investigation. We explained that we were only an investigating organ, not a court, and that the final decision lay in their hands. They let us go with a warning that we should expedite the process and dispatch these leboch (thieves) to their deserved fate!

Understandably, some members of the Commission showed anxiety and began to question whether the legal process was necessary. Strenuous efforts were made by members of the political committee of the Derg to convince us to accept a new law that would have retroactive effect, exacting the death penalty for the "crimes" of the Wollo disaster. We refused, instructing them on one of the fundamental principles of the rule of law—that laws are not to have retroactive effect. In this some of the Derg's members, like the Eritrean police captain Michael Gebrenegus, and Berhanu Bayeh, quietly encouraged us. The reason for suggesting a new law carrying the death penalty was that the law that the Commission used as the framework of its enquiry was the Penal Code of Ethiopia, under which the maximum penalty for the kind of offences the Commission was investigating was fifteen years imprisonment. That was not acceptable to the Derg.

In the end the Commission wrote a report finding five among all those questioned to be responsible for the Wollo disaster and recommending that they be charged under the applicable Penal Code. The maximum penalty under the Code is fifteen years imprisonment. But before the Commission's report reached them, the radical elements of the Derg executed fifty-seven of the detainees plus two of its own members who disagreed with its decision. It has since been claimed by Mengistu and some of Mengistu's supporters that the execution was carried out on the basis of the Commission's recommendation. This patent and malicious lie flies in the face of the record and is designed to absolve Mengistu and his collaborators of the crime they committed. It is a case of Might, in desperation, trying to pay homage to Right retroactively. Mengistu's single-minded pursuit of power at any cost used people, including General Aman to a certain extent; but in the matter of legality and due process, Aman refused to be part of the crime and he paid for it with his life. In this, only Mengistu and his close associates in crime are answerable before law and history, and nothing that he or his supporters can say will change this.

Saturday Night Massacre

It was one of those memorable days—a uniquely and tragically memorable day. You remember the exact time and place where you were on such a day. It was Sunday, November 24, 1974, and I had spent the night at the home of my friend Asseghid Tessema in the Kechene locality of Addis Ababa, off Prince Mekonen Street. I had hardly slept and, because I expected some bad news in the morning, I turned on the radio to hear the eight o'clock news. Asseghid and his wife, Sally, were up and came to hear the news in their pajamas. In view of the events of the previous day, we all expected bad news, but what the radio announced exceeded my worst expectations.

Addis Ababa had been gripped with fear and anxiety. Disturbed by rumors of dissension within the top leadership of the Derg, with threats of violence as a real possibility, many of the city's dwellers were engaged in panic buying of essential goods like food, petrol and cooking oil. As if to lend credence to the rumors, gunfire erupted suddenly on Saturday, the evening before, in parts of the city. I personally saw tank units moving in the streets and some were deployed outside the entrances of the Menelik Palace where the Derg had installed itself and was holding its meetings.

At about six in the evening on Saturday, I had made my way to Aman's house. I saw that a military security detail had cordoned it off. I stopped to ask what was going on, and a stern looking and helmeted soldier told me it was none of my business and ordered me to move on. All I could do was to glare at him and curse him under my breath as I obeyed his order and drove away in the direction of my brother-in-law Abate's house. I had been advised to change places of residence as a security precaution; I used at least three places. Abate was not in, so I talked to the children for a few minutes and left, heading for the center of the city. Things seemed normal around the piazza, and as I waited at a red light, Amare Gugsa, my friend Chaneyalew Gugsa's younger brother, hooted his car's horn and pulled up alongside me. Amare told me that Chanyalew had been looking for me and wanted to see me. Would I join them for dinner? I agreed and followed Amare to Chaneyalew's house in the Kebenna area.

Chaneyalew was very happy to see me and thanked his brother for bringing me to him. "No offense to Amare," I said, "but you should rather thank the gods of the righteous who see to it that the righteous meet without an appointment, whereas the evil ones don't make it even to their appointed time and place, as the saying of our fathers has it."

"True," Amare said, "I will not take offence; it was the good gods that got us together." Chanyalew served us Scotch whisky and called his beautiful wife to ask for dinner to be served. His wife came to greet me and then disappeared into the kitchen. Over dinner, Chanyalew expressed deep worry about Aman, whom he admired immensely. He said he was particularly concerned because he knew something about Mengistu's character and background. I trusted Chanyalew's judgment and insight, so I listened intently to what he had to say. I cannot reproduce the exact words of what he said that evening, but the gist of it was that Mengistu's character was warped by his deprived and despised upbringing as a *baria* (slave), and that he was out to seek revenge and he would start by killing the best of the nation. And according to Chaneyalew, Aman represented the best in the nation that Mengistu hated. He concluded by urging me to warn Aman and tell him not to trust the "*baria*." Now, there was a time when I would have contested Chanyalew's use of the word *baria* and chided him for it. But that evening I kept quiet, fearful that Chanyalew's insight into the psychology of Mengistu might be right.

Was it too late to warn Aman?

The last time I had seen Aman was Thursday, November 21st, at his sister Tsion's house, where he ate most of the time, since he was separated from his wife. It was exactly a week since he'd had his final showdown with the Derg and walked out of their meeting never to return, despite several attempts to persuade him to go back and finish the business of the revolution. We were sitting in the living room of Tsion's villa reviewing the events of the past few weeks, when he handed me an envelope "for safe-keeping." He told me that he'd had it with the Derg. He looked warn out and very sad. When I started reading the note he said I could read it later, and asked me to move to Tsion's smaller waiting room, because he was expecting a guest. As I left the living room, Tsion ushered in the Sudanese military attaché, Colonel Tajeddin, who greeted him volubly in Arabic. Aman introduced me to Tajeddin and I left them to join Tsion.

Two days later, on Friday morning, I talked to Aman on the phone briefly before he cut me off saying, "The roof is leaking," our code for telephone tapping. That afternoon Tsion told me that they had cut off the telephone line, and when she tried to take food to him they refused to let her in and said they would take it to him. Concerned that he might be poisoned, Tsion took back the food and headed home in distress. After she told me all this, I tried the phone myself; it was indeed cut off. So was the water and electricity, she later informed me. I spent little time at the Commission's office, which had been moved to a building on the Bole road. The atmosphere at the office was tense. Nobody could concentrate on work; the sense of hopelessness and confusion was palpable. One of the Commissioners, Baro Tumsa, a six-foot-six giant of a man from Wolega, told me to be careful what I said on the telephone; a good friend of his who was a member of the Derg had told him that they had played tapes of my phone conversations with General Aman.

Saturday came and went, taking with it my sense of mission and confidence in the future. I went to my friend Asseghid's house for lunch and spent the afternoon reflecting on what to do in the event of unexpected happenings. About six o'clock in the evening, I drove to Aman's house to see what was happening and ran into the cordon that I described above. Nothing made sense. I came to help, and now both my friend and I were rendered helpless. Would that I could find a time machine to take me back to Washington—to be with my family and forget everything that had happened in the past four months.

On that fateful Sunday morning, at eight o'clock, I turned on the radio in the living room at Asseghid's house, as I wrote above. I was anxious to hear news about any developments of the previous night. As soon as the music started, Asseghid and Sally came in their pajamas to listen to the news. The radio program began with the usual martial music, then it shifted to a song that would become the signature tune presaging grave news, a sort of an overture for tragic happenings. The tune was "*Yefiyyel WeTeTye*" (The Young Male Goat), based on an Ethiopian fable about a young goat that challenged a tiger with the inevitable result. As the tune played the radio announcer outlined the crimes of the human goats that had challenged the tiger Derg. The voice of the announcer, Assefa Yirgu, was particularly odious that morning as he told the public that the people whose names he was going to read had suffered death with the sword of the revolution. He then began to read the names of the "counter-revolutionaries and traitors" to whom revolutionary justice had been meted out. Heading the list was my friend, Lt. General Aman Michael Andom. The names of fifty-nine others followed, including Prime Ministers Aklilu and Endalkachew and most members of the Aklilu cabinet, generals of the army and the police.

The martial music, which played on under the announcement of the executions, became like poison to my ears. Murder! Murder, most foul! Murder! I intoned as my friends watched me with concern. As if they could ease the pain I felt, I kept repeating these words.

How cruel fate can be! One bloody Saturday, men with guns who had usurped power, unleashed a reign of terror on an unsuspecting public. Even those of us who thought we knew them and trusted them had been taken completely by surprise. The outrage of betrayed trust as much as the evil deed itself brought home to me, with blinding clarity, the simple truth that we were heading to disaster. I was soon to be a target, so I did not have the luxury of choice between several alternatives. There was only one choice. Escape.

Meanwhile, family members of the victims of the massacre tried in vain to recover the remains of their loved ones in order to give them a decent burial. It was impossible. Nor could they mourn for them in the proper traditional way, in the proven ritual that alleviates grief through communal sharing. The perpetrators of the blood bath had dumped the victims in a mass grave inside the prison compound known as *Alem Bekagn* (End of the World) where they had executed them.

There had been nothing like it in living memory. It was the madness of mob justice; men drunk with suddenly acquired power decided to kill simply because they could do it. Not that the victims were saintly figures, but even those who had committed wrongs had the right to a hearing, to legal process in accordance with traditionally sanctioned practice, as well as in terms of the modern laws. Wasn't the Commission of Enquiry formed for that purpose? But law and justice were not available, only naked violence.

In solemn silence I wondered whether people would ignore or come to terms with the stain of this crime. Why did it come to this? Why kill Aman, the very person who had provided a rational and charismatic leadership to the revolution, who had guided it from the start? Mengistu and company also killed many innocent men for merely being at the wrong place at the wrong time. At that point, I remembered Robert McNamara's admonition to me, and his remark about revolution's tendency to devour its children.

Everyone wanted to know what went on inside the Derg that led to the Saturday night massacre. And I was particularly anxious to know what the public reaction would be. The perpetrators of the massacre apparently expected the public to come out in massive support. They were bitterly disappointed; instead of cheering, the Addis Ababa citizens came out dressed in black as sign of mourning. The Derg then ensconced itself inside the Menelik Palace with tanks deployed at strategic positions throughout the city. I was faced with a cruel dilemma. What should I do? Death had stalked me like a dark shadow since Bloody Saturday. For six days, I had lived in fear, in daily expectation of arrest. Every night I changed places among friends and relatives to avoid the

dreaded midnight knock and being dragged out to face the firing squad. During the day, I carried a loaded gun even when I went to the office of the Commission, where I sat near the window of my office overlooking the entrance of the five-story building. I had decided that if the worst came to the worst, and they came to get me, I would take them with me, saving the last bullet for myself.

The survival instinct in me urged me to find a way out of the death trap. A couple of friends spoke in support of this instinct. One of them, Dr. Mekonen, a wise veterinarian who had a brother in the Derg, was particularly insistent. I remember the look of apprehension when he ran into me in a pharmacy opposite the Commercial School. "What are you doing here? You should get out of town," he told me in a whisper. "Get out before they get you."

Dr. Mekonen's emphatic remark confirmed my instinctive reaction and decision to escape. Although he gave me no specifics, I suspected that he knew something from his brother. I had come to appreciate Abby's prescience in counseling changing cars and houses; in fact I decided to use one more safe house in which pass the night. Gebrehiwet Woldearegai, a lawyer and former student of mine, offered his office and gave me spare keys for that purpose. I had a .38 special with fifty bullets, Aman's gift, and Chanyalew's "pineapple" hand grenade, given to me when I confided him that I was planning to leave town. In those days of madness, I had decided that if they came to get me, I would take them with me. Thus the gun and the hand grenade.

Chapter 14

JOURNEY TO THE UNKNOWN

The Die is Cast

It is a sunny and warm afternoon in late November 1974, under the blue African sky. Two cars are seen entering the compound of the central YMCA of Addis Ababa. The first, a light blue Peugeot 403, is driven to the eastern end of the compound and parked facing the street. The second, a silver Fiat, is parked in the middle of the compound, several cars away from the first car. Some ten minutes later, the driver of the Fiat gets out, looks around as though he is looking for someone, then walks towards the area where the first car is parked and sits in the passenger seat.

A casual meeting? Anyone watching the scene, as I am doing now in my mind's eye, might assume so. That at least was our hope. For in fact I was one of the two men and I was headed for a rendezvous with destiny. I was in the first car, the Peugeot, which I had borrowed from Abby. Abby, a good Samaritan to a fault, had insisted that I drive his car two or three days a week, leaving my own at home in order to confuse the "guardian angels," his word for the security people.

Beneath the warmth and calm of that glorious afternoon, there lurked fear and anxiety in the city. After the trauma of the Saturday night massacre, the city convulsed like a patient writhing in an epileptic seizure. Subjected to the violent rhetoric punctuated by martial music, the people were utterly confused and expected the worst. The work of the Commission of Enquiry that had given rise to such hope of setting the revolution on a rational course was given short shrift. The promise of the rule of law was denied in the sudden eruption of violence and chaos.

The man in the other car, the Fiat, was my very good friend Desta Woldekidan, who had volunteered to help me. Desta not only urged me to leave town; he actually offered to help me escape. Our meeting at the YMCA compound was the beginning of our plan. After he joined me in the blue Peugeot, we waited and surveyed the place for any signs of the security goons who might be in the compound. We were not sure who the people meeting inside the hall of the YMCA were. Hence our caution; you couldn't be too careful in the circumstances. Nothing was what it seemed. So much had changed in one act of madness, turning everything topsy-turvy. Anything was possible; anything could happen to anybody, and nobody knew what to expect. Or what to do when the arbitrary hand of the mighty struck.

The "Good Old Days" were gone forever—gone the way of His Imperial Majesty who had seemed eternal and solid as the rock of Lalibela. Now he and his imperial regime were consigned to oblivion and those who derived vitality and meaning under his system were reduced to nothing, overnight. Formerly dynamic men of business and arrogant men of government now moved aimlessly, stooped and dazed and wearing forced humility.

Sic transit gloria mundi, I mused in silence, remembering my meager Latin. The bottom had fallen from underneath the world that these wretches knew and which they thought they controlled forever. The old order that had defined their daily rhythm with certainty and regularity lay in ruin. The Emperor, who was the lynchpin of the old system and of their sense of security was in chains, living at the mercy of military officers whose careers he had fashioned. I must now leave all this behind. Better run for it and escape or even die in the attempt, rather than meet an ignominious end at the hand of the cruel junta. I must get out of town.

I was thus on the run.

When Desta joined me in the Peugeot, I pointed to the traveling bag in the back seat and asked him to take it to his car. I said he was to follow me some five minutes after I left.

"Then what? Where are we going to meet?" he inquired.

I told him to drive into the University College compound in front of the Arts Building and wait for me there. I would deposit Abby's car and walk to where his car was parked. We would leave from there together in his car. In order to avoid detection in case we were followed, we would drive southward towards Casa Incis and make a detour through a different route, and hit the Asmara highway.

"Okay?" I asked.

"Okay," Desta said, smiling with excitement.

I had told Abby's guard that I was going to Dire Dawa for the weekend for a short rest. In fact, the morning of the same day, I had driven to Bishoftu (Debre Zeit) and had lunch at the Ras Hotel, where most of the waiters were presumed to be paid security agents. Using the hotel telephone at the front desk, and speaking loudly, I had made reservations at the Dire Dawa Ras Hotel. I asked for a room for a week starting the next day. I learned years later that the following Monday, when I did not report to work at the Commission office, all hell had broken loose and they were looking for me everywhere, including the Dire Dawa Ras Hotel.

Would our luck hold? Would we pass the roadblocks undetected, or would we be caught and handed over to the Derg? My friend Desta had volunteered to go with me fully aware of the danger. *The die was cast. I was on my way to a hazardous journey.* It was an act of friendship bordering on the heroic and for which I could find no words sufficient to express my gratitude. As a token of my appreciation, I named the principal character of my novel, *Riding the Whirlwind,* Desta, and wrote the following opposite the dedication page:

"The name of the protagonist, Desta, was chosen by the author to memorialize his deep gratitude to his friend Desta Wolde Kidan. The latter risked much to save the author's life in November 1974 by driving him out of Addis Ababa, all the way to the North, putting him in touch with Eritean liberation fighters."

Escape From Addis

We drove on the Asmara road toward Kebena, past the British Embassy. No one stopped us, and our passage out of the city center to the outskirts went without incident until we reached a roadblock before the Kotebe Secondary School. I asked Desta to slow down, while I reached for my 38 special and grenade, just in case. Both were concealed under the seat. Looking back now, I marvel at the sheer madness of it all!

We stopped in front of a wooden pole suspended across the road. A soldier walked slowly out of a small observation post. He took his time to come closer to the car and looked at us as we greeted him, smiling amiably. His glazed eyes studied us with the practiced detachment of a veteran police interrogator. Then he walked slowly back to his post and lifted the pole without saying a word.

"Obviously he decided we are not counter-revolutionaries," I said facetiously as we drove off.

"Or reactionaries," Desta answered, and we laughed more in relief than amusement.

One hurdle down, I thought, and said so, turning to Desta who simply sighed and drove on silently for a while. I turned my gaze to the countryside. The fields had turned brown and there were a few trees here and there. When we reached the approaches of Debre Birhan, a center of the Ethiopian Territorial Army (or militia), the thought crossed my mind that we might face problems. Desta was sure there would be no problems there because, he explained, the people were still confused, the Emperor was still alive and the country folks around the area were loyal to the Crown.

"You may be right; let us hope you are right," I said and we drove on. He was right; there was no roadblock of any kind, and we passed the town without incident, without anybody even noticing us.

Two hurdles down.

As we drove on, cutting across the rolling hills of central Shoa, and passed sheep and cattle grazing on field after green field with shepherds tending their flocks, I experienced the first feeling of ease, a sense of escape from the death trap that had been weighing heavily on my mind for a whole week. But we had a long way to go yet—six hundred kilometers before leaving Shoa and Wollo and entering the more friendly territory of Tigrai, and another three hundred kilometers before reaching Eritrea, my destination.

As we became more at ease, Desta and I chatted about the events of the past weeks. I told him about the few people in whom I had confided regarding my intention to escape. Taking money out of my bank account was out of the question, because it would attract attention. When I confided my predicament to my friend Berhane Gebremedhin, a businessman, he did not hesitate to give me the money I needed, adding that I must leave immediately. Armed with the generous amount of cash, I made sure that we had enough petrol for the journey as well as other provisions such as some medical supplies.

There was only one other person who knew my intentions—my childhood friend Habtegiorghis Indrias. Habtegiorghis offered to help by arranging a meeting with an Italian business client who had a private Cessna airplane and might agree to take me to Somalia or the Sudan. I thanked him and told him I would think about it, but in my heart I knew it would be too risky. I did not even tell my brother-in-law, Abate, or Abby who had done so much to help me by putting his car at my disposal. I did not tell my best friend Asseghid either. The less my friends and relatives knew, I thought, the better for them.

There was, of course, my fellow commissioner (and fellow Eritrean) Mewael Mebrahtu, who had quietly asked me if I had considered the idea of escape to Eritrea, the day after the massacre. I had responded with caution in the form of question as to how we could escape even if we wanted to. Mewael told me that he had connections with the Eritrean Liberation Front (ELF). Although I trusted him, I told him only that I was "exploring" the idea, and that if I decided it would probably be after a week. In actual fact, I was leaving the following day. Mewael had nothing to fear because he had no association with General Aman, and indeed, he stayed in Addis Ababa for a whole year, unharmed, before he joined the Eritrean Liberation Front.

Desta and I were both familiar with the road and the landscape and were determined to pass the Tarma Ber tunnel before sunset, and begin our descent to the lowlands of northern Shoa. And we did pass the tunnel around six o'clock. I related to Desta the story of the heroic resistance of the Ethiopian patriots at Tarma Ber in 1936, holding the Italian troops at bay for several days before superior arms and air attacks forced them to retreat. That was before the Italians built the tunnel, following their victory. Before we knew it, we were launched into a dialogue on the impact of Italian rule in Ethiopia.

"One thing the Italians are good at is road building," I said.

"I know," Desta said, "have you seen the Lemalemo Road in Gondar? It is incredible."

"I have seen it," I said and told him that a certain fanatic Ethiopian governor of the province had ordered the demolition of the monument erected by the

Italians to honor those who died building it. That raised the question of whether the country would be better off without the legacy of Italian rule. I told him a story of my Ghanaian friend, Kwaku, who saw Addis Ababa for the first time in 1963, during the founding conference of the OAU. When he and I were students in the university in the 1950's, he used to tell me how fortunate Ethiopians were for maintaining their independence from European rule, while the rest of Africa was colonized. After he saw Ethiopia's backwardness, he was so shocked that he said maybe colonization was not a bad thing, after all. He said, if this is the result of three thousand years of Ethiopian civilization, then Ghana and other African countries are better off without it.

I said that Kwaku and I had a long and bitter argument on that point, and asked Desta what he thought. He said that maintaining one's national pride is better than all the material advancement Europeans could bring. He cited the Japanese who took from Europe its technological know-how but kept their cultural heritage. This was one of those questions on which you could argue till kingdom come and never reach agreement. So we left it there.

In any case, we were missing the amazing beauty around us. The sight of the lowland valleys was pleasing to the eye and soothing to the nerves. Soon we were negotiating the winding road, snaking round the hills and riverbeds. We slowed down as we crossed narrow passes. We could now feel the warm air of the lower altitude, which was invigorating and induced a change of mood in us; we even became enthused with our journey, seeing it more and more as an adventure.

Before we knew it, the sun was slipping down the ochre sky to the west of us, above the mountains of Menz. By the time we reached Robit, dusk had fallen; the early night enveloped the landscape and we were awed by the dark hulking shadows of huge trees and sleepy buildings. We decided to spend the night there.

Robit was a new settlement town that had suddenly sprouted in the wake of a large plantation project. It was later used as a military camp and, after the failed coup of December 1960, as an internment camp for a few hundred Imperial Body Guard officers and enlisted men who had participated in the attempted coup. The presence of soldiers and plantation workers gave birth to the sprawling town, with the usual small shops and eating-houses and bars. All of which attracted young local women, who are known for their beauty and amorous temperament.

Music was blaring from some of the bars when we arrived. We chose the first available motel, which was probably the only decent one. I went straight to the room while Desta registered us for the night under his name. The motel had its own bar, and Desta lingered there a while, listening for information and getting a sense of the temper of the town. When he came back after an hour or so, I was dozing for I had hardly slept the previous night. He had nothing special to report; no unusual troop movement or police inquiries about anybody.

Safe Passage Through Wollo

After a restful night, we woke up at five in the morning and decided to leave before any of the city dwellers saw us. The bill had been paid upon checking in. I volunteered to drive this portion of the journey and we headed north for Dessie. We had breakfast at Kombolcha, at the junction with a road leading to Asab. We did not want to take any chances, so Desta ordered breakfast for two to be served in the car. A sleepy-looking waitress took our orders while I lay my head on the wheel, pretending to be asleep. We had a generous portion of *Fitfit* made of *Injera* and *Doro Wat* plus some coffee with milk. We also bought some bread, fruit and mineral water. Then we filled the tank with petrol, and added a spare can to see us through to Mekele.

We reached Dessie before ten in the morning. We grew tense as we drove through the piazza, but it was Sunday morning and the city center was empty; on Sundays, people go to church and stay indoors most of the day. And as soon as we were safely out of the city limits, we shouted "hurrah" at the top of our voices like two schoolboys cheering the victory of their favorite football team. We were now in Wollo, and Wollo was safer than Shoa for historical reasons.

The people of Wollo always felt neglected by Shoan rule, epitomized by the Emperor's oldest son who was Wollo's nominal governor. Historically Shoans questioned their loyalty. The Emperor never forgave them for attacking him when he was on the run, fleeing pursuing Italian troops after his defeat at the battle of Mai Chew in 1936. He was forced to make a detour and pass through the region inhabited by Amharas. In attacking the Emperor in his desperate hour, the people of Wollo were avenging their defeat at the battle of Seghele, earlier in the twentieth century, when their king was defeated by the Emperor's army and taken captive, from which he never recovered. In my hour of need, therefore, I reckoned that no Wollo man or woman would betray us if worst came to the worst and I was recognized. It was for that reason that my friend Chanyalew (a native and nobleman of Wollo) had written a note to one of his kinsmen, a local chieftain, asking him to give me safe passage out of Wollo, in case of need. Fortunately, it never came to that; I did not need such assistance.

We passed the beautiful area of Lake Haiq, a site of historic churches. Further north is Lake Ashenghe, which was on the route taken by the Emperor in his flight from Fascist Italian forces in 1936. This area of Wollo is one of the most beautiful parts of Ethiopia with imposing mountains and valleys. One of these is the strategic mountain pass near Woldia. We passed Woldia and the narrow pass leading out of it. We then crossed the bridge of the river Milley, and before long reached the famous Alewuha River, the historic dividing line between Wollo and Tigrai. We stopped and sat watching the water rolling in the deep gorge of the river, and I told Desta the story of a famous Tigrayan feudal lord who had been kept a virtual prisoner in Addis Ababa for many years, by order of Emperor Menelik.

The story goes that the man, whose name was Tedla Aba-Guben, feigned illness and tricked Menelik into letting him go to his native Tigrai to die and be

interred there. The strategem he used was a masterpiece of acting. He ordered one of his loyal servants to slaughter a sheep, then had him save some of the sheep's blood in a small cup. He then sent the servant to Menelik's palace with instructions to inform the Emperor that his master was dying of a serious illness. Menelik sent a messenger to find out if the story was true. When Menelik's messenger was ushered into the bedroom, the wily man started coughing violently and spat up a shower of blood. Whereupon the spattered messenger hurried back to the Emperor and reported what he had seen.

The Emperor granted Tedla Aba Guben's wish, and the old man left for home, thanking the Lord and the slain sheep. On his way back to Tigrai, Tedla Aba Guben stopped at the Alewuha River and ordered one of his servants to fetch him a pail of water. When asked what for, he said that he wanted to wash out his mouth, cleansing from it all the false words he had uttered, including addressing "many a slave" as "my lord." He had done all this, he said, in order to survive. Indeed, Tedla Aba Guben survived Menelik and was still alive when the Italians occupied Ethiopia. When asked how he was faring during that time, the witty old man is reported to have remarked that every one, including all the commoners, was better off except himself and the hares, which the Italians loved to hunt and eat. (The locals did not eat hares, following the biblical injunction. In this respect, the Ethiopian Orthodox Church follows Mosaic Law to this day).

As we made our way toward the wide plains of Alamata valley, Desta wanted to make a short detour to visit his mother and older sister who lived in a village near Waja, off the main highway. We did so and found his mother, his sister and a couple of other relatives. They were surprised to see us and wanted to render the usual Ethiopian hospitality—slaughter a sheep, etc. We told them we were in great hurry, but they would not budge; they were so insistent that the only way we could get out of the place was by promising that we would visit them at leisure on our way back. Desta's mother, a striking noblewoman, warned her son to keep his promise and said something highly complimentary about his Yugoslav wife, before she released us to leave.

It took us an hour to cross the Alamata plains and reach the foot of Ambalaghe Mountain. The area had been the scene of drought and famine the previous year, but seemed to be recovering with good rains. This part of Ethiopia (northern Wollo and southern Tigrai) has been a meeting point of three ethnic groups (Amhara, Oromo and Tigrawai), and is a fascinating mix of cultures. For example, the inhabitants of the Alamata environs, the Raya, who wear leather or cotton kilts, instead of trousers, are of Oromo stock; but they speak a Tigrigna dialect laced with Amharic words.

Mekele—Close Encounter of a Special Kind

We arrived in Mekele, the capital of Tigrai, a little after seven in the evening on Sunday. We had lingered on the way so that we could get in after it grew dark. According to Desta the safest place for me to stay while finding ways for safe conduct to Eritrea, was in his sister's house. Being the grandson of Abraha

Tsa'eda, one of the illustrious noblemen of Tigrai, he was well known and had relatives all over Tigrai. The biggest hotel in Mekele, the Abraha Castle Hotel was named after his grandfather. For all his aristocratic birth, Desta had always been a humble and earthy person; in fact, his sympathies lay with the common people, and against the ruling class, a factor that was critical in our friendship. His education in Yugoslavia, during Tito's time reinforced these sentiments.

Long before we entered Mekele, Desta devised a plan for hiding me while he explored contacts for safe conduct to Eritrea. As an employee of the Ministry of Agriculture in charge of an important department, he had access to people and resources in the Mekele branch of the ministry. He also knew Eritreans living and working in Mekele who had contacts with the Eritrean Liberation Front (ELF). It was a time when the youth of Eritrea and Tigrai, who have cultural and linguistic ties, were creating a common front against their oppressors. Eritreans living in Tigrai were generally treated with respect and when in need provided with the necessary help.

Desta first saw to it that I was comfortably settled in his sister's house. I stayed there undisturbed for five days, mostly staying indoors during the day. He made it absolutely clear that no one was to know I was staying in the house. He told his sister and her domestic helpers, particularly a manservant, (a godchild of his oldest brother), that I was a professor at the University of Addis Ababa and that I had suffered a nervous breakdown. Therefore, he told them, I needed peace and quiet and was not to be disturbed by anybody. During the day, I passed the time reading and writing, while in the evenings Desta would join me for dinner, and at least on a couple of occasions, he took me for a ride in town, against my objection. In the evenings, we were twice joined for dinner by women relatives of his. One of them, a beautiful young divorcee was asked by him to call on me during the day, "to break the monotony," as Desta put it. My friend thought of everything.

During one of those occasions when the women came to visit, an interesting thing happened. The conversation had turned to the work of the Commission of Enquiry and its members. One of the women said, "I hate the way that Dr. Bereket was harassing the poor Ministers with hard questions". Desta and I looked at each other and smiled while the lady went on criticizing my work. She was obviously an avid listener to the radio program on the investigation, which had become a kind of soap opera. It was lucky for me that, whereas in Addis people had seen TV shows of the Commission's work and people knew my face, TV service had not begun in Mekele at the time.

We considered two alternative routes of escape from Mekele to Eritrea. One possibility was through the north West via Shiraro and the Badme area, and thence to the ELF-held areas in western Eritrea. That was the safest. The other was to travel by car on the Asmara road, and cross over the border to Eritrea, another ELF-held area. That was the more dangerous. Preferring the first option, Desta and I considered who could give me assistance for a safe passage. Desta thought of the governor of the region, Dr. Haile Selassie Belay.

Haile was an old friend and, although he may not have known it, I had had a small hand in his appointment by commending him to General Aman.

The governor was willing to see me, and Desta arranged a meeting in the compound of the Abraha Castle Hotel. It took courage for Haile to agree to see me, and we discussed my predicament and the possibility of his assistance. Partly because he was a newly appointed governor, and in part perhaps because of the risk of betrayal involved, Haile said he was not able to help me escape. That was the end of the matter as far as escape through the west was concerned, leaving us to consider the other alternative. Indeed we had no choice. Desta was bitterly disappointed and angry at Haile, but I understood his problem and held no grudge. But we had to move fast. Desta contacted two ELF-supporters in Tigrai. One was a small business owner living in Mekele. The other was working as a driver for the Tigrai branch of the Ministry of Agriculture. The first was the head of the ELF underground cell in Mekele. Desta made an elaborate arrangement one evening for me to meet him. He took me to a small house in a dimly lit dark neighborhood, introduced me to him and withdrew.

The man welcomed me, but said he had to ask me some questions in order to make sure that I was a genuine Eritrean trying to join the movement. He was more than surprised when I told him who I was. He then asked me where I was born, and I told him. The following is a sample of the interview, to the best of my recollection.

"Your village of birth is Adi Nifas, I think you said. Can you tell me the names of the villages bordering Adi Nifas?"

"Adi Abeyto, Beleza and Imba Deho," I answered.

"What is the name of the artificial lake to the west of Addi Nifas?"

"Kelai Abi."

"Does your family own farmland other than the ones in the highlands?"

"Yes. We have land in BaHri."

"What is the name of the biggest mountain in that area?"

"Ri'esi Adi."

"Good. Now, how does your father call your mother—does he call her by her name?"

"No, he called her 'Hanna.'"

"Called her?"

"Yes, my father has long been deceased."

"I am sorry to hear that....But who is Hanna?"

"My oldest sister."

"And how did your mother call your father?"

"Tekeste; that is my oldest brother's name."

The questioning continued—he asked me what kind of grain grows in our area, what I did before I left my village, how many brothers and sisters I had, and so on. Then with a smile signaling his satisfaction about my authenticity, he offered me his hand of welcome. He talked about himself, telling me that his village of origin was Tera Imni, in Seraye province. He expressed regret that he could not offer me tea or coffee, but hoped I would understand. He was cool and warm at the same time. Before I rose to leave, he said he would make all the necessary arrangements for my journey to Eritrea and wished me all the best. I thanked him and joined Desta who was waiting for me outside. We walked to our car, which was parked some distance away, and drove to my hiding place at his sister's home.

The next day, Desta awakened me early. I was to leave that afternoon. The house was not secure, so I spent the morning in a Eucalyptus grove with my gun on my lap and heart beating hard in my chest. While waiting there, a local man approached me and wanted to know if I needed any help. I thanked him and said, I did not need any help. He looked suspicious and moved on, leaving me devoutly wishing for Desta to come back before this man informed the authorities. Finally, Desta—what a relief! He told me that I was to travel in a Land Rover with a trusted driver who was an ELF underground member, together with a young ELF cadre who would take me all the way to the ELF base. I rode with him in his car back to town, and later on in the afternoon, we set out continuing my hazardous journey to the unknown. On a hill, overlooking a valley, we stopped to say our goodbyes. He introduced me to the two people in the Land Rover, then took a folded Mekele *gabi* (shawl) and handed it to me, saying it would be good for the cold nights ahead and it would remind me of Mekele. We shook hands and hugged. It was a bittersweet moment, and we would not see each other again for sixteen years.

Transition

I left Mekele in the early afternoon of a Thursday, five days after arriving there. As we started our journey, I felt a keen sense of uncertainty about the fate awaiting me ahead. After the murder of my friend Aman, I had no choice but to escape for the shadow of death hovered over my head. To escape from death there were two alternatives: one was betrayal and compromise of my principles in order to survive; the other was to leave town. I chose the latter, and as I looked back, I was reminded of what an American humorist said: "if you reach a fork in a road, take it." I could now laugh at the humor, being out of danger. I made a decision and was now facing the consequences flowing from that decision, including the uncertainty of the fate awaiting me in the wilds of Eritrea.

We traveled for about an hour without much talk, except for occasional remarks on the landscape and its rugged nature. There were many twists and turns on the Mekele-Adigrat road. The driver, called Mekonen, told me that he was an employee of the Ministry of Agriculture, and the other said he was ELF cadre working as a recruiter and guide. His name was Gebrehiwet. The driver was coached on what to say if we were stopped. He was told to say that I was a World Bank expert on a project trip in Eritrea. In support of this story, I carried my World Bank identity card with my picture taken at the time I joined

the Bank and could show it in case anybody required proof. I knew enough about the Bank's projects in Ethiopia and Eritrea to make the story credible. The important thing was that nobody knew my face outside of Addis Ababa.

In fact, I had considered using the same ruse earlier, during the first desperate moments after the Saturday Night Massacre. Mr. John Malone, the World Bank Representative in Addis, a man I had befriended, had volunteered (bless him!) to drive me all the way to the Sudan border through the Addis Ababa-Gondar route. The idea of my escape—its urgency—was first suggested by David Sassoon, one of the Bank's attorneys, who happened to be on a Bank mission to Ethiopia at the time and whom I met at the Addis Abba Hilton Hotel, the day after the massacre. I remember David being quite agitated when he saw me, and telling me that I should "get the hell out of town by any means possible." He offered to help me, adding, "If you need money, I am willing to give it to you, but get out, for God's sake." At that particular moment, this man who had previously appeared to me arrogant and unsociable assumed the aura of a saint. The next day, he talked to the Bank representative who, in turn, called and invited me to his house for dinner at which he made the suggestion of escape through Gondar. I thought the Gondar option too dangerous and, by that time, Desta had made his offer to help me escape. But I thanked my Bank colleagues, to both of whom I feel indebted.

Now, I was stuck with the only available escape route and was hurtling toward what could be a disastrous end. The real test would come when we reached Adigrat, the last town before the Eritrean border. Long before we approached the outskirts of Adigrat, thinking aloud, I asked if there might be any obstacles in Adigrat. Mekonen said with a broad smile that there would be no problem: that he had done this kind of work, taking new recruits past Adigrat and into Eritrea. Gebrehiwet, who was eighteen years old and articulate, reassured me even more enthusiastically. Neither of them asked me questions of a personal nature; it would have been contrary to custom for them to do so. To begin with, an elder is not subjected to questioning beyond what he volunteers, according to custom. Secondly, the freedom fight in which they were engaged required secrecy and discipline. About three in the afternoon, we reached the edge of the escarpment above Adigrat, which we could see far below. Our descent along the winding road was slow and it was an hour before we reached Adigrat, a garrison town.

As we entered Adigrat, my traveling companions became quiet and tense, naturally inducing anxiety in me. We stopped at a police outpost, which was also presumably a checking point for customs officials. From past experience, I knew that such outposts were used for extracting bribes by low-paid police and customs officials. And true enough, things began to happen; no sooner had we stopped than an elderly uniformed policeman approached the car and greeted Mekonen, who greeted him heartily, but with nervous smiles. Both of my companions got out of the car and went behind and spoke to the officer. The conversation and whatever else happened did not take more than ten minutes. I sighed with relief as we drove away.

About half an hour after we left Adigrat, the car stopped. A young man appeared seemingly from nowhere. He had been hiding behind a ridge waiting for the car. After making sure that there was no other vehicle on the horizon, he came toward us, carrying half a sackfull of something. My companions helped him put it up on the luggage rack. I caught a glimpse of a fair-skinned, good-looking youth in his twenties. Naturally, I didn't ask any questions about him or the stuff he carried. For all I knew, it could be ammunitions or provisions for the guerillas. I was later told by one of my traveling companions that he was a teacher in a local elementary school.

We were in Eritrea and Mekonen said to me quietly that he had done his part. From now on, he said to me with a smile, I would be in the good hands of Gebrehiwet. Dusk had fallen by the time we got to Hawlti, the place with the ancient ruins a few miles south of Senafe. Gebrehiwet took my bag out of the car and asked me to follow him on foot. I thanked Mekonnen and said goodbye.

Gebrehiwet was incredibly nimble and fast, even though he was carrying my bag. We walked eastward along a narrow path. He wore rubber sandals that the freedom fighters called Kongo. I walked in my city shoes, which eventually proved difficult. Very soon, it became too dark for me to walk fast enough, so Gebrehiwet adjusted his pace to mine. "Mind you don't step on a stone," he would say repeatedly as we walked on and on. It was extremely hard for me to walk in the dark along a rough country road; but my young guide was amazing in the ease with which he could find the way and walk as though it were daylight. He was obviously used to walking in the dark and he certainly knew the way. I was fairly hardy and could walk long distances, but I found it difficult in the dark, with those city shoes. The macho spirit in me, sedulously inculcated from childhood, would not let me show weakness; so I struggled to keep up. Once, I stepped on a stone and slightly sprained my ankle. He heard me moan and inquired if I was okay. "Okay," I said and stuck it out, even though my ankle was hurting.

We crossed a small dry valley and began climbing up a hill. Gebrehiwet took pity on me and said we would rest a while, which was a Heaven-send. Without telling him about my sprained ankle, I took my shoes off, pretending to remove dust and sand, but actually rubbing my ankle so that I could finish the journey with my dignity intact. After about an hour's climb, we arrived at the top of a hill where I saw lights and heard goats bleating.

"We have arrived. This is Ad Agheb," said Gebrehiwet, leading me to a small compound. He knocked at the gate and a man came to open the gate. It was the owner of the house. He ushered me into a small room where I put my bag on the floor and sat waiting while Gebrehiwet chatted with the man outside the house and a woman, presumably the wife, set about preparing dinner. I was tired and hungry and lay down on a rough wooden bed. After about an hour, they awakened me and we were served a dinner that was meager but filling. At least my hunger was satisfied.

My hosts were a Saho family. The man spoke fairly good Tigrigna but spoke to his wife in Saho. Although I assumed that they had been expecting us, I knew nothing about where I would go or what I would do the following day. Gebrehiwet left to sleep in another part of the compound, and I spent a sleepless night, being the victim of bedbugs. I must have been heard tossing in my bed, for the master of the house called out in the dark, offering to spray the bed to kill the bugs. I agreed, and he came and sprayed something with a pungent smell, which was suffocating. I had to step out into the open air. I sat it out the remainder of the night.

Sunrise revealed a breathtaking landscape. To the southeast of us, loomed Ambasoira, the highest mountain of Eritrea, which lay just across the valley below. To the west was Senafe, nestled at the foot of a huge rock outcrop, which looked like a giant whale with its back caught in a noose of early morning light while its base was hauntingly dark. The sound of cocks crowing and goats and sheep bleating in a nearby village heralded the coming of dawn and, to the local inhabitants, the start of a new workday. It was beautiful; I felt at peace with myself and with my surroundings for the first time in a long while.

I stepped out of the house to answer nature's call a little distance down the hill in a secluded place. I returned to the house to find Gebrehiwet and the owner of the homestead. The man apologized for the bedbugs, but I assured him (white lie) that I had slept well and thanked him for the Fleet. We went inside to have tea and locally made bread. While we were having breakfast, Gebrehiwet announced that he was returning to duty and that, from that point on, I was under the care of the Eritrean Liberation Front (ELF). The man responsible for the area would come later in the day, or at the latest, the following day, to tell me what came next.

I was sorry to see Gebrehiwet leave; he was a fine young man who performed his duty diligently and expressed himself articulately and with passion. Before we said goodbye, I revealed to him who I was, and I could discern his happiness. The truth was, as he told me later, that he already knew about my identity. He gave me a short history lesson on the ELF and its rival, the newly formed Eritrean Peoples Liberation Front (EPLF), a group that had splintered from the ELF. He referred to the EPLF as *Tsere Gedli* (counter revolutionary), which was the term the ELF leadership used to describe the rival organization. I would hear this term used often by other ELF cadres during my months in the ELF-held territories. Gebrehiwet wished me well and departed towards Senafe, leaving me wondering how long I would have to wait in this village with a people whose language I did not speak and who did not know me. But the momentary worry disappeared as I remembered what I had heard and read about the Eritrean struggle including what Gebrehiwet had told me passionately during our long walk from Senafe to Ad Ageb. According to him, the Saho and the other ethnic groups of Eritrea were fighting for a common cause transcending ethnic and religious difference. The common goal was freedom of their country from alien rule and that the ethnic diversity did not present any problem in their quest for self-determination.

Into the Arms of the Guerillas

I spent the entire day waiting for the expected ELF chief of the area. Sometime before noon, another young cadre (whose name escapes me), came to tell me that the chief of the area, called Omar, would come the following day. Meanwhile the young cadre took me down the hill and across a valley in the direction of the Ambasoira mountain range. I noticed that he was equipped with an hourglass-shaped Chinese hand grenade. As we climbed down the hill, we saw a couple of people coming toward us from the direction of Senafe. He stiffened and clutched the grenade with his right hand, unfastening it from it s leather holster tied to his belt. He concealed the grenade under his light green *kushuk* (shawl). Only when he saw that they were people he knew, did he relax and put it back into its holster. I could see then that these fighters were living on the edge of danger, even though they moved among their own people, like the proverbial fish in the sea.

He greeted the people in Saho and they chatted for a brief moment exchanging news about events in the town, as he explained to me later. We went up and down a rough, boulder-filled valley for about half an hour before we reached a well-built *hidmo*, tucked at the foot of the mountain. The name of the place was *Argudolega*. We saw a group of young boys sitting around a man who was showing them how to disassemble and put together a weapon, using an old rifle. My guide greeted them in Saho and the man rose to greet us. When he saw that I was a stranger who did not speak Saho, he said in Tigrigna, half in jest, that he was preparing the next generation of revolutionaries.

We sat under the shade of an acacia tree, and I asked one of the boys his name and when he would like to become a freedom fighter. He said with a smile tomorrow, if he was given the chance. The others joined in saying the same. As proof that he was ready, the boy said that he could disassemble the weapon after being shown only once. The teacher was challenged and gave the boy the rifle. As the boy started taking it apart, two elderly men came from down the valley and greeted us. One of them was a sheikh. When he saw what the boy was doing he rebuked us, complaining that the boys should be taught the Holy Qur'an before everything else: that the national call for freedom must be answered in the right way. First, boys must be educated before they are taught how to use arms. One of the boys told the Sheikh that they went to a Qur'anic School in the afternoon, and the Sheik blessed him, repeated his admonition and continued on his journey towards Senafe, saying "*Assalamu 'Alekum!*" We all responded in unison, "*Wa'Alekumu'Salaam.*"

We were then greeted by a young man holding a baby, who asked us to his house. Inside the house, his wife was preparing food and making tea. She greeted us and asked us to make ourselves at home. At that time we were joined by two *tegadelti* (freedom fighters) one of whom was carrying a rifle. They too were asked to make themselves at home. The house was obviously frequented by *tegadelti* and the owners were part of the freedom fight. Soon we were offered tea, the staple of the *tegadalai*. As tea was served we were also joined by the father of the house owner.

As we started sipping our tea, my guide told the others that I was a guest of the ELF passing through and waiting to meet Omar. The young husband who spoke good Tigrigna welcomed me and offered me an olive twig for brushing my teeth, saying it was cut from the best olive tree in the area. I accepted with thanks. When he saw that my hair had not been combed, he also offered me a beautifully carved wooden comb. I accepted with great appreciation and even greater thanks, to the amusement of the company including the young bride. My face must have betrayed my eagerness and desperate need. And how kind and prescient the young man was!

The two *tegadelti*, at times joined by my guide, spoke about the politics of national unity (and disunity) in the Eritrean struggle, as well as about some of the ELF's exploits in recent months. The man with the rifle spoke about the betrayal of the revolution by the *tSere Gedli* (counter revolutionaries), meaning the EPLF. He repeated pretty much what Gebrehiwet had told me about the EPLF leadership's betrayal. The primary targets of the charge were: Osman Saleh Sabbe, the head of the EPLF's Foreign Mission, and Isaias Afewerki, head of its military wing. I would hear the charge in different forms again and again, and would eventually confront the two who were the targets. These kinds of charges were part of the politics of the time. Indeed, charges and counter-charges, group formation and splintering, information and disinformation (and counter-disinformation) were part of the menu of liberation theology, as I would find out soon enough to my utter disgust.

I spent two days and nights at *Argudolega,* a strategically located safe haven, as guest of that gracious Saho family. And there were no bedbugs this time, for which I was grateful, after the sleepless night I passed at *Ad Ageb.*

The Saho are one of Eritrea's nine ethnic groups, or nationalities, as the guerillas liked to call them then, following Marxist usage. The other eight are (in alphabetical order): Afar, Bilen, Hidareb, Kunama, Nara, Rashaida, Tigre and Tigrigna. The Afar and Saho belong to the Eastern Kushitic linguistic group, related to the Somali and Oromo. The Saho are essentially highlanders, combining farming and cattle and camel herding as their way of life. The Afar inhabit the hot Denkel (Danakel) region adjoining the Red Sea. There are also Afar in Ethiopia and Djibouti. The Bilen inhabit the Keren area, while the Hidareb, Kunama and Nara inhabit the western lowlands of Eritrea. The Rashaida, the smallest ethnic group, is of Saudi Arabian origin and inhabits the northern part of the Red Sea coastal region. The Tigre and Tigrigna, who constitute eighty percent of the Eritrean population, are related. The Tigre live in the central and northern highlands, engaged in farming as well as livestock herding, while the Tigrigna, who inhabit the central and southern highlands, are settled farmers.

These nine ethnic groups were brought together as one nation under Italian colonial rule. Each one had (and still has) its own customary laws governing the lives of its people, covering all areas except criminal and administrative law. The colonial rulers appropriated the latter and also introduced a new code of commercial law to regulate their commercial enterprises. Alien occupation brought the nine nationalities together as one nation and, succeeding rulers (British and Ethiopian) brought them even closer, thus paving the way for a united struggle for independence.

In the morning of the third day, my young guide said that Omar was *in Ad Ageb* and wanted me to come. I noticed a number of young people running in and out of the house carrying notes that the young cadre read, and then hurrying off with his answers. It was clear to me that they had no modern means of communication, like a radio or walkie-talkie, so that communications took time to go from one place to another. After one boy brought a note my young guide told me that Omar was waiting for us at *Ad Ageb*. And no sooner had he read the note, than he sent the boy back with a verbal message. By the time we were halfway up the stiff hill to *Ad Ageb*, I felt sure that the young boy who ran like a mountain goat had already reached his destination.

We reached *Ad Ageb* around midday and found Omar waiting for us. He received me warmly and asked the lady of the house to give us tea. Omar was a short, stoutly built man in his mid-to-late twenties. He spoke fluent Tigrigna; as we came to know each other more, he told me that he had gone to school in Asmara up to the eleventh grade. Like most Muslims, he of course had gone to a Qur'anic school before joining the government school and he spoke and wrote Arabic. The spoken Arabic was a result of his involvement of the armed struggle with the ELF. Arabic was the language of instruction in the training camps in the earlier history of the ELF, and remained the language of communication among the leadership and senior cadre at the time I met Omar.

I briefed Omar on the reason for my coming to Eritrea. In response, he expressed great pleasure in seeing me safe and sound. He said he had followed the radio program on the Commission of Enquiry's investigation and had wondered what had happened to me after the massacre of the sixty people by the Derg. His curiosity was restrained; he was not inquisitive but waited for me to volunteer my views and provide information. He struck me as the perfect lieutenant who performed his assigned duties diligently but discreetly. After our brief encounter, he said he had to leave me for a while because he had to arbitrate between two conflicting group of villagers. He said he would see me the following morning. Another night at *Ad Ageb*! Ah well, I must be stoic and face the bedbugs. But I was daunted by the prospect of an unequal struggle with these creatures, so I spent the night outside again, and my good friend Desta's gift of the Mekele *gabi* came in handy.

The following day, the fifth day after my arrival in the area, Omar told me everything was arranged; I was to leave for an undisclosed destination to meet with the leader of the ELF in the Akeleguzai region. He wrote a letter and gave it to my guide who was joined by another *tegadalai*.

The three of us set out in a northerly direction. We began our journey in the early afternoon, walking along the edge of the mountain range, overlooking a valley to our west where we could see the Senafe-Asmara road and Adi KeyiH, the regional capital. After some four hours of rough terrain, we reached a village called *Da'Ero Galba*, where we stayed overnight. Our hosts were a young *tegadalai* and his beautiful wife, and they slaughtered a goat for us and we had a feast.

The whole area is so rough that, even though it was not far from the city centers, it was not easily accessible to government troops or police. For that reason, it was defined by the *tegadelti* as a semi-liberated area.

As the sun went down over the western horizon, there appeared on the Senafe-Asmara road a convoy of several military trucks; we counted twenty. The *tegadelti* began discussing the meaning of this troop movement. My guide translated for me; one of the fighters who was also a fluent Tigrigna speaker, helped in translation. He said that in his views, the Derg was going to launch a new offensive in Eritrea. The question was where it would start. The others were curious to know my opinion. I then told them about the dissention within the Derg on the question of how to resolve the Eritrean war, with a minority led by General Aman supporting a peaceful solution while the majority was adamantly for a military solution. Since Aman lost out and was killed, it means an all-out war, I said.

"You see, I told you," said one *tegadalai*.

Chapter 15

AMONG THE GUERILLAS—
A LAWYER TURNED OUTLAW?

We spent a restful night at *Da'Ero Galba*, and early in the morning on Monday, we set out for a place called Alil, which served as a kind of a relay station for messages, judging by the number of young boys coming in and going out with written notes. From Alil we started on a long journey and, after an exhausting day, hiking over high mountain ranges, down steep valleys and across dry riverbeds, my guide and I finally arrived at a place called *Mindegle*. It seemed our final destination; I prepared to meet with the leader of the ELF in charge of the Akeleguzai front. His name was Mohamed Ahmed Abdo, former chairman of ELF's Central Command, known as *Qiyada Al Amma*. From about 1965, the ELF High Command had divided the fields of operation into five guerilla zones, adopting the Algerian model of *willayas,* and Akaleguzai was one of the five, under Mohamed Abdo.

Mohamed Abdo's "headquarters" consisted of a small cave nestled on a clearing at the base of a mountain, a cave shaded by a middle size acacia tree. He was listening to the BBC news in Arabic when we arrived. The guide, who obviously respected him, told me to wait outside until the news was over. Then he went inside the cave with the letter from Omar, and came back to usher me in. Mohamed Abdo was gracious, receiving me warmly and congratulating me for deciding to join the ELF. "Welcome home to the mother Front," he said, in faltering Tigrigna.

"I am a guest of the ELF, not a member," I told him.

"That is alright, we were all guests when we started," he said with an intriguing smile, which raised loud laughter from my guide and another *tegadalai* who was sitting with Mohamed Abdo. I was intrigued by all this and, for a brief moment, I wondered if these people would ever let me go. I was assailed by the nagging sense of uncertainty that I had felt since setting out on my journey from Mekele.

Mohamed Abdo said something in Saho and the second man left us. He then started speaking in Arabic, with my guide translating. He spoke of his student days at Cairo's Al Azhar University. I told him about myself and then asked him about his life in the ELF. As our conversation became more informal and cordial, he confided in me that when Eritrea attained its independence, he would like to be the Eritrean ambassador to Egypt. I decided I liked him—his candor and simplicity.

He talked about some of the leading personalities in the struggle, beginning with the elder statesmen like Idris Mohamed Adam and Woldeab Woldemariam; and then his peers like Osman Saleh Sabbe. On occasion, he interspersed his Arabic with Tigrigna words to emphasize his point, particularly when speaking about people he did not like. A detail that sticks in my mind, evidence of the ferocity of factional politics, is that he called Woldeab *tebelatsi* (Tigrigna for opportunist). Now Woldeab was a revered elder statesman, regarded as one of the fathers of Eritrea nationalism, who had sacrificed much, including his own family, for the cause of Eritrean freedom and dignity. It was galling to hear him called an opportunist. When I pointed this out to Mohamed Abdo, he seemed to relent and tried to explain his reasons. He saw that his explanations left me cold and thus changed his tune and started abusing another personality—Osman Saleh Sabbe, whom he called *adharhari* (reactionary).

These were some of the stock terms of abuse that fighters flung at one another across factional lines. Both Woldeasb and Sabbe, I would discover later, belonged to the rival front, the EPLF, and most ELF members saw Sabbe as the villain of the piece, though some defected to his faction after he broke with the EPLF. It all sounded very complicated to me until I met Sabbe and the other leaders of the EPLF, as I will explain.

Mohamed Abdo and his ELF comrades tried their best to recruit me, in the pursuit of which they spared no efforts to paint the rival front in the darkest of colors. The *TSere Gedli* (counter-revolutionary) EPLF was an agent of US imperialism and was allied with the Zionists—proof positive that it was promoting the cause of Ethiopia. Isaias Afewerki, the EPLF leader, had been seen at Kagnew, the US communications base in Asmara; he was clearly an American agent. There were variations on the theme; and these assertions were not limited to the Saho-based ELF branch led by Mohamed Abdo. After I climbed to the highlands around Asmara, I would hear similar charges from Tigrigna-speaking members of the ELF.

We left Mindegle after three days and nights and went back to Alil (the relay station). After two days and nights at Alil, I was taken to a village called *Abigrat*, which lies on the Senafe-Asmara road. After spending a day there I was met by four ELF activists who came by car from Asmara. They had decided to smuggle me to Asmara, and they did not even consider consulting me. As far as they were concerned, if an ELF leader of the area sent word that I was coming, I must be a *tegadalai*, and a *tegadalai* does what he is told by the leadership.

Four cadres from among the ELF's underground operators in Asmara, including two girls, waited for me at a point between Adi KeyiH and Segeneiti and took me in a car to Asmara. One of Mohamed Abdo's minions, who must have been informed about my identity, told them they were to say that I was a peasant, an uncle of one of them, who needed medical care in Asmara. I was suitably dressed for the role, with a grizzled beard and emaciated face. With the *netsela* that Desta had given me suitably soiled and wrapped around me, I looked very much like a poor peasant.

We headed for Asmara.

It was a crazy act, one that I had not anticipated. I felt like a cipher in a game played by invisible hands and there was nothing that I could do to influence the course of events. I was in their hands and simply hoped and prayed that they were right. But I couldn't help wondering why they were tempting fate? Why take me into an enemy-occupied city after all that I had been through—after my miraculous escape from Addis Ababa and my hazardous journey. When these young and reckless cadres came with a car, I thought they were taking me to the outskirts of Asmara to meet the leaders who, I had been told, were in hiding not far from the city. I never in my wildest dreams expected them to take me into the city. When I protested, pointing out the risk, they all laughed and one of the girls, a University of Asmara student, said that the police and everybody else were ELF sympathizers.

"Don't worry, uncle," she said, "nothing will happen to you," I could do nothing but keep quiet. The only comforting thought was that they did not know my identity. At least that was what I thought. Then the talkative girl, the University student, gave me cause for concern. "Did you hear about Dr. Bereket's escape from Ethiopia?" she announced suddenly, adding: "He is probably coming to Eritrea. But some also speculate that he escaped to Somalia."

Could she have suspected about me? Nah, how could she! They couldn't possibly suspect that the poor peasant they called uncle, a man in his early forties, was in fact Dr. Bereket? I feigned ignorance of what they were talking about, covering my head with the *netsela*, but smiling at the irony of the situation—just as I had smiled when one of Desta's relatives was bad-mouthing me in Mekele for being an aggressive interrogator at the Commission of Enquiry.

And my luck held—we were moved through the police roadblock. After we entered the city, they stopped at the door of a restaurant and cheerfully led me to the basement—an underground meeting place, no doubt—where I was given a hearty meal. I was then taken to the home of an activist where I had a bath, shaved and put on the blazer and khaki trousers I had brought with me from Addis Ababa.

My memory of what happened next in the following four days, and especially of my last day in the occupied city, is as fresh and clear as if it happened yesterday.

Into the Jaws of Death

On the evening of the first day of my arrival, a fighter named Fissehaie, who was one of the "escorts," asked me if I wished to see anyone. I told him that there were three people I wanted to see, the first being my old friend Dr. Isaac Abraha who was working at the Empress Menen Hospital, to which he offered to take me immediately. So someone took us by car from where I had washed and shaved and left us some distance from the hospital gate. We walked toward the hospital, avoiding the street lights. I was thrilled to walk in the city of my youth in the bracing December night air, but in constant fear of being noticed by someone who knew me. It was a strange feeling of exhilaration mixed with anxiety, akin to the feeling you get on your first date with a beautiful girl about whom you are not sure. After we entered the hospital compound, I wrote a note to Isaac and asked Fissehaie to deliver it by hand. I waited outside under the shadow of a tree.

After about ten minutes, Isaac emerged, dressed in his doctor's white overalls. Fissehaie followed him from a safe distance and then passed him going in the direction where he had left me. Isaac was happy to see me, but anxious about possible discovery. He spoke later about the gleeful smile he saw on Fissehaie's face when he glanced up after reading my note. He suggested we go to his apartment, which was a few minutes' walk from the hospital. Before he left us, Fissehaie asked for and received Isaac's home phone number; I also gave him my kinsman engineer Yohannes Haile's number, in case of need. Isaac expressed great surprise at my daring to enter the occupied city. And who is this Fissehaie, he wanted to know, and how can I trust him? If he were to betray us, it would be a horrific understatement to say that we would be in grave danger. In supreme confidence born of desperate hope, I did all I could to reassure Isaac that a *tegadalai* like Fissehaie is sworn to secrecy and fidelity to his cause and comrades. Never, I told him, would a *tegadalai* betray his comrades. As I reassured him, I was also reassuring myself and hoping that I was right. It remained to be seen if I was.

I spent the night at Isaac's house; his young wife, whom I knew from her childhood and who was expecting a baby, welcomed me warmly. I spent the next day reading in the bedroom, and Isaac took me to my kinsman Dr. Nerayo in the evening. I spent the night at Nerayo's and the following evening he took me to engineer Yohannes Haile's house.

On my fourth night in Asmara, Fissehaie took me to a secret meeting at the home of an activist named Haregu Zere. It had been called by Tareke Beraki, a senior ELF cadre and former Addis Ababa University student. There were four of us at the after-dinner meeting; Haregu's husband joined us for dinner, but was absent during the meeting. It seemed that, unlike his wife, he was not an ELF activist. In our society, it is rare for a wife to become a member of an underground movement if the husband is not; yet he did not object to his wife's activities.

During our meeting, I told the three ELF cadres that I was saddened by the ongoing "civil war" between the ELF and EPLF. I had been sufficiently briefed about the situation by Isaac, Nerayo and Yohannes, and had made up my mind to stay outside the factional fight and act instead as mediator to help bring the conflict to an end. I had been told that the public had launched mediation efforts and I wanted to be part of that. My plan was, of course, to go back to America to join my family, following a successful mediation. When I made my position clear proposing a mediating role, I saw disappointment on their faces, for they had assumed that I had joined the ELF. But none of them objected; indeed they expressed willingness to help in any way they could in my mediation efforts.

After the meeting, they decided to take me on a quick tour of the city; so the four of us—Tareqe, Fissehaie, Haregu and myself—drove to the city center in Haregu's car. I felt uneasy and asked them to take me straight to Yohannes Haile's house where I was staying, but they brushed aside my worries and insisted on giving me a last-minute tour of the city. Then while we were driving on the main highway of the city, Haregu made a fanciful suggestion, which was to prove fateful. She stopped her car outside one of the bars on Haile Selassie Avenue (today's Liberation Avenue), and with a broad smile, announced that she was going to treat me to a glass of whiskey, as a token both of welcome and farewell. The others loudly cheered in agreement. Although I was getting extremely anxious about the whole venture, I had no choice but to accept. But I said that we must have the drinks in the car, which they found amusing.

Haregu lost no time in saying, "But of course," adding in a teasing tone: "Do you think we want to take you to the bar and get you arrested?" She blew the horn and the waiter came out. I hid my face as she ordered the drinks. From the very moment that she came up with the suggestion, I had felt extremely uneasy; that silent "sixth sense" was sending danger signals that rang in my head. When the drinks came, I downed my whiskey in three or four gulps and said, "Let us go, please." Surprised and somewhat disappointed, the others reluctantly finished their drinks and Haregu started the car. We drove westward along Haile Selassie Avenue, past the cathedral to our right, continuing past the Ministry of Education, to our left, and made a turn to the left in the direction of the Hamasien Hotel.

That was when we saw a crowd of people milling around a couple of cars. Ethiopian army personnel were hassling the crowd, and hauling out drivers and passengers from the cars.

My heart leaped to my mouth. My worst fears were being realized; it was a nightmarish situation, as in a dream when you desperately want to run but your legs won't move. It was not possible to turn the car around on that narrow street, and anyway it was too late. An Ethiopian army officer and a couple of soldiers with rifles were running toward us. Fissehaie, who was seated on my right in the back seat, flung the car door open, leaped out and fired a round of shots at the approaching soldiers—then took off, crying "*nihdem*" (Tigrigna for let us run) at the top of his voice.

Having escaped being hit by Fissehaie's volley, the army officer and his men pounced on us, ordering us out of the car. The officer was extremely agitated, shouting, "*tessera, tessera*!" (Italian for ID card). After what Fissehaie had done, the officer could have easily ordered his men to shoot us dead there and then.

In the face of death, your mind works a thousand times faster. You think about the things that mean most to you. I saw my life running in front of me like a fast moving film. I thought of my family—my poor children who would grow up without a father. I did not even think of the horrible death I would die if I were caught and brought before Mengistu Haile Mariam, who had reportedly pounded his desk in rage upon hearing of my escape and had put a price on my head.

I was in the back seat behind the driver, Haregu. Tareke was in the front beside her. When the officer demanded ID cards, Tareke said he was a student (in Amharic) and the officer struck him on the head, cursed him and dragged him out. Everything happened so fast. I had been carrying a .38 Special with me all the way from Addis Ababa. I got rid of it by slipping it underneath Haregu's seat. When the officer asked me for an ID, I took out my World Bank ID and calmly, and in perfect Amharic, told him that I was a World Bank officer on a mission of project evaluation. "Here, look" I said handing him the card. I got out slowly out of the car and told him that I had met these people in a bar and they had kindly offered to bring me to my hotel.

"Shut up!" he said and walked away, telling the two soldiers to guard us. Tareke and I were ordered to sit on the ground. Meanwhile an Eritrean police officer had come toward the car and was engaged in conversation with Haregu. Obviously, he knew her and wanted to help. Tareke was quietly apologizing to me for putting me in this mess, and I was whispering to him to keep quiet, afraid he might blow my disguise. Suddenly, Haregu gunned the engine and sped off in reverse. Tareke then wished me good luck and sprung to his feet; he ran like a hunted rabbit, weaving left and right. One of the soldiers chased him, firing shots, and I was left sitting beneath the one remaining soldier, who stood guard, obviously shaken. Everyone's nerves were on edge, especially those of the Ethiopian soldiers.

It was time for me to make a move, and fast. It was going to be do-or-die. I made some remark about how hot it was and watched the soldier's reaction. He nodded nervously. He was young and this was probably his first experience in such turmoil. Suddenly, I made a quick calculation.

"Do you mind if I take off my raincoat," I asked amiably. He shrugged his shoulders, whereupon I slowly got up and took off the raincoat and placed it on my left arm. It was a very nice off-white raincoat loaned to me by my kinsman, Dr. Nerayo. The soldier was standing to my right, looking straight ahead. I planted the raincoat on his face, hit him on the throat with a right hand karate chop, and ran like Hell toward Haile Selassie Street. I heard shots firing and bullets whizzing over my head. I started weaving left and right, plunged into the traffic, and disappeared into the next street.

I turned right on the next street and kept running in the direction of the main Post Office. I turned back and when I saw no one following me, I stopped to catch my breath and began to walk, breathing heavily. I turned down an alley, where I saw a couple of prostitutes sitting on the kerb warming themselves over a stove. I greeted them and stopped to make small talk, then bid them good night and moved on. I then saw a barber shop with the owner standing at the door. I asked him if I could come in; he let me in. I was still breathing heavily, which he must have noticed because he asked me a question,

"Are you from our family?" (*kab sidrana diKa?*), that I took to mean was I a fighter? I said yes and he shut the door. A couple of army jeeps drove past and then everything went quiet. We must have remained there in the dark, in silence, for over an hour. The barber opened the door and said that it was safe to move. He lived in the Paradiso area, he said, and could take me there to spend the night with his family if I wished. I thanked him kindly but left alone, slowly making my way to Yohannes Haile's house.

By the time I reached the house and the gate-keeper let me in, it was long past midnight. But upon hearing the gate open and close, someone turned on the bedroom light. Abrehet, Yohannes' wife, opened the door to let me in and said that they were worried about me. Someone called Fissehaie had been calling all evening. "Who is he and what happened?" she asked, anxiety written over her delicate face.

"I just came out of the jaws of death," I told her, sitting down on the sofa. Yohannes came out in his pajamas, looking equally worried, and wanted to know what had happened. I related to them the unreal happenings of the evening. When I told them what happened, who Fissehaie was and what he did, Yohannes exploded into expletives, cursing Fissehaie and the whole gang who put my life in danger.

After he regained his composure, Yohannes said, "You must leave town at once; you must leave early in the morning." He said that the Ethiopian military had been searching homes and would continue in the following days. He explained the reason for the evening's agitation, why the Ethiopian armed forces were stopping and arresting people in many parts of the city. His house was surely on the list.

"Yes, but how do I get out? " I asked.

"I'll smuggle you out in my car." Yohannes then proceeded to explain. He would put me in the luggage compartment and drive his daughters (Helen, age 7 and Lea, age 6) to school—then take me to a safe place, out of the city. "I know just the spot," he said; his engineer's mind was working fast. We agreed on that; Abrehet gave me a double helping of Johnny Walker, after which we all went to bed.

We were up well before six in the morning. While Abrehet prepared the girls, feeding them and grooming them, Yohannes and I discussed alternative routes for me to take to link up the EPLF fighters. After I had informed him that I was intent upon helping in the mediation efforts between the ELF and EPLF, he had sent his sister Nitsihti to inform one of the leaders who was in the environs of Asmara about my intentions and plans.

We had a hasty breakfast; I was anxious to get out of the occupied city before they started the house-to-house search. So I got up and urged that we leave. Yohannes then went to the bedroom and came back holding a jacket which he handed to me, saying I would need it since I had sacrificed the one Dr. Nerayo had loaned me. He then sent the night guard on an errand so that he would not see me getting into the luggage compartment of the car. Then we left, and I could feel the car stopping at traffic lights and hear Yohannes greeting people on the way, until we finally reached the school where he left the girls. He came to the back of the car and, leaning on the luggage compartment, asked me if I was okay. I said yes, and he started the car and drove some distance until he stopped at what turned out to be a secluded area sheltered by eucalyptus trees.

I got out, heaving a sigh of relief. I remember joking, asking if this spot was where he used to bring his dates before marriage. At that moment of small triumph I felt the warmth of gratitude to a wonderful human being; I just looked at him almost in tears before we hugged and said our silent goodbyes. We had agreed on the next steps; accordingly, I put my Mekele *netsela* on top of the jacket, and started walking toward Wekidibba. I had exchanged my city shoes for the plastic sandals they call *kongo,* and I looked like a real peasant walking all the way to Mesfinto, Yohannes's village of origin, where he had arranged for me to meet with EPLF leaders. I arrived there in the early afternoon and was shown the house of the parents of my kinsman Yohannes Haile. They were out, so I sat down to rest under the awning of their *Hidmo.*

Leteberhan, Yohannes's mother, arrived while I was dozing off on the porch. She awakened me from my slumber and examined my face closely, wondering who I was. When I told her, she was overcome with joy mixed with surprise. She was about to break into the customary ululation, but I stopped her in time. She understood immediately and led me inside, where I told her the story of my escape and why I had come to Mesfinto. Aya Haile, her husband (Yohannes's father), joined us later. After hearing about the reason for my coming, he left to make arrangements for me to meet with the area EPLF cadres.

A Nation at War With Itself

When I left Addis Ababa in a hurry in late November 1974, the driving emotion that propelled me was fear—fear of being killed by the military junta who had killed my friend Aman Andom and many other innocent people. My fear was coupled with hatred of the military, not only for their murderous deeds, but also for high-jacking a promising popular revolution. The fear subsided, gradually diminishing, but reappeared as I was arbitrarily detoured into Asmara by the ELF cadres; it climaxed in the near-death experience at the hand of the Ethiopian military. I was free from fear only after I was safely smuggled out of Asmara by Yohannes Haile.

After I was safely out in what the *tegadelti* called the 'semi-liberated area' around Asmara, fear was replaced by sadness and anxiety. My original plan was to secure the assistance of the liberation fighters for safe passage back to the USA to rejoin my family. Now two unpleasant facts stared me in the face. First, Eritreans were decimating one another in a tragic fratricidal war. Second, the

Ethiopian military was enjoying this spectacle and confidently looking forward to the prospect of Eritrean guerillas finishing each other off.

To my utter dismay, I found an Eritrean nation at war with itself, a condition worse than war against an occupying enemy, which was bad enough. In the face of this crisis, neither of the fighting factions was willing to accord me safe passage out of the country and back to Washington; nor was I insistent once I saw the tragic situation of brother killing brother and wailing mothers desperately suing for peace and reconciliation. I had no choice but to bide my time, at the same time doing my part in helping to stop the factional fight.

Meanwhile, Eritrean elders throughout the countryside were organizing meetings aimed at mediating between the fighting factions. Their counterparts in the cities could not hold open meetings, but sent words of encouragement and material support to sustain the movement for peace and reconciliation. I decided to join the public efforts to stop the uncivil war between the ELF and EPLF and to help unite them. I entertained fond hope that these efforts would bear fruit in a matter of months—three or four, at most.

It was not to be.

At that point, I knew very little about the causes of the internecine conflict, though I witnessed its tragic consequences. When I began to ask and probe deeper, I discovered two totally opposed explanations and justifications for the war with incredible depth of mutual hatred and suspicion. The leadership on both sides seemed intransigent, whereas ordinary fighters were eager to end the conflict and get reunited, even though some of them repeated slogans demonizing the rival Front.

The tendency among the public was to define the rival fronts in terms of their respective leaders. The public referred to the ELF as *ganta Herui* (Hirui's team) and the EPLF as *ganta Isaias* (Isaias' team). Some of the older citizens identified each faction in terms of earlier Eritrean leaders who had competed for leadership in the 1940s. For example, when I went to visit Aboy Bahta of Geremi (my sister Bissrat's father-in-law), who was blind at the time, he asked me an interesting question. He wanted to know whether the man from Tselot (meaning Isaias) was on the side of Woldeab or Tedla Bairu. Woldeab and Tedla were the chief protagonists during the late 1940s—the former seeking Eritrean independence, the latter being in favor of union with Ethiopia. And Tedla, whose village of origin was Geremi, happened to be the father of Herui. I later found out that there was a reversal of roles, a generational evolution—Woldeab was on the side of *ganta Isaias*, not the other way round. Indeed, truth be told, Isaias resented the public adoration of Woldeab as the "father of the Eritrean nation." More on this later.

As soon as news spread of my involvement in the public efforts to stop the factional war, I received words of encouragement from various segments of the Eritrean public—religious leaders and village elders engaged in the mediation efforts, and youth groups associated with one or the other of the factions. Everyone wanted the fighting to stop and the two fronts to unite their forces against the common enemy. As I traveled throughout the length and breadth of the Hamasien highland, I was joined by people who offered their services to help in the mediation efforts. Elders came from as far as Segeneiti in the south and Keren in the north to help in these efforts. As people saw us passing by their villages, they would bring food and water for us, the women ululating and invoking the name of the Holy Mother of God to lend us "her healing hand."

On the Ethiopian side, the leaders were obviously not happy with the mediation efforts and made attempts to frustrate them through various methods, including selective assassination. I received warnings from several people; it seemed that word was out to have me kidnapped or killed. EPLF cadres warned me not to travel without armed guards and not to reveal where I spent the night. It is possible that it was then that Mengistu Haile Mariam, the junta leader, issued a price on my head, as the following story of an attempt to poison me seems to indicate.

Sometime in January 1975, after we launched the mediation efforts, there was a wedding in Shimanegus, a village that I frequented because my sister Mebrat lived there. Now the EPLF leaders had been monitoring the movements of a couple of villagers whom they had reason to suspect of being enemy agents. The leader of this group was a man by the name of Gebresilassie (nicknamed Hankish, because he limped). He had himself elected as an elder in a mediation committee to help in the mediation representing his village of *Adi SheKa*, a village with a small dam and a police unit—on the face of it, to protect the dam, but suspected of acting as a center for recruitment of local agents. Another suspect, named Berhe, if memory serves me well, was from *Shimnegus La'Elai* (my sister's village). One of his younger relatives was also under suspicion. The EPLF monitored the movements and activities of these people with the help of its local agents.

Their plot, as it turned out, was to have me invited to a wedding in *Shimanegus La'Elai* and poison me there. The EPLF, who were ready, spotted the younger relative of Berhe with a glass of poisoned *siwwa*, ready to hand it to me. Armed EPLF cadres caught the culprits red-handed and arrested them. I never found out exactly how the EPLF determined that the glass of *siwwa* was poisoned, but they did. There is no doubt in my mind that their vigilance saved my life; another reason, perhaps, why I decided to join them eventually.

A few days later, I saw Gebresillasie and Berhe at a detention place in Quazien, looking dejected. True to character, the EPLF leaders did not tell me anything about what they did or how they found out the plot. But I suspect that they wanted me to see the physical evidence of their diligence, which was why they ushered me to a room where the culprits were kept before they were taken to Bahri Bara and executed. I don't know what happened to the third man.

An example of the EPLF's method of indirect communication was when I was summoned to witness an interrogation of another suspect, a villager from Adi SheKa. It appeared that some poison was found in his house, and I assumed that, by inviting me to observe the interrogation, the EPLF leaders were indirectly informing me about how and why they arrested the culprits.

The interrogation took place in the open air outside the village of Wekki, on the edge of the escarpment. Isaias did the interrogation of the man, aged around 45, who was asked to explain how and why he had the poison. He kept saying he bought the poison for protection against rodents that had been eating his crops. The interrogator was not satisfied with the answer and warned the detainee that unless he told the truth, he would be flogged severely (The words Isaias used were: *HiQoKa kisa'E zQileT kitgref iKa!*) The man denied any criminal act or intention and persisted in protesting his innocence.

A couple of times one of the two young cadres, nicknamed "Somal," hit the man on the head with a stick to emphasize the threat of flogging. The man winced but kept his dignity and protested his innocence. I was disgusted and turned away as the interrogation continued. I asked Isaias later what happened to the man. He told me he was found to be innocent and released. He must have noticed the disgust on my face and we never mentioned the incident again; but I was to witness another "interrogation" in Sahel, this time by the notorious Haile Jebaha. I will return to this subject later.

As for the attempts of the Ethiopian authorities to have me killed, there is anecdotal evidence to that effect. For instance, in June 1980 I traveled to Freetown, Sierra Leone, on the occasion of the 18th summit of the Organization of African Unity, and was distributing pamphlets describing the atrocities of the Ethiopian military in Eritrea. The head of the Ethiopian delegation had me detained at the Pademba Road prison by the Sierra Leone authorities, on trumped up charges that I was a terrorist. The accusation was challenged and dismissed as ridiculous by the leader of the Somali delegation, who agitated on my behalf and had me released in the nick of time before the police began their torture. All I suffered was an intense "third degree" interrogation and a couple of slaps on the face, accompanied by a promise of a worse fate unless I confessed to being a terrorist!

Amare Tecle, an Eritrean who was at the time on the Ethiopian side and a member of the delegation, later heard Mengistu express regrets that they had not been able to have me killed and that it must still be carried out. To his credit, Amare sent word through the appropriate channels relating Mengistu's threat and warning me to be careful.

The Guerilla Leaders and Issues of Contention

As an important part of the mediation efforts, I needed to gain access to the top leaders of both factions. I decided to begin by meeting the EPLF leader, Isaias Afewerki.

It proved more difficult than I had expected. I had higher expectations because Iyob Gebrelul, the man that Yohannes' sister contacted on my behalf before I was smuggled out of Asmara, was among the first group of EPLF cadres I met in Mesfinto—a group led by Mesfin Hagos. At the time I had no idea who Mesfin was or what position in the hierarchy he occupied; the EPLF people did not introduce themselves to strangers and they certainly did not talk about themselves. I spent a whole evening and a good part of the night with the group, learning about the history of the EPLF and asking probing questions. The EPLF cadres put the entire blame on the ELF leadership for launching the "war of liquidation," as they called it. As for the necessity of ending the fratricidal war and reconciliation, they were all non-committal. They deferred such decisions to the "proper organ" of the front.

Mesfin asked me what group I represented in my mediation efforts. When I told him I represented myself, he just smiled and said nothing. In later years we joked about that incident with me teasing him about the EPLF's "group-think" approach and he reminding me of the limits of individual roles. But on one occasion he did express regrets not only for doubting me, but also for the manner and tone of his questions (*defirnakka!*). I was grateful for his candor, which was rare in EPLF circles.

It was more difficult to gain access to the top leadership of the EPLF. To begin with, they spoke in collective terms—"leadership" not leaders—and when I asked to meet the leader in my first encounter with a group of EPLF *tegadelti* in Mesfinto, two of them spoke at the same time and said, "We are all leaders," with the rest nodding in agreement. I was intrigued by this response and by the idea of collective leadership. At first I thought someone was pulling my leg, and when I questioned the idea of all being leaders, there was a benign smile betokening mild pity mixed with pride of place—"Here comes a city slicker," they seemed to say, "who does not understand the ABCs of the EPLF organization!" I turned it in my mind over and over again, wondering whether it was a case of these hardy types pulling the wool over the eyes of a "city slicker" like me who came barging into their private domain. Or perhaps it was a governing myth by which they lived.

On closer examination in the days that followed, as I walked among the *tegadelti* from Mesfinto to Geremy, and then to Quazien, Azien and elsewhere, I began to see beyond the veil of collective "we." I observed that only one of them wore a watch, the one who was assigning the rest places to sleep. He turned out to be the company commander (*MeraH Haili*). The formation of the military organization at the time had not gone beyond company. The commander of the company I first met and traveled with was Ibrahim Afa, with Weldenkiel Haile as "political commissar." These two and Iyob gave me a rough idea of the status of the guerilla war and some insight into the nature and origin of the "civil war." None of them would commit himself in terms of agreeing with my ideas of ending the fratricidal war and about reconciliation and unity.

It took over two weeks for me to see the top EPLF leader, Isaias Afewerki. I first met Isaias in a secure place called Sabur Seghi. Our talks ranged over the history of the conflict between the two factions and why the group he led decided to split from the ELF. As for the issue of the on-going fight between the two, he did not oppose my plea to both fronts to lower the temperature of the propaganda war, and stop calling each other by derogatory terms (such as *tSeri gedli* for the EPLF, and *amma* for the ELF). To show that he accepted my plea,

Isaias told me that I could tell Herui, the ELF leader at the time, that he should not worry, whatever that meant. His exact words were, "*NiHerui deHan'yu bello* (Tell Herui it is okay). In later years, while dealing with Isaias in different capacities, I would discover that ambiguity is his favorite mode of communication, which some attribute to an ingrained feudal mentality.

Why did Herui need the reassurance of Isaias? One of the accusations leveled against Herui was that he had presided over the meeting of the ELF leadership where they decided to hunt down the EPLF and liquidate them. In telling me to tell Herui "it is okay," Isaias was in effect saying, "Let us bury the hatchet."

Herui did not seem to reciprocate. When I saw him a few weeks later in Adi Gebrai and told him what Isaias had said, he was dismissive, saying that he did not trust Isaias. But he did agree to lower the temperature of factional propaganda war by not calling the EPLF "*tSeregedli.*" So did several of his top cadres like Tareke BeraKi and Tesfamariam Woldemariam, who happened to be in Adi Gebrai. Also present in Adi Gebrai at the time was Redazghi Gebremedhin, who had decided to be part of the mediation efforts. From then on he and I tried to coordinate our efforts and, whenever possible, to travel together. Redazghi, from a devout Protestant family, was a sincere humanitarian whose simple human approach was appealing. Together, we would later form the Eritrean Relief Association (ERA).

The history of my involvement with the Eritrean liberation struggle begins at this point— first as a mediator, then as relief organizer and finally as a full-fledged member of the EPLF. But I did not find out till much later that the liberation war had a darker side, masked by the mystique of revolutionary struggle. My plan of uniting the fronts was to prove unrealistic due to this masked reality, and my hope of joining my family soon would also prove illusory. The carnage caused by the factional fights and its demoralizing impact on the Eritrean nation had its root in the inordinate ambitions of guerilla warlords and the psychosis of unchecked power, which stood in the way of realizing the two legitimate goals.

Unfortunately, while the reality of carnage was visible to the naked eye, the root cause (the power psychosis) was not easily discernible. As I tried to probe deeper to understand the issues dividing the two fronts in order to bring them together, it was not clear to me at first that the conflict did not necessarily have to do with ideological issues. In time it became clear that personal ambition and rivalry was equally to blame. But the cadres of both fronts emphasized ideological and other differences. Each front charged the other with arbitrary killings. Ideologically, EPLF cadres sought to distinguish their organization from the ELF by describing the rival leadership as backward and reactionary. In response, ELF cadres claimed that the EPLF was in the pay of the Ethiopians and their Zionist allies. And so on and so forth, ad nauseam.

These charges and counter charges were part of the problem that our mediation efforts had to overcome, before we could arrange a meeting. The meetings had to be held first between lower cadres at the platoon level, followed by a meeting of the higher leadership. The first breakthrough at the platoon level took place on January 19, 1975 in Adi Shimagle. The mixed group of *tegadelti* then came together to Hazega where, to everyone's disbelief, the members from both sides joined in a celebratory dance. Redazghi beamed with satisfaction and hugged me warmly. It was indeed a rare joyful moment.

This joyful event was marred by tragedy when a *tegadalai,* who was dancing with a loaded AK-47, accidentally touched the trigger and two people fell dead and two others were wounded. The names of the dead were: Tesfagiorghis Habtemariam and Kidane Tekie, both of the Hazega village. The wounded were Bereket Misghina, an ELF fighter, and Tekleab, a Hazega villager. The dead were buried the following day and we raised money from both fronts and from individuals, including myself, to be given to the families of the deceased. As for the wounded, only one needed medical attention. I sent word to Dr. Nerayo to come from Asmara with the necessary medicine and instruments. He came in the evening of the same day and treated the wounded man, after which he slipped back to Asmara with the help of experienced *tegadelti*. It would be Dr. Nerayo's epiphany, his rehearsal for his eventual decision to join the EPLF and become one of the architects of the field hospital in Sahel that amazed all visitors.

The meeting of the *tegadelti* at the platoon level continued under my chairmanship, with Redazghi keeping minutes of the meeting. The joint meeting passed a resolution affirming their belief in reconciliation and unity, and requesting that the meetings continue at the level of higher leadership. They urged that a joint defense committee be formed to plan military tactics and strategy. There was a spirit of optimism and hope, inducing one of the leaders of the EPLF contingent, Girmai Gebremeskel, to make a remark that moved everybody and that has stuck in my mind. He said, "This meeting of fighters on the road to unity and out of a terrible war is our first independence." We all said "Amen" to that, and went about facilitating more meetings.

The low-level meeting of the ELF and EPLF cadres was followed with several meetings between the higher leadership. One face-to-face meeting took place at the home of my sister Mebrat in Shimanegus La'Elai, attended by Isaias from the EPLF and Abdulqadir Rommodan representing the ELF. It was a cordial meeting, clearing the way for others that were held in quick succession, climaxing in the final meeting that took place in AmetSi on February 7, seven days after the Ethiopian military launched their offensive. At that meeting the ELF was led by Herui who had come all the way from Adi Neamen. He was accompanied by Ibrahim Totil and several other cadres. Isaias came with only two: one was Zerimariam Sheqa, nicknamed Waldheim, and the other was called Laeke. Both Laeke and Waldheim were apparently sharpshooters and both were martyred not long after. Several decisions came out of the meeting, including joint or coordinated attacks and defense operations, and a common policy of helping civilian victims of enemy attacks, displaced from their villages. That was when the idea of creating a relief organization was born.

From Mediation to Relief Work

News of the successful meeting between the rival Fronts spread far and wide, giving rise to public expressions of joy and renewed hope of liberation. The news also spurred the enemy to prepare an offensive against positions held by the guerillas. Ethiopian military units launched a coordinated attack on several positions around Asmara, burning villages as they pushed forward toward the temporary trenches where the guerillas were dug in. This naturally caused a massive exodus of displaced villagers that came seeking shelter behind the guerilla-held lines. Assisted by air cover, the Ethiopian army caused considerable damage to life and property. It was in response to this emergency facing the displaced civilian population that the leadership of both fronts agreed to authorize the creation of an entity to organize relief work, even as they prepared for the defense of their positions against the oncoming Ethiopian military offensive.

Accordingly, top representatives of both fronts met in the village of Deqetros to agree on a plan of action. The participants were Isaias Afewerki and Asmerom Gerezghiher on the EPLF side, and Ibrahim Totil and Ahmed Mahmud on the ELF side. The plight of a mass of humanity displaced by war was staring them in the face; so in addition to issues of defense and future counteroffensive, the leadership of the two fronts discussed relief options. Redazghi Gebremedhin and I had suggested the creation of a joint relief entity to mobilize support both inside Eritrea and abroad. The original understanding was that I would represent the EPLF and Redazghi would act on behalf of the ELF. For political reasons not made clear to us at the time, the participating leaders decided that it would be better to work under the sponsorship of one or the other of the factions. Isaias told me later that Ibrahim Totil had told him it would be acceptable if we worked under EPLF sponsorship. We were given full mandate to organize relief efforts locally and internationally and to employ all appropriate and lawful methods in fulfillment of our mission.

The Ethiopian offensive continued to intensify, with the use of tanks and heavy artillery against the light arms of the guerillas. It would be another ten years before the EPLF could acquire the military capability in heavy armory and weaponry to engage the enemy in classical positional war, including tank battles. But even in 1975, extraordinary acts of heroism were demonstrated; young men armed only with AK47s and Bren guns routed better armed and more numerous enemy soldiers in battles around Beleza and Adi Nifas. One of the most dramatic events in the battles of Adi Nifa and Beleza was when the EPLF *tegadelti* shot down an F-86 fighter. I saw the pilot eject and his parachute open as the jet crashed near Mai HuSa. There was wild jubilation among the guerrillas and the public and the event had a galvanizing effect on the young villagers pulling them to become guerilla fighters. From then on the fighter jets (F-86 and F-5) and the smaller aircraft like the T-28s as well as the Canberras were forced to fly very high to avoid being shot down with small arms fire.

An important document describing the enemy's plan of attack and secret codes was found on the body of an Ethiopian officer who was killed in the battle around Beleza. I was surprised to find my name mentioned in the document as one of the leaders of "Jebha" (ELF). The document was to prove useful in our "diplomatic" work a few weeks later, as I shall explain. What amazed me most was the morale of the *tegadelti* who came back from battle smiling and burst into spontaneous dances, as if the dance served as substitute for their dinner. Indeed, one of the popular songs sung by Tiberih Tesfahuney contained lyrics to that effect: *Laloye, laloyye- Quinat wi'Ilom guayla zidirarom!....etc*

As far as I could tell, the guerillas never left their dead and wounded behind. They took care of the wounded and buried the dead quickly. And they were light-hearted about it all, behaving as though nothing had happened. They never spoke of a fighter being killed; they said instead that he had "fulfilled his duty." A fighter was martyred not dead, and this new language intrigued the peasants and in time had became part of their vocabulary, occasionally giving rise to some comic relief. For instance, one day a peasant in Quazien approached a group of *tegadelti* asking for assistance. He said, in all seriousness, that he needed help to dispose of a donkey that lay martyred in front of his house. He was puzzled by the hilarious laughter with which they greeted his remarks, even as they willingly helped him dispose of the "martyred" donkey.

The Ethiopian military launched a two-pronged attack from Asmara—to the west in the Deqeteshim area held by ELF units, and to north in the Karnishim area held by EPLF units. They proceeded first to displace the ELF from their positions. From the high point in the Zaghir village, I could see villages in Deqeteshim burning, as the Ethiopian military torched them one after the other. A couple of days later, I saw the village of my birth burning, as the Ethiopians torched it in revenge for their humiliating defeat the day before at the hand of EPLF fighters. The Ethiopian military advanced displacing the *tegadelti* and pushing them further onto the escarpments around Zaghir and Weki. The day Redqazghi and I were to leave for Sahel, Quazien was taken, following pitched battles in which some of the best fighters were killed, including the renowned fighter and platoon leader Kidane Teklom (Wedi Teklom) of Defere. He had vowed, "I will rather die defending Quazien than see the enemy take it." He was true to his word. Also martyred was Zerimariam (Waldheim). When we reached Zagre, we saw a number of wounded soldiers, among them the former university student, Tesfu Kidane, with whom I had had very interesting discussions on revolutionary tactics and strategy. He had been wounded in the head and Dr. Nerayo told me there was little hope of recovery. He died before we resumed our march to Sahel.

The Hard Road to Sahel

My journey to Sahel was physically the most challenging in all my life. The following account is written to give a flavor of some of the trials the guerilla recruits were forced to go through right at the outset before they began their training. "The road to Sahel" or "the Sahel test" are phrases understood by EPLF *tegadelti* with no need for explanation. I kept a journal from the day I left

Addis Ababa in late November 1974 all the way to Sahel and beyond, and the following is an abbreviated account of the journey.

I started from Weki on the edge of the Hamasien highland, escorted by five *tegadelti,* including one crazy girl named Meriem Gual Dirfo. I call her crazy because she almost killed me while we were resting the day after we left Weki. We were resting at a point between Wina and BaHri Bara, when she started showing off, examining a Sonoval rifle and the gun went off and the bullet whizzed over my head. She also gave me a foretaste of "the class struggle" that I would experience later, by criticizing me for having spare trousers while she and the others only had one pair each. What I said to her in response is not fit for printing. A fine beginning of a journey to Sahel!

My escorts and I had to leave without Redazghi because he was away on some errand at the time; I was told that he would meet us on the way. We started from Weki in the afternoon of March 3, 1975, climbing down the steep hills of Midri Zen. When it grew dark at times we were forced to crawl, and had to spend the night in a hut offered by a kind peasant. Early the next morning, we climbed further down and crossed the Digsana Valley, after which we climbed up a mountain and reached Wina and, further up, Bahri Bara, which was used as a secondary training camp. The head of the camp was Sebhat Efrem who told us that we would leave the following morning in the company of five hundred trainees travelling to Sahel. He saw that my *kongo* shoes were worn out and offered to give me his, which I thankfully accepted. The following morning, March 5, we began our march to Sahel and arrived at Zagre three hours later. Solomon, the guide responsible for the journey—a tough former commando soldier—ordered a stop at a beautiful spot where we stayed much of the afternoon. I found Redazghi, who had traveled with the lorry that brought some wounded guerillas, accompanied by Dr. Nerayo.

We left Zagre and after marching for some four hours stopped and spent the night at a place, the name of which I did not write down. Zagre was to be the last forest area with cool mountain water that I would see until I was out of Sahel. The journey to Sahel is a test even to the hardiest among men, and many a city slicker was sorely tested, threatening to give up the journey. Only it was not possible to give up; you either forged ahead trudging along in the desert for days with little water, or were left behind to die of dehydration.

The following morning, March 6, we started at 5 a.m. We passed Gedghed at 7 and arrived at Laba riverbed at about 9:30. Many of the trainees were tired, hungry and above all dying of thirst. All we had for breakfast was a cup of tea each, and morale was beginning to be a problem. We left Laba at 4 p.m. and an hour later arrived at Mai Ule, where we spent the night, then rested all the next morning and part of the afternoon.

The next day, March 7 (the fourth day of the march), we left Mai Ule at 3.30 pm ; it was a cloudy afternoon so the heat was less oppressive. Walking behind camels loaded with provisions of rice, sugar, and tea, we marched for seven hours non-stop and reached the next water-point, called Ablet, at the foot of a dry riverbed called Abarara. We spent the night there, where a spring was supposed to be found; we were all dying of thirst and dug in the sand only to find that there was not much water to drink. We left Ablet and walked for seven hours and reached another water-point called Me'ETir. This leg of the journey was probably the toughest, because the hot sand heated the plastic *Kongo* and burned our feet. At age 43, I was the oldest in the whole group and I walked with great difficulty, tolerating the pain out of sheer will power and tenacity.

Our guide was changed; we were now in the care of one Teklu Berhe, an Asmara "lumpen" who openly boasted of having knifed an American soldier to death after a bar brawl. My naïve idea of a *tegadalai* as a sort of angel began to change. Yet, despite such background, Teklu seemed more compassionate than Solomon in treating the trainees who complained and threatened to give up the walk. He reasoned with them, encouraging them to hang on and promising that there would be plenty of water and food at the next water point—knowing full well that it was not true. We had become close, and he told me with a smile, "It is as true as you want to believe it is."

I don't need to go on describing the rest of the journey. Three more days of the same march over hot sands in a "God-forsaken" landscape passed like a nightmare, at times tantalized with the appearance of mirages on the desert. The recruits, mostly young men in their late teens and early twenties, walked like zombies, limping and dragging their feet, probably cursing the day they decided to join the armed struggle, gasping for air with open mouths and cracked lips, barely able to speak. Watching them, I wondered whether they would survive the military training that awaited them. I would find out months later that they did survive and had become physically fit and adept at desert warfare. Moreover, they had turned a corner, having been purged of what their trainers called "petty-bourgeois" sentiments and aspirations, and armed with a new ideology drummed into them during months of training. Whatever else one might say about Marxism, it had a powerful mobilizing capacity, promising the world to the "oppressed masses" and, at best, making them a potent weapon of struggle—or at worst, an instrument of the inordinate ambitions of unscrupulous individuals.

In any case, the hard road to Sahel was a well-conceived test, preparing the recruits for what was to come.

Journey's end at last! We reached our destination, Bleqat, at 7 pm on Tuesday, March 11, seven days after we started from BaHri Bara. When we arrived, a man with an emaciated face and eagle-like eyes watched us as the trainees passed by and were told to sit for a welcome speech. The man's name was Solomon Woldemariam and he neither made a welcome speech nor showed any sign of welcome. Apparently this, too, was part of the Sahel test. Our guide, Teklu, whispered something to him, as a result of which he approached me and Redazghi. I gave him the two letters that Isaias had given me, as well as the packet given to me by Sebhat Efrem at BaHri Bara. We were then taken to a hut where we spent the night.

I slept like a log. The following morning, Solomon took us to meet with the members of the provisional leadership: comprising Romodan Mohamed Nur, Solomon Woldemariam, Abu Teyyara, and Abu Ajaj. These were the Sahel segment of the provisional leadership of the EPLF; one of them, Ali Said Abdalla, had gone to the highlands with some foreign journalists; we actually met him at Zagre. The others were: Isaias Afewerki, Mesfin Hagos, Asmerom Gerezgher, and another man, a lowlander, whose name escapes me.

In contrast to Isaias and Mesfin, whom I found to be taciturn and secretive, Romodan was refreshingly open and talkative. Such characteristics reflect men's natural character as well as their regions of origin. Both Isaias and Mesfin were highlanders, whereas Romodan was from the lowland region of Semhar where the people are open and sociable. Abu Teyara and Abu Ajaj, who spoke in Arabic, were to defect a year later when the head of the EPLF's Bureau of Foreign Affairs, Osman Saleh Sabbe, split from the EPLF. By defecting they were conceivably spared the periodic purges that Isais Afewerki would execute on his comrades-in-arms over the years, until he was left standing alone. Among the first to be purged was Solomon Woldemariam, a tough-minded and wiry highlander. A year later, in the spring of 1976, I was in the FaH area of Sahel awaiting the reorganization of ERA, when I heard about wide-spread practice of torture under Solomon's watch. I dismissed the rumors as enemy propaganda, or factional spite.

But on one occasion, while I was walking toward a place where I habitually went to answer nature's call, I heard cries of agony from the bush. Curious to find out, I approached the bush where the cries came from. And there, to my horror, I saw Haile Jebha,(Solomon's Deputy Chief of Security), beating another man repeatedly on the head with a thin stick. The victim, whose hands and feet were tied and who apparently knew me, called me by name and begged to be rescued. Without a moment's hesitation, I rushed to his rescue, whereupon Haile angrily warned me not to interfere in "the business of the *Hafash*"(masses). But he at least stopped the beating and took the prisoner Goitom Berhe (BitSai) back to the headquarters. Later on, at the headquarters where I stayed, I was surprised to hear Haile asking Goitom (his erstwhile victim) if there was enough sugar in his tea, to which Goitom answered quietly by nodding his head. I made it my business to find out what crime he had committed and began to chat with him in Haile's absence, but was rebuked by a young *tegadalai,* a teenager named Mekonnen, who seriously advised me never to talk to *guguyat (*wrong doers). When I asked him why not, he said that it would give them a sense of support and harden them in the process of interrogation.

I went away wondering whether we were creating monsters. I must also note that I was informed years later that Haile too was purged and executed along with Solomon and others dubbed "Right Wingers." The "Left Wingers" had been executed earlier dubbed as *Menka'E* or leaders of *A'Enawi Minqisqas* (destructive movement). Here, I will say, in parenthesis, that it is time that some one armed with all the facts write about this dark side of the armed struggle. The deafening silence on this topic has been an obstacle to the movement toward democracy.

One day, I referred to the interrogation conducted by Isaias a couple of weeks earlier in Weki, and asked Solomon Woldemariam about the practice of torture in the struggle. He advised me to stay away and not to intervene in these things in the future, if I knew what was good for me. When I said that it was my business to intervene and condemn torture, he responded with contemptuous laughter, adding something about "petty bourgeois sentiments." I was disgusted, and mentioned this to some of the more mature members of the EPLF; the standard answer was that the CIA and their agents in Asmara had tried to penetrate the EPLF, and that people like Goitom BiSai had to be dealt with severely for the protection of the revolution. The department of security was itself called *Halewa Sewra* (Protection of the Revolution).

Once more, I confronted the question: does the end justify the means? Not in my philosophy, but the question remains. In a revolutionary situation, when (or if) the life of a whole movement as the embryo of a future nation is at stake, can torture and other practices prohibited by universal principles of international law be justified or excused? The leadership of the movement seemed to think so, my objections notwithstanding. They seemed oblivious to the fact that, apart from its moral repugnance, torture as a method of interrogation does not necessarily produce the right result. For under torture, a person will confess to anything, true or false.

I will leave this issue there for the moment.

From Sahel to Aden and Beyond

At the meeting with the leaders in Bleqat, we discussed some of the problems of bringing relief to the field. The first problem was points of entry. If the Sudanese government was willing to help, the way to Sahel and Barka would be smooth, so the first step was to meet with and persuade the appropriate Sudanese authorities. In that respect I thought that my work was cut out for me, but discovered later that it was not as hard as I had thought, as I will explain below. Failing Sudanese cooperation and in case of urgent need, the points of entry to Eritrea from the Red Sea were discussed by the leaders who knew the geography of the place.

A related problem was transporting and distributing the food to people in the highlands. Several solutions were suggested, including using camels as far as the edge of the highlands and donkeys from there onwards. Clearly, a relief operation involved not only getting supplies but also logistical questions of transportation and distribution, points that ERA would work out later.

At 5:30 a.m. on March 14, the fourth day after our arrival in Bleqat, we left camp on our way to Aden, Yemen, in the company of Romodan Mohamed Nur and Weldenkiel Gebremariam, chief of the EPLF office in Aden. Also with us were three Ethiopians—Assefa Habtu, Efrem, and Petros, members of the opposition movement in Ethiopia. After three days of leisurely march, avoiding points occupied by Ethiopian troops, we arrived at BeriTe, an oasis on the edge of the Red Sea. There we boarded an EPLF boat, also named *The Red Sea*. The sight of the Red Sea and its fresh air revived our spirits making us light-hearted, indulging in jokes and horseplay.

On board the boat, we met some wounded *tegadelti* on their way to Aden for medical treatment. We were treated to a delicious dinner of rice and fish served by smiling Afar men, members of the fledgling naval force of the EPLF. The captain of the boat, called Vasco, was delightful.

After a voyage that took us first east and then south, we passed the strait of Bab-el-Mendeb on Friday, March 20. We arrived at Aden the following day at 3:30 p.m.. Feeling dizzy, we made our way out of the boat and were taken to the EPLF headquarters, where we found some twenty Eritrean recruits waiting to go to Bleqat by the next boat. I remember thinking, "At least they will be spared the grueling march on the sands of Sahel!" The EPLF office was a beehive of activity with the famous Hiwet, a middle-aged woman, as manager and moving spirit.

On Sunday, March 23, Osman Saleh Sabbe came from Beirut to meet us and make all the necessary arrangements for our relief efforts. A slightly built man in his mid-forties, Sabbe was an affable, ever-smiling, energetic man who inspired trust, making us feel that all he thought about was our needs. His detractors, who were many in both the ELF and the EPLF, described him as a chameleon who changed his mood to suit the moment, a supreme opportunist. He might have had a touch of opportunism, but in my assessment of him based on months of observation, it was opportunism in the service of a cause: Eritrean freedom. He was a committed Eritrean nationalist, even though he made use of his Islamic and Arabic language heritage, and his "Semitic" visage.

The first logistical question facing us was travel documents, and Sabbe said he would take care of that, through his contacts in the Somali Embassy. Redazghi and I took passport photos. Meanwhile, Woldenkiel arranged for us to meet with the delegate of the International Committee of the Red Cross (ICRC), a Swiss national named Dominique Dufour, whom we met on Saturday, March 29. His advice on potential sources of relief in Europe and on modes of approach was very helpful, including the list of names he gave us of people we needed to see in Geneva.

I asked Dufur if he could mail a postcard for me; he agreed and so I wrote a few lines to my Swiss friend Christian Walser at the World Bank in Washington, DC. Using a pen name but making reference to something only he and I knew, I informed him that I was safely out and asked him to inform my wife and the head of our department at the World Bank

Dufour suggested that we meet with ELF leaders who were visiting Aden at the time, led by Ahmed Nasser, a suggestion we accepted willingly. We met Ahmed Nasser and Ahmed Salah the following day and briefed them on our relief mission. Ahmed Nasser briefed us on the situation on the ELF side in Barka, and supported our efforts and wished us well. He did not imagine, anymore than we did, that the hardliners in the ELF leadership would decide a few weeks later to create a rival relief entity in the name of the ELF, a decision that would create problems for ERA's relief mobilization efforts for the better part of 1975. Ibrahim Totil's agreement that ERA, sponsored by the EPLF, could work for all Eritrean refugees and displaced persons, was rescinded by those in the ELF leadership who put factional and personal ambitions above national interest.

The same day, Sunday, March 30, Ahmed Tahir Baduri, the assistant head of the Aden EPLF office, brought us our Somali passports; so we were ready to leave for Beirut where Sabbe was waiting for us. Early in the morning on Monday, March 31, Baduri took us to the airport; we arrived in Beirut around 3 p.m. We were met at the airport by Grasmach Asberom Abraha, the Foreign Mission's treasurer, who took us to the Atlas Hotel in central Beirut. Later in the day, Sabbe came to see us and he took Redazghi and me out for dinner.

The Birth Pangs and Growth of ERA

After meeting us in Aden, Sabbe had summoned the other members of the EPLF Foreign Mission to Beirut, for a meeting. Present with us were: Woldeab Woldemariam and Taha Mohamed Nur from the Cairo office; Tsegai Kahsai from Rome; and Adam Idris, Mohamed Ali AfArora and Ibrahim Mantay from the Beirut office. To these assembled members of the EPLF Foreign Mission, I gave a detailed account of our mediation work and told of the humanitarian situation created by the escalation of the war by the Ethiopian military around Asmara. Sabbe informed the assembled group about the captured document that we brought with us and promised to translate parts of it into Arabic himself. It was then that I learned that, in his youth, he had lived and studied in Addis Ababa and knew Amharic well.

Three proposals came out of the meeting. The first was for us to meet with diplomatic representatives of as many countries as possible and give interviews to the press in Beirut. Second, we should tour Arab countries in the neighborhood, especially Syria and Iraq. Sabbe would arrange all that; clearly, he was a skilled operator, who enjoyed fixing problems and cultivating relationships.

The third proposal was based on our own recommendation of the need to create a permanent official Eritrean relief entity. In fact I had drafted a constitution for the Eritrean Relief Association (ERA) while we were in Eritrea and given a copy to Sabbe. I had also written a long report on the humanitarian situation in Eritrea as well as on our mediation work. Sabbe suggested that a relief organization be formally established as soon as possible and he promised to help in having it registered in Beirut. He also suggested that we include as members of the board of directors people representing both "factions of the ELF," as he liked to refer to the two Fronts.

To that end, he proposed that we should go to Khartoum, Sudan, where he and some of the other members of the Foreign Mission were going soon. We agreed on this and went about meeting diplomats and journalists in Beirut after which we traveled to Syria and Iraq. The visits to Syria and Iraq lasted ten days, and at the end of the visits we left for Khartoum on Sunday, April 20.

In Khartoum, we met members of both EPLF and ELF and briefed them about our Middle East tour as well as of our planned relief work. We divided our work into three parts. The first was meeting with Eritreans and identifying potential members of the ERA board of directors as well as organizing relief committees in various parts of Sudan where there was a large Eritrean refugee population. The second was contacting appropriate Sudanese individuals, including members of the government, who could help us in our relief work. The third concerned visits to European countries and the United States to establish branches of ERA; and, with the help of Eritreans in those countries and their friends, collecting relief goods and funding to finance their shipment.

In pursuit of these ends, we first contacted Eritreans living in Sudan who could become members of the board of directors of ERA. Later, we sought out individuals who could form relief committees in Khartoum, Kessela, Gedarif and other places where there was a large concentration of Eritreans. Redazghi and I took a bus to Kessela and found several Eritreans who were willing to help in relief work. Unfortunately, it was in Kessela that we first experienced frustration in the form of ELF resistance to ERA's work. We were advised by one of the ELF representatives, Jimi'E, to write a letter to Hirui Tedla who was attending the ELF Congress inside Eritrea, asking him to confirm the ELF-EPLF agreement about ERA's mandate to work for all Eritreans. Romodan Mohamed Nur had written a letter of delegation in Beirut confirming the agreement reached between Isaias and Totil, mandating us to work for all Eritrean victims of displacement caused by the war.

I wrote a letter to Herui regarding this matter and gave it to Jimi'E, who promised to send it immediately. He never did—welcome to double-faced intrigue, Eritrean style! Not that Herui would have done anything to help: he was facing his own crisis; in fact, unbeknownst to us, he was being ousted from leadership by the ELF hardliners at the time I wrote the letter.

Our problem was complicated by the fact that the ELF cadres considered Kessela their special preserve and that the Sudanese authorities never did anything having to do with Eritrean affairs without first consulting the ELF representatives. In fact, on one occasion, we were detained the whole day in police headquarters because some ELF informer had told the police that we were Ethiopian spies. It was only after I threatened to complain to Khelifa Kerrar, the Chief of Security, and my friend Zaki Mustapha, the Attorney, General that the Kessela police chief released us, having first confirmed that I was not bluffing: that I did indeed know both of the officials.

We agreed that Redazghi would remain in Kessela, to organize relief committees and conduct research on the conditions of Eritrean refugees in Kessela and nearby refugee centers, and that I go to Khartoum where a lot of work awaited me. After much negotiation and cajoling, I managed to obtain a permit from the immigration branch of the police for Redazghi to visit the refugee camps in the area. Redazghi did excellent work in contacting individual Eritreans and recruiting some of them to help in relief work.

I took a bus to Khartoum on May 6, and the following day, contacted my old friend Zaki Mustapha, Sudan's Attorney General. Zaki received me in his office warmly, if somewhat puzzled that I was looking so emaciated. He knew me in my days of "glory," when I had what someone called my "ministerial substance," which was now gone. Before being enticed by Sudanes President Jafar El Nimeiry to become his Attorney General, Zaki had lived in Addis Ababa teaching at the Law School for a while, a position for which I had recommended him.

I briefed Zaki about the humanitarian needs of Eritrean refugees and internally displaced persons and showed him a copy of the constitution of ERA. He agreed to have one of his former law students to translate it into Arabic. Zaki also made several phone calls, contacting a number of people in the government whose duties included matters pertaining to security, foreign affairs and refugees. Most of all, he made arrangements for me to meet with both President Nimeiry and Rashid Al Tahir, Speaker of the People's Assembly. After making all these arrangements, Zaki took me to his home where we had lunch. He and his wife had been our guests in Addis Ababa, and his wife insisted that I call my wife Koki from their house, which I did.

The next day, I saw Khalifa Kerar, head of security, and briefed him on what we had done and what we needed. He promised to call Kessela and order that the necessary permit be given for Redazghi to visit the refugee centers. On Thursday, May 8, I met Mr. Abdullahi Al Hassan Al Khider, who I had been told was a key figure in the President's inner circle. I briefed Hassan Al Khider about our needs and asked him if we could register ERA as a non-profit organization. He told me no, so I immediately told Sabbe, who was in Khartoum, to go ahead and register ERA in Beirut. ERA was thus registered as a non-profit, non governmental organization (NGO) in Beirut.

The following day, I was received by the Speaker of the House, Mr. Rashid al Tahir, who told me that he had been a supporter of the Eritrean cause from the beginning. He made a car and a driver available whenever I wanted to meet people in Khartoum. He and Zaki also took me to meet with President Nimeiry, whom I briefed about the reason for my coming to Khartoum and our need of assistance. Although he was non-committal, he said that both Zaki and Rashid would see to it that everything possible would be done. He was affability itself, even joking that Rashid's forehead and mine were similar, which led him to speculate that we might have had a common ancestor. Who knows!

The same day, in the evening, Khalifa Kerar came to visit me in my hotel and said that he had received an urgent report from his informer at the Ethiopian embassy that the military government of Ethiopia had sent several people with orders to assassinate me, Osman Sabbe and General Goitom. He said that he had posted a special security detail to guard the Metro Hotel where I was staying, and advised me never to leave it without notifying him. An Eritrean veteran fighter who lived in Sudan advised me strongly to move out of the hotel, saying that I would be safer among my people. He took me to an area where a number of Eritreans lived, Khartoum Telata. I stayed there until my mission in Sudan was completed.

I flew out of Khartoum to Beirut on May 10. I stayed in Beirut for a week, writing a progress report on our work in Sudan as well as reviewing and refining a special booklet prepared by Redazghi, showing ERA's needs, for distribution among international relief organizations. I also applied for visas to travel to Europe and the USA. On May 17, I left Beirut for an extensive European tour, beginning with Geneva where a number of international relief organizations are headquartered, including the International Red Cross (ICRC), the World Council of Churches, and the UN High Commission for Refugees. I visited these and other organizations, submitting appropriate documents, including the report and my credentials. We discussed logistical problems and ways of overcoming them. In this respect, the most helpful person was Mr. Jacques Moreillon, senior counsel at the ICRC, who made several helpful suggestions. According to the ICRC, the critical point as far as shipments of relief was concerned, was a properly functioning organization to receive such shipments at Port Sudan, with storage facilities and transportation to take the goods to the intended victims. Mr. Moreillon drafted a memorandum of understanding between ICRC and myself covering such logistical issues that would prove helpful vis-à-vis the Sudanese authorities. The critical role of the ICRC was indicated by the fact that all the other organizations, as well as government departments, asked what the ICRC's response was to our request. It is sad to note that UNHCR was a huge disappointment; not only was it unresponsive, its bureaucratic maze would try a person with the patience of Job and send him vowing not to see its forbidding door again.

An enduring lesson we learned from the Geneva experience was that smaller non governmental organizations (NGOs) responded more quickly and effectively. Another, related lesson was the need for relying on our own people in the diaspora. After Geneva I traveled to Paris and several other European capitals where I contacted Eritreans urging them to form committees to mobilize relief on behalf of ERA. The response was amazing: relief committees bearing different names emerged in many countries, including Italy, Sweden, Germany, Denmark, the Netherlands, Norway, the UK, the USA, Canada and (later on) Australia. These organizations became the point of entry for mobilizing relief from government and non-government sources, such as national Red Cross organizations and church groups throughout the world, and helped to save millions of lives over the years until Eritrea's independence in 1991

One of the most effective relief committees, and one that moved with amazing speed and effectiveness in response to our urgent call, was the one created in Germany. I have selected and reproduced below a memorandum written on September 7, 1976, by the founding chairman of the German-based relief committee, *Eritrea-Hilfswerk in Deutschland e. V.* (EHD).

In December 1975 when Dr.Bereket Habte Selassie was in Europe, he contacted and advised us to establish an Eritrean Relief Organization here in Germany, which should serve for the benefit of the Eritrean refugees and displaced persons. During the annual Eritrean meeting in Frankfurt on 4th January 1976, this recommendation was introduced to the conference and unanimously supported by the committee. On March 16th, 1976 the *Eritrea-Hilfswerk in Deutschland e. V.* (EHD) was officially recognized by the German Government. EHD is composed of 10 members, five of whom are German and five Eritrean nationals. Meanwhile, we have prepared necessary materials, such as pamphlets, materials, donation receipts etc. Moreover, we have contacted numerous institutions in Germany and abroad as well as news agencies. All members are determined to contribute great efforts to achieve successful results.

(Signed)
Colonel Wolde Selassie Berhe, Chairman

Although remarkable for the speed with which it began and went about mobilizing assistance, EHD was not the only relief committee. Others followed and began relief work and continued on a sustainable basis in all the countries mentioned above. But EHD's speed and effectiveness had a galvanizing effect on other Eritrean relief organizations. I cannot overstress the enormous contributions these organizations made in helping Eritrea and Eritreans for over sixteen years. ERA itself became a model relief organization respected throughout the donor communities. The man who succeeded me as its chairman, Paulos Tesfagiorgis and his team should be commended for the historic role ERA played, a role that the EPLF leadership has failed to recognize, let alone commend. Again, that is another story for another day.

Nation, Family and Self—A Conflicted Involvement

When I was engaged in the mediation work, walking from village to village throughout the length and breadth of the Hamasien highlands, and, like the priestly pilgrims of old, sleeping at the homes of peasants, sharing their food, and receiving their blessing and best wishes in "the blessed work" of peacemaking and reconciliation, I did all that with a feeling of excitement and a keen sense of higher purpose. And I imagined that, my task accomplished, after the end of the fratricidal war and reconciliation, I would be off to America to rejoin my family. Accordingly, I did not feel the pang of guilt that would assail me later as I walked in the harsh sands of Sahel and during all my tours in search of relief for Eritrean victims of war.

In Sahel I passed sleepless nights lying on the sand alongside young *tegadelti* who slept without a care in the world; I would have slept like them too, but for the constant concern over my family. I often thought of my three children, remembering each one, my mind lingering over their faces and each time feeling a sharp pain inside me. Sleeping on the sands of Sahel, I often cried softly, "What the hell am I doing here!"

Of the many challenges that I faced in the course of my service to the Eritrean cause, the problem concerning my family was the most critical. The creation and consolidation of ERA was a challenging experience, of course. So were the diplomatic and logistical hurdles that we had to pass in order to facilitate the flow of relief goods to those who needed them. Naturally, a rebel movement engaged in a struggle to defeat the army of an internationally recognized government must face immense difficulties; and a relief organization associated with such a rebel movement is always suspect and must pass the most rigorous test before securing the assistance of any donor, even for humanitarian purposes.

In facing such difficulties my professional training as a lawyer as well as my experience in legal and government affairs was helpful. Indeed when Sabbe managed to obtain Somali passports for us, I had considered adopting a *nom de guerre* as a precautionary measure. However, both Sabbe and the chief of the Aden office of the EPLF insisted that I use my own name, considering my name recognition as an asset for the cause. As a result, on many occasions, I was questioned rigorously by immigration officials, especially when I traveled to Europe coming from the Middle East. The question in their minds was: how can a person with a name like "Selassie" be a Somali national? In fact a Kenyan immigration officer once asked that very question, and kept me for hours until the Somali embassy assured him that the passport was genuine.

But as I have already mentioned, by far the greatest challenge facing me was the painful conflict between my service to nation and obligations to my family. The diplomatic and logistical hurdles, and the insistence by the EPLF leadership that I remain to help remove them, meant that my original plan to join my family was postponed to the bitter disappointment of my wife, who even threatened to leave Washington and go back to Ethiopia on a couple of occasions. And who could blame her? Originally, my plan was to rejoin my family at the end of the mediation efforts. When the escalation of the war created a catastrophic humanitarian situation, the two-to-three month delay was extended to six months. I visited my family in June 1975 and promised to return in a matter of two months. Far from being resolved, however, the refugee problems kept increasing, and so did the demand for my presence in the field and the need to keep knocking at the doors of donor organizations. The demands of the EPLF leadership became more insistent, often becoming shrill. At the same time every time I called my wife, she expressed desperation and anxiety over the fate of our children in words and tone that were heart-rending.

I was caught in a double bind. It was a classic case of a person torn between conflicting obligations—family and nation. In my own case, the conflict was particularly acute in view of the fact that I had been the sole breadwinner when I left my family in the summer of 1974, and my wife had stopped working; so there was no income on which my family could depend. My salary from the World Bank was not available after I left for Ethiopia in July 1974.

It was at this time that Sabbe's generous offer to send money to my family seemed to offer hope of resolving my dilemma. When I first met Sabbe in Aden, I had explained to him the difficulties that I imagined my family would be facing. He was very sympathetic and promised to help. When we met in Beirut, I was surprised that the first thing he mentioned to me was his decision to send money to my family until I could go back to support them myself. The fact that he gave priority to resolving personal problems said a lot about the man's leadership qualities, as well as his humanity. In contrast, when I raised this matter to the EPLF chief of the Aden office, his response was as callous as it was unrealistic; he said, "All family problems will be resolved in the context of the resolution of the national problem, with the liberation of the country." It was a standard mantra that I would hear again and again. Incidentally, I raised this issue with a couple of high-ranking EPLF cadres after liberation, when they themselves had families. One of them was honest enough to own up to the naivete and cruelty of their previous views and attitudes. He even wondered how I had managed to keep going despite the conflicting claims of family and nation.

I must note here, for the record, the fate of the money that Sabbe ordered to be sent to my wife. Sabbe said that he instructed his treasurer to send her $1,000 at the time we met in Beirut and $500 a month thereafter until further notice. To that end, I had given the treasurer my wife's name and our Washington address. When I asked her if she received the money, she said she did not receive any money. To this day, this matter has remained a mystery to me, but I desisted from pursuing it because fortunately in the meantime, my wife found employment at the World Bank.

Before she found employment, she had thought of going back to Ethiopia, and that was the time when I put an ultimatum to the EPLF leadership that I could not go on seeing my family suffering in a foreign land. In the autumn of 1976, I met Isaias Afewerki in Khartoum during one of his visits there, and showed him a letter my wife had written in which she threatened to leave for Ethiopia. I made it clear to him then that I had decided to go back. By that time, Paulos Tesfagiorgis had taken over from me; I had toured Europe with him and Berhe Tesfamariam (Mariano) for over two months, introducing them to all the relief agencies with which I had created good working relationships. Isaias reluctantly agreed and said that there was a great deal of "diplomatic" and publicity work to be done anyway, and that I could serve equally well in those fields. So I tied up the loose ends of the work before I left for Washington, writing or rewriting progress reports on the humanitarian situation in Eritrea and requesting assistance. Paulos and Berhe knew the ropes by then and could be relied upon to continue the work, as they eventually did with flying colors. I left Khartoum and made my way to Washington, where I found a family that had been hurt by my absence. I set out to remedy the situation as best I could.

Chapter 16

TRANSITION TO NEW LIFE AND WORK

When I met Osman Saleh Sabbe in Beirut, in the Spring of 1975, he tried very hard to persuade me to join his EPLF Foreign Office team. Sabbe was a consummate diplomat and a brilliant publicist. However, his performance was handicapped by two problems. The first was that his domain was limited to the Arab world, which he wanted to remedy by having me act as head of Europe and North America. Second, he was perceived to be a one-man show. The guerilla leaders whom he called the "Field Command," thought of him as a primadonna, a lone star who "stole the show." They resented his sole control of the financial aid coming from some Arab sources and complained bitterly even as they took the material assistance that he was procuring.

I did not accept Sabbe's offer for two reasons. First, I was aware of the hidden rift between him and the "Field Command," and I had no desire to be used by him against them. Whatever their faults, they were engaged in the hard and hazardous work of guerilla fighters, while he operated abroad, out of harm's way. Moreover, I was in sympathy with the socialist leanings of the guerillas. Much as I admired Sabbe's service to the Eritrean liberation struggle, I did not share his conservative and highly personalized approach to politics.

In retrospect, while I do not regret for one moment the position I took to support the guerillas in the field, I find that Sabbe's prediction that the "Field Command" would establish a Stalinist dictatorship proved prescient. His detractors might say that he too was determined to establish an Islamic republic. Yet, in all fairness, apart from the fact that Sabbe was a realist who knew that an Islamic republic in a country half Christian and half Muslim would not work, his detractors' claim falls in the realm of historical speculation whereas Isaias Afewerki's dictatorship today is a tragic reality.

The second and more compelling reason why I did not accept Sabbe's offer had to do with my family. As I mentioned in the preceding chapter, of the many challenges that I faced in the course of my service to the Eritrean cause, the problem concerning my family was the most critical. As I noted previously, the creation and consolidation of ERA was a challenging experience, of course; so was the problem concerning the diplomatic and logistical hurdles that we had to pass in order to secure and facilitate the flow of relief goods to those who needed them. But the problems affecting one's family is particularly poignant when in conflict with the national call.

The "National Call" Versus Family Obligation

Again, as I mentioned already, Osman Sabbe's offer to send money to my family seemed to offer hope for resolving my dilemma. In our Beirut meeting he confirmed the promise he made in Aden; in fact I was pleasantly surprised that the first thing he mentioned to me in Beirut was his decision to send money to my family until I could go back and take care of them myself. Those were his words; there was no reason for me to suspect that his proposal was conditioned on my acceptance of his request for me to join his team. I did not take steps to find out what happened to the money. For one thing, Sabbe had, in the meantime, broken with the EPLF (in the spring of 1976); for another, Koki had found employment in the World Bank, thanks to the intercession of my friends there and her own qualifications. So the matter of Sabbe's promised money remains a mystery to this day.

At last, a nightmarish experience was now behind me. For all the relief I felt, however, I knew the transition was not going to be smooth. This time, it was family first, then nation. Having tied all loose ends and handed over complete responsibility of ERA to my successor, I left Khartoum.

It was a gray November afternoon when I arrived at Dulles International Airport. I stepped out of the airplane to be greeted by a cold wind that went right through to my bones, a stark contrast to the hot Khartoum weather. Riding the bus to downtown Washington and then a taxicab to our residence, I enjoyed the typical autumn scene with the wind blowing the multi-colored leaves. I arrived in the late afternoon at our residence to find the front yard filled with leaves, whereas the yards of the neighbors were clean, a rude reminder of my absence. There and then I resolved that the first thing to do the next day would be to clear the yard; in fact, I looked forward to that simple, prosaic domestic chore—raking and collecting the leaves and shoving them into trash bags. Don't homeowners feel relieved or even validated when engaged in such simple chores? Perhaps this is limited to those of us who do not do much to help the womenfolk in the domestic area, being a relief of our sense of guilt.

I rang the bell and the door was opened; Hirut, Koki's younger sister, stood there speechless at seeing me back, tearfully hugged me and took my bags to the bedroom. My son Asgede, age 14, had a separate bedroom to himself. Finot (age 9) and Sebene (age 6) shared one bedroom. Hirut then told me that Bahrnegash, Koki's 20-year-old nephew), had come to stay for a while, and was sleeping in the basement.

I made an inspection tour of the house, beginning with the girls' bedroom, where there were cute pictures of many different kinds of animals hanging from the walls. It was touching to see these simple things.

Koki was at work and Hirut told me the children were at the Lafayette Elementary School participating in some school event. I couldn't wait to see them, so I asked Hirut to take me there. We found Sebene on the playground. She had grown into a tall, stunningly beautiful six-year old, with long braided hair hanging over her shoulders. She was astonished to see me and when she laid her eyes on me it was as if an arrow pierced through my heart and I felt myself swept by a sudden exultation. As I recovered and moved forward, stretching my arms to hug and kiss her, she ran off, saying something about wanting to find her sister Finot. Hirut ran after her and brought both of them and we went home together holding hands and silently looking at each other.

The next few days several of our friends and neighbors came by in the evening to celebrate my homecoming. Those who came the first few days were the closest friends. They were: Belkis Woldegiorgis, Haile Gerima and Abiyi Ford. Belkis was a graduate student, and Haile and Abiyi were professors at Howard University. There were also two couples: Jarso and Etete Mekonen, and Getachew and Brutawit Abdi. Jarso and Etete were graduate students at Howard University, while Getachew and Brutawit worked at the World Bank. Having children of Sebene's age, the two couples were frequent visitors and, with the other family friends, had formed an important support system during my absence.

Another friend I saw was Christian Walser of the World Bank. Christian told me how he and Ronnie Broches, the Bank's General Counsel and Vice President, had agonized about me and my family when I disappeared from the scene in Addis Ababa following the execution of my friend General Aman. In a moving journal he later sent me, Christian recorded those difficult days as follows:

> It was a bitter cold evening in Upper Montclair in New Jersey, in November 1974, just a day or two before Thanksgiving. I had taken a week off to travel with my wife and my two children to visit friends in New York, and we were then staying for a long Thanksgiving weekend with one of our oldest friends from the Gymnasium days (in our native Basel, Switzerland), just across the river from Manhattan in New Jersey. As we were having drinks in our friends' kitchen, helping the hostess prepare dinner, there was a phone call for me from my boss Ronnie Broches,...who much to my surprise, asked me to find out from Bereket's wife, Koki (whom he did not know) whether she had had any news from Bereket in the last few days; she had not. With a leave of absence from the bank, Bereket had returned to Addis Ababa in July to head an investigation commission which was looking into the misdeeds by members of the Haile Selassie government. (By way of background, Ronnie explained the latest developments in Addis, which being on the road most of the

time in the preceding days, we were only vaguely aware of, namely that General Aman had been killed by Mengistu and his people, and that the Bank had just received a message from Mr. Gardner of the UN Economic Commission for Africa in Addis, confirming that Bereket, being in grave danger himself, had gone into hiding, and asking whether there was anything that the Bank could do to help. Ronnie read to me a draft he said McNamara, the Bank's President, was willing to sign, in which the bank informed the authorities in Addis that Bereket's leave of absence had expired, that the Bank needed him back in Washington, and that the Bank asked for any help the authorities could provide to facilitate his safe return...As I understood it, that letter was dispatched the following morning, but to my knowledge no reply was ever received. In fact, it took many more months until Bereket's family and friends, all anxiously waiting for a sign of life from him, finally got the news we all had hoped for: It came in the form of picture postcard addressed to me...I recognized Bereket's hand writing and immediately informed Koki and all of Bereket's friends in the Bank.

The "authorities" referred to in the letter were, of course, Mengistu and company. And far from giving me safe conduct, as Christian, Broches, and McNamara asked, Mengistu was after my blood. If I had relied on the good will of "the authorities" and lingered in Addis, instead of leaving town as I did, I would have been speedily dispatched to meet my Maker!

* * *

Now that I was safely back with my family, I set out to make it up to them as best I could. The first question in that regard was to find a suitable employment. There was no question of returning to my World Bank job. I had decided to help the Eritrean cause from the Washington end, and since working for the World Bank precludes involvement in politics of any kind that was not an option open to me. The best solution was to find employment in an area university and combine teaching with "diplomatic" work. Accordingly, I applied for a position at Howard University and was accepted as an Assistant Professor at the African Studies Department

I had crossed from one phase of my life and career into another, one that would become my chosen career for the rest of my life. It is a life that involved much reading, writing, lecture tours and travel and work in what might be called the diplomacy of the oppressed. This life of endless movement and ceaseless activities lasted until Eritrea was liberated in May 1991. More important, I was now back with my family picking up the "broken pieces," making amends for the absence of the past two years.

One year after I started work at Howard University, Abate Menkir, Koki's older brother, who worked at the Nairobi office of the World Bank, was transferred to Washington in the engineering department of the Bank. He and his four children (Esete, Tekle, Seble and Fikirte) lived in our neighborhood thus helping create a close-knit community and providing an Ethiopian/Eritrean cultural milieu for the children. Whenever Abate traveled we would look after his children's needs, and vice versa.

The contentment of family life (what the French call *joie de la famille*), has its ups and downs. All families go through moments of tension occasionally involving rows, some more than others. This is part of a normal family life. In our own case, it was complicated by the experience of my "disappearance" and the absence felt by my family. Every time Koki and I had a row, I was reminded of the sad days the family went through as a result. The compelling reason for my "disappearance" was grudgingly accepted as extenuating if not excusing my "wrongs"; but at times when tempers ran high, it would be dismissed and I would be reminded of my past wrongs. This was particularly true during the first few months after my return, while I was looking for a suitable job.

Whenever the subject of my "disappearance" was mentioned among our circle of friends, opinion was divided between those who supported me and those who did not. Those who supported me—mostly men—not only accepted the compelling reason, but also commended me for answering to the call. Those who did not support me—mostly women—asserted the primacy of family obligations. No extenuating circumstance was acceptable. Period. For my part, I chose to keep a respectful silence waiting for the healing hand of time to take care of things, as it eventually did. Years later, Asgede who had been silent all the time, surprised me by putting it in terms of his own religious belief according to which the order of priority is: God first, then nation, then family, and last the individual self.

One issue related to my family obligations that I had to settle concerned Finot's schooling. Once again my American friends came to the rescue, beginning with Harris Wofford. Harris wrote a letter of recommendation to Mr Sargent Shriver, asking him to help facilitate Finot's admission to the Joseph Kennedy School for the Handicapped in the Washington DC area. Harris followed his letter with a phone call and urged me to call on Mr. Shriver in his law office at the Watergate building, which I did. Mr. Shriver was very gracious and sympathetic with my request, assuring me that he would help. And he did; Finot was admitted to the school.

Mr. Shriver, who was vice-presidential candidate of the Democratic Party in the 1972 election, is husband of one of the Kennedy sisters, and the school is named after the late Joseph P. Kennedy, older brother of John F. Kennedy. The Kennedy School was created because the Kennedys are partial to the needs of mentally handicapped people (nowadays called mentally challenged) in consequence of the fact that one of their sisters suffered from such disability.

Academic Life and Politics of Liberation

As I resumed my parenting role and my family life became stable, I began a number of contacts that would prove useful for my future work to advance the Eritrean cause. I was careful to strike the right balance between my family and service to the cause of Eritrean liberation. It was not always easy, particularly as more reports came out of the war zone and a news-hungry press discovered our struggle at last. All wanted to know the answers to some nagging questions of conflict and intervention of foreign powers in the affairs of the Horn of Africa sub region in general and Eritrea in particular. I did my best to fulfil my family obligations, while at the same time helping in the struggle.

Fulfilling family obligations meant, among other things, spending "quality time" with the children and showing them that you care. In the culture in which I was raised, a man does not make overt expressions of love to his wife and children; instead, he shows it by body language and deeds. But being in America we had to make adjustments, especially in the case of children who were born or raised in the United States from a young age. Children know, of course, when you love them, even as they miss you in your occasional absence due to work away from home. In my case, the teaching job gave me ample time to devote to the needs of my family and be close to my children, in terms of attending important school events.

My classes at Howard University were for graduate students enrolled for the MA or Ph.D. in African studies. In the fall semester of 1977, I started teaching two courses: "Politics of Development in Africa" and "Law and Social Change." The courses I taught changed from semester to semester, but one course I taught every semester was a seminar on "The African World." A year later I was hired as adjunct professor at Georgetown University's School of Foreign Service where I taught "Legal Order and Political Change," for many years. At Georgetown I made good friends, most notably, Chester Crocker, who would become Assistant Secretary of State for African Affairs, and Carol Lancaster who also held important posts in the government under Presidents Carter and Clinton. Both of these good people gave me moral support and sound advice.

I have always enjoyed teaching and Howard was not the first university where I taught. I taught a course on "Constitution and Government" for over ten years, as adjunct professor at Haile I Selassie University (renamed Addis Ababa University). I have also taught summer courses, including one at Queens College, New York, in the summer of 1973. But Howard was my first full time teaching job. Apart from my love of academic inquiry, research and writing, what I found appealing in the University teaching profession is first the flexibility of time; it is not a 9 am to 5 pm work schedule. Moreover, the long summer vacation, as well as the Christmas and Easter Break provide with ample time resources. I used this time resource to attend to family matters, as needed, and to help in the Eritrea cause.

I started teaching at Howard with the rank of Assistant Professor, with a salary corresponding to that rank, which was not much. However, as I had already published a peer-reviewed book and some articles, I was promoted to Associate Professor, within a year, and to full Professor three years later, following the publication of two more books. But even then, my salary did not remotely approximate to what I would have earned had I gone back to my World Bank job. It was a conscious choice I made for a cause, and far from regretting it I was determined to make the most of the time resources and contacts forthcoming from my academic life for a greater cause.

During the eight months between December 1976 and August 1977, before I started work at Howard, I spent time in the Library of Congress, as well as creating new contacts and renewing old ones. At the Library of Congress and at times in the local public library, I started writing about my experience. Among the institutions I contacted was the Institute for Policy Studies (IPS), a liberal think tank where I eventually became an Associate Fellow and conducted seminars on African issues, including the Horn of Africa. My book, *Conflict and Intervention in the Horn of Africa* came out in 1980 published by the Monthly Review Press, principally as a result of the positive recommendation made on my behalf by members of IPS. The IPS community included some of the best writers and commentators on national and international policy issues, such as Peter Wise, Marc Raskin, Richard Barnet, the late Eqbal Ahmed, Robert Borosage, Saul Landau and Roger Wilkins.

As I grew closer to many of these good people, I created a better awareness among them and the larger IPS community about the Eritrean cause. The one exception was Saul Landau. Saul had a close connection with Cuba and his aversion to the Eritrean cause came about after Cuba intervened on Ethiopia's side in the 1977-1978 war between Ethiopia and Somalia. Cuban forces had also been sent to Eritrera to act as replacement for Ethiopian troops in Asmara, so that the Ethiopian forces could go to fight Eritrean guerillas. When we pointed this out to Cuban sympathizers, their answer was that no Cuban was fighting Eritreans; it was also Landau's line.

Another line of activity was related to academic meetings. I attended the annual meeting of the African Studies Association (ASA) for the first time in Baltimore in November 1978. This meeting brought me face to face with many African and Africanist academics and policy experts. I presented a paper on the principle of self-determination to a panel convened and chaired by an Egyptian academic. The paper was later revised and published in *The Horn of Africa* journal edited by Somali publisher Osman Ali. This first venture into international academic conferences and the prevailing ethos of progressive politics in the academy gave me an idea of the need for a general strategic plan on telling the Eritrean story and gaining support among intellectuals and policy makers. The strategy was based on a two-front-line of attack, to use a military metaphor: (a) organizing Eritreans in the diaspora, or relying on the already organized associations, and (b) mobilizing support of friends of Eritrea in Europe and North America.

I made it a point to participate in every annual meeting of ASA and also to persuade the growing number of other Eritrean academics to participate. By the beginning of the 1980s, there was a significant number of Eritrean academics and others who made their presence felt at these important academic meetings. Many organized panels on the Eritrean cause. Eventually, a critical mass of Eritreans and other academics from the Horn of Africa region who began organizing panels at ASA on the liberation movements, including the Tigray Peoples Liberation Front (TPLF), and the Oromo Liberation Front (OLF). Somali academics and activists also organized panels on Somalia and the "Ogaden question."

As far as Eritrean liberation is concerned, the first international meeting that drew attention was one that took place in London in January 1979 of which a book came out under the title *Behind the war in Eritrea*, edited by Basil Davidson, Lionel Cliff and myself. The book was translated into Arabic as was the book I published in 1980, *Conflict and Intervention in the Horn of Africa*. These and other works, as well as the continual reports on the ongoing war of liberation, began to draw more attention to the work of the EPLF. The EPLF leaders realized, perhaps for the first time, that academic activity carried within it politics of a different kind, enabling the liberation movement to gain access to hitherto unreachable diplomatic and political forces. The AK-47 (Kalashin, as the *tegadelti* called it adoringly) has a decisive role in liberation; but the notion of power coming "out of the barrel of the gun" (to paraphrase Mao Tse Tung), has its limitations when we are talking about diplomacy. The root causes of a liberation war need to be articulated. And articulated they were in annual academic conferences, in lecture tours, in special seminars, symposia and other forums organized by Eritreans and their friends in cities throughout the United Sates, Canada and in Europe.

International meetings produce academic papers on critical issues to all interested people. Just as the 1979 London conference produced a book, there have been many other meetings from which books or booklets came out that were used for submission to policy makers. In this respect the Research and Information Center of Eritrea (RICE), initiated by Eritrean academics and eventually taken over by the EPLF, established an office in Rome and produced much material that was useful for diplomatic purposes. This success encouraged Eritrean academics in America and Europe to pay attention to academic endeavor as an important weapon of struggle, a matter that they had hitherto neglected or even, in some case, discouraged.

Eritreans for Liberation and "Diplomacy of the Oppressed"

In the United States of America, Eritrean students had established an association known as Eritreans for Liberation in North America (EFLNA), at first almost entirely made up of students. Their counterparts in Europe established Eritreans for Liberation in Europe (EFLE). These organizations, especially EFLNA, played an important role in providing material support to the armed struggle, including clothes, walkie talkies and other communications equipment, as well as money. I had heard of these organizations when I was working at the World Bank in 1973-1974, but I was not sanguine about their capacity or their seriousness until I went to the field where I was told about the crucial help they provided. Indeed, in February 1975, I met a few former members of EFLNA in Sahel, including Haile Menkerios, Naizghi Kiflu and Stifanos Seyoum, who had joined the armed struggle. Among the members of EFLE, Eritreans who were studying in the Soviet Union and Eastern Europe had adopted a policy of going to the Field to join the armed struggle immediately upon completing their studies, unless a special dispensation was made exempting them.

On the occasion of my visit of my family in June 1975, the leadership of EFLNA heard of my presence in Washington and arranged for me to address their members, which I did both in Washington and New York. According to them I was the first Eritrean to come out from the field and give a first hand account of the situation there, including the humanitarian situation. After I returned and settled in Washington, I made it my business to visit their offices in Washington and seek out ways we could cooperate for the common cause. I was soon able to size them up, noting their strengths and weaknesses. Their main strength was their single-minded dedication to the cause of Eritrean liberation. Their weakness was a rigidity of approach, itself based on a rigid Marxist-Leninist ideology. This narrowness of approach and rigidity was further aggravated by a lack of experience in, and appreciation of, the power of subtle persuasion. They believed that the more strident you are, the more successful you will be, a militancy that was reinforced by the guidelines coming out of the Field, which the EFLNA leaders followed religiously, after their decision in 1976 to become attached to the EPLF.

Until 1976, they had operated as a separate organization giving support to the armed struggle but not taking orders from it. The change was prompted by a demand from the "Field Command" of the EPLF, faced by Sabbe's open blandishments to the student organizations in Europe and North America. Sabbe attended the annual meeting of EFLE in Bologna, Italy, in August 1975 and addressed the meeting; I also attended, sharing the platform with him and others. It was quite clear that Sabbe was courting the organizations and had in fact persuaded some branch leaders to see things his way. This was a wake-up call for the "Field Command" who perceived Sabbe's move as a bid to control their alternative sources of material aid. It became a life-or-death struggle for them, inducing them to go "the whole hog" and insist that the mass organizations become affiliated with the armed struggle.

Among those who went along with Sabbe's approach were early critics of the EPLF leadership and its record of "human rights abuse" going back to the so-called "Menka'E movement." There were also members who resisted, unsuccessfully, the move to be integrated with the EPLF because they believed that a mass organization should maintain its autonomy and provide support from a safe critical distance. This minority counsel of the wise was overwhelmed and decisively dismissed by the passionate majority, who were eager to provide maximum help to the armed struggle unencumbered by "bourgeois ideas of autonomy." In the armed struggle, obedience was all.

I will also mention in passing two other student organizations, one Eritrean and the other Ethiopian, which are relevant to the discussion of student role in the armed struggle. The first was an Eritrean student organization in the Middle

East, known as GUES (General Union of Eritrean Students), divided into the Cairo faction and the Baghdad faction. GUES supported mainly the Eritrean Liberation Front (ELF) until its demise in 1981. The principal rivals among the earlier Eritrean leaders campaigning for influence in GUES were Osman Saleh Sabbe and Idris Gelawdeos. As a spin-off of this behind-the-scenes power struggle, I was a victim of attack at the hands of Eritrean students in Iraq when I addressed their meeting in a township in the outskirts of Baghdad, on April 18, 1975, during my first Middle East tour organized by Sabbe. The vast majority were Gelawdeos supporters, and they poured venom on Sabbe and on me whom they considered as a Sabbe surrogate.

I had been warned by Weldenkiel, the EPLF head in Aden, to avoid the students in Bhagdad like the plague, but I defied his admonition, saying, "They are my compatriots and I will make my case before them," my case being unity of the Eritrean struggle and a united approach to relief work, a task I had just undertaken. I paid for my principle, being subjected to a torrent of verbal abuse by many of the students although many of them were won over by the spirited defense I put up for my case. Some, like Dr. Oumer Jabir, even came to me afterward and apologized for the behavior of the zealots. It was an experience I would never forget, and a foretaste of the ideological passions that I would also encounter in America. Ideologically, the Eritrean students in Iraq at the time were divided between the nationalists, a silent majority, and an effective minority of Baathists. They were all scholarship beneficiaries of the Bathist government of Iraq. The Baathists considered the EPLF an outright Marxist organization, which made it suspect. Even though Bathists professed socialism as their guiding ideology and shared a similar worldview with Marxists, in reality it was an uneasy alliance, which ended when Saddam Hussein eliminated all Marxists.

The Ethiopian organization was ESUNA (Ethiopian Student Union in North America). Until the emergence of the EPLF in 1970, many Eritreans studying in the United States of America were members of ESUNA, and many studying in Europe were members of ESUNA's European equivalent. Then came the parting of the ways, with most Eritreans leaving these organizations and forming or joining EFLNA and EFLE. Indeed, for the first few years of their establishment, EFLNA and EFLE were engaged in a running battle with Ethiopian organizations on the issue of Eritrea's right to independence. Some of their prominent intellectuals, like Andreas Eshete, were adamantly opposed to Eritrea's independence, until much later when EPLF's military victory became more than a possibility. Within ESUNA itself there was a minority of young leaders who not only accepted Eritrea's right to self-determination in principle, but also made it a point of contention, leading to a crisis in the organization and even the mysterious murder of one of the best young leaders, Mesfin Habtu. ESUNA never recovered its earlier dynamism after that event.

There was a Marxist-Leninist core in both EFLNA and EFLE that determined the content and style of politics. Marxist-Leninist ideology was fashionable in those times, and different expressions flowered in Europe and North America, some aligned with the Chinese, others with the Soviets and still others professing Albanian or other versions. It was in the midst of this ideological profusion (or rather confusion) that I ventured into the field of the diplomacy of the oppressed—itself an offspring of the pedagogy of the oppressed—in the late 1970s. The instruction manual of Eritreans for liberation reflected the teaching material the EPLF had prepared and used for its *tegadelti*, particularly after 1976 when both student organizations became EPLF mass organizations.

In these instructional materials, the alliance of workers and peasants was the center of the struggle, and the "petty bourgeoisie" were always suspect and had to be watched with vigilance by the true revolutionary cadres. The fact that students and teachers belonged to the petty bourgeoisie did not seem to pose problems to the true believers, even though the majority of the cadres belonged to that class. Many espoused Amilcar Cabral's dictum that the petty bourgeoisie must commit class suicide in order to become a truly revolutionary instrument of the masses. Never mind the difficulty of committing class suicide—people could claim that they committed class suicide by a simple declaration to that effect.

These guidelines, and their literal application by the cadres, were problematic when it came to the practice of diplomacy and liberation politics in general. Even in the field of research and publicity, the rigidity and lack of appreciation of the different requirements presented problems of cooperation and coordination. Simply put, though the mass organizations were an important part of the struggle, at times their cadres, with whom I was forced to deal by circumstances, only made things more difficult. Luckily, some among the top leaders of the EPLF knew the value of an experienced hand in advancing the cause of Eritrean liberation. Accordingly, a division of tasks was devised under which I was encouraged to go ahead and conduct my quiet diplomacy of the oppressed. Particularly helpful in this respect was Mr. Sebhat Efrem, member of the EPLF's Political Bureau and at the time in charge of mass organization affairs, who told me to go ahead and establish contacts and cultivate relationships with US policy makers at all levels, and especially at the State Department.

The Great Fallout

I suspect that the decision to encourage me to engage in quiet diplomacy was triggered by the fallout of the summer of 1978. In August, EFLNA, led by Mengisteab Isaac, broke away from the EPLF. The split shook the movement in North America to its foundation, creating one of the most serious crises the EPLF faced at a crucial time in the Eritrean struggle for independence. I happened to be in Italy attending the EFLE annual meeting, addressed by the EPLF's Sebhat Efrem. Sebhat and I discussed the crisis created by EFLNA's split and what needed to be done to minimize the damage. He was uncharacteristically harsh in his condemnation, dismissing outright my suggestion for "diplomacy" in approaching the breakaway leaders. I remember him raising his voice and saying, "We will not deal in diplomacy!"

Speculations abound as to Mengisteab's motives in taking such a drastic step at a time when the EPLF needed all the assistance it could muster. A graduate, like myself, of the elite school of Addis Ababa, the General Wingate Secondary School, Mengisteab was an influential member of EFLNA's leadership. In 1975, he was one of two emissaries EFLNA sent to the Field to inquire into rumors that EPLF leadership had violated the rights of some prominent members who had challenged Isaias.

In 1978 Mengisteab and his close-knit group of leaders of EFLNA decided that the EPLF withdrawal from the liberated zone was a tactical mistake. Moreover they accused the EPLF of revisionism, a cardinal sin among some Marxist-Leninists at the time. In August 1978 they issued a declaration condemning the EPLF leaders and renouncing EPLF membership. EFLNA split into two factions, one supporting Mengisteab and his group, the other remaining loyal to the EPLF. As soon as I got back from Italy, I sought out dissident members in the Washington DC area and joined in the efforts to win them back to the EPLF. It did not take long to win back the majority, but a vocal minority of Mengistrab's followers held out, charging the EPLF leaders with defeatism. The strategic retreat was portrayed as capitulation. The loyal majority of EFLNA members convened a series of meetings in the major cities of the United States, electing new leaders and rebuilding the branches. In the face of two rival factions competing for support, each side arguing its case, the Eritrean public in North America and the diaspora in general was confused.

Andemicael Kahsai, EPLF Central Committee member, addressed the largest meeting which I arranged for him at Howard University's campus Church. The rival faction was refused admission for fear that they would disrupt the meeting, whereupon they started agitating outside, singing and beating drums and hurling unprintable epithets at Andemicael and the rest of us. It was ugly, as ugly as the worst factional war, the only difference being that no shots were fired.

Reasonable people, even those who admired Mengisteab, wondered why he and his group condemned EPLF's strategic retreat as defeatism, when not to have retreated would have meant a massacre of the EPLF army by a Soviet backed Ethiopian offensive. According to some reports, Romodan Mohamed Nur had explained the military situation to Mengisteab in a phone conversation. Obviously, the explanation did not convince Mengisteab. It is hard to believe that the strategic retreat was the only or even the main reason for Mengisteab's disaffection and drastic step. I am forced to speculate that there was another reason and I am reminded of recent writing reporting that Mengisteab and another companion who had made a field trip to Sahel in 1975 were informed of some unsavory facts concerning the EPLF's treatment of some of its members.

Mnegisteab and Paulos Tesfagiorgis were sent to the Field by EFLNA to investigate reports of human rights violations by the EPLF, especially concerning the so-called Menka'E movement. Referring to this matter British writer Michela Wrong writes as follows.

> It was Paulos' first visit to the Front and he found it psychologically overwhelming. The purge had created an atmosphere of fear and suspicion he could feel but barely understand. In daytime he was kept under strict escort, but at night manqa (Menka'E) sympathizers sidled up to him to mutter 'Don't believe everything you hear.' He was awed by the austerity of life at the Front, humbled by the Fighters' sense of purpose. Above all, he was agonizingly aware that while he—a spoilt member of the educated bourgeoisie—was free to return to a cushioned existence in the West, former classmates who possessed no more than the clothes on their backs were staying behind. To question it all would have felt like gross disloyalty.

The writer then quotes Paulos as saying:

> In our report we said: 'Those executed were guilty of incitement and creating division. Our report created a calmness. We were the first people from the North American community who had been there, so no one could challenge us. Our word was the word. Single-handed, we made the Front look fantastic.

It seems plausible to suggest that Mengisteab, Paulos' companion in the trip to the Front, was suddenly seized with remorse for the suppression of the EPLF's alleged wrongs. Perhaps Paulos can clarify this point and supply the answer; meanwhile, however, it is reasonable to suppose that a feeling of guilt for making the EPLF "look fantastic" might have induced Mengisteab's desperate final actions, including his suicide barely a year after the fateful decision to break from and condemn the EPLF.

Mengisteab's suicide left his group disoriented. By the time the August annual meeting of EFELNA was held in August 1979, his group had been considerably weakened, with many of its adherents coming back to the EFLNA. I met Sebhat Efrem, member of the Political Bureau of the EPLF and head of Mass Organizations, during the August 1979 meeting, and that was when he encouraged me to go ahead and start informal diplomatic contacts with officials of the US government.

Under US law, any activity conducted on behalf of a foreign political organization is required to be registered under US federal law in the name of an agent. The agent is then required to notify the Department of Justice of all contacts and communications or submissions made to US government officials on behalf of the organization he or she represents. I contacted my old friend Marty Ganzglass, of the law firm of O'Donnell, Schwartz and Anderson, for advice on how to go about the registration. Marty, a former Peace Corps volunteer in Somalia, volunteered to do the registering on a pro bono basis. He had become a supporter of the Eritrean cause after an international conference held in Mogadishu, Somalia, which we both attended and where I had made a presentation on the right of the Eritrean people to self determination. Marty had acted as legal advisor to the government of Somalia and subsequently written a book on Somalia's criminal law. In addition to our meeting in Mogadishu we also discovered that we were living in the same neighborhood; we thus became close friends.

Marty rendered legal advice to us free of charge until Eritrea's liberation. He even participated in demonstrations on behalf of Eritrea, such as the one in front of the Israeli embassy to protest Israel's military sales to Ethiopia, including internationally prohibited weapons. After liberation, I invited Marty to lunch with Hagos Gebrehiwet who had been appointed Eritrean representative to the United States. I was not surprised to learn later that Hagos had indeed asked Marty to become official legal advisor to the Eritean embassy. Hagos, who is no fool, saw the usefulness of such a friend.

Diplomacy of the Oppressed, Bertrand Russell Style

Bertrand Russell, the renowned British philosopher, organized the "Russell Tribunal" at which the United States was the defendant, charged with war crimes and crimes against humanity for its war in Vietnam. The Tribunal was like a serious moot court without legal sanctions, but with tremendous moral force in terms of mobilizing world opinion against the Vietnam War. With the death of Bertrand Russell, Italian philosopher and Senator, Lelio Basso, took over and moved the venue of the Tribunal from Stockholm and London to Milan.

Now we had the good fortune of befriending a number of people in Europe as well as in America—people who went out of their way to help us by providing support of different kinds. One of these was an Australian-born Englishwoman, Victoria (Vicky) Bawtree. I first met Vicky in Rome where she was employed by FAO. I was introduced to her by two old friends, Italian scholar Alessandro (Sandro) Triulzi and his wife, Gloria. Gloria, in particular, insisted that I meet Vicky and tell her the Eritrean story, having just come, from the war zone in 1975. Young Europeans at the time were mostly Left-leaning and had a romantic view of liberation movements such as those in Mozambique, Guinea Bissau and Eritrea.

After hearing my story and the status of the war in Eritrea, including the humanitarian situation, Vicky suggested that we meet with other interested people. During several other meetings, I explained to Vicky and other friends about the needs of the struggle—humanitarian and diplomatic. In a series of meetings Vicky arranged for me with some of her influential friends, I gave in-house seminars on the situation in Eritrea and Ethiopia, and the future of the people in the region of the Horn of Africa. One of the best suggestions Vicky made was that we should start an information publication, which she volunteered to edit. That was how *Eritrea Information*, a monthly bulletin about Eritrea got started. Later on, Vicky cooperated with Arefaine Berhe, who became head of the Research and Information Center of Eritrea (RICE), to sustain the work of informing world public opinion on Eritrean affairs in general and the liberation war in particular.

Then Vicky introduced me to Italian Senator Lelio Basso and others who were associated with him. Organizing a Tribunal on Eritrea was Vicky's idea, which she pursued with single-minded drive and energy. She convinced the Lelio Basso Foundation to sponsor it, and in May 1980, the Permanent Peoples' Tribunal of the International League for the Rights and Liberation of Peoples (Session on Eritrea) was held in Milan with great success. The proceedings of the Tribunal came out as a book, *The Eritrean Case*. Fourteen papers were submitted to the Tribunal, covering the history of Eritrea and its peoples' struggle for self determination. The tribunal was presided over by Professor Andre Rigaux, with Ruth First and Armand Uribe acting as Vice Presidents. The other members were: Amar Bentoumi, Antonio Cassese, Andrea Guardina, Francois Houtart, Louis Joinet and Edmond Jouve—all eminent jurists and writers.

I was among the presenters with my paper, "Eritrea and the United Nations." Having reviewed the submissions as well as the opinions of the Ethiopian side based on various publications and official statements, the Tribunal issued its verdict on October 3, 1980, in the form of an "Advisory Opinion." The Tribunal made a thorough review of the facts and the law before it issued its verdict. Its verdict was an admirable summing up of Eritrea's legal case and it exerted moral force on all thoughtful and well informed circles throughout the world.

Clearly, there could be no better way to help advance the cause of Eritrea in the legal/diplomatic struggle that we were facing than this verdict. We set about our duties to use its moral force to extract the legal recognition that we were denied principally because of Ethiopian diplomacy, which defined us as a secessionist movement. International public opinion, especially in Africa, was dominated by Ethiopian diplomacy, but with the help of the Tribunal's verdict and the continued successes scored in the military field by our liberation fighters, we were able to challenge this dominance and begin to score victories for the case of Eritrean independence.

In the military field, the Ethiopian army, which had become Sub-Saharan Africa's largest by the early 1980's, launched several offensives to encircle and finish off the armed struggle. In 1983, the so-called "Red Star" offensive was expected to deal a deadly blow to the Eritrean struggle. By that time only the EPLF remained in the field; the ELF had left the field in 1981, having lost out to the EPLF in the last internecine war fought between the two national liberation fronts. "Red Star" proved a disaster for the Ethiopian army, albeit costly to the Eritrean side also in terms of heavy casualties. Ethiopian leader Mengistu Haile Mariam was confident of victory and when "Red Star" failed to yield the expected victory, his best officers planned another offensive, known to Eritreans as "*SelaHta Werar*" (Stealthy Offensive). It, too, ended in failure, though it was also costly to the Eritrean side in casualties. During the following five years, there were several military engagements, none of them decisive until the EPLF victory at Afabet in 1988. Afabet changed the balance of power in favor of the Eritrean side.

By 1988, Eritrean diplomacy had succeeded in putting Ethiopian diplomacy on the defensive; we had changed the terms of the debate by insisting on the Eritrean question being accepted as a colonial one, not as secession. As our fighters were scoring victories in the field, Eritreans in the diaspora, were mobilizing public support wherever they lived and worked. Taxi drivers in Washington DC carried pamphlets and leaflets bearing news and analysis of the Eritrean situation and handed these to senators and others in positions of authority. Academics and other professionals took part in debates and discussion groups wherever they saw an opportunity. The annual meeting of the African Studies Association (ASA) became a "battle ground" in which the contending forces fought out the issues concerning Eritrea and other parts of the Horn of Africa.

By the mid to late 1980s, the time when pro-Ethiopian academics dominated the field, propagating one-sided views, was over.

In this respect one particular event is worthy of special mention—the One-Day Conference on the Horn of Africa held at the Blackburn Center of Howard University, August 25, 1984. As the principal convener, I had a hand in selecting the topics and subjects to be addressed. Jointly sponsored by the African Studies and Research Program of Howard University and the Institute for Policy Study, it was also organized by an ad hoc committee, the Committee to Organize a Horn of Africa Conference (COHAC), comprised of Eritreans, Tigrayans and Oromos, notably the late Sisai Ibsa.

The basic assumption of the conference organizers was that change will soon come in the region and that the liberation movements will replace the then-reigning dictatorships in Ethiopia/Eritrea and Somalia. This assumption was reflected in the issues discussed at the conference. There was a Special Current Issues Panel made up of government envoys and representatives of liberation movements. The success of the conference was measured not only by the positive comments voiced by participants and observers, but also by the negative reaction of the Ethiopian embassy. The Charge d'Affairs of the Ethiopian embassy in Washington wrote a letter of protest to the President of Howard University complaining that Howard had given a forum to a bunch of " secessionists and trouble makers." The Academic Vice President called me to his office and showed me the letter. He said that the people who wrote the letter clearly did not know about First Amendment rights of citizens and residents of the United States.

Even as victories were being scored in various fields of endeavor by Eritreans in the Diaspora, there was also some frustration among members of the Eritrean mass organizations, particularly in North America. I was closely connected with these organizations as a member of the Washington DC chapter of NUESNA (National Union of Erirean Students in North America), a successor to ELFNA. I attended meetings regularly in the DC chapter as a member. The axis of division in the mass organizations was along democratic versus bureaucratic lines, though it was more complicated than that. The contradiction in the Diaspora reflected the internal struggles in the Front back in Eritrea.

This is a topic that forms part of a larger question concerning the dynamics of revolutionary process as demonstrated by the Eritrean experience, a subject I intend to deal with another time. Suffice it to say for now that I was on the side of the democratic faction, demanding accountability of leaders at all levels, beginning with leaders of chapters. Accountability included financial accounting. A common complaint among members was that they did not know how much money was raised from the public and other sources, and what happened to that money. This question together with the general running of the organization became a bone of contention. There was no transparency, and leaders were accused of arrogance and intimidating tactics. There was a pervasive sense of "Us" and "Them," of insiders who had access to privileged information and outsiders who were denied such privilege.

Though I tried to concentrate on assisting the cause by providing professional service – preparing memoranda, writing briefs, conducting seminars and giving lectures on the Eritrean question, making personal contacts with people of influence, etc—I could not avoid being affected by the general malaise in the movement in North America. Occasionally, I wrote letters to Isaias Afewerki, with what I considered important information, at times attaching useful documents procured from privileged sources. I was struck by the fact that Isaias never responded in writing. One long letter that I sent him (by hand of writer Dan Connell) was an analysis of the general malaise in North America, naming one particular person as the principal cause of the malaise and that he should take steps to change that person whom I described as very unpopular. This is not the place for going into details on this subject, but it is worth mentioning that in that letter I said that unless the situation was rectified, I was considering resigning from membership in the movement.

In response, Isaias instructed Sebhat Efrem to call me and ask me to be patient, that there would be an important change. Sebhat called me from Milan where he was engaged in resolving a conflict between factions within the Eritrean member organizations in Italy. I noticed from our conversation that Sebhat did not know why Isaias had told him to call me, for he asked me what I had written; I told him to ask Isaias. At any rate, what he had called "an important change" came to pass soon after our phone conversation.

Assignment to the United Nations

In March 1985, I received a letter of appointment, signed by Alamin Mohamed Said, head of Foreign Affairs in the EPLF Political Bureau. The letter designated me as the EPLF representative at the United Nations; it was renewed two years later by the new head of Foreign Relations of the EPLF, Mr. Ali Said Abdalla. The letter read as follows:

> The Eritrean Peoples Liberation Front (EPLF) wishes to confirm to all concerned that Dr. Bereket Habte Selassie has been designated as the official representative to the United Nations. We call on political parties, embassies, organizations, institutions and personalities who are sympathetic to the just struggle of the Eritrean people to avail him of the support he will need in the fulfillment of his duties.

There was no question asked by anybody whether I was willing to do the job; obviously the EPLF leadership considered me a *tegadalai*, a soldier who must obey commands. As for me, I saw an opportunity for service to the cause in accepting the assignment, though I remember jokingly calling it "Mission Impossible." I remember showing the letter to my mentor, veteran Eritrean Freedom Fighter, Woldeab Woldemariam, during one of my visits I paid him when he was staying with his daughter BriKti and her husband Dr. Petros Hadgu, near Atlantic City, New Jersey. He welcomed the news with a smile and a mordant remark: "Thank God. At last, they have started assigning the right man to the right job."

Many a truth is told in a joke, as the saying goes; there was a sense in which my assignment could indeed be called Mission Impossible. Consider the following:

First and foremost, the United Nations is an organization of governments, not of nations in the sense of peoples. So, as a representative of a non-governmental, political organization, I could not gain access to the United Nations, let alone demand accreditation. Second, it was the United Nations that had frustrated the Eritrean people's quest for self-determination, joining it with Ethiopia in a lopsided federal arrangement falling short of independence. Logically, therefore, the organization was biased against Eritrean claims or demand for recognition. Third, even when its own handiwork (the federation) was violated by Emperor Haile Selassie, and Eritreans protested, the United Nations ignored Eritrean protests thus encouraging the Emperor to deliver the *coup de grace* to the dying federation and declare Eritrea an Ethiopian province, obliterating its separate identity.

Thus it seemed foolhardy to expect different treatment now.

Nonetheless, we were determined to challenge the United Nations and its betrayal of a trust. In this tale of betrayal, the last words of Anze Matienzo, the UN Commissioner for Eritrea, who had been assigned the task of drafting an Eritrean constitution and overseeing the formation of an Eritrean government, are prophetic. Quoting the panel of experts who helped him draft the constitution, Matienzo noted in his final report to the UN General Assembly that if the terms of the UN Resolution and the federal arrangement were violated, the UN was still charged with a responsibility. In the words of the panel of experts, *"The United Nations Resolution on Eritrea would remain an international instrument and, if violated, the General Assembly could be seized of the matter."*

Our strategy was based on our belief in the justice of our cause and our conviction that we would overcome one day. On the strength of that simple conviction we conducted ourselves in accordance with the military adage: "Despise the enemy strategically, but respect him tactically." And in that respect, again to use a military metaphor, any means of breaking the ramparts of the UN fortress was acceptable: any direct or circuitous route of entry must be used to gain access.

Immediately after I began work, I approached the head of the Somali Mission to the UN, Mr. Abdullahi Osman, seeking his advice and assistance. It is a matter of record that all Somalis in positions of authority provided help to the Eritrean cause. Incredible as it may seem, Ambassador Abdullahi Osman invited me to join the Somali delegation and attend the UN General Assembly. That I had carried a Somali passport since 1975 was, of course, helpful in case any one asked for my documents. All EPLF officials used Somali passports for traveling and the Somali government officials from the president on down, were not only aware of this fact, they gave it their unequivocal approval. Somali embassies throughout the world put their facilities at our disposal. We felt at home in their offices and were frequently invited to their homes. Eritreans are ever grateful for this help and hospitality.

At the UN, using my status as a "Somali delegate" I made several useful contacts and distributed documents helping the Eritrean cause, including the verdict of the Milan Tribunal. I also wrote several memoranda addressed to African and Arab delegates in which I summarized the legal basis and legitimacy of the Eritrean case, with appropriate historical background. Inevitably, members of the Ethiopian delegation saw me and began lodging complaints with the UN security department. As long as I was attached to the Somali delegation, there was nothing they could do. This lasted for a little under a year. Unfortunately, Somali President Syiad Barre and Ethiopian leader Mengistu Haile Mariam reached a rapprochement, which eventually affected my status as a "Somali delegate." Ambassador Osman regretfully informed me that he could no longer oblige me as he had done up to that time; he had his instructions.

I had to look for another means of access. One possibility was to befriend one or more of the representatives of the NGOs accredited to the UN; to that end, I cultivated a number of individuals. This became very useful when in May 1986 an international conference of world NGOs, including several African NGOs, was held at the UN headquarters. Tesfalem Seyoum, the head of the Eritrean Relief Committee in the US, and I were invited as observers. Tesfalem, with his cheerful personality, helped me in mobilizing support among the civil society organizations. We met with many of the heads of African NGOs and briefed them about the war in Eritrea and the humanitarian problems it caused. We succeeded in getting the Eritrean situation on the conference agenda. This was in and of itself a mark of recognition for the Eritrean cause. In its historic resolution the NGO Conference called upon the United Nations to play a more active role to resolve the conflict between Eritrea and Ethiopia, and more specifically, to undertake immediate discussion to bring an end to the war and thus help avoid further suffering "through a just and peaceful resolution of the conflict."

The conference resolution also took note of the then anticipated Soviet-backed Ethiopian military offensive in Eritrea. This resolution was second only to the Milan Tribunal's verdict in helping us to break the spell of silence imposed by Ethiopian diplomacy on the Eritrean case. For the first time, African intellectuals and leaders of civil society organizations began to articulate Eritrea's case in its proper light.

"Eritrea's case is the same as that of Namibia," declared one delegate. The head of the Senegalese delegation said, "Eritrea is an African problem; so we Africans must help provide an answer to the problem." The same delegate summed it all up by declaring, "Eritrea must be free and shall be free." It is not every day that one meets a prominent African intellectual and civic leader who can make such a principled declaration—and with such verve and conviction that affected all present.

"*Vive le Senegal; vive l'Afrique!*" I cried with emotion to the amazement of the audience.

A person I had contacted for advice earlier was Mr. Ramon Horta, representative of FRETILIN, the East Timor liberation organization. Representation at the United Nations of non-governmental political organizations such as FRETILIN or the EPLF can only be granted on the basis of an observer status. Such status was granted to the African National Congress (ANC), the Palestinian Liberation Organization (PLO), the Namibian SWAPO, among others, because these organizations were supported by governments and the UN recognized their cause as legitimate. FRETILIN was granted observer status because the UN recognized the justness of the cause of East Timor, despite Indonesia's protests. Ethiopia's abolition of the federation and occupation of Eritrea was illegal, and our conviction was that we should also be granted an observer status, at the very least. Alas! There was no possibility of this happening.

Our task was to research ways of influencing a critical mass of member nations who could see the betrayal that Eritrea had suffered and the plight of its people as a result of that betrayal. We had to diversify and refine our method of struggle, reaching out to more people and groups in order to create such a critical mass. This included writing and distributing documents that briefly stated Eritrea's case for independence, submitting periodic reports of Ethiopian atrocities committed against Eritrean civilians, as well as reporting the military victories our guerilla armies were scoring—this latter in order to show hard-nosed diplomats who were trained to respect power that we were on the winning side of history, and thus induce them to send reports to their respective governments.

In order to achieve these goals in a proper and timely manner, I called on the assistance of four Eritrean professionals living in the United States to help me as members of an advisory panel. These were: Kassahun Checole, Kibreab Habtemichael, Rezene Gebreyesus, and Woldai Futur. We met periodically to review events and discuss strategies and tactics, sharing duties in research and analysis. Kibreab and Rezene, being lawyers, handled human rights issues, while Kassahun and Woldai acted as general advisors, generating and vetting ideas and tactics. They all gave of their time unstintingly. And during the last two years, Kidane Woldeyesus, a quiet and thoughtful graduate of Toronto University, joined me to act as my assistant.

We all, in our different ways, worked to tap all our contacts to mobilize support, particularly in gaining access to important individuals representing governments that carried influence. Since the primary responsibility rested with me, I targeted Western governments. To that end we supplied them with the necessary documents periodically, including legal arguments and reports of military success of the EPLF armed forces..

It is interesting to record that the level of the officials I could meet was lowest in the American case, but that it kept going higher as news of spectacular victories of our guerilla army kept coming. Things changed dramatically after the EPLF scored a decisive victory at Afabet in 1988 when the balance of power shifted in favor of our forces. Our supporters were heartened and others began seeking us out; and our adversaries at the UN headquarters began to think of desperate tactics to minimize the impact of our progress towards victory.

All the while the Ethiopians and their Soviet allies were following my movements, and I was arrested on three occasions by the UN security. Each time, I was told that I could not get into the UN without the appropriate permit. One of the security people, a man with a Caribbean accent, informed me one day that the UN mission of an important government was following my movements closely and that I should be careful.

Soon after that, someone claiming to represent the New York Police Department phoned me at my office and demanded that I meet him and a colleague of his, suggesting a hotel not far from the UN headquarters.

I went to the hotel at the appointed hour and waited in the lobby near the front desk. A few minutes later I saw two men dressed in civilian clothes approaching me from different directions. One of them asked for my name and introduced himself as Detective Parola. His companion joined us, and I asked them to sit down. Detective Wayne T. Parola took out a card and handed it to me; under his name the card read:

Joint Terrorist Task Force. 26 Federal Plaza, New York City, 10278.

On the top left hand corner was the insignia of the Department of Justice, Federal Bureau of Investigation (FBI). And on the top right hand corner there was the insignia NYPD.

Terrorism? What had that got to do with me? Why did these fine looking officers want to talk to me? For a fleeting moment, my mind went back to Pademba Road, Freetown, Sierra Leone, June 1980, where I had been arrested by the local police at the instigation of the Ethiopian delegation to the OAU Summit meeting, as I have already related.

Detective Parola did most of the questioning. He asked me a number of questions to establish my true identity and the reason for my presence in New York. One question he asked that has stuck in my mind was what I thought of terrorism. I said I abhor terrorism; all acts of terror." The two detectives looked at each other; then Parola asked me what exactly I was doing in New York and what business did I have at the UN headquarters. I gave a long lecture on Eritrea and its just cause and informed them that I represented the EPLF at the United Nations. They not only believed my story but in the end they wished me luck, advising me to obtain the proper permits before I entered the UN headquarters.

Before they left, I asked them why they had decided to interrogate me. Parola said that "a UN member government" had complained that I represented a threat to their safety. They both smiled as Parola told me this, as if to indicate that the story was not well founded. Again they wished me well and left.

Although my work at the UN was at times frustrating and annoying, as the above story illustrates, there was hardly a dull moment. The six years went by quickly and I carried on until victory day in May 1991.

Free At Last!

When news of Asmara's fall to our liberation forces broke to the world, I was at Howard University, meeting with a graduate student. The telephone rang and an excited Rezene Medhane broke the news; he was calling from the EPLF office in downtown Washington, DC. He handed the receiver to Tesfai Girmzion, EPLF deputy representative in the US (in actual fact, he was the real representative, though Hagos claimed the rank, harvesting the fruit of the toil of others). Tesfai's crackling voice was at its most crackling, this time teasing me—what the Hell was I doing at Howard when the whole world was celebrating! Come on, he said, we are opening the champagne; we can't wait all day! So I went to join the others at the office where a second bottle was being opened and people were drinking and hugging each other boisterously.

I was dazed and felt out of place. All of a sudden I felt a sense of anti-climax. Was it because the adrenalin that flowed and kept me going throughout the years of struggler was drained out? Wasn't success supposed to bring joy? I was happy of course: happy that the war was over, and hopeful that the people of Eritrea and Ethiopia would now live in peace. Even as I sipped the champagne and saw the others celebrating, the title of a project suggested itself "From Conflict to Concord—Cooperation in the Horn of Africa." Indeed, that was a project that I submitted for my Fellowship at the US Institute of Peeace a year later and convened an international symposium on it in Addis Ababa in July 1993.

As the others celebrated noisily, with people coming in and going out all the time, suddenly—out of the blue—the idea of going to church came to me. Going to church and making some kind of homage to a higher power seemed to me at that point to be better than drinking champagne. I left the celebrating group quietly and got into my car. I remember turning on the ignition and driving. Without thinking, I found myself driving toward the cathedral of Catholic University of America. It was as if the car had its own will and took me there itself. I parked the car and walked inside. I am not Catholic, but I went to the chapel, lit a candle and sat there for a very long time.

That act seemed to fulfill a deeply felt but unarticulated spiritual need. As I left the chapel I felt a huge weight was lifted off my head. I was at peace at long last! I also discovered that the front of my shirt was drenched with tears that must have flowed while I sat in the chapel.

One week after liberation, the EPLF leadership summoned three of us—myself, Rezene Medhane, and Amare Tekle—to the Field. We were joined by two Eritrean professionals, Professor Asmarom Legesse and Dr. Belainesh Araia. We all flew from Washington to Khartoum, and then were driven across the Sudanese-Eritrean border, through Barentu, Aqurdet and Keren, to Afabet.

The landscape was littered with thousands of dead Ethiopian soldiers who had perished while fleeing toward Sudan. Presumably they all died of thirst. It was a frightful sight and the stench was overpowering; we were forced to put wet handkerchiefs over our noses until we passed Aqurdet. As we got closer to Keren, there were fewer and fewer corpses. The horror of war! These corpses were left to rot or for hyenas to feed upon.

We passed Keren, making our way toward Afabet by night. At one point, our driver missed a turn and almost got us blown up in a mine field. The EPLF forces had cordoned off that road, but the driver did not know. We were just lucky; some guardian angel made him pull back and take a different direction.

We stayed overnight at Afabet and were told to proceed to Asmara, via Keren, which we did. In Keren we stayed in the main hotel, which had no running water. I had known the hotel in its better days; it had become a shell of its former self, the result of war and an Ethiopian army of occupation.

On our way from Keren to Asmara, we saw several carcasses of abandoned vehicles and tanks—the scars of war.

We entered Asmara at about 4 p.m. on Tuesday, June 11, 1991. Asmara, which I had not seen for almost sixteen years, looked run down, with the paint peeling off the houses. The inhabitants looked gaunt but nonetheless delirious with joy, still celebrating with drums sounding everywhere two weeks after liberation day.

We checked in at the Nyala hotel but, although exhausted from the long journey, we just could not stay inside the hotel. Rezene and I walked the streets of our fair city, absorbing the scenes and observing the pedestrians and motorists shouting greetings at one another. It was like a dream. Amid drums sounding and people dancing everywhere, we started visiting our relatives who welcomed us with jubilation, the women ululating.

Obituary of the Martyrs

Not long after that, families were told of their children who had been killed, or martyred as people learned to say; practically every family was affected. If it was not a son or a daughter, then a cousin or nephew or niece had been killed in the long war of liberation. Our jubilation was modulated by that fact. In my own family, my older sister Bisserat had sent four sons to join the struggle; two of them never came back. When I visited her, although she was happy to see me and her surviving two sons safe and sound, I could feel the bitter sweet spirit enveloping the atmosphere in the household. So it was also with Senbetu Asfaha, one of my favorite cousins. All of Senbetu's five sons never made it back; they were all killed as was her son-in-law, leaving her a small orphaned boy to raise. Senbetu was still dazed when I visited her in Adi Nifas; she could not get up to greet me.

These are small samplings of a general condition affecting tens of thousands of Eritrean families. Some hardy souls bore the brunt of the sad news and went about their daily lives as best they could; while others, like my cousin Senbetu, were crushed by sorrow. One woman, a former teacher, who had lost two sons, was asked by a journalist how she felt. She answered that she was not the only one who had suffered a loss and she was proud of her sons. Then she added a sentence that has been quoted time and again by many a commentator. She said:

> *"But if the country for which they paid the ultimate price were to become the plaything of a few, then I shall weep."*

Today, these memorable words sum up Eritrea's post-liberation blues. Indeed, these words may serve as *obituary to our martyrs and a painful reminder of what we have lost and why we have lost our way.*

The next volume of my memoir will probe the questions implied in this loss and how we came to be where we are today.

END OF VOLUME ONE

Index

Aba Woldeab 32, 33, 35, 36
Abate Mengiste 67
Abate Menkir 271, 330
Abby 279, 281, 282, 284
Abdullahi Al Khider 322
Abdullahi Gelmo 226
Abdullahi Osman 345
Abebe Bikila 198
Abebe Kebede 238
Abebe Retta 101, 103, 106, 236
Abebe Teferi 148
Abigrat 300
Abiyi 329
Aboy Bahta 307
Aboy Geresus 38
Aboy Hailu 8, 9
Aboy Seleba 43
Aboy Tirfe 47
Abraha Castle Hotel 288, 289
Abraha Gebreselassie, 32
Abraha Tedla, 203
Abraham Geresus, 30
Abrams, Norm 204
Abrehet 305
Abu Ajaj 317
Abu Teyyara 317
Ad Agheb 292
Adam Idris 320
Adama 50
Addei Tiblets 53, 54, 56, 57

Addis Ababa 36, 38, 43, 44, 46, 48-50, 52, 54, 56, 57, 60, 61, 67, 75, 83, 85, 98, 103-109, 113-119, 121-123, 129, 133, 136, 138, 144, 145, 147-149, 151, 160, 170, 171, 173, 178, 179, 181-185, 188, 189, 191, 192, 195, 197, 200, 202, 204, 205, 207-209, 215, 216, 219, 220, 230, 232, 233, 236, 243, 244, 257, 259, 260, 264, 266, 267, 270, 275, 278, 281, 283-286, 288, 291, 301, 302, 304, 306, 315, 320, 322, 329, 332, 338, 348
Addis Ababa Law School 200, 205, 216
Addis Hilton Hotel 291
Aden 318-320, 325, 326, 328, 336
Aden Abdella 188
Adere 54, 223, 226, 227, 231
Adey Itye Sebene 11
Adi Abeyto 289
Adi Grat 45, 47
Adi Nifas 3, 12, 21, 23, 27, 30, 45, 48, 60, 289, 313, 350
Adi SheKa 308
Adi Shimagle 312
AdifiChen 30
Adoa 42, 43
Adolf Hitler 154
Advent 33
Afabet 341, 347, 349
Afar 295, 319

Afarora 320
Afersata 195, 196
Afewerk Tekle 123, 124
African National Congress (ANC) 177, 197, 212-214, 346
African Union 190
Agamido 233, 234
Ahmed Mahmud 313
Ahmed Nasser 319
Ahmed Salah 319
Ahmed Tahir Baduri 320
Aida Desta 115
Aide de camp 116, 161
Akalework 108-110
Akeleguzai 297, 299
Aklilu Habte 175, 223
Aklilu Habtewold 61, 152, 153, 185
Akpata 176
Al Azhar 300
Alamata 47, 287
Alamin Mohamed Said 343
Aleka Lemma 53, 97
Alemaya 52, 148, 222
Alemaya College 231, 232
Alemeselassie (Aleme-Selassie) 126, 127
Alemseghed Hiruy 104, 114, 151
Alewuha River 286, 287
Alexander Dimitrov 147-149
Algerian Liberation War 94
Ali Said Abdella 317, 343
Alil 299, 300
All African Peoples Conference 71, 72, 93, 94, 145, 148, 174-179, 184
Allied Troops 31, 112
Allott 209
Almaz 83
Aman Andom 147, 171, 204, 268, 269, 306
Amare Gugsa 276

Amare Tecle 309
Ambalaghe 47, 52, 287
Amdemichael Dessalegne 106, 112, 117
AmetSi 312
Amhara 9, 48, 54, 85, 104, 106, 128, 160, 174, 226, 227, 231, 264, 287
Amharic 9, 32, 33, 36, 46, 49, 51, 53, 65, 66, 68, 97, 113, 124, 125, 136, 137, 143, 169, 178, 182, 192, 211, 223, 264, 267, 287, 304, 320
Amir Kanji 86
Andemicael Kahsai 338
Anton Jonsson 44, 53, 55
Apostle Paul 8
Arabian Peninsula 4
Arab-Israeli War 84
Arabs 4, 54, 234
Araia 38, 142, 349
Arbegna 56, 128, 129, 133, 139, 168, 195
Arefaine Abraham 45, 147, 340
Argudolega 294, 295
Ariam 49
Arsi 185, 270
Asberom Abraha 320
Asegedech Alamiro 189
Asfaha Woldemichael 105, 113, 161
Asgede 3, 27, 73, 194, 204, 211, 216, 233, 259, 260, 264, 328, 331
Ashenghe 43, 286
Asmara 3, 10, 12, 13, 22-24, 26, 31, 36, 39, 43, 45, 48-50, 52, 53, 59, 60, 84, 104-108, 113, 115, 146, 167, 178, 179, 181, 220, 282, 283, 288, 296, 297, 300-302, 305, 309, 312-314, 316, 318, 320, 333, 348, 349
Asmerom Gerezgher 317
Asmerom Legesse 108

Asrate Kassa 147, 149, 152, 160, 166
Assefa Ayana 146
Assefa Demisse 168
Asseghid Tessema 236, 275, 277, 284
Astatke Tassew 127, 128
Ato Menkir 119
Attorney General 74, 134, 136, 137, 146, 150-153, 157-161, 184, 192, 193, 196, 197, 200-202, 208, 209, 222, 229-231, 269, 271, 321, 322
Auriot 170
Awash 50
Awassa 168
Awate 191
Axis Powers 31
Aya Geresus 49, 50
Aya Haile 306
Ayele Gebre 132, 133, 143, 156
Ayya (Aya) Leggese 48
Azien 310

Baathists 336
Babu 178, 198
Badme 288
Bahlquist 264, 265
BaHri 4, 41, 289, 308, 315, 316
BaHri Bara 308, 315, 316
balabats 47
banda 48, 49, 68, 128
Bandung 186
Baria 276
barley 13
Barnabas 52, 53, 56
Bashai (Pasha) 10, 21, 28, 29
Bashai Tedla 4, 192, 193
Basso, Lelio 340, 341
Bath 42, 96

Bawtree 340
beans 13, 15, 20
Bechuanaland (Botswana) 91, 177
Bego Adragot 239
BeHailai 30
Beirut 54, 108, 151, 319-323, 326-328
Bekele Getahun 124
Belachew Asrat 136-138, 152, 244
Belai Abai 85
Belai Zeleke 128, 129
Belainesh 349
Belete Gebre 142
Belete Gebretsadik 108
Beleza 12, 17-19, 289, 313, 314
Belkis 329
Bella, Ben 186, 188
Benamir 47
Bereket Goitom 55, 56
Bereket Manna 119
Bereket Misghina 312
Berhane Gebremedhin 284
Berhanu Bayeh 275
Berhanu Dinke 208
Berhe 53, 308
Berhe Assegahegne 111
Berhe Tesfamariam 326
Bevan 91, 92
Beverly Hills Bar Association 193, 205
Beyene Solomon 169
Beyene Woldegabriel 85
Biba 197
Bible 8, 32, 33, 38, 53
Bilen 295
Bimpe 98, 100
Biniam 49
Birheen 12, 18, 19, 21
Bissrat 7, 39, 43, 60, 105, 203, 307
Blata Kitaw 147

Bloody Saturday 278
Botega 52, 225, 233
Botsio, Kojo 93
Boundaries 29, 46
Bourguiba, Habib 188, 189
Bretton Woods 262
BriKti 344
British Broadcasting Corporation (BBC) 195, 269, 299
British Council 65, 66, 85, 87, 191, 209, 210
British Empire 89, 90
British Military Administration 95
British Traveler 3, 4
Broches, Ronnie 260, 263, 264, 270, 329, 330
Brockway 93
Brooke, Edward 202
Bruce, James 4
Brutawit 329
Buhagiar 138
Bulcha 241
Bunia 112
Burma 95, 261

Caesar 25
Cairo 84, 136, 194, 300, 320, 335
Cambridge University 98, 115
Cambridge, Mass. 203, 207, 208
Camp Hall 99
Canada 59, 323, 334
Casa Incis 257, 282
Casablanca 184
Catholic 4, 17, 18, 22, 23, 25, 42, 132, 147, 154, 184, 221, 348, 349
Chanyalew Gugsa 102, 103, 276, 279, 286
Chaplin, Charlie 197
Chatelanat 617

Che Guevara 270
Chelenko 226
Chewa Sew 227
Chickpeas 13
Chilalo 270
Christian Era 4
Christianity 4, 11
Christmas Day 8
Churchill 35, 89, 127
COHAC 342
Commission of Enquiry 268-272, 278, 281, 288, 296, 301
Communist Manifesto 37
Communists 37
Connell, Dan 343
Constitutional Commission 10, 45, 202
Constitutional Law 101, 201
Copts 18
Criminal law 30, 204, 340
Croydon Polytechnic 60, 86

Daily Worker 91
Daniel 7, 8, 10
Dar-es-Salaam 191, 197, 209
David, Rene 153, 157
Davidson, Basil 334
Dawit Abraha 55, 57
Dawit Gebru 192
Dawit Ogbazghi 26, 42
Dean Maxwell 204
Dean of the Law School 153, 216
Debre Sina 49
Debre Zeit 267, 282
Democratic Party 200, 201, 331
Dengogo 221
Denkel 295
Denning 200
Deqi-Asgede (also Deqisgede) 3, 27

Derg 84, 246, 247, 267, 268, 271, 272, 274-279, 283, 296, 297
Dessie 45, 47, 48, 286
Desta Woldekidan 46, 281
Development 55, 61, 62, 103, 135, 156, 158, 167, 168, 175, 184, 188, 205, 209, 231, 237, 258, 259, 261, 262, 270, 332
Development Unlimited 61
Dewelle 170
Dickens, Charles 123
Dien Bien Phu 94
Digsana 315
Dimbleby, Jonathan 269, 273
Dire Dawa 24, 50-52, 57, 148, 170, 220, 221, 239, 282
Djibouti 50, 170, 220, 225, 295
Doman, Glenn 265
Dominique Dufour 319
Dr. Afewerki 31
Dr. Boyd 86, 87
Dr. Mekonen 279
Dynamic Party 176

East Timor 346
Efrem Teweldemedhin 42
Egyptians 5, 38, 95, 185, 333
El Nimeiry, Jafar 322
Elders 4, 6, 9-11, 22, 23, 26, 29-31, 34, 42, 50, 56, 93, 106, 192, 193, 233, 243, 307, 308
Elias 7, 253
Ellen 38
Emanuel, Victor 24
Emperor Teodros 41
Emperor Yohannes 41
Endalkachew Mekonen 59, 267-269, 271, 278
England 10, 25, 37, 42, 44, 45, 57, 59, 60, 65, 66, 68, 70, 71, 83, 85-87, 89-91, 93-97, 99, 104, 105, 107, 109, 113-119, 121, 123, 124, 129, 145, 147, 168, 169, 191, 197, 200, 201, 203, 208, 209, 214, 215, 218, 220, 236
English Legal History 101
Ephrem Isaac 203
Epistle 8
Eritrean Liberation Front (ELF) 191, 233, 234, 248, 249, 284, 288-290, 293-297, 299-303, 305-307, 310-314, 319-321, 336, 341
Eritrean Relief Association (ERA) 311, 317, 318, 320-325, 328
Eritreans for Liberation in North America (EFLNA) 334, 335, 338
Esete 330
ESUNA 203, 206-208, 336
Etete 329
Ethiopian Embassy 37, 84, 93, 96, 102, 161, 197, 322, 342
Ethiopian Students Association 91
Evangelical School 55
Ewing, Bill 216, 266
Ezra 136

Fallers 201
Fanon, Franz 94, 175, 176
Fascism 17, 24
FBI 347
Federal Supreme Court 138, 139, 168
Field Command 327, 335
Fikirte 330
Filseta, Mary 239
Finot 211, 238, 239, 241, 249, 250, 259, 260, 264-267, 328, 329, 331
Finsas 257
Firqi 6
First, Ruth 197, 213, 265, 266, 341

Fissehaie 301-303, 305
Fissehaie Bahta 39
Fitawrari Manna 191
Flax 13
Ford Foundation 200
Fort Hare 196
France 25, 87, 90, 94, 95, 100, 102, 123, 214
Frederick, Wayne 200
French Revolution 91, 270
Friends House 101
Front de la Liberation Nationale (FLN) 94, 176
Funeral 9, 10, 33, 98, 123, 136, 141, 192, 230

Gabi 3, 21, 290, 296
Gabre 49, 50
Galba, Da'Ero 297, 299
Ganzglass, Marty 339
Gashaw Kebede 234
Ge'ez 97, 131
Gebreab Garoy 35
Gebrehiwet Woldearegai 279
Gebrehiwet Woldemichael 248, 290-293
Gebreselassie Hankish 308
Gebretsadiq 10
Gebrewold Ingidawork 138
Gedarif 321
General Goitom 322
General Union of Eritrean Students (GUES) 335, 336
Geneva 25, 96, 210, 211, 319, 323
Geremi 307
Germame Neway 125, 127, 129, 141, 142
Germany 31, 87, 214, 323, 324
Getachew Kibret 184

Getachew Mekasha 174
Getahun Tessema 75, 237, 274
Geza Banda Habesha 38
Geza Kenisha 24, 26, 31, 35, 38, 39, 96
Geza Nistrom 39, 60
Ghana 93, 94, 97, 173, 174, 177, 184, 185, 198, 285
Ghana Trade Union Congress 177
Ghizot 223
Girma Belew 119
Girmachew 178, 179
Girmai Gebremeskel 312
Girmai Melelik 34
Goats 6, 18, 19, 277, 292, 293
God 8, 18, 21, 24, 35, 48, 51-53, 234, 240, 241, 308, 316, 331, 344
Gohoho 174
Goitom Berhe 317
Goldwater, Barry 201
Gonder 55
Graham Tyer 195
Gravin, Jean 153
Greece 261
Greeks 5, 187
Guatemala 95
Guiana 211
Guinea 90 177, 182, 187, 211
Gurage 54
Gurnell 65, 66

Habeshas 5
Habte Selassie 9, 10
Habteab 123, 124
Habtegiorgis 39, 122, 284
Habtetsion 44, 45
Hadis Alemayehu 111
Hagman Don 76, 204
Hagos Gebrehiwet 340

Index

Hagos Gebreyesus 207
Haile Arficio (Arficho) 214
Haile BeraKi 43, 48
Haile Fida 214
Haile Gerima 329
Haile Jebha 317
Haile Kahsai 36, 38
Haile Keleta 67
Haile Menkerios 334
Haile Selassie Belai 148
Haile Selassie University 175, 205
Haileab 53
Haileab Tseggai 197
Hailegebriel Negero 134
Hailu Alemayehu 122
Hailu Bahru 114
Hakim Gara 76-78, 232, 257
Haleqa Tewelde-Berhan 8
Halliday, Fred 271
Hamasien 3, 27, 303, 308, 315, 324
Hanna 7, 8, 10, 289
Haraka 182
Harar 7, 24, 39, 44, 48-59, 67, 76, 78, 79, 97, 108, 110, 114, 119, 136, 139, 148, 154, 161, 171, 185, 217, 219-224, 226, 227, 230, 231, 233, 234, 237, 257, 266, 267, 272,
Harari 54, 226
Haregu Zere 302
Harlem Renaissance 206
Harvard 202, 203
Harvest 6, 9, 14, 15, 26, 27, 181, 348
Hasen Hirsi 229
Hausner, Gideon 150
Hayter 261, 263
Hazega 312
Helen 307
Herodotus 3
Hirut 328, 329
Hirut Imru 175

His Imperial Majesty (see Emperor)
Hiwet 340
Hoffa, Jimmy 201
Holeta Officers 112
Hollywood 36, 205, 206
Holy Mother 17, 18, 306
Home Office 103
Homer 5
Horn of Africa Journal 333
Houphuet-Boigny, Felix 90
Hughes, Langston 206
Hyde Park 89, 90

Iasu Gebrehawariat 52, 53, 55-57, 116
Ibrahim Afa 310
Ibrahim Mantay 320
Ibrahim Sultan 31, 96
Ibrahim Totil 249, 312, 313, 320
Idris Mohamed Adam 300
Il Duce 25
Iliad 5
Imam Musa 24
Iman 44, 49, 50
Imperial Palace 126, 132, 182, 231
India 36, 86, 88-90, 110, 129, 153, 175, 212, 261
Indians 36, 90
Indigeno 25
Individualized Education Plan (IEP) 267
Indonesia 186, 346
Inkoyye 56
Inspector General of Justice 134, 180
Institute of Policy Studies (IPS) 333
International Confederation of Free Trade Unions (ICFTU) 169
International Monetary Fund (IMF) 262

International Red Cross (ICRC) 319, 323
Iraq 229, 261, 263, 320, 321, 336
Irfi 6, 7
Isaac Abraha 39, 43, 44, 48-53, 55-57, 108, 113, 118, 121, 203, 219, 302, 337
Isaias Gebreselassie 146, 192
Islam 4, 226, 319, 327
Italian colonial rule 31, 41, 42, 46, 296
Italians 12, 17, 26, 31, 41, 47, 48, 49, 52, 84, 95, 111, 112, 115, 128, 158, 284, 285, 287
Iteghe Hotel 107, 118, 127
Ives 98
Iyob Gebrelul 309

Jarso Mekonen 329
Jesus 18
Jimi'E 321
Jimma 185, 191, 195
Joanna 201, 202
Journal of African Law 205
Jubilee 61, 63

Kabaka 197
Kagnew 300
Kahsai Tesfai 58, 83
Kalafalla Rashid 210
Kalamazoo 202
Kalekristos 142
Kasabubu 187
Kassahun Checole 346
Kaunda, Kenneth 144, 173
Kebede Gebre 146
Kebede Tessema 146
Kebero 27

Keita, Modibo 188
Kelemu Bahru 114
Kennedy, John F. 167, 201, 331
Kennedy, Robert (Bobby) 200-202
Kentiba Ghidey 6
Kenya 53, 55, 84, 89, 91, 92, 144, 173, 176, 196-198, 325
Kenya Africa National Union (KANU) 173, 196
Kenyatta 91, 187, 196, 197
Keren 205, 308, 349
Kessela 321, 322
Khama, Seretse 91
Khartoum 47, 320-323, 326, 328, 349
Khelifa Kerrar 321
Kiano 176
Kibreab Habtemichael 346
Kidane Haile 35, 36
Kidane Tekie 312
Kidane Teklom 314
Kidane Woldeyesus 347
Kifle Hagos 237, 238
Kifle Worku 269
King Farouk 133
Koinange, Mbuyu 91
Koki Menkir 117
Kombolsha 48
Korry, Edward 167, 168, 172
Kotebe 57-60, 83-85, 129, 283
Kumlachew 106, 113, 114
Kunama 295
Kunene, Mazizi 212
Kushitic 295

Labor Party 91, 176
Laeke 312
Lake Maniara 197
Lakew 67

Lancaster Gate 124
Land of the Thousand Villages 3, 4
Landau, Saul 150, 333
Lawrence, Harry 58, 63-66, 83
League of Nations 25, 42, 96, 154
Lee, Jenny 91
Leghar 50, 221
Leteberhan 306
Letehaimanot Negassi 10
Levine, Don 201
Leys, Colin 197, 198
Libya 41, 95
Lidet 14
Lion Cub 66, 89
Littler 65
London 7, 36-38, 58-60, 66, 71, 85-87, 89, 93, 96, 97, 101, 104, 105, 107, 109, 123, 124, 150, 191, 196, 197, 205, 208, 209, 211-214, 218, 223, 229, 241, 245, 258, 259, 264, 334, 340
London School of Economics 36, 85, 93, 124
London University 97, 209
Lorenzo Taezaz 25, 42, 104, 111, 194
Lucien Matte 109
Lumumba University 178
Lumumba, Patrice 148, 177, 178
Lutheran 11, 39, 44, 52, 55
Lyons Restaurant 87, 89

Madagascar 188
MaHber ShewAte 182
Mai Chew 286
Mai HuSa 313
Mai Ule 315
Maize 13
Majete 175
Makerere College 108, 197, 198

Mali 188
Malone, John 291
Mamo Habtewold 221
Mandela, Nelson 212, 213
Maputo 214
Marble Arch 87
Mariam Gunbot 21
Marshall, Burke 202
Marxist-Leninist 335, 336, 338
Mason and Asher 261
Mathew, Charles (Sir Charles) 134, 153, 232
Matriculation 58, 68
Mau Mau 89, 91
Mauritania 261
Mboya, Tom 144, 145, 173, 176, 196
McGill Law School 136
McNamara, Robert 270, 278, 330
Me'ETir 316
Meaza Workineh 84, 85
Mebrahtu Fisseha 49
Mebrat 7, 8, 10, 308, 312
Medallions 17, 18
Medhane-Alem 226
Mehal Sefari 128, 131
Meharenne Minda 234
Mehreteab 54, 79
MEISON 214
Mekbib 49
Mekele 46, 47, 286-290, 296, 299, 301, 306
Mekonen Hagos 233, 235
Mekonen Zewde 57, 58
Melaku Bekele 144
Mellinkoff, Ruth 205
Menage, Victor 60, 65, 66
Menbere 55, 57, 58
Menelik 41-43, 110, 137, 174, 215, 225, 226, 276, 278, 286, 287

Mengisteab Isaac 337-339
Mengistu Haile Mariam 24, 46, 146-148, 152, 155, 162, 190, 214, 271, 275, 276, 278, 304, 308, 309, 329, 330, 341, 345
Mengistu Lemma 53, 56, 57, 85, 93, 96, 97, 107, 123, 124, 130, 131, 168
Mengistu Neway 129, 142, 147, 162, 171
Menka'E 317, 335, 338, 339
Meriem Gual Dirfo 315
Meselles 6
Mesfin Embaye 229, 233
Mesfin Gebrehiwet 31, 33
Mesfin Gebremichael 169
Mesfin Woldemariam 145, 169
Mesfinto 306, 309, 310
Meshalokia 222, 267
Meskel 312
Metahara Sugar Workers Union 170
Mewael Mebrahtu 270, 284
Michael Gebrenegus 275
Michael Imru 151, 152, 268, 274
Midri BaHri 4, 41
Midri Zen 315
Milan Tribunal 345, 346 (See also Russell Tribunal)
Mindegle 299, 300
Minister of Public Works 170
Minister of Security 219, 220, 227, 229
Minister of the Pen 126, 127, 132, 133
Ministry of Foreign Affairs 26, 174, 184
Ministry of Justice 125-127, 130, 131, 133, 135, 136, 138, 147, 149, 151, 153, 156, 157, 160, 168, 180, 191, 193, 196, 208, 222, 230
Missionaries 4, 17, 22, 26, 42, 55, 221

Mogadishu 161, 339, 340
Mogues Wube 134, 137
Mohamed Abdurahman 153
Mohamed Ahmed Abdo 299
Monastery 33
Monfreid 226
Monique 100
Monrovia Group 184
Montpelier University 25
Moreillon, Jacques 323
Morocco 177, 190, 261
Morris, Herbert 204
Moshi 197
Moumie, Felix 173
Mpanga, Freddie 197, 198
Mrs. Holland 87, 101-103, 122
Mrs. Startin 86
Muezzin 24
Mugabe, Robert 92
Mulugeta 171
Muluwork 230
Murray, Iain 209, 241
Muslim 4, 12, 24, 154, 185, 193, 227, 231, 296, 327
Mussolini 24-26, 42, 43, 92, 95, 112, 154, 207

Naizghi Kiflu 334
Namibia 177, 346
Nara 295
Nasser, Gamal Abdel 95, 171, 185
Nazi Ideology 150
Nazret 50
Nebiat Teferi 238, 265
Needler Hall 98, 99
Neo-Destour Party 175
Nerayo 60, 265, 302, 304, 306, 312, 314, 315

Nerayo Isaias (Esseyas) 127, 131, 133, 136, 152, 153, 230
Netsela 3, 301, 306
New Statesman and Nation 91
New Testament 18
New York 96, 198-200, 329, 332, 335, 347, 348
Ngorongoro 197
NIEO 262
Nifas BaHri 4
Nifas BereKa 4
Nigussay Ayele 207
Nile 4, 5
Njonjo, Charles 196
Nkrumah, Kwame 55, 93-95, 144, 145, 174-178, 185-187, 189, 190, 210
Nobel Peace Prize 168, 172
Non-Aligned Movement 18
Norway 95, 323
Nurick, Lester 260
Nyala Hotel 349
Nyerere, Julius 55, 144, 145, 173, 178, 188, 197

Obote, Milton 188, 197
Odinga, Oginga 196, 197
Ogaden 161, 174, 188, 225, 228, 229, 334
Okello 197, 198
Olympos 5
Omar 294-296, 299
Omar Mukhtar 41
Organization of African Unity (OAU) 90, 94, 184-187, 189-191, 194, 197, 209, 216, 285, 347
Oromo 47, 48, 51, 54, 218, 223, 226, 227, 287, 295, 333
Oromo Liberation Front (OLF) 334

Orthodox 4, 8, 11, 12, 18, 22, 32, 42, 231, 234, 287
Orthodox Christian Scholars 8
Osborne Hotel 85, 86
Osman Ali 333
Oxford University 65
Pademba Road 309, 347
Pakistan 95, 263
Pan-Africanism 94
Pankhurst, Richard 93
Pankhurst, Sylvia 92, 93, 96
Paris 37, 85-87, 94, 95, 101, 102, 105, 210, 211, 323
Parola, Wayne T. 347, 348
Pastor Tron 26
Paul, Jim 194, 200, 202, 204, 205, 216-218
Paulos Tesfagiorgis 324, 326, 338
Peace Corps 167, 265, 339
Penal Code 153, 158, 160, 161, 275
Persians 90
Petros Bekhit 108
Petros Hadgu 344
Philips and Randall 85
Plough 6, 7, 13
Political Bureau 337, 339, 343
Port Sudan 105, 323
Priestly, J.B. 123
Princess Tenagnework 104, 113, 114
Procuratore Generale 158
Protestant 4, 10, 11, 17, 18, 22, 25, 26, 31, 33, 38, 42, 44, 53, 65, 123, 135, 136, 146, 171, 184, 311

Qarsa 15
Qemis 12
Qeshi 10
Qeshi Abraha 44
Qolo 18

Qottu 54
Quazien 308, 310, 314
Queen Helena 14
Queens College 332

Ras Abebe 128, 143
Ras Desta Hospital 147-149, 152
Ras Hailu 129
Ras Imru 79, 103, 104, 109-112, 115, 117, 129, 175, 257, 258, 268
Ras Mekonen 57, 225
Ras Mekonen School 57
Ras Teferi (Tafari) 25, 42, 110
Rashaida 295
Rashid Al Tahir 322
Red Sea 3, 4, 95, 165, 295, 318, 319
Redazghi 249, 311-313, 315, 316, 319-323
Republican Party 201
Research and Information Center of Eritrea (RICE) 334, 340
Revised Constitution of 1955 135, 153, 161
Rezene Gebreyesus 346
Rezene Medhane 348, 349
Rhodesia 92
Ri'si Adi 4
Rigby 98
Robit 285
Roman law 101
Romodan Mohamed Nur 317, 318, 321, 338
Rose, Vernon 212
Rousseau 183
Russell Tribunal 340

Sabur Seghi 310

Sahel 27, 268, 309, 312, 314-319, 324, 325, 334, 338
Saho 293-295, 299, 300
Saleh Sabbe 295, 300, 317, 319, 320, 322, 325-328, 335, 336
Santa Monica 204
Sassoon, David 291
School of Oriental and African Studies (SOAS) 66, 205, 209
Schwartz, Murray 194, 200, 204
Scott, Hugh 241, 258-260
Scuola Vittorio 22, 23, 39, 42
Seare Kahsai 32
Sebene 249, 259, 260, 266, 328, 329
Sebhat Efrem 315, 316, 337, 339, 343
Seble Desta 104, 105, 113-115, 122, 218, 330
Segeneiti 300, 308
Selamawit 223
Selassie Hamle 12
Sella, Piero 260
Semhar 4, 317
Semnna Work 192
Senafe 292-294, 297, 300
Senbetu Asfaha 350
Senghor, Leopold 90, 188
Seraye 290
Seyoum Haregot 105, 145, 184, 243
Shaw, Bernard 65, 87, 89, 92, 123, 183
Sheep 6, 18-22, 185, 283, 287, 293
Shell Oil 197
Shelton 98
Shils, Edward 201
Shimanegus 308, 312
Shimelis Adugna 236, 238, 239
Shiraro 288
Shoan Amhara 85, 104, 128
Shobero 181

Shriver, Sargent 265-267, 331
Sickles 6
Sidamo 185, 237, 267
Sidetegnas 128
Sierra Leone 309, 347
Simret 7, 8, 10, 23, 47
Sisai Ibsa 342
Siyad Barre 190
Slades School 124
Slovo, Joe 197, 212-214
Smith, Ian 92
Solomon Deresa (Deressa) 61
Solomon Gebrehiwot 15, 22
Solomon Woldemariam 316-318
Somali 52, 79, 160, 161, 174, 188, 221, 223, 225, 229, 230, 295, 309, 319, 320, 325, 333, 334, 345,
Somalia 95, 148, 149, 160, 174, 188, 190, 228, 229, 284, 301, 333, 334, 339, 340, 342
South Africa 95, 177, 196, 212-214, 265
South African Communist Party 213
Soviet Allies 347
Soviet Bloc 186
Soviet Union (USSR) 26, 166, 194, 213, 334
Soyinka, Wole 98
Speakers' Corner 89
Stalin 35, 110, 327
Stark 56, 105, 328
Stifanos Seyoum 334
Sub-Saharan Africa 93, 176, 187, 341
Sudan 31, 36, 47, 93, 105, 112, 151, 177, 182, 185, 190, 202, 210, 277, 284, 291, 318, 320-323, 349
Sun King 181
Sunni Islam 4
SWAPO 346

Swedish Mission 7, 26, 31, 39, 44, 49, 53, 55

Taddese Negash 131-133, 143, 182
Taddesse Mengesha 138
Taff 13
Taha 320
Tahir Imam Musa 24
Tajeddin 277
Takele Woldehawariat 138, 139, 168, 169, 171, 191, 192, 195
Talbot, David 144
Tamrat Yigesu 149, 151, 152
Tareke Beraki 302, 311
Tarma Ber 49, 284
Tasew 55, 56
Teachers Training Institute (TTI) 233, 235
Tecletsadik 66
Tecletsion Debas 35
Tedla Aba-Guben 286
Tedla Bairu 37, 93, 96, 106, 123, 307
Tedla Tebeje 72, 175
Tedla Zewoldi 192
Tegadelti (Tegadalai) 295, 297, 306, 310, 312-315, 319, 324, 334, 337
Tegbaru 60
TeHambeley 14
Tekeste 6, 7, 9, 252, 289
Tekeste Dirar 22, 23
Tekleab 312
Teklu Berhe 316
Tera Imni 290
Territorial Army 283
Tesfa Gebremariam 169
Tesfai 21
Tesfalem Seyoum 345
Tesfalul 58, 60, 68, 83, 85
Tesfamariam 30, 311

Tesfazghi 39, 55-58
Tesfu Kidane 314
Teshome Gebre-Mariam 184
TewesseT 15
Tewolde 8, 9, 26, 251
The Dome 199
The Eritrean Case 341
Third World 36, 186, 213, 258, 260-263
Ti'gist 49
Tiberih Tesfahuney 314
Tigray Popular Liberation Front (TPLF) 333
Tigre/Tigray 41, 45-47, 136, 137, 233, 235, 286, 295 333, 342
Tigrigna 4, 13, 22, 24, 32, 34, 42, 46, 47, 109, 113, 137, 182, 207, 233, 287, 293-297, 299, 300, 303
Tilahun Gizaw 67, 235
Tilahun Kassaye 108, 117
Timbi 15
Timket 14
Toure, Sekou 90, 182, 183, 187
Tribune 91
Triulzi (Gloria and Sandro) 340
Tsegai Iasu 116
Tsegai KaHsai 170, 320
Tsegaye (Qes) 52, 169
Tsighe Dibu 146
Tsion 252, 277
Turkish 28, 54, 66, 84
Tutu Imru 122

UCLA 76, 193, 194, 202-208, 212
UCLA Law School 76, 194, 202-204, 208
UN General Assembly 95, 96, 138, 154, 262, 344, 345
UNHCR 323

United Kingdom (UK) 133, 236, 265, 323
United Nations (UN) 95, 107, 138, 154, 180, 186, 189, 260, 262, 323, 330, 341, 343-348
United States 10, 59, 85, 108, 110, 133, 153, 154, 159, 166, 167, 175, 178, 186, 189, 194, 196, 198, 200, 202, 203, 208, 220, 229, 231, 262, 264, 321, 332, 334, 336, 338, 340, 342, 346
United States Information Agency (USIA) 194, 200
University College Addis Ababa 109, 129, 171, 207, 282
University College London 101, 124, 150
Upper Volta (Bukina Faso) 261

Vasco 319
Ventimale 12, 13, 21
Village girls 10, 11, 14, 27, 28
Village values 32, 56

Wadla-Delanta 8, 9
Wainwright 66
Waja 287
Waldiba 33
Walser, Christian 259, 260, 319, 329
Warren, Earl 202
Washington Consensus 270
Wass 156
Watts riots 206
Webb, Jean 260, 261
Wefera 6
Weizanski, Charles 200
Weki 314, 315, 318
Wells, H. G. 123
Weqro 47

Index

West (East-West rivalry) 186
West Indian 88
Westwood Village 207
Wheat 13, 18, 43
Wilson, Harold 92
Wina 315
Wingate School 39, 44, 55, 57-68, 83-85, 92, 96, 123, 126, 144, 147, 148, 218, 338
Wofford (Harris and Clare) 200, 265-267, 331
Woizero Bruke 222-224
Wolamo (Wolaita) 54, 129
Woldai 19, 346
Wolde Selassie Berhe 324
Woldeab Woldemariam 26, 31-33, 96, 136, 170, 251, 300, 320, 344
Woldia 286
Wolfowitz, Paul 263
Wollo 46, 268-275, 286, 287
Wollo Famine 268-270, 272-274
Wonji 169, 170
Workineh Gebeyehu 130, 142
Workineh Woldeamanuel 79, 222
Worku Habtewold 44, 57, 58, 64, 68, 83
Worku Mekasha 58
World Bank (IBRD) 258, 262
World Council of Churches 323
World War II 7, 44, 62, 85, 95, 112, 166, 262
Wright, Stephen 65, 66, 93, 144
Wysbich 87

Yale Law School 216
Yemisrach 104, 111
Yeneta Yohannes 23, 24, 39
YMCA 129, 281, 282
Yohannes Admasu 206

Yohannes Haile 302, 303, 305, 306
Yohannes Menkir 59, 271
Yoke 6
Yoseph Gebremicael 25, 38

Zaghir 314
Zagre 314, 315, 317
Zaki Mustapha 202, 321, 322
Zalambesa 46
Zanzibar 175, 176, 178, 198
Zegeye Mengesha 221
Zeleka 148
Zerai Deres 111
Zerimariam Sheqa 312
Zerit 32
Zeus 5
Zewde Gebrehiwot 236, 274
Zewde Gebreselassie 37
Zewde Haile Mariam 86, 90
Zewde Seyoum 58

367